History and

THE CODEX CHIMALPOPOCA

History and Mythology of the Aztecs

THE CODEX CHIMALPOPOCA

Translated from the Nahuatl
by JOHN BIERHORST

THE UNIVERSITY OF ARIZONA PRESS

Tucson

The University of Arizona Press
© 1992 John Bierhorst

www.uapress.arizona.edu

Library of Congress Cataloging-in-Publication Data
Codex Chimalpopoca. English.
History and mythology of the Aztecs : the Codex Chimalpopoca /
translated from the Nahuatl by John Bierhorst.
p. cm.
Companion volume to: Codex Chimalpopoca.
Includes bibliographical references.
ISBN 978-0-8165-1886-9 (pbk. :acid-free paper)
1. Codex Chimalpopoca. 2. Aztecs — History. 3. Aztecs — Religion and
mythology. 4. Manuscripts, Aztec — Facsimiles. 5. Mexico — History —
To 1519. 6. Colhuacán–History. I. Bierhorst, John. II. Title.
F1219.59.C62   1992
972'.018 — dc20   91-42267

Manufactured in the United States of America on acid-free,
archival-quality paper.

16   15   14   13   12   11   9   8   7   6   5   4

Contents

rediscovered the ending of the Codex in the León y Gama copy at the Bibliothèque Nationale in Paris. As a result, the edition in hand is the first in any language to present the Legend of the Suns in its entirety. I am grateful to Professor Tschohl for an offprint of the 1989 paper that announces his find; and I thank Monique Cohen of the Bibliothèque Nationale for permission to transcribe and translate from the León y Gama manuscript.

Along the way, numerous individuals and institutions have answered calls for help. I thank them all, especially R. Joe Campbell, John Ceely, Mary Clayton, Marc Eisinger, Willard Gingerich, and Michael E. Smith, all of whom shared unpublished research.

History and Mythology of the Aztecs

THE CODEX CHIMALPOPOCA

Introduction

In approximately the year 1430, as the new Aztec capital called Mexico
Tenochtitlan consolidated its power and began to make far-reaching conquests, its ruling elite decided to burn the old pictographic histories. According to the traditional explanation these accounts contained "false-
hoods" that could have undermined the realm. Presumably the books that
replaced them exaggerated the deeds of the upstart Mexica and codified
the legend that the Mexica themselves had founded Tenochtitlan, though
we may only guess what changes appeared in the new histories or what
earlier records, if any, survived to contradict them.[1]

A hundred years later the books were burned again, this time by Spanish
missionaries who, in the wake of the Conquest of 1521, rushed to elimi-
nate whatever might remind the native people of their pre-Christian past
and might thus inhibit the work of conversion.[2] Once again, new histories
rose out of the ashes. And it is this second wave of history writing, much
of it preserved, that forms the basis for our remarkably detailed, if somewhat colored, knowledge of the rise of Aztec civilization.

Revisionist elements in the new histories are not always easy to isolate.
Among them, evidently, are the numerous references to comets, eclipses,
Cassandra-like oracles, and other omens foretelling the arrival of the Spaniards as early as a generation before the fact. More subtle novelties are to
be looked for in the treatment of Aztec religion, which became a subject
of considerable sensitivity after the Conquest. It will be noticed that the
author of the Annals of Cuauhtitlan (though not the author of Legend
of the Suns) repeatedly disparages the old gods as "sorcerers" or even
"devils"; we are given to understand that the "devils" tricked people
into making human sacrifices, in opposition to the somewhat Christlike
deity, Quetzalcoatl.[3] But even such mundane matters as the succession of
Mexica kings (ca. 1350–1521), including their names and the approximate

---

1. FC bk. 10, ch. 29, section entitled "The Mexica" (p. 191), is the source for the Aztec
book-burning tradition. For discussion see Graulich, "Las peregrinaciones," pp. 311–12 and
347–48; Brundage, *A Rain of Darts*, pp. 107–8.

2. The matter is discussed at length by García Icazbalceta, *Don fray Juan de Zumárraga*,
ch. 22 (vol. 2, pp. 87–162). See also notes 5 and 6, below.

3. I am indebted to Louise Burkhart for making this point. For detailed information see
Subject Guide: Sorcerers.

dates of their reigns, may have been manipulated by the post-Conquest historians.[4]

At the very least, it is obvious that there are variations in the record. The discrepancies can be explained, in part, by the competing claims of the different city states, each of which had its own record keepers. Within the city of Mexico itself there was rivalry between Tenochtitlan and the decidedly weaker, if older, borough, Tlatilolco. Sharing control over the far-flung Aztec empire in a kind of triple alliance were the city of Tlacopan, just four kilometers west of Mexico, and the important Acolhua town of Tetzcoco, some thirty kilometers to the east. Tetzcoco, which had nearly, some would say just, as much power as Mexico, maintained its own traditions, often at variance with those of the Mexica. Still within the Valley of Mexico—a highland basin 120 kilometers north to south and half that distance east to west, centering on the city of Mexico—were such towns as Cuauhtitlan, Cuitlahuac, and Chalco Amaquemecan, all of which preserved records that have survived. Outside the Valley, such nations as Tlaxcallan and the city state of Cuauhtinchan also bequeathed histories during the early colonial period.

Although each chronicler followed his own version, there was agreement on a fundamental chain of events. Tollan, the old imperial capital at the northern edge of the Valley, was thought to have collapsed in the twelfth or thirteenth century A.D. At about the same time, tribesmen from the deserts north of Tollan were said to have begun migrating southward, gradually establishing or gaining control of Tetzcoco, Cuitlahuac, Mexico, and other towns. By the early 1400s the Tepaneca, whose home cities lay in the western part of the basin, were subduing their neighbors and building a small, regional empire. Led by Mexico, or by Mexico and Tetzcoco, an allied army beat back the Tepaneca in about 1430. It was then that the old histories were burned and the Mexica inaugurated their glorious era of expansion. By the time Cortés and his men arrived in 1519 the new empire had outposts on the Gulf of Mexico and the Pacific Ocean and as far south as Guatemala. The typical chronicler, in compiling his manuscript account of these events, added up-to-the-moment annals for the post-Conquest years and, in some cases, began the story with the myth of the four primeval ages, or suns, thus providing his readers with what might be called a history of the world.

A number of the new manuscripts, like the Codex Telleriano-Remensis, ca. 1563, or the Codex Aubin of 1576, hark back to a pre-Cortésian style in which a string of year symbols follow one another in chronological se-

---

4. A theory that the succession of Mexica kings (as preserved in post-Conquest chronicles) was adapted to an ahistorical, ritualistic pattern is developed in Susan Gillespie's *The Aztec Kings: The Construction of Rulership in Mexica History*.

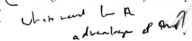

quence, each accompanied by pictographs representing noteworthy For the convenience of sixteenth-century readers the scribe adds a commentary in the alphabetic script learned from missionaries. Possibly some of these painted chronicles were adapted from old books that had escaped the autos-da-fé. Fray Diego Durán states emphatically that none did.[5] Fray Bernardino de Sahagún, a usually more restrained witness, claims that there were many and that they were available for reference.[6] Be that as it may, no certifiably pre-Cortésian history book from the Valley of México has survived to the present.[7]

A second class of chronicle, more modern and more expansive, dispenses with the pictographs, giving instead the narrative the symbols were supposed to call forth. Incorporating vivid descriptions, conversations, speeches, and song texts, these fuller histories offer a rich sampling of the old Aztec oral literature, for which the pictographic codices must have served as prompt books.

Among the prime representatives of this second category are the Anales de Cuauhtitlan (Annals of Cuauhtitlan) of 1570 and the Leyenda de los Soles (Legend of the Suns), dated 1558[8]—both preserved in the manuscript now widely known as Codex Chimalpopoca.

Annals of Cuauhtitlan

In his *Monarchía indiana* of 1615 Fray Juan de Torquemada could write of Cuauhtitlan as "a large community with much jurisdiction in those days [the 1530s] and one of the finest towns at the present time"; similarly, Cortés on the eve of the Conquest had described the city as both "large" and "beautiful."[9] Apart from Tetzcoco, Cuauhtitlan together with its suburb Tepotzotlan was the first outlying district to be missionized after the fall of Tenochtitlan.[10] The well-known Fray Toribio de Benavente, called Motolinía, served among the Franciscans stationed in Cuauhtitlan, and it was there that Motolinía began writing his *Memoriales*, or "Historia de los indios de la Nueva España," perhaps as early as 1532;[11] Cuauhtitlan, he

5. RITOS, Prólogo, p. 6; DCAL, ch. 2, p. 226.
6. CF bk. 10, ch. 27; or FC Introductory Volume, p. 82.
7. See Glass, "A Survey of Native Middle American Pictorial Manuscripts," pp. 11–12; Dibble, "Writing in Central Mexico," pp. 322–23. Both Glass and Dibble base their remarks on Donald Robertson, *Mexican Manuscript Painting of the Early Colonial Period*.
8. On the dating of the two works, see 16:26 (side 16, line 26), 16:30, 31:42, 50:54, 75:4, and 122:6–9.
9. TORQ, bk. 19, ch. 3, p. 306; Cortes, tercera carta, p. 130.
10. Motolinía, "Historia," tratado 2, ch. 1; Mendieta, bk. 3, ch. 33, p. 259.
11. *Memoriales* (ed. O'Gorman), p. 64, n. 3; p. 75, n. 2.

3

explained, had been fourth among the cities of the Aztec empire, ranking next after the triple cities of Tenochtitlan, Tetzcoco, and Tlacopan.[12] Later, when Sahagún was naming the four Indian linguists who had enabled him to prepare his encyclopedic *Historia general*, no less than two, Alonso Vegerano and Pedro de San Buenaventura, were identified as natives of Cuauhtitlan.[13]

Evidently this imposing town—whose name may be vulgarly Englished as Woodside, Tree Town, or Forestville—shared at least marginally in the post-Conquest renaissance that fostered the brief, golden age of Nahuatl letters. It comes as no surprise, therefore, that a major sixteenth-century chronicle should have been written from the point of view of a Cuauhtitlancalqui, or native of Cuauhtitlan.

But the anonymous author tells more than the story of his own nation. Drawing upon the records of Tetzcoco, Cuitlahuac, and Colhuacan, which he acknowledges by name, he builds a comprehensive history of the Valley of Mexico, with occasional sidelights from towns beyond. He uses his sources critically, dismissing the reports of those who "talk much" at 17:46 (side 17, line 46); admitting at 2:3 that his informants had "trouble remembering"; accepting a Tetzcoco tradition at 32:10, while rejecting Tetzcoco data at 4:31 and 12:53. He makes an effort to distance himself from the patently fabulous, inserting a circumspect "it is said" wherever a disclaimer seems needed. The result, nevertheless, is a traditionary account, rich in mythopoetic as well as historical values. Today it is best known for its colorful variant of the legend of Topiltzin Quetzalcoatl, priest-king of Tollan, who became drunk in the company of his sister, fled in shame, and was changed into the morning star.

Though pausing to spin a yarn like the Quetzalcoatl story, or to lay out a genealogy or a tribute list, the work takes the basic form of a pre-Cortésian *xiuhpohualli* (year count), with the entries arranged in chronological order, each bearing the number and name of its corresponding year. Since there are only thirteen numbers by which a year may be known—1 through 13—and only four names—Flint, House, Rabbit, Reed—there can be no more than 13 × 4, or 52, number-and-name combinations. Hence the cycle that begins 1 Flint, 2 House, 3 Rabbit, 4 Reed, 5 Flint, etc., ending with 13 Reed, begins again with 1 Flint after the passing of 52 years.

Near the close of the work, the author correlates the date of Cortés' arrival, 1 Reed, with the date A.D. 1519, enabling the industrious reader to count backward, assigning a Christian date to every entry that has gone

12. "Historia," tratado 3, ch. 7.
13. CF bk. 2, Prólogo; or FC Introductory Volume, p. 55.

4

before, all the way to the earliest, 1 Reed = A.D. 635. This yields a linear chronology that may be taken at face value for events of the 1500s and 1400s, since many of the dates are more or less corroborated by other sources. But the earlier sequences of the 52-year rounds, or "year bundles," become increasingly artificial, leading back to the creation of the present sun, in 13 Reed = A.D. 741, and the initial date mentioned above, A.D. 635, which marks the mythical emergence of tribal ancestors. It must have been accounts such as this, though probably not the one in hand, that prompted Sahagún to write in 1576, "they knew and had records of the things their ancestors had done and had left in their annals more than a thousand years ago." [14]

The ancestors who emerged in A.D. 635, or earlier, are referred to as *chichimeca* (Chichimecs), a term that recurs throughout the chronicle in a variety of contexts, obviously with more than one meaning. In its broadest sense, 'Chichimec' refers to any Indian inhabitant of the Valley of Mexico and of the adjacent highlands, especially to the north and east, whether Nahuatl-speaking or not. More narrowly it refers to the rude tribesmen of the northern deserts who migrated into the Valley at the time of the Toltec collapse, eventually settling Tetzcoco, Cuitlahuac, Mexico, Cuauhtitlan, and other cities. Thus the Toltecs of Tollan may be contrasted with the *chichimeca*, even though both groups are Chichimecs in the broad sense. With its double-edged connotation of rusticity and hardihood, the term could be used either contemptuously, when referring to simple villagers, or pridefully, when recalling the shared heritage of migration and conquest. [15]

As the chronicle opens, Chichimecs (in the narrow sense) come forth from Chicomoztoc (Seven Cave Place); their supernatural leader, Mixcoatl, cremates the old Chichimec goddess Itzpapalotl; and the tribesmen begin their wanderings. The account is unusual in that it has the Chichimecs emerging before the start of the Toltec era. In fact, the world is still dark at this time. In 751 the sun rises, and in 1 Flint (752) the Toltecs inaugurate their first ruler.

Exactly fifty-two years later, in 804, the Chichimecs are said to be breaking up into separate nations. One infers that the Cuauhtitlan people were the parent stock, since the earlier Chichimec chieftains are said to have been Cuauhtitlancalque (the plural of Cuauhtitlancalqui). The succession of these Cuauhtitlan rulers is carefully recorded, though the founding of the city of Cuauhtitlan is still far in the future.

The author pauses now to consider the life of Topiltzin Quetzalcoatl (817–95), whose disgrace and exile, brought about by sorcerers, paves

14. CF bk. 10, ch. 27; or FC Introductory Volume, pp. 82 (quotation) and 84 (date).
15. For references see Concordance: Chichimecatl.

the way for the Toltec collapse. Quetzalcoatl's successor, Huemac, also flees in disgrace, and the Toltecs dispand in 1064.

In the year 1 Rabbit (1090) the Mexica enter the story as marauding wanderers, eventually founding their capital, Mexico Tenochtitlan, in 1318. Other tribes are hostile to these newcomers. But not the people of Cuauhtitlan, whose friendship with the Mexica is one of the chonicle's persistent themes.

Meanwhile the Cuauhtitlancalque have become engaged in a protracted, hundred-years' struggle with Xaltocan (ca. 1297–1395), resulting in impressive territorial gains for Cuauhtitlan. With the influx of sophisticated emigrés from Colhuacan (ca. 1348), the old Chichimec culture of Cuauhtitlan is modernized, and the building of the city of Cuauhtitlan begins.

The death of the Cuauhtitlan ruler Xaltemoctzin, at the hands of Tepaneca assassins (1408), marks a decline in Cuauhtitlan's fortunes. Through a policy of murder and usurpation, the Tepaneca begin to build an empire, terrorizing the entire Valley.

Once again the narrative interrupts the *xiuhpohualli* format, slowing its often breathless pace to recount the legend of the child hero Nezahualcoyotl. We learn here that the boy's father, King Ixtlilxochitl of Tetzcoco, has been assassinated by the Tepaneca, who now seek to murder the child. After a hair-raising chase through the countryside, the boy is sequestered in Mexico, where, in a vision, he is informed by sorcerers that he has been chosen to put an end to the Tepaneca tyranny. With the help of his mentor, the faithful Coyohua, the boy taunts the Tepaneca ruler, Tezozomoctli, allows himself to be captured, cleverly escapes, and eventually leads the campaign that crushes the Tepaneca in 1430.

By 1432 Nezahualcoyotl has been installed as ruler of Tetzcoco. Meanwhile, Itzcoatl is serving as king of Tenochtitlan. And these two, following the defeat of the Tepaneca, begin to hold sway over the Valley of Mexico (together with the city of Tlacopan, a somewhat inferior third partner, not acknowledged in these Cuauhtitlan annals until the triple-city tribute lists near the end of the text).

The doings of Cuauhtitlan continue to be mentioned as the annals proceed, but now in the shadow of the mighty Mexica of Tenochtitlan, whose kings become the chronicle's principal figures: Itzcoatl's successor, Moteuczomatzin (r. 1440–68); Axayacatzin (r. 1469–80); Tizocicatzin (r. 1481–85); Ahuitzotzin (r. 1486–1502); and Moteuczomatzin the younger (r. 1503 until the arrival of the Spaniards).

The chronicle closes with a series of tribute rolls and a brief recapitulation of Mexica history, perhaps added by a different author. In sum, a complex and very dense work, enlivened by the myth of the five suns (2:2–52), the Nezahualcoyotl saga (34:33–39:53), the scandals of Moquihuix (55:16–48), the story of the origin of the skull rack lords of Cuitlahuac (62:11–63:22), and, of course, the famous legend of Topiltzin Quetzalcoatl (3:49–8:4). As pure chronicle, the text is significant for its rare histories of Cuauhtitlan, Cuitlahuac, and Xaltocan, as well as for its voluminous treatment of the Tepaneca War, which (as tradition suggests) laid the groundwork for the Mexica empire. And, finally, as ethnography, the work offers information on Aztec land tenure, statecraft, the tribute system, the role of women, warfare, religion, and, especially, human sacrifice. (These and other topics can be traced in the Subject Guide.)

Legend of the Suns

It is more than likely that the author of the Annals of Cuauhtitlan had access to pictographic sources in addition to oral accounts. In fact, at 51:31 he speaks of what had been "painted," and in a list of greeting gifts at 28:28–34 he is apparently struggling to read picture writing without the aid of a gloss. But in Legend of the Suns, the second of the two Nahuatl texts preserved in the Codex Chimalpopoca, the reliance on pictures is much more obvious. Here the author speaks to us as though we were looking over his shoulder, while he points to the painted figures. "This sun was 4 Jaguar," he writes; "these people . . . were blown away"; "here's when . . ."; "this is when. . . ." In places the text reads like a sequence of captions, as though the unseen pictures could carry the burden of the tale. Yet the narrative relaxes into an easier style wherever the story implied by the paintings happens to be already on the author's lips. The overall effect is of a knowledgeable traditionalist making his way through a single, well-integrated work of mytho-history. (Despite moments of awkwardness, Legend of the Suns is one of the finest, one of the purest sources of Aztec myth that has come down to the present time. Moreover, it is the only creation epic to have survived in the Nahuatl language.)

Since the author uses the phrase "we today who are Mexica" (79:1), it would appear that he identifies with Mexico City; and, certainly, his text, with its focus on Tenochtitlan, is a Mexica document. This is not to say that it records an official dogma. Myth fragments preserved in a wide range of texts, mostly Spanish, make clear that variants were tolerated. Or, to put the matter differently, the dogma was flexible within certain limits.

Although isolated myths of creation are to be found in the various other sources, there are only two, in addition to the Legend of the Suns, that can be called creation *epics*: the Spanish-language "Historia de los mexicanos por sus pinturas" and the "Histoyre du Mechique," known through a sixteenth-century French translation of a lost Spanish original. Of these, the "Historia" is the more complete, and since it is remarkably similar to the Legend of the Suns, it serves as an aid to the interpretation of the Legend, and vice versa: [16]

As the Legend opens, the author declares in a short preamble that he will tell "how the earth was established," a promise he does not fulfill. *But the "Historia" explains that the gods created the earth from the body of a reptilian monster. Afterward, the god Tezcatlipoca became the sun.*

The people who lived in the time of the first sun were eaten by jaguars, and the sun itself was "destroyed." *The people were giants, according to the "Historia," and it was Tezcatlipoca in the form of a jaguar who consumed them after he had been knocked out of the sky by Quetzalcoatl. Then Quetzalcoatl became the sun—the second sun.*

In the time of the second sun, the people were blown away by wind and changed into monkeys. The sun also was blown away. *The sun, actually Quetzalcoatl, was kicked out of the sky by Tezcatlipoca, whereupon the rain god, Tlalocanteuctli, became the third sun.*

During the time of the third sun the people were destroyed by a rain of fire. *The fire was sent by Quetzalcoatl. The rain god's wife, Chalchiuhtlicue, became the next, or fourth, sun.*

The fourth sun ended as the "skies came falling down," causing a world flood. Only one man and one woman survived, having been warned to seek refuge in a hollow log; [17] later, disobeying instructions, this couple ate all the corn that had been given to them, roasted fish when they were hungry, and suffered the punishment of being changed into dogs. When the flood waters subsided, the skies were again "established." *The heavens were lifted to their former position by Tezcatlipoca and Quetzalcoatl.*

During the second year after the flood, the year 2 Reed, Tezcatlipoca drilled fire. *Hence the origin of the new-fire ceremony, celebrated every fifty-two years.*

In order to repopulate the earth, Quetzalcoatl descended to the underworld to fetch the bones of earlier generations. With these the gods created a new race of humans. *"The gods created humans as they had been before."*

To provide food for the newly created people, Quetzalcoatl follows an ant into the interior of "Food Mountain" and discovers a cache of corn

16. Another comparison of the Legend of the Suns and the "Historia de los mexicanos por sus pinturas" may be read in Mercedes de la Garza's "Análisis comparativo," *Estudios de Cultura Náhuatl*, 1983.

17. The story of the man and the woman who escaped the flood is missing from the "Historia de los mexicanos por sus pinturas," but the couple is mentioned in "Códice Vaticanus 3738," plate 1.

kernels; the rain gods split open the mountain, gaining control over the corn and other crops as well. *(The myth is not mentioned in the "Historia" or in any other Aztec source, though it is well known in modern Mexican and Central American folklore.)* [18]

The world has been dark since the flood. The gods now bring forth a new sun from the flames of the "spirit oven" at Teotihuacan, also a moon from the less-hot ashes at the flames' edge. With their own blood the gods nourish the sun so that it can rise into the sky. *Immediately prior to the creation of the sun, Tezcatlipoca makes four hundred men and five women; the men are sacrificed to provide the sun with its initial nourishment, but the women survive to play a role later in the story (see below).*

After the sun has risen, four hundred Mixcoa are born, then five more Mixcoa, who make war on the four hundred in order to give the sun a "drink." *The god Mixcoatl creates four hundred Chichimecs plus a war party of five to prey on them, "so that the sun will have hearts to eat."*

Of the four hundred Mixcoa only a few survive the massacre, including Xiuhnel and Mimich. *The surviving Chichimecs Xiuhnel and Mimich are joined by the god Mixcoatl (also called Camaxtle), who himself becomes a Chichimec.*

A pair of two-headed deer descend from the sky. *A two-headed deer descends from the sky.*

The pair of deer become women; Xiuhnel (and Mimich?) engage these dangerous women in sexual intercourse, with the result that Xiuhnel is killed and Mimich is reduced to tears. Mixcoatl, by contrast, acquires a sacred bundle, which he carries with him as his charm, pacifying enemies and making conquests. While on the warpath, he subdues the so-called Huitznahua women, one of whom he assaults sexually; this woman, Chimalman, gives birth to the hero Ce Acatl. *Mixcoatl carries the two-headed deer into battle as his charm, thus making easy conquests. His enemies, eventually, seize the deer while he is distracted by one of the five women who had been created just before the fifth sun (see above); by Mixcoatl this woman gives birth to the hero Ce Acatl, i.e., Topiltzin Quetzalcoatl.*

Mixcoatl, his luck gone, is killed by his three hateful brothers, Apanecatl, Zolton, and Cuilton—three Mixcoa who survived the massacre after the creation of the fifth sun. Seeking revenge, Ce Acatl confronts the three brothers and craftily kills them. *The episode finds its parallel not in the "Historia de los mexicanos por sus pinturas" but in the "Histoyre du Mechique": Mixcoatl, it seems, has three hateful sons, who kill their father when they learn*

---

18. Two modern Nahuat versions from the Sierra Norte de Puebla are published by James Taggart, who compares them with the story in Legend of the Suns (Taggart, *Nahuat Myth and Social Structure*, pp. 87–97). Twenty variants ranging from central Mexico to El Salvador are cited in Bierhorst, *The Mythology of Mexico and Central America.*

that he favors his fourth son, Quetzalcoatl. In revenge, Quetzalcoatl kills the three brothers.

Ce Acatl (Quetzalcoatl) performs an operation of ritual sacrifice on the brothers' corpses. *In the words of the "Histoyre": "Because he introduced the custom of sacrifice, he was held to be a god [by the people of Tollan], whom he taught many good things, [constructing] temples for himself and other [monuments], and he lived as the god of that country for 160 years." According to the "Historia," this Ce Acatl lived as lord of Tollan and built a great temple; but four years after the temple was finished the god Tezcatlipoca came to him and advised him that he would have to leave.*

Proceeding eastward, Ce Acatl reaches Tlapallan, where he dies and is cremated. *"Historia": He proceeds to Tlapallan, where he takes sick and dies.*

After the departure of Ce Acatl, i.e., Topiltzin Quetzalcoatl, Tollan is plagued by omens of doom: a stinking corpse that cannot be moved, four years of drought, a little old woman selling banners, and a prophecy delivered by the rain gods to the effect that the Mexica are to inherit the land. *The "Historia" (ch. 11) mentions only the old woman selling banners.*

Meanwhile the Mexica have set out from Aztlan, their point of origin, and are migrating southward. After passing through the neighborhood of Tollan, they reach Chapoltepec, suffer hardships in the country of the Colhuaque, and eventually establish the city of Tenochtitlan. *The "Historia" recounts the migration more fully, telling how the Mexica are guided by their tribal deity Huitzilopochtli.*

The rulers of Tenochtitlan are named, together with the towns that each ruler conquered. First, Acamapichtli, then Huitzilihuitl, Chimalpopocatzin, Itzcoatzin, and so forth, down to Moteuczomatzin the younger, in whose time the conqueror Cortés arrives. *The "Historia" covers the same ground, concluding with the events of the Conquest and its aftermath, down to the year 1529.*

The Manuscript

Codex Chimalpopoca, or Códice Chimalpopoca, has been catalogued as Colección Antigua no. 159, of the Archivo Histórico, Museo Nacional de Antropología (under the auspices of the Instituto Nacional de Antropología e Historia), Mexico City.[19] Its present whereabouts, however, are in doubt. Apparently it has been lost since at least 1949.[20]

19. HMAI, vol. 15, p. 432.
20. HMAI, vol. 15, p. 333. Ojeda Díaz (*Documentos sobre Mesoamérica*, p. 39, n. 50; quoted in Tschohl, p. 270) writes that the manuscript "fue extraviado por Salvador Toscano en septiembre de 1946, cuando era Secretario del INAH." But Angel M. Garibay, in a pub-

Before being transferred to the Archivo Histórico, the Codex was housed at the library of the Museo Nacional de México, where Walter Lehmann examined it in 1909 and again in 1926.[21] "In its present condition," he wrote, "it is at most 22 cm. high and 15 cm. wide. The paper is thin and yellowed, finely ribbed, longitudinally, at intervals of about 1 mm., and considerably flawed; thus little pieces have crumbled away at the edges, especially below."[22]

Until the manuscript again becomes available, if it does, the photographic facsimile published by Primo F. Velázquez in 1945 must be regarded as the optimum source. In the 1975 reprint of Velázquez's work the plates are reduced to about three-quarters original size, with a slight loss in legibility. The present edition has been based on the facsimile of 1945—with help from the León y Gama copy of the Codex Chimalpopoca (Bibliothéque Nationale de Paris, ms. FM 312), which preserves the text of the manuscript's long-lost side 85. Modern scholarship had been unaware that side 85 was recoverable until the work of Peter Tschohl, whose "Das Ende der Leyenda de los Soles und die Ubermittlungsprobleme des Códice Chimalpopoca" appeared in 1989. The forty-two folios of the Codex as it was known to Lehmann and Velázquez make for a manuscript of eighty-four sides, written front and back, and these are numbered consecutively, 1 through 84. The so-called Anales de Cuauhtitlan occupies sides 1–68; the Leyenda de los Soles fills 75–84. Sides 69–74, excluded from the Velázquez facsimile, contain a work in Spanish by the sixteenth- and early seventeenth-century Indian cleric Pedro Ponce de León. Called "Breve relación de los dioses y ritos de la gentilidad," Ponce's work is thematically unrelated to the Anales and the Leyenda, which, though by different authors, are both world histories written in Nahuatl. The "Breve relación" is a collection of short notes on Aztec gods, rites of passage, incantatory medicine, farmers' rituals, and other, miscellaneous lore.[23]

In addition to the manuscript's eighty-four page, or side, numbers, there is an older foliation on the recto sides, clearly establishing that folio 1 is missing. Thus "side 1" of the new foliation is really side 3 of the Codex in

---

lication of 1965 (*Teogonía e historia de los mexicanos*, p. 17), spoke of the Codex as though it were still in the archive: "Este manuscrito se halla en la Biblioteca del Instituto de Antropología e Historia" (see also note 23, below). My own inquiry of 1985 failed to clear up the question.

21. GKC, 2d ed., p. vii.

22. GKC, p. 2.

23. For editions of Ponce's work, see Ponce, "Breve relación" (1892) and Ponce, "Breve relación" (1953). Angel M. Garibay reprinted the text in 1965, claiming to have corrected the errors of the earlier editions in light of the text in the Codex Chimalpopoca (Garibay, *Teogonía e historia de los mexicanos*, pp. 17, 121–40).

its original state. Nevertheless, the present edition abides by the new numbers, following the custom set by Lehmann and Velázquez.

Guard leaves, in a different hand, preserve a genealogy of the family of the seventeenth-century historian Fernando de Alva Ixtlilxochitl; and a latter-day title page, dated 1849, assigns the rubric Códice Chimalpopoca (with a note in a contrasting hand explaining that the Abbé Brasseur de Bourbourg had so named the Codex in honor of the early nineteenth-century academician Faustino Galicia Chimalpopoca, who made a pioneering attempt to translate it).[24]

Obviously the manuscript itself, all in a single hand, must be a copy of earlier works. Old marginal glosses have even been swept into the text at 48:53, 49:13, 49:35, and possibly 59:2–3 and 59:43. Moreover, the old, presumably Franciscan, orthography has been converted to a Jesuit style, which did not take hold until the 1590s at the very earliest.[25] The sound /w/, as in English 'water', written *u*, *v*, or *o* in the old style, has become *hu*; and the glottal stop, formerly written *h* or indicated by a circumflex over the preceding vowel, is now indicated by a grave accent. Occasionally, the scribe neglects to make the conversion, and we find *vactli* (rather than *huactli*) at 3:15 and *tlahçolyaotzin* (rather than *tlàçolyaotzin*) at 57:34.

If the year of Ponce's "Breve relación" could be established, the earliest possible date for our manuscript might be pushed forward to the period 1610–28. In 1610 Ponce was commissioned by the archbishop of Mexico to investigate idolatry in the region of Teutenango (resulting in the "Breve relación"?); and 1628 is the year of Ponce's death.[26]

If the Alva Ixtlilxochitl genealogy preserved in the guard leaves is to be taken as a clue, then the copyist might have been the famous historian himself. But although Don Fernando de Alva Ixtlilxochitl (d. 1650) has often been mentioned as the likely scribe, the troubling fact remains that he does not demonstrate an acquaintance with the Codex Chimalpopoca in either his *Relaciones* or his *Historia de la nación chichimeca*.

Working backward from the time of Brasseur de Bourbourg and Galicia Chimalpopoca, the manuscript's history can be sketched with only a fair degree of certainty. The Mexican scholar Antonio de León y Gama, as evidenced in his work on the Aztec calendar, dated 1792, had the manuscript in his hands and of course made the copy already mentioned; and

24. The genealogy and the title page are included in the Velázquez facsimile; the genealogy is transcribed in GKC. For the partial translation by Galicia Chimalpopoca see *Anales de Cuauhtitlan* (1885).

25. On Jesuit orthography see Bierhorst, *Cantares Mexicanos*, pp. xi-xiii, 8.

26. Information on Ponce is given in HMAI, vol. 13, p. 83; HMAI vol. 15, p. 356; and Garibay, *Teogonía*, pp. 16–18. Garibay (p. 17) states that Ponce's work was composed in 1569; HMAI, vol. 15, p. 677, says it was "probably composed in 1597."

the Jesuit historian Francisco Javier Clavigero seems to have been aware of its existence, at least, some twenty years earlier.[27] Both León y Gama and Clavigero evidently had access to the very same document described by Lorenzo Boturini Benaduci in his *Idea de una nueva historia general* of 1746:

> Una historia de los reinos de Culhuacan y México, en lengua Nahuatl y papel europeo, de autor anónimo, y tiene añadida una breve relación de los dioses y ritos de la gentilidad, en lengua castellana, que escribió el bachiller don Pedro Ponce, indio cacique beneficiado que fue del Partido de Tzumpahuacan. Está todo copiada de letra de don Fernando de Alba, y le falta la primera foja. (A history of the kingdoms of Colhuacan and Mexico, in the Nahuatl language, on European paper, by an anonymous author; and added to it is a brief *relación* on the gods and rites of heathen times, in the Spanish language, written by the *bachiller* Don Pedro Ponce [de León], Indian cacique and curate, of the district of Tzumpahuacan. The whole is copied in the hand of Don Fernando de Alva [Ixtlilxochitl], and the first folio is missing.)[28]

This, with its lost first folio, sounds very much like the item named by Brasseur de Bourbourg and later catalogued as ms. 159 at the Museo Nacional de Antropología. An earlier inventory of Boturini's collection adds the information that the manuscript contained forty-three leaves, clinching the identification with ms. 159, which would comprise forty-two leaves plus (as we now know) one missing leaf.[29]

Accepting Boturini's descriptive title, Lehmann called his edition *Die Geschichte der Königreiche von Colhuacan und Mexico* (The History of the Kingdoms of Colhuacan and Mexico). This, of course, refers only to the first part of the Codex, which, aptly, had already been dubbed Anales de Cuauhtitlan by the nineteenth-century historian José Fernando Ramírez.[30] The title Leyenda de los Soles, for the third part, was put forth by Francisco del Paso y Troncoso in his edition of 1903.

Confusingly, the entire manuscript has sometimes been referred to as Anales de Cuauhtitlan, the name that actually designates the first of the three texts. Since the Velázquez edition, however, the nomenclature in

27. On León y Gama and Clavigero see Moreno, "La colección Boturini y las fuentes de la obra de Antonio León y Gama"; also GKC, pp. 12–13, 17.

28. Boturini, *Idea*, p. 119 (Catálogo, párrafo VIII, no. 13).

29. As established by Tschohl, "Das Ende der Leyenda de los Soles." See especially pp. 203–4.

30. Velázquez, *Códice Chimalpopoca*, p. xi.

general use has been Códice Chimalpopoca for the whole compilation; Anales de Cuauhtitlan for the first part; Leyenda de los Soles for the third. Strictly speaking, neither the present edition nor that of Velázquez should have been called Chimalpopoca, since the manuscript's middle part, the *relación* of Ponce, is not included. But at this writing I may argue—as Velázquez could not—that the popularity of his *Códice Chimalpopoca*, comprising just the two Nahuatl works, has given the name a valid second meaning.

Guide to the Translation

The English version appearing in this volume is what language scientists call a free translation, as opposed to a lexical or morphemic analysis. But it is not free in the sense that students of literature apply the term; rather, it attempts to be strictly faithful to the text, unbeautiful where the text is unbeautiful, ambiguous where the text is ambiguous. As for a close lexical analysis, the underlying assumption is that this is unnecessary if the version adheres to grammatical rules. My belief is that it does, unless I have been careless, and that the Glossary and Grammatical Notes in the companion volume provide whatever additional support is needed to make the reading acceptable to specialists in the early 1990s—even if it cannot, at this point, be called definitive. Special features of the translation are as follows.

Paragraphing and subheads. For ease of reading, the monolithic copy blocks of the manuscript have been broken into paragraphs, mostly short, serving as topical units. Further, to assist readers in finding their way through a complex of narrative strands, subheads have been inserted, enclosed in square brackets to show that they are extraneous to the text.

Line numbers. Numbers in the left margin, at the beginning of each paragraph, key the English version to the Nahuatl text as it appears in the manuscript. For example, the number 51:20 means that the paragraph in question starts in the twentieth line of side fifty-one of the physical paleograph. The reason for this numbering method is that the Codex Chimalpopoca is so compactly and messily written that it would otherwise be nearly impossible (for those who must do so) to compare the translation with the original. Those who are using only the English translation should find the numbering sufficiently serviceable, even if references need to be sought within a range of two or three lines of the cited number (since the English often runs a little ahead or behind the Nahuatl).

Word order. Naturally, the textual word order must often be changed in the translation. For example, at 1:12–14 the text, literally, has "And then into her hands they fell, who ate them, Itzpapalotl, the four hundred Mixcoa, she finished them off. Only White Mixcoatl, called Mixcoatl the Younger, ran away, escaped from her hands." To make this understandable I have written, "And then they fell into the hands of Itzpapalotl, who ate the four hundred Mixcoa, finished them off. White Mixcoatl, called Mixcoatl the Younger, was the only one who escaped, who ran away." The changes should require no comment, except for the last two verbs, which I have transposed to avoid an anticlimactic word order in English. Under the assumption that this is a potential point of interest, all such cases have been noted in the translation.

Christian dates. Throughout the Annals of Cuauhtitlan, native-style dates such as 1 Flint or 8 Rabbit are accompanied by Christian-style equivalents added in square brackets. These follow the native author's own correlation (see above) and are inserted here, just as Lehmann inserted them in his German edition, to help orient the reader. From the modern point of view these dates, especially the early ones, have literary rather than historical value—as Willard Gingerich has recognized in his perceptive study, "Quetzalcoatl and the Agon of Time: A Literary Reading of the *Anales de Cuauhtitlan*."

Personal names. Names of persons have been left untranslated, except in rare cases where the writer seems to be striving for a pun or some other special effect. The English text preserves the varying forms of a particular name, such as Tezozomoctli, which may be apocopated (Tezozomoc) or enhanced by the honorific suffix *-tzin* (Tezozomoctzin). For further comments on personal names see Grammatical Notes, sections 3.4–5, in the companion volume.

Group names. Since the names of most ethnic, tribal, or national groups have not been Anglicized in the translation, the reader should have some awareness of the derivation of these terms and of the differences between singular and plural forms. A few examples will illustrate the more common types: a Mexicatl (pl. Mexica, variant pl. Mexitin) is a native of Mexico; a Chololtecatl (pl. Chololteca) is a native of Cholollan; a Cuauhtitlancalqui (pl. Cuauhtitlancalque), of Cuauhtitlan; an Acolhua (pl. Acolhuaque), of Acolhuacan. For further particulars see Grammatical Notes, sections 3.2–3, in the companion volume.

Place names. Wherever there is a clear indication to do so, variant spellings of geographical names have been regularized in the translation in order to minimize ambiguity. The reader who came upon "Chiapan," and later "Chiyapan," might wonder if the same place is meant. It is, and the more usual spelling, "Chiapan," has been adopted throughout the translation. For the sake of completeness, variant spellings in the paleograph are entered in the Concordance in this volume and, of course, preserved in the Transcription in the companion volume.

The recurring "etc."   The Latin et cetera appears frequently in the Annals of Cuauhtitlan, evidently with differing shades of meaning. At 2:1 it seems equivalent to "more of the same," while at 3:26 it implies "and so forth, as stated previously." Apparently at 6:27 it means "et al." But most often, as at 8:46 and 12:5, it suggests that the author (or the copyist?) is cutting short his source, as if to say that the matter is not worth pursuing or that the story is too well known to need retelling.

Annals of Cuauhtitlan

Contents

Contents

[The goddess Itzpapalotl speaks: ca. A.D. 635][1]

:1 " . . . a yellow eagle, a yellow jaguar, a yellow snake, a yellow rabbit, a yellow deer.

:2 "Shoot to the south, to the southlands, the garden lands, the flower lands. There you must shoot a red eagle, a red jaguar, a red snake, a red rabbit, a red deer.

:5 "And when you have done your shooting, lay them in the hands of Xiuhteuctli, the Old Spirit, whom these three are to guard: Mixcoatl, Tozpan, and Ihuitl.[2] These are the names of the three hearthstones." Thus Itzpapalotl taught the Chichimecs.

:10 And when the Chichimecs come, the Mixcoa, the four hundred Mixcoa,[3] are in the lead. That's how they issue forth from Chiucnauhtilihuican [Nine Hills], from Chiucnauhixtlahuatl [Nine Fields, i.e., the underworld].

:12 And then they fell into the hands of Itzpapalotl, who ate the four hundred Mixcoa, finished them off. White Mixcoatl, called Mixcoatl the younger, was the only one who escaped, who ran away.[4] He jumped inside a barrel cactus.

:15 And when Itzpapalotl seized the cactus, Mixcoatl rushed out and shot her, calling to the four hundred Mixcoa,[5] who had died. They appeared. They shot her. And when she was dead, they burned her. Then they rubbed themselves with her ashes, blackening their eye sockets.

:19 And when their bundle[6] was finished being made, they all decorated themselves in a place called Mazatepec.

---

1. The teachings of the goddess, continued from the missing first folio, are recapitulated in lines 3:16–29 below.
2. The translation follows Lehmann and Velázquez. But Sullivan, plausibly, has "And when you have shot your arrows, place in the hands of Xiuhtecutli [the god of fire], the Old God, the three who are to guard him—Mixcoatl, Tozpan, and Ihuitl."
3. For the textual *mixcoat* read *mixcoa* or *mixcoâ*. See GN sec. 1.1.
4. Anticlimactic word order reversed in the translation.
5. For the textual *mixcoã* read *mixcoâ*.
6. A sacred bundle containing the ashes of Itzpapalotl is mentioned in line 50:36 below. See also lines 80:10–19.

[The beginning of the year count: A.D. 635–93]

:22   Then the four year counters got started. The first is Reed. The second, Flint. The third, House. The fourth, Rabbit.

:24   1 Reed [635]. This is when the Chichimecs came out of Chicomoztoc [Seven Caves], so it is told, so it is related in their narratives.

:25   The year count, the day sign count, and the count of each twenty-day period were made the responsibility of those known as Oxomoco and Cipactonal. Oxomoco means the man, Cipactonal means the woman. Both were very old. And from then on, old men and old women were called by those names.

:31   2 Flint. 3 House. 4 Rabbit. 5 Reed. 6 Flint. 7 House. 8 Rabbit. 9 Reed. 10 Flint. 11 House. 12 Rabbit. 13 Reed. 1 Flint. 2 House. 3 Rabbit. 4 Reed. 5 Flint. 6 House. 7 Rabbit. 8 Reed. 9 Flint. 10 House. 11 Rabbit. 12 Reed. 13 Flint. 1 House. 2 Rabbit. 3 Reed. 4 Flint. 5 House. 6 Rabbit. 7 Reed. 8 Flint. 9 House. 10 Rabbit. 11 Reed. 12 Flint. 13 House. 1 Rabbit. 2 Reed. 3 Flint. 4 House. 5 Rabbit. 6 Reed. 7 Flint. 8 House. 9 Rabbit. 10 Reed. 11 Flint. 12 House. 13 Rabbit.[7]

:37   13 Rabbit [686] was the beginning of Tetzcoco's year count, [the beginning of] their Chichimec period.

:38   1 Reed [687] was when Chicontonatiuh (of Cuauhtitlan) was made ruler. At Quetzaltepec he assumed the rule.[8]

:40   2 Flint. 3 House. 4 Rabbit.

    5 Reed [691]. This was the year the Cuauhtitlan Chichimecs arrived in the region, at Macuexhuacan Huehuetocan. It has already been told, already been mentioned how they came out of Chicomoztoc and how it was known that the year count of the Cuauhtitlan Chichimecs began in a year 1 Reed.

:44   And when these Chichimecs arrived in the year 5 Reed, they were hunters on the move. They had no houses, no lands, no clothes that were soft goods.[9] They just wore hides and long moss.[10] And their children were brought up in mesh bags and pack baskets. They ate large prickly pears, barrel cactus, spine silk, sour prickly pears.

:49   They suffered much during all the 364 years before they arrived in the country of Cuauhtitlan, and it was then that the dynasty of the Cuauhtitlan Chichimecs began and got started.

:52   Now, it must be said and it is to be understood: with regard to the

---

7. Marginal gloss: 52.
8. The translation agrees with Sullivan. See GLOS: tlatocati.
9. For *yanmanqui* read *yamanqui*.
10. *Tillandsia* sp. (Spanish moss).

above year-time, it was actually in that time, in that year, 1 .
they were still on the road, that they got themselves a ruler.[11]

1:54   During these years that the Chichimecs lived, it is told and 1
there was still darkness.

1:55   There was still darkness, so it is told, because they had no fai   , no
renown. There was no happiness. They were still on the move, etc.

2:2   6 Flint. 7 House.

[The five suns: A.D. 694–751]

According to their stories, which they had trouble remembering,[12] the
old ones knew that the land, or earth, had its beginning and was established in the first age.

2:5   8 Rabbit [694]. The fourth sun, the sun whose day sign is 4 Wind.
9 Reed. 10 Flint. 11 House. 12 Rabbit. 13 Reed. 1 Flint. 2 House.
3 Rabbit. 4 Reed. 5 Flint. 6 House. 7 Rabbit. 8 Reed. 9 Flint. 10 House.
11 Rabbit.

2:8   The second age is told and related to be the fifth sun, or age.

2:9   12 Reed. 13 Flint. 1 House. 2 Rabbit. 3 Reed. 4 Flint. 5 House.
6 Rabbit. 7 Reed. 8 Flint.

2:10   The third age, sun five of 4 Wind.

2:11   9 House [721]. At this time the Colhua Chichimecs established their
own nation.

10 Rabbit. 11 Reed. 12 Flint.

2:12   13 House [725]. Chicontonatiuh rules in Cuauhtitlan. The town is at
Macuexhuacan.

2:14   1 Rabbit [726] is when the Toltecs began. Their year count started in
1 Rabbit.

2:15   It is said that life had been created four times.

2:16   So the old ones knew that in the fifth age,[13] in the time of 1 Rabbit,
earth and sky were established, and they knew that when earth and sky
were established, people had existed four times, life had been created four
times. So they knew how each of the suns had been.

2:21   And they said that the one they called their god made them, created
them, out of ashes. This they attributed to Quetzalcoatl. 7 Wind is the day
sign of the one who made them, created them.

11. See line 1:38 above.

12. The passage that follows, down through line 2:10, is indeed confusing. A more
coherent version of the myth begins with line 2:24 below.

13. The intrusive CCCC, written with an overline in the manuscript, appears misplaced.
At 1:13 and 1:17 the same figure means 400.

24   4 Water is the day sign of the first sun that there was in the beginning. And its name is Water Sun. All those who were created in its time were swept away by water. All the people turned into dragonfly nymphs and fish.

2 : 27   4 Jaguar is the day sign of the second sun that there was, called Jaguar Sun. It happened that the sky collapsed then,[14] and the sun did not continue. It happened at midday. Then there was darkness, and while it was dark, the people were eaten.

2 : 31   And giants were alive in the time of this one, and the old people say that their greeting was "Don't fall!" because whoever fell would fall for good.

2 : 34   4 Rain is the day sign of the third sun that there was, called Rain Sun. In the time of this one it happened that fire rained down, so that those who were there were burned. Also gravel rained down. They say that the gravel we find was strewn at this time. Also the lava stone boiled. And the various rocks that are red were deposited then.

2 : 39   4 Wind is the day sign of the fourth sun, the Wind Sun. In its time people were blown away by the wind, people were turned into monkeys. Those who remained, the monkey people, were scattered in the forest.

2 : 42   4 Movement is the day sign of the fifth sun, called Movement Sun, because it moves along and follows its course. And from what the old people say, there will be earthquakes in its time, and famine, and because of this we will be destroyed.

2 : 46   2 Reed. 3 Flint. 4 House. 5 Rabbit. 6 Reed. 7 Flint. 8 House. 9 Rabbit. 10 Reed. 11 Flint. 12 House. 13 Rabbit. 1 Reed. 2 Flint. 3 House. 4 Rabbit. 5 Reed. 6 Flint. 7 House. 8 Rabbit. 9 Reed. 10 Flint. 11 House. 12 Rabbit. 13 Reed.

2 : 49   They say the sun that exists today was born in 13 Reed [751], and it was then that light came, and it dawned. Movement Sun, which exists today, has the day sign 4 Movement, and this sun is the fifth that there is. In its time there will be earthquakes, famine.

[Early history of Cuauhtitlan: A.D. 751–816]

2 : 52   13 Reed [751] is when Chicontonatiuh died in Macuexhuacan. He had ruled Cuauhtitlan for sixty-five years.

2 : 54   In the year 1 Flint [752] the Toltecs got themselves a ruler. They took Mixcoamazatzin as their ruler, and he initiated the Toltec rule.

2 : 55   Also in this year Xiuhneltzin was inaugurated as ruler of Cuauhtitlan in

14. For the *tla-* impersonal verb with specific third-person subject see GRAM sec. 5.9.

Ximilco.[15] They were there for one year and moved to Cuaxoxouhcan. This was during the era of the devil Mixcoatl, who was still with them at that time. And it was then that Xiuhneltzin set up his boundary markers. Afterward [Mixcoatl] sent the Chichimecs away, and they went from town to town. He took leave of them, giving them his gear and apparel.[16]

3 : 5   2 House. 3 Rabbit. 4 Reed. 5 Flint. 6 House. 7 Rabbit. 8 Reed. 9 Flint. 10 House. 11 Rabbit. 12 Reed. 13 Flint. 1 House. 2 Rabbit. 3 Reed. 4 Flint. 5 House. 6 Rabbit. 7 Reed. 8 Flint. 9 House. 10 Rabbit. 11 Reed. 12 Flint. 13 House. 1 Rabbit. 2 Reed. 3 Flint. 4 House. 5 Rabbit. 6 Reed. 7 Flint. 8 House. 9 Rabbit. 10 Reed. 11 Flint. 12 House. 13 Rabbit. 1 Reed. 2 Flint. 3 House. 4 Rabbit. 5 Reed. 6 Flint. 7 House. 8 Rabbit. 9 Reed. 10 Flint. 11 House. 12 Rabbit. 13 Reed.

3 : 12   In 1 Flint [804] the Cuauhtitlan Chichimecs got themselves a ruler. Thus began a new Chichimec rule in Cuauhtitlan. They made Huactli their new ruler in a place called Necuameyocan.

3 : 15   Now, this is the story that was told by the Chichimec old people:

3 : 16   When the rule of the Chichimecs began, a woman named Itzpapalotl spoke to them and said, "You must make Huactli your ruler. Go to Necuameyocan and build a thorn house, a maguey house. And there you will spread the thorn mat, the maguey mat.

3 : 20   "And then you must go to the east, and there you must shoot.

3 : 21   "Likewise to the north, to the desert lands, and there you must shoot.

3 : 22   "Likewise to the south [should be west?], and there you must shoot.

3 : 23   "Likewise to the garden lands, the flower lands [i.e., the south?], and there you must shoot.

3 : 24   "And when you have done your shooting and have taken the holy ones, the blue, the yellow, the white, and the red, the eagle, the jaguar, the snake, and the rabbit, etc., then you must put Tozpan, Ihuitl, and Xiuhnel to guard Xiuhteuctli, etc. That's where your captured ones will be cooked. When Huactli has observed his four-day[17] ruler's fast, your captured ones will be needed."

3 : 29   And those Chichimecs who got themselves a ruler are named here: Mixcoatl, Xiuhnel, Mimich, Cuahuicol. And then these: Itztlacoliuhqui, Necuametl, Amimitl, Iquehuac, Nahuacan.[18] And the Chichimec women were Coatl, Miahuatl, Coacueye, Yaocihuatl, Chichimecacihuatl, Tlacochcue.

---

15. Follows Lehmann. Velázquez reads Temilco.

16. In later times Cuauhtitlan Chichimec warriors and ritualists would dress themselves as Mixcoatl. See lines 25 : 47 and 56 : 25 below.

17. The reading follows Velázquez, who conjectures that the numeral 9 in the manuscript is a copyist's error for "4," which would merely reinforce the *nahuilhuitl* (four days). According to Alva Ixtlilxochitl, the ruler's four-day inaugural fast was instituted by Topiltzin. See IXT 1 : 387.

18. Lehmann reads Iquehuac Nahuacan as one person.

3 : 33   And so then they installed a Chichimec prince, who would always lead them. And they made an egret banner for their leader to carry wherever he might go, wherever he might settle, so that he could be seen and they could rally around. This was not to be the place where he would stay.

3 : 37   And when that was done, in the very year 1 Flint, the Chichimecs dispersed, going everywhere, from one country to the next: Michhuacan, Cohuixco, Yopitzinco, Totollan, Tepeyacac, Cuauhquechollan, Huexotzinco, Tlaxcallan, Tliliuhquitepec, Zacatlantonco, Tototepec.

3 : 41   And some of them turned around and went to Cuextlan, and some went to Acolhuacan. They went in all directions, traveled in all directions.

3 : 43   Tepolnextli, Tlancuaxoxouhqui, and Xiuhtochtli, who are said to have taken the lead among those who went to Huexotzinco, were separated in Cuaxoxouhcan by that devil, who took them to different towns.

3 : 46   In order to finish the above story, it must be said that it was when Xiuhneltzin was ruling that Cuaxoxouhcan was the seat of Cuauhtitlan.

3 : 48   2 House. 3 Rabbit. 4 Reed. 5 Flint. 6 House. 7 Rabbit. 8 Reed. 9 Flint. 10 House. 11 Rabbit. 12 Reed. 13 Flint.

[The life of Topiltzin Quetzalcoatl: A.D. 817–95]

3 : 49   1 House [817]. In that year the ruler of the Toltecs died, the one who started the dynasty, the one whose name was Mixcoamazatzin. Then Huetzin was inaugurated, and he ruled in Tollan.

3 : 52   2 Rabbit. 3 Reed. 4 Flint. 5 House. 6 Rabbit. 7 Reed. 8 Flint. 9 House. 10 Rabbit. 11 Reed. 12 Flint. 13 House. 1 Rabbit. 2 Reed. 3 Flint. 4 House. 5 Rabbit.

3 : 54   6 Reed [835]. This is when Quetzalcoatl's father died, whose name was Totepeuh. And at this time Ihuitimal was inaugurated, and he ruled in Tollan.

3 : 56   7 Flint. 8 House. 9 Rabbit. 10 Reed. 11 Flint. 12 House. 13 Rabbit.

   1 Reed [843]. According to what they tell and what they say, this was when Quetzalcoatl was born, called Topiltzin Priest Ce Acatl Quetzalcoatl, and his mother they say was named Chimalman. And from what they say about him, Quetzalcoatl was placed in his mother's belly when she swallowed a piece of jade.

4 : 3   2 Flint. 3 House. 4 Rabbit. 5 Reed. 6 Flint. 7 House. 8 Rabbit.

4 : 4   9 Reed [851]. It was in 9 Reed that Quetzalcoatl looked for his father. When he was nine years old and had some awareness,[19] he said, "What is my father like? May I see him? May I look at his face?"

19. Anticlimactic word order reversed in the translation.

28

4 : 6   "He's dead, he's buried over there," was the answer. "Take a look." So Quetzalcoatl went there. And he looked for the bones. He dug them up.[20] And when he had removed the bones, he went and buried them in the temple mound of [the spirit] known as Quilaztli.

4 : 10   10 Flint. 11 House. 12 Rabbit. 13 Reed. 1 Flint. 2 House. 3 Rabbit. 4 Reed. 5 Flint. 6 House. 7 Rabbit. 8 Reed. 9 Flint.

4 : 11   10 House [865]. In that year Huactli died, who had been ruler of Cuauhtitlan. He had ruled for sixty-two years. This was the ruler who did not know how to plant edible corn. Also, his subjects did not know how to make tilmas. They still wore hides. Their food was just birds, snakes, rabbits, and deer. As yet they were homeless. They just kept going, kept moving from place to place.

4 : 17   In 11 Rabbit [866] the lady Xiuhtlacuilolxochitzin became ruler, and she had her straw-house in Tianquiztenco. Where it was is now Tepexi-tenco. And the reason the nation had been left to this lady, they say, is that she was Huactli's wife—also she knew how to invoke the devil Itzpapalotl.

4 : 21   12 Reed. 13 Flint. 1 House.

4 : 22   In 2 Rabbit [870] Quetzalcoatl arrived in Tollantzinco. He spent four years there and built his house of fasting, his turquoise house of beams. From there he came out toward Cuextlan, and in order to cross a certain river he built a bridge of stone that stands to this day, so it is said.

4 : 25   3 Reed. 4 Flint.

5 House [873].[21] This was the year the Toltecs went to get Quetzalcoatl to make him their ruler in Tollan, and in addition he was their priest. The story of it has been written elsewhere.

4 : 27   6 Rabbit.

7 Reed [875]. Xiuhtlacuilolxochitzin, the Cuauhtitlan lady, died at this time. She had ruled for twelve years.

4 : 29   8 Flint [876]. That year Ayauhcoyotzin was inaugurated as ruler of Cuauhtitlan at a place called Tecpancuauhtla.

4 : 30   9 House. 10 Rabbit. 11 Reed. 12 Flint. 13 House. 1 Rabbit.

4 : 31   2 Reed [883]. According to stories from Tetzcoco, Quetzalcoatl To-piltzin of Tollan Colhuacan died at this time.[22]

4 : 32   It was in 2 Reed that Topiltzin, or Ce Acatl Quetzalcoatl, built his house of fasting, his place of penance, his place of prayer. Four in number were the houses that he built: his turquoise house of beams, his house of red-shell, his house of whiteshell, his house of quetzal plumes. There he prayed, did penance, and kept his fast.

20. Anticlimactic word order reversed in the translation.
21. Marginal gloss: Ihuitimal died.
22. Marginal gloss: These are not valid here.

4 : 36 And just at midnight he would go down to the water, to the place called Water Shrine, or At-the-Water-Weed.

4 : 37 And he punctured himself with thorns[23] on top of Xicocotl and Huitzco and Tzincoc and Mount Nonoalco. And he made his thorns of jade and his needles of quetzal plumes. And for incense he burned turquoise, jade, and redshell. And the blood offerings that he sacrificed were snakes, birds, and butterflies.

4 : 42 Now, it is told and related that it was to heaven that he prayed, that he worshipped. And the ones he called out to were Citlalinicue, Citlalatonac, Tonacacihuatl, Tonacateuctli, Tecolliquenqui, Eztlaquenqui, Tlallamanac, Tlalichcatl.[24]

4 : 45 Well, as they knew, he was crying out to the Place of Duality, to the Nine Layers,[25] which is how the sky is arranged. And so those dwellers yonder knew that the one who was calling to them and praying to them had really been keeping up his humility, keeping up his contrition.

4 : 49 What is more, in his life and in his time he introduced great riches, jade, turquoise, gold, silver, redshell, whiteshell, quetzal plumes. And cotingas, roseate spoonbills, troupials, trogons, and herons.

4 : 53 In addition he introduced cacao of different colors and different-colored cotton.[26]

4 : 55 And he was a great craftsman in all his works: his eating dishes, his drinking vessels, his green-, herb-green-,[27] white-, yellow-, and red-painted pottery. And there was much more.

5 : 2 And during the time that he lived Quetzalcoatl started and began his temple; he put up the serpent columns. But he did not finish it, he did not build it to the top.

5 : 4 And in the time that he lived he did not show himself in public. He was guarded in a chamber that was hard to reach. Many were the places in which the pages who were guarding him had sealed him up. And wherever

23. For the textual *onmohuitztlaliliaya* read *onmohuitztlaliaya*. The rite of puncturing one-self with thorns, or maguey spines, in the wilderness as a devotional offering is described in FC bk. 3, app. ch. 8; and HG bk. 3, app. ch. 8. Cf. line 6 : 52 below.

24. The names may be translated Star Skirt, Star Shine, Food Woman, Food Lord, Dressed in Charcoal, Dressed in Blood, Earth Founder(?), and Earth Cotton. *Citlala-, eztla-,* and *tlalla-* are here taken to be modified combining forms of *citlalin, eztli,* and *tlalli*. See GRAM sec. 7.2.

25. Twelve layers are mentioned in FC 10 : 169 : 2. According to HG bk. 10, ch. 29, sec. 1, the lord and lady of duality (Ometeuctli and Omecihuatl) were in the topmost of these layers.

26. FC 3 : 14 : 13–24 mentions naturally colored cotton that did not have to be dyed and "flower cacao" (see NED: xochicacahuatl).

27. "Green-, herb-green" is evidently a single color (see GLOS: xoxoctic 2). Since "green" can also be blue, the writer needs to make clear that he means green like the grass, not green like the sky (see NED: ilhuicaxoxohuic 2). I am indebted to the archaeologist Michael E. Smith for advising me that blue-glazed pottery is not found.

he was sealed, some of his pages were there. And that's where the jade mat was, the plume mat, the mat of gold.

5:8   Now, it has been told and mentioned that the houses for fasting that he built were four in number.

5:9   Well, it is told and related that many times during the life of Quetzalcoatl, sorcerers tried to ridicule him into making the human payment,[28] into taking human lives. But he always refused. He did not consent,[29] because he greatly loved his subjects, who were Toltecs. Snakes, birds, and butterflies that he killed were what his sacrifices always were.

5:15   And it is told and related that with this he wore out the sorcerers' patience. So it was then that they started to ridicule him and make fun of him, the sorcerers saying they wanted to torment Quetzalcoatl and make him run away.

5:18   And it became true. It happened.

5:19   3 Flint. 4 House. 5 Rabbit. 6 Reed. 7 Flint. 8 House. 9 Rabbit. 10 Reed. 11 Flint. 12 House. 13 Rabbit.

5:21   1 Reed [895] was the year Quetzalcoatl died. And it is said that he went to Tlillan Tlapallan in order to die there.

5:22   Afterward, a certain Matlacxochitl was inaugurated as ruler, became ruler of Tollan.

5:23   Then they tell how Quetzalcoatl departed. It was when he refused to obey the sorcerers about making the human payment, about sacrificing humans. Then the sorcerers deliberated among themselves, they whose names were Tezcatlipoca, Ihuimecatl, and Toltecatl. They said, "He must leave his city. We shall live there."

5:27   "Let us brew pulque," they said. "We'll have him drink it and make him lose his judgment, so that he no longer performs his sacraments."

5:28   Then Tezcatlipoca said, "Myself, I say we should give him a way to see his flesh."[30]

5:30   They agreed that they would do it.

    Then Tezcatlipoca went first. He took a two-sided mirror, a span wide,[31] wrapped it up. And when he had come to where Quetzalcoatl was, he said to the pages who were guarding him, "Announce to the priest: A young man[32] has come to show you, come to present you,[33] your flesh."

---

28. "Payment" refers to human sacrifice. See also 5:24 below. Compare the "payment" made in the Cantares Mexicanos (see NED: patiuhtli).

29. For the textual *àma çiz* read *àmo çiz*.

30. Lit., let us give him how he will see his flesh. For *quitoz* read *quittaz*. Lehmann, followed by Sullivan, translates "Let us give him his flesh. How shall he see it?"

31. The "span" is a unit of measure equal to about 14 cm. See GLOS: cemiztitl.

32. A play on words. "Young Man" (Telpochtli) was another name for the god Tezcatlipoca.

33. Anticlimactic word order reversed in the translation.

5:34 The pages went inside and repeated it to Quetzalcoatl, who said, "What's that, grandfather page? What's my 'flesh'?" Take a look at what he's brought, and then he may come in."

5:36 But he refused to let them see it. "I must show it to the priest myself," he said. "Go tell him that."

5:37 They went and told him: "He refuses, and he very much wants to show it to you."[34]

5:38 "Let him come, grandfather," said Quetzalcoatl.

5:39 They went and called Tezcatlipoca. He entered, greeting him. He said, "My child,[35] Priest Ce Acatl, Quetzalcoatl, I greet you. And I've come to show you your flesh."

5:42 "You've wearied yourself,[36] grandfather," said Quetzalcoatl. "Where do you come from? What is this 'flesh' of mine? Let me see it."

5:43 "My child, O priest, I, your servant, have come from the foot of Mount Nonoalco. May it please you to see your flesh."

5:45 Then he gave him the mirror[37] and said, "Know yourself, see yourself, my child, for you will appear in the mirror."

5:46 Then Quetzalcoatl looked and was terrified. "If my subjects saw me," he said, "they might run away." For his eyelids were bulging,[38] his eye sockets deeply sunken, his face pouchy all over—he was monstrous.

5:50 When he had looked in the mirror, he said, "My subjects are never to see me. I must stay right here."

5:51 Then Tezcatlipoca left him and came away.[39] And in order to make fun of him he consulted with Ihuimecatl.[40]

5:53 Ihuimecatl said, "Let the featherworker Coyotlinahual be the one to go."

5:54 They repeated it to him, that he was to go. "Very well," said the featherworker Coyotlinahual, "I'll go see Quetzalcoatl." And so he went.

5:56 He said to Quetzalcoatl, "My child, I say you must go out. Let your subjects see you. And for them to see you, let me dress you up."

6:1 He said, "Grandfather, do it! I'd like to see it."

6:2 And so he did it, this featherworker, this Coyotlinahual. First he made

---

34. Read *mitzmottitiliznequi*. Cf. lines 5:34 and 5:37 above, and 5:41 below.

35. The alternate translation "my prince," seems less appropriate in light of the usages in FC bk. 6, where the ruler is addressed by subordinates as "child" or even "grandchild" (see FC 6:51:23). At 6:42 below, Quetzalcoatl's sister is also addressed as "my child."

36. A standard greeting to visitors, often translated "Welcome!"

37. Lehmann notes, "*Tetzcatl* is a variant of *tezcatl* [mirror], especially in the speech of Tetzcoco."

38. Lit., his eyelids were rounded greatly. "Rounded eyelids" (*ixcuatolli mimiltic*) describes the normal condition per FC 10:101.

39. Anticlimactic word order reversed in the translation.

40. A "named partner" construction allowed by Andrews (p. 201), evidently not allowed by Carochi (see CAR 490 or CAROC 86v, GRAM sec. 10.11). Lit., And Ihuimecatl [and he] consulted with one another as to if they [might] not be able to make fun of him.

Quetzalcoatl's head fan. Then he fashioned his turquoise mask,[41] taking yellow to make the front, red to color the bill.[42] Then he gave him his serpent teeth and made him his beard, covering him below with cotinga and roseate spoonbill feathers.

6:7   When he had prepared it—the way the attire of Quetzalcoatl used to be—he gave him the mirror.

6:8   Seeing himself, Quetzalcoatl was well pleased. At that very moment he went out from the place where he was being guarded.

6:9   Then Coyotlinahual, the featherworker, went to Ihuimecatl and said, "I have brought Quetzalcoatl out. Now go!"

6:11   "Very well," he said. Then he befriended a certain Toltecatl, and when they were ready to go, they set off together.[43]

6:13   Then they came to Xonacapacoyan[44] and lodged with the man who worked the fields there, Maxtlaton, the keeper of Toltecatepec.[45] Then they also stewed greens, tomatoes, chilis, fresh corn, and beans. And it was all done in just a few days.

6:16   There were also magueys there, which they requested from Maxtla. In just four days they made them into pulque, then they decanted it. They were the ones who discovered the little hives of tree honey, and it was with this[46] that they decanted the pulque.

6:20   Then they went to Tollan, to the house of Quetzalcoatl, bringing all their greens, their chilis, and so forth. Also the pulque. When they got there, they tried to enter, but Quetzalcoatl's guards would not let them.[47] Twice, three times they turned them away. They were not admitted. Finally they were asked where their home was.

6:24   "Over at Tlamacazcatepec, at Toltecatepec,"[48] they replied.

6:25   Hearing them, Quetzalcoatl said, "Let them come in."

6:26   They went in.
Well, they greeted him, and at last they gave him the greens, etc. And when he had eaten of it, they urged him once again, giving him the pulque.

---

41. The Quetzalcoatl mask that Moteuczoma sent to Cortés was a "serpent mask of turquoise mosaic" (*coaxaiacatl, xiuhtica tlachioalli*)—FC 12:11:10 and HG. But the description in our text seems closer to the Quetzalcoatl masks shown in the pictographic codices, with their long bird bills, sometimes red, set with alligatorlike teeth or merely a pair of serpent fangs, and surrounded by a fringelike beard. The area of the eyes and forehead, either yellow or some other contrasting color, perhaps corresponds to the "front" mentioned here. For a guide to pictorial representations of the deity see León-Portilla, *Quetzalcoatl*.

42. Word order reversed in the translation.

43. Anticlimactic word order reversed in the translation.

44. Lit., place where onions are washed.

45. Lit., Toltec mountain.

46. Read *yehuatl inic*.

47. Lit., they tried, but Quetzalcoatl's guards would not allow them to enter.

48. Lit., at priest mountain, at Toltec mountain.

6 : 28   But he said, "No, I mustn't drink it. I'm fasting. Is it intoxicating? Or fatal?"

6 : 29   "Taste it with your finger," they told him. "It's piquant."[49]

6 : 30   Quetzalcoatl tasted it with his finger. Finding it good, he said, "Let me drink, grandfather." And when he had drunk one draught, the sorcerers said to him, "You'll drink four." And so they gave him a fifth draught, saying, "This is your portion."[50]

6 : 33   Well, when he had drunk it, then they served all his pages, and they drank five draughts apiece.

6 : 35   When the sorcerers had gotten them completely drunk, they said to Quetzalcoatl, "My child, may it please you to sing, and here's a song for you to recite." Then Ihuimecatl recited it for him:

6 : 38   I must leave[51] my house of quetzal, of quetzal, my house of troupial, my house of redshell.

6 : 39   When he had gotten into a happy mood, he said, "Go get my sister[52] Quetzalpetlatl. Let the two of us be drunk together."

6 : 41   His pages went to Mount Nonoalco, where she was doing penance, and said, "My child, lady, Quetzalpetlatl, O fasting one, we've come to get you. Priest Quetzalcoatl is waiting for you.[53] You're to go be with him."

6 : 44   She said, "All right, let's go, grandfather page." And when she got there, she sat down beside Quetzalcoatl. Then they served her the pulque. Four draughts and one more, a fifth, were poured for her.

6 : 47   And when Yhuimecatl and Toltecatl had made everyone drunk, they presented a song to Quetzalcoatl's sister. They recited it for her:

6 : 49   My sister, where are you?[54] O Quetzalpetlatl, let's be drunk, aÿya ÿya ynye an.

6 : 50   Having made themselves drunk, they no longer said, "Let us do penance." No longer did they go down to the water. No longer did they go out to puncture themselves with thorns. From then on they did nothing at daybreak.

49. Lit., indeed it's a sharp stone(?), indeed it's a thorn. Perhaps a pun is intended, since "thorn" (*huitztli*) is a synonym for pulque.

50. Four draughts were allowed; a fifth was considered the mark of a drunkard (HG bk. 10, ch. 29, section entitled "De los mexicanos").

51. The *ya* in *ticyacahuaz* is a nonsense syllable.

52. Lit., elder sister.

53. Read *mitzmochialia*.

54. *Cā tiyanemeyan = can tinemi* (where are you?; the *ya* and *yan* are nonsense syllables). This is a standard expression in Aztec songs, used to invoke an absent spirit, especially the supreme deity. For parallel passages, see NED: nemi 3.

6 : 53   Well, when dawn came, they were filled with sadness, their hearts were troubled. And Quetzalcoatl said, "Alas for me!" And then he sang a lament, composing a song about how he would have to go away. Then he sang it aloud: [55]

7 : 1   Never [56] a portion counted [57] in my house. [58] Let it be here, ah, let it be here, here. [59] Alas. May the realm endure. Alas. There's only misery and servitude. Never will I recover. [60]

7 : 3   He sang aloud the second stanza of his song:

7 : 4   Ah, she used to carry me, alas, my mother, ah, Coacueye, the goddess, the noble one. I am weeping, ah.

7 : 5   When Quetzalcoatl had sung, then all his pages were saddened. They wept. And they, too, sang, saying: [61]

7 : 8   They made us rich, they, our lords, and he, Quetzalcoatl, who shined like a jade. Broken are the timbers, his house of penance. [62] Would that we might see him. Let us weep.

7 : 11   And when Quetzalcoatl's pages had sung, he said to them, "Grandfather page, enough! I must leave this city. I must go away. Give the command. Have them make a stone chest."

7 : 14   Then quickly a stone chest was carved. And when they had carved it and it was finished, they laid Quetzalcoatl in it.

7 : 16   But he lay only four days in the stone chest. When he felt discomfort,

55. Rewritten as I understand it, with vocables italicized, the song text is as follows: aic-*on* pohual[li] ce tonal[li] nocallan ma nican *aya* hue-*ya* ma nican-*o* nican-*an* ma-*ye* ommani *ye* hue-*hua* tlall-*a* hue çan *ya* cococ tlacoyotl aic-*a* ninozcaltiç-*a*.

56. It is by no means clear that the copyist has stricken "htli," though it seems to be smudged or blotted in the manuscript. Lehmann reads *ayahtli*, interpreting this as *ayahtle* or *ay ahtle*, in which case the translation might be "Ay, at my house a portion is counted as nothing." The catchword *aya* at the bottom of side 6 lends weight to Lehmann's reading.

57. The two characters preceding the word are illegible. The reading *on pohual* follows Lehmann's guess.

58. Freely, "pulque has never been served (or esteemed) in my house" (?). In a variant of the story, a sorcerer addresses Quetzalcoatl, calling the pulque "your portion" (*motonal*, FC 3 : 16 : 22).

59. The diction of this and the following two sentences has echoes in the Cantares Mexicanos. With such phrases mortals leaving the earth express both nostalgia and anguish.

60. Alternate translation: "Never will I sober up."

61. My reconstruction of the song text: *aya* techon-*ya*-cuiltonoca yehuan noteuchuan yehua [i]n quetzalcoatl-*an* mochalchiuhpopo[ya]hu-*a* cuahuitl iezzocan-*a* tlapa[n] ma tic-*ya*-itzcan *yehuan* ma-*n* tichocacan *ean*.

62. Marginal gloss: house of Quetzalcoatl.

he said to his pages, "Enough, grandfather page! Let's go. Everywhere conceal and hide what we once discovered, the joy, the riches, all our property, our possessions. And his pages did so. They hid it where Quetzalcoatl's bathing place was, at the place called Water Shrine, At-the-Water-Weed.

7 : 22   Then Quetzalcoatl departed. He got up, called together his pages, and wept over them. Then they set out, heading for Tlillan, Tlapallan, Tlatlayan.[63]

7 : 25   And he went looking everywhere, exploring. Nowhere was he satisfied. And when he reached the place he had been heading for, again he wept and was sad.

7 : 27   Now, this year, 1 Reed, is when he got to the ocean, the seashore, so it is told and related. Then he halted and wept and gathered up his attire, putting on his head fan, his turquoise mask, and so forth. And as soon as he was dressed, he set himself on fire and cremated himself.[64] And so the place where Quetzalcoatl was cremated is named Tlatlayan [land of burning].

7 : 32   And they say as he burned, his ashes arose. And what appeared and what they saw were all the precious birds, rising into the sky. They saw roseate spoonbills, cotingas, trogons, herons, green parrots, scarlet macaws, white-fronted parrots, and all the other precious birds.

7 : 37   And as soon as his ashes had been consumed, they saw the heart of a quetzal rising upward. And so they knew he had gone to the sky, had entered the sky.

7 : 39   The old people said he was changed into the star that appears at dawn. Therefore they say it came forth when Quetzalcoatl died, and they called him Lord of the Dawn.

7 : 43   What they said is that when he died he disappeared for four days. They said he went to the dead land then. And he spent four more days making darts for himself. So it was after eight days that the morning star came out, which they said was Quetzalcoatl. It was then that he became lord, they said.

7 : 47   And so, when he goes forth, they know on what day sign he casts light on certain people, venting his anger against them, shooting them with darts.[65] If he goes on 1 Alligator, he shoots old men and old women, all alike.

7 : 50   If on 1 Jaguar or 1 Deer or 1 Flower, he shoots little children.

7 : 52   And if on 1 Reed, he shoots nobles. The same with everybody, if on 1 Death.

7 : 53   And if on 1 Rain, he shoots the rain. No rain will fall.

63. Lit., red land, black land, land of burning.
64. Anticlimactic word order reversed in the translation.
65. Anticlimactic word order reversed in the translation.

7 : 54   And if on 1 Movement, he shoots youths and maidens.

7 : 55   And if on 1 Water, there is drought,[66] etc.

7 : 56   So each of these [day signs] was venerated[67] by the old men and the old women of former times.

8 : 1   As for the one called Quetzalcoatl, his entire lifetime was such that he was born in 1 Reed and also died in 1 Reed, so that his life was counted altogether as fifty-two years.

8 : 3   So, it is finished in the year 1 Reed [895].

8 : 4   It was said that Matlacxochitl succeeded him and ruled in Tollan.

[The fall of Tollan: A.D. 896–1070]

2 Flint. 3 House. 4 Rabbit. 5 Reed. 6 Flint. 7 House. 8 Rabbit. 9 Reed. 10 Flint. 11 House. 12 Rabbit. 13 Reed. 1 Flint. 2 House. 3 Rabbit. 4 Reed. 5 Flint. 6 House. 7 Rabbit. 8 Reed. 9 Flint. 10 House. 11 Rabbit. 12 Reed. 13 Flint. 1 House. 2 Rabbit. 3 Reed. 4 Flint. 5 House. 6 Rabbit. 7 Reed. 8 Flint. 9 House.

8 : 9   10 Rabbit [930]. Ayauhcoyotzin, ruler of Cuauhtitlan, died in that year. He had ruled for fifty-five years. Matlacxochitzin, ruler of Tollan, also died then, and Nauhyotzin was inaugurated, succeeding him as Tollan's ruler.

8 : 13   11 Reed [931]. The Cuauhtitlan ruler Necuamexochitzin was inaugurated in that year. His palace was in Tepotzotlan Miccacalco. The reason it was called Miccacalco [At the House of the Dead] is that lightning struck there, killing noblemen and ladies, and so they changed residence. Nothing was left standing but the Chichimec rulers' straw-house. They did not dare go[68] back to their palace.

8 : 19   12 Flint. 13 House. 1 Rabbit. 2 Reed. 3 Flint. 4 House. 5 Rabbit. 6 Reed. 7 Flint. 8 House. 9 Rabbit. 10 Reed. 11 Flint.

8 : 21   12 House [945]. It was the year the Cuauhtitlan ruler called Necuamexochitzin died. He had ruled for fifteen years. Also at that time the Tollan ruler, Nauhyotzin, died, and Matlaccoatzin was inaugurated, succeeding him.

8 : 24   13 Rabbit [946]. In that year Mecellotzin was inaugurated as ruler of Cuauhtitlan. His palace was built in a place called Tianquizzolco Cuauhtlaapan.

8 : 27   1 Reed. 2 Flint. 3 House. 4 Rabbit. 5 Reed. 6 Flint. 7 House. 8 Rabbit. 9 Reed. 10 Flint. 11 House. 12 Rabbit. 13 Reed. 1 Flint. 2 House. 3 Rabbit. 4 Reed. 5 Flint. 6 House. 7 Rabbit. 8 Reed. 9 Flint. 10 House. 11 Rabbit. 12 Reed. 13 Flint.

66. Read *tlahuaqui*.
67. Read *quitenyotiaya*. Cf. line 9 : 55 below.
68. The textual *yaz* should be *yazque*.

8 : 30   1 House [973]. In that year the ruler of Tollan, who was called Matlac-coatzin, died. Tlilcoatzin was inaugurated as Tollan's ruler.

8 : 32   2 Rabbit. 3 Reed. 4 Flint. 5 House. 6 Rabbit. 7 Reed. 8 Flint.

8 : 33   9 House [981]. In that year the Cuauhtitlan ruler Mecellotzin died. He had ruled for thirty-six years.

8 : 35   10 Rabbit [982]. In that year Tzihuacpapalotzin was inaugurated as ruler of Cuauhtitlan. His palace was built in Cuauhtlaapan.

8 : 37   11 Reed. 12 Flint. 13 House. 1 Rabbit. 2 Reed. 3 Flint. 4 House.[69] 5 Rabbit. 6 Reed. 7 Flint. 8 House.

8 : 38   9 Rabbit [994]. At that time, in the time of 9 Rabbit, the Tollan ruler Tlilcoatzin died. And then Huemac was inaugurated, and his official title became *atecpanecatl*.[70] Many more stories about this are to be heard from a certain book: at the time he was inaugurated he got married, taking to wife a certain Coacueye, a *mocihuaquetzqui*,[71] who received instructions from the Devil at a place called Coacueyecan; it was there that this woman known as Coacue had her home; her buttocks were an arm-span wide, etc.[72]

8 : 46   And when that occurred, they went to Xicocotl and got a high priest, whose name was Cuauhtli. Then they came back and set him up on the mat and throne of Quetzalcoatl.[73] Thus he was made his successor, he became the Quetzalcoatl of Tollan: it was he who became priest, succeeding Huemac. Indeed, he became Quetzalcoatl.

8 : 50   When female sorcerers set out to make fun of [Huemac] and mock him, [Huemac] cohabited with them. The sorcerer Yaotl and the one called Tezcatlipoca, who lived in Tzapotlan, were the ones who came there. When they deceived Huemac by changing themselves into women, he did cohabit with them. Then he stopped being Quetzalcoatl. It was said that that is how Cuauhtli succeeded him, etc.

8 : 56   10 Reed. 11 Flint. 12 House. 13 Rabbit. 1 Reed. 2 Flint. 3 House. 4 Rabbit. 5 Reed. 6 Flint. 7 House. 8 Rabbit. 9 Reed. 10 Flint. 11 House. 12 Rabbit. 13 Reed. 1 Flint. 2 House. 3 Rabbit. 4 Reed. 5 Flint. 6 House.

9 : 1   7 Rabbit [1018]. Here began the sacrifice of the human streamers.[74] At

69. Marginal gloss: In [4?] House Tollan was destroyed, according to stories from Tetz-coco. Not valid.

70. Marginal gloss: huemac atecpanecatl.

71. Defined by Sahagún as "valiant woman" (*mujer valiente*), the term was applied to women who, having died in childbirth, rose to the sky as ghost warriors and descended at night to haunt the earth. See HG bk. 6, ch. 29.

72. According to the *Historia Tolteca-Chichimeca*, Huemac desired a woman with but-tocks "four [hand-]spans" wide. This led to a conflict that caused the downfall of Tollan (HTCH secs. 18–32).

73. Lit., Then it was he who came to be set up on the mat and throne of Quetzalcoatl.

74. "Streamers" refers to the little children sacrificed on mountaintops as offerings to the rain gods (FFCC 1:68, FC 2:42–43). The marginal gloss simply reads: human sacrifice. See GLOS: tetehuitl, tlacatetehuitl.

that time, in the time of 7 Rabbit, a great famine occurred. What is said is that the Toltecs were seven-rabbited. It was a seven-year famine, a famine that caused much suffering and death.[75]

9 : 6   It was then that the sorcerers requisitioned Huemac's own children and went and left them in the waters of Xochiquetzal and on Huitzco and on Xicocotl, thus making payment with little children.[76] This was the first time that the sacrifice of human streamers occurred.

9 : 10   8 Reed. 9 Flint. 10 House. 11 Rabbit.

9 : 11   12 Reed [1023]. The Cuauhtitlan ruler called Tzihuacpapalotzin died at this time. He had been ruling for forty-two years.

9 : 12   13 Flint [1024]. In that year a Cuauhtitlan lady named Itztacxilotzin was inaugurated to govern the nation.[77] Her mound and her straw-house were in Izquitlan Atlan. At her side were many ladies who paid her honor. It was in this manner that the Chichimecs attended her, etc.

9 : 17   1 House. 2 Rabbit. 3 Reed. 4 Flint. 5 House. 6 Rabbit. 7 Reed. 8 Flint. 9 House. 10 Rabbit.

9 : 18   11 Reed [1035]. In that year the lady Iztacxilotzin died, having ruled for eleven years. Then Eztlaquencatzin was inaugurated, succeeding her. In Techichco he built himself a new straw-house, or palace house. That is where he started it, and so that is where the rulers' residence was, etc.

9 : 23   12 Flint. 13 House. 1 Rabbit. 2 Reed. 3 Flint. 4 House. 5 Rabbit. 6 Reed. 7 Flint. 8 House. 9 Rabbit. 10 Reed. 11 Flint. 12 House. 13 Rabbit.

9 : 25   1 Reed [1051]. At that time the Chalca came out of Xicco:[78] the founder Acapol, his wife Tetzcotzin, their children Chalcotzin, Chalcapol, etc.

9 : 27   2 Flint. 3 House. 4 Rabbit. 5 Reed. 6 Flint. 7 House.

9 : 28   8 Rabbit [1058]. In that year there were a great many evil omens in Tollan. Well, it was the same year that sorcerers arrived,[79] the so-called *ixcuinanme*, the female devils. And according to the stories of the old people, which tell how they came, they issued forth from Cuextlan. And at so-called Cuextecatlichocayan [Place Where the Cuexteca Weep] they spoke to the captives they had taken in Cuextlan and made them a prom-

75. Lit., it was a seven-year famine; at that time (*yc oncanin*) this one (*ye*), the famine, afflicts people in general, this one hides (i.e., kills) people in general. See NED: tla- 2, tlatia:te. The expression *ye tlatlatia* could also be translated "this one burns people in general." On the burning sensation caused by hunger during a famine see HG bk. 6, ch. 8 (FC 6:37:15–19).

76. For *yca* read *ÿca*.

77. See AND 293 for examples of this purposive syntax.

78. Marginal gloss: The Chalca left Xicco.

79. Arrived in Cuextlan? According to 9:40 below, they did not reach Tollan until the following year.

ise, saying, "We are going to Tollan now. You will go with us, and when we get there, we will use you to make a celebration,[80] for there has never been an arrow shoot. And we are the ones who are going to start it[81] by shooting you."

9 : 37   When the captives heard this, they wept, they grieved. Then the arrow shoot[82] began, and in this way a feast used to be celebrated in honor of the *ixcuinanme* at the time of the so-called Izcalli.[83]

9 : 40   9 Reed [1059]. It was then that the *ixcuinanme* arrived in Tollan, bringing their captives with them.[84] There were two whom they shot with arrows. Well, the Cuexteca captives were the husbands of those sorcerers, those female devils. That was when the arrow shoot was founded.

9 : 44   10 Flint. 11 House. 12 Rabbit.

13 Reed [1063]. At this time there were many evil omens in Tollan. At this time, too, was the beginning of the war that the devil Yaotl started. The Toltecs were engaged [in battle] at a place called Nextlalpan. And when they had taken captives, human sacrifice also got started, as Toltecs sacrificed their prisoners. Among them and in their midst the devil Yaotl followed along. Right on the spot he kept inciting them[85] to make human sacrifices.

9 : 50   And then, too, he started and began the practice of flaying humans. This was when he sang songs at Texcalapan.[86] Then, to start with, he seized an Otomi woman, who was washing maguey fibers at the river, and flayed her. Then he made one of the Toltecs named Xiuhcozcatl wear the skin, and he was the first to wear[87] a *totec* skin.[88]

9 : 55   Indeed, every kind of human sacrifice that there used to be got started then. For it is told and related that during his time[89] and under his authority,[90] the first Quetzalcoatl, whose name was Ce Acatl, absolutely refused to perform human sacrifice. It was precisely when Huemac was

---

80. Lit., By means of you we are to arrive in the region, by means of you we are to make a feast day. Cf. 9 : 41 below.

81. Read *ticpehualtitihui*.

82. Marginal gloss: sacrifice of the ones shot by arrows.

83. The feast of the *ixcuinanme* is mentioned in FFCC bk. 1, ch. 12. For the twenty-day feasting period, or "month," of Izcalli see FC bk. 2 and DCAL. Arrow sacrifice is described in RITOS ch. 14.

84. Lit., It was then that the *ixcuinanme* arrived in Tollan; they arrived in the region by means of (or in company with) their captives. For *yca* read *ÿca*. Cf. 9 : 35 above.

85. Read *quinitlahueltitinenca*.

86. The story is fully told in FC bk. 3, ch. 21. During the last days of Tollan the sorcerer mesmerized the people with his singing, causing them to dance near the edge of a gorge at a place called Texcalpan (sic). Many fell and were killed. Flaying, however, is not mentioned in the FC version.

87. Read *quimaquiaya*. Cf. line 7 : 56 above.

88. The victim of flaying was called a *totec* (FC bk. 2, ch. 21).

89. The expected form is *ymatiyan*.

90. Anticlimactic word order reversed in the translation.

ruler that all those things that used to be done got started. It was th
who started them. But this has been put on paper and written dov
where. And there it is to be heard.

10:5 1 Flint[91] [1064] is when those who had been Toltecs disbanded. It
happened in Huemac's time, when he was ruler. And when they were on
their way, traveling, they came to Cincoc. And there at Cincoc, Huemac
sacrificed a human streamer, thus making payment. Its name was Ce Coatl.

10:9 And on the road at Tlamacazcatzinco he tried to enter a cave but was
unable to do so.

10:10 Then he left and came to Cuauhnenec, where Huemac's wife, whose
name was Cuauhnene, gave birth. For this reason it is now called Cuauhnenec [Place of Cuauhnene].

10:12 Then he left and came to Teocompan [Place of the Pot Cactus]. There
on a pot cactus stood the sorcerer Yaotl, calling together his friends, saying, "Rest here, friends. Let the Toltecs go ahead. You must not go on, O
friends."

10:16 Well, the ones he called together were: first, Icnotlacatl; second, Tziuhmazatl; third, Acxocuauhtli; fourth, Tzoncuaye; fifth, Xiuhcozcatl; sixth,
Ozomateuctli; seventh, Tlachquiahuitl Teuctli; eighth, Huetl; ninth, Tecol
Teuctli; tenth, Cuauhtli; eleventh, Aztaxoch; twelfth, Aztamamal; thirteenth, Icnotlacatl's mother.

10:21 And the Devil brought together many more of his poor friends there at
Huecompan [At the Great Pot Cactus].

10:22 Now, when the Toltecs had gone, the Devil sent forth his friends for
the purpose of settling them in Xaltocan,[92] saying to Icnotlacatl and all the
others:

10:25 "Don't become arrogant. Remember all the work we did in Tollan. You
are to keep on doing it.

10:27 "You are a poor man indeed, Icnotlacatl.[93] Do not be proud.[94] If you
people become proud, I will mock you, destroy you, the way I mocked
Maxtla, who lived at Toltecatepec, who had two daughters, Quetzalquen
and Quetzalxilotl, whom he kept in a jeweled cage. I got them pregnant with twins,[95] and they gave birth to two creatures in the form of
opossums.

10:33 "Likewise I mocked Cuauhtliztac, the keeper[96] of Oztotempan, and
Cuauhtli, the keeper of Atzompan. It was I who destroyed them."

10:35 And when the devil Yaotl had sent forth his friends in order to estab-

91. Marginal gloss: Tollan was depopulated.
92. Compare the purposive syntax in lines 9:13–14. And for confirmation see lines
10:36–37.
93. The name Icnotlacatl literally means "poor man."
94. I follow Lehmann, who reads *ma tatlamâ*. The expected form is *ma tatlamat*.
95. Read *niquincocohuapilhuati*.
96. Read *tlapiaya*. Cf. 7:56 and 9:55 above.

lish them in Xaltocan, he went and got them settled—down yonder, in
Xaltocan.

10 : 39   And as for the Toltecs, they went on. They went to Coatliyopan, they
went to Atepocatlalpan, they went to Tepetlayacac.

10 : 40   They went to old Cuauhtitlan, where they served Atonal, who lived in
Tamazolac and was the keeper of that place. And he governed them together with his other subjects.

10 : 43   Then the Toltecs departed and went on to Nepopohualco, Temacpalco,
Acatitlan, Tenamitliyacac, Azcapotzalco, Tetlolincan, at the time when
Tzihuactlatonac was ruler. There they left two Toltec elders, Xochiololtzin
and Coyotzin, who gave the ruler a gold medallion so that they could
settle in his territory.

10 : 49   Then the Toltecs went on to Chapoltepec, Huitzilopochco, Colhuacan.
They went to Tlapechhuacan Cuauhtenco.[97] And when they entered a
country, some of them settled down—in Cholollan, Teohuacan, Cozcatlan, Nonoalco, Teotlillan, Coaixtlahuacan, Tamazolac, Copilco, Topillan,
Ayotlan, Mazatlan, so that they settled everywhere in the land of Anahuac,
where they are today.

11 : 3   And 1 Flint [1064] was also the time when all[98] the Colhuaque went
their own way.[99] And their ruler, whose name was Nauhyotzin, was in
the lead.

11 : 5   2 House. 3 Rabbit. 4 Reed. 5 Flint. 6 House.

11 : 6   7 Rabbit [1070] is when Huemac killed himself at Chapoltepec Cincalco.[100] In the year 7 Rabbit the Toltecs' years came to a close. For seven
years they went wandering everywhere, from place to place, establishing
themselves and settling down. The Toltecs existed for 339 years.[101]

11 : 11   Well, the year 7 Rabbit was when Huemac committed suicide by hanging himself. It was then that he lost hope, there in the cave at Chapoltepec.
First he wept, grieving, when he saw no more Toltecs drawing up behind
him. Then he killed himself.

[The Mexica reach Chapoltepec: A.D. 1071–1240]

11 : 15   8 Reed [1071].

9 Flint [1072]. This was when the Colhuacan ruler Nauhyotzin died.
Nauhyotzin's son, Cuauhtexpetlatzin, was inaugurated, and Nauhyotzin

---

97. Cf. 11 : 19.
98. For çe read çē, i.e., *cen* (all).
99. Marginal gloss: The Colhuaque went by way of another country.
100. Cincalco was the name of a cave at Chapoltepec (HG bk. 12, ch. 9).
101. This probably means from the founding of Tollan to the death of Huemac, as in
ZCHIM 1 : 4, where the span is reckoned as 342 years.

died at Coatolco Ayahualolco. The Colhuaque had spent nine years[102] at Tlapechhuacan Cuauhtenco.[103] And it was there that Cuauhtexpetlatzin was inaugurated and became ruler of Colhuacan.

11 : 21 10 House. 11 Rabbit. 12 Reed. 13 Flint. 1 House. 2 Rabbit. 3 Reed. 4 Flint. 5 House. 6 Rabbit. 7 Reed. 8 Flint. 9 House. 10 Rabbit. 11 Reed. 12 Flint. 13 House.

11 : 23 1 Rabbit [1090]. The Mexitin set out from Aztlan.

11 : 24 2 Reed [1091]. That was the year the ruler Eztlaquentzin died. He had ruled for fifty-seven years. During the time of Cuauhtexpetlatzin of Colhuacan, while on the road, a year-bundle feast was celebrated at a place called Xochiquilazco.[104] As for the Mexitin, this was the time they arrived at Cuahuitlicacan.

11 : 28 3 Flint [1092] was the year that Ezcoatzin was inaugurated as ruler in Cimapan Tehuiloyocan—the straw-house town in Techichco.[105]

11 : 30 This was also the time that Aca died, ruler of Chalco when they were still at Xicco. And so then, Tozquehua Teuctli was inaugurated. He ruled for forty years.

11 : 32 4 House. 5 Rabbit.

6 Reed [1095]. In that year the Mexitin reached Tepetlimonamiquiyan [Where Mountains Come Together].

11 : 33 7 Flint. 8 House. 9 Rabbit. 10 Reed. 11 Flint.

11 : 34 12 House [1101]. At that time the Mexitin reached Tepetlmaxaliuhyan [Where Mountains Divide].

11 : 35 13 Rabbit. 1 Reed. 2 Flint. 3 House. 4 Rabbit.

5 Reed [1107]. In that year the ruler Ezcoatzin died. He had ruled for sixteen years.

11 : 37 6 Flint [1108]. In that year the ruler Teiztlacoatzin was inaugurated, and his straw-house was in Xoloc.

11 : 38 7 House.

8 Rabbit [1110] was when the Mexitin arrived in Coatlyayauhcan.

11 : 39 9 Reed. 10 Flint. 11 House.

11 : 40 12 Rabbit [1114] is when the Mexitin arrived at Zacatepec.

11 : 41 13 Reed. 1 Flint. 2 House.

3 Rabbit [1118] is when the Mexitin arrived at Tematlahuacalco.

11 : 42 4 Reed. 5 Flint. 6 House.

7 Rabbit [1122] is when the Mexitin arrived at Coatepec.

11 : 43 8 Reed. 9 Flint. 10 House. 11 Rabbit.

---

102. Read *chiconnauhxiuhtique*, for which the textual *9-xiuhtique* is an abbreviation.
103. Cf. 10:51 above.
104. The year-bundle feast, or *toximmolpilia* ("our years are tied"), marked the end of a fifty-two year cycle. See FC 4:143, 7:25.
105. The translation follows Velázquez. Evidently the Cuauhtitlan people are still in Techichco, as in 9:21 above.

11 : 44   12 Reed [1127] is when Cuauhtexpetlatzin arrived in Colhuacan. And then he sent subjects of his to live in Ocuillan and Malinalco.

11 : 46   13 Flint.

1 House [1129]. That was the year the Colhuacan ruler Cuauhtexpetlatzin died, and Huetzin was inaugurated. And when he was inaugurated there in Colhuacan, the prince Acxocuauhtli, who was the younger brother of Nauhyotzin, set forth, etc.

11 : 50   2 Rabbit [1130]. The Xochimilca and the Colhuaque had provoked each other, and [the Colhuaque] chased the Xochimilca and left them at Teyahualco. That was how they drove them away.

11 : 52   3 Reed [1131]. In 3 Reed, while they were still at Xicco, the Chalco ruler Tozquihua died. Then Acatl was inaugurated. All those who are now known as Chalca arrived during his time, etc.

12 : 2   4 Flint [1132]. In 4 Flint the Mexitin came to Chimalcotitlan. It was also in 4 Flint that the Chalca Tenanca arrived and obtained land. Island town. Cima. He conquers, etc.[106]

12 : 5   5 House. 6 Rabbit.

7 Reed [1135]. In 7 Reed the Chalca Mihuaque, who were Huitznahua Chichimecs, arrived, etc.

12 : 6   8 Flint [1136]. In 8 Flint the Mexitin arrived.

9 House.

12 : 7   10 Rabbit [1138]. In 10 Rabbit, the Tlahuacan Chalca arrived, traveling with the magician's staff,[107] Mixcoatl. Now, in that same year Chalca and other nations arrived together.

12 : 9   11 Reed. 12 Flint.

12 : 10   13 House [1141]. In 13 House the Xochimilca got rid of the ones who ferried across, who reached Colhuacan.[108]

12 : 11   1 Rabbit [1142]. In 1 Rabbit the Xochimilca chased those Colhuaque whom they had conquered and scattered them where they live today.

12 : 13   2 Reed. 3 Flint. 4 House.

5 Rabbit [1146]. The Mexica reach Tollan.

12 : 14   6 Reed. 7 Flint. 8 House.

9 Rabbit [1150]. That was the year the Colhuacan ruler Huetzin died.

106. This seems to mean that the Chalca Tenanca arrived in the region of Lake Chalco and obtained land when their leader, Cima, conquered an island town. The name Cimatzin, though not in connection with the Tenanca, is attested in ZCHIM 1:54 and HTCH sec. 223.

107. Lit., they and the magician-staff Mixcoatl went. In which case the text should read *yaque [i]n nahualcuauhtli mixcoatl*. The expected form, *nahualcuahuitl*, seems to mean "sorcerer's staff" at FC 2:77:9; and HMPP (ch. 8) speaks of "una vara de Mixcoatl, al cual tenían por dios, y por su memoria tenían aquella vara." On the interchangeability of *cuauhtli* and *cuahuitl* see NED: cuāhuitl.

108. Lit., the Xochimilca left him who ferried people hither, who reached Colhuacan. Cf. 12:11–13 below.

And at that time the Mexitin arrived at Atlitlalaquiyan. And when Huetzin was dead, Nonoalcatzin was inaugurated as ruler of Colhuacan.

12 : 17   10 Reed. 11 Flint. 12 House.

12 : 18   13 Rabbit [1154]. Some say Huetzin died at this time.

1 Reed [1155]. That was when the Mexitin came here to Cuauhtitlan. In 1 Reed the Chalco ruler Acatl died, and Tlalli Teuctli[109] was inaugurated. Here in this vicinity, in 1 Reed, the Mexitin got to Citlaltepec and Tzompanco, where they spent ten years.

12 : 21   2 Flint. 3 House. 4 Rabbit. 5 Reed. 6 Flint. 7 House. 8 Rabbit. 9 Reed. 10 Flint.

12 : 23   11 House [1165]. At that time the Mexica were in Ecatepec.

12 Rabbit [1166] is when the Mexitin got to Coatitlan.

13 Reed.

12 : 24   1 Flint [1168]. The Chalca Tlacochcalca arrived at that time. Yaotl obtained [lands]. Then, too, was the beginning of rulership in Tepeyacac and in Cholollan.

12 : 26   2 House. 3 Rabbit.

4 Reed [1171]. In that year the Colhuacan ruler Nonoalcatzin died. Then Achitometl was inaugurated as ruler of Colhuacan.

12 : 29   5 Flint [1172]. The Mexitin were in Tolpetlac.

6 House.

7 Rabbit [1174]. In that year the Cuauhtitlan ruler Teiztlacoatzin died. He had ruled for fifty-seven years.

12 : 31   8 Reed [1175]. It was then that the elder Quinatzin was inaugurated at Techichco, and his palace house was in Tepetlapan Tequixquinahuac Huixtompan.

12 : 33   9 Flint [1176] was when the Mexitin got to Chiquiuhtepetlapan Tecpayocan.

12 : 34   10 House. 11 Rabbit. 12 Reed. 13 Flint. 1 House. 2 Rabbit. 3 Reed. 4 Flint.

12 : 36   5 House [1185]. In that year the Colhuacan ruler Achitometl died. Then Cuahuitonal was inaugurated as ruler of Colhuacan.

12 . 38   6 Rabbit [1186]. In that year the Mexitin reached Tepeyacac.

7 Reed. 8 Flint

9 House [1189]. In that year the Mexitin reached Pantitlan. Then they withdrew to Popotlan Acolnahuac.

12 : 40   10 Rabbit. 11 Reed. 12 Flint.

13 House [1193]. Since the Toltecs had disbanded, the Colhuaque had been on their own for 125 years.

12 : 42   1 Rabbit [1194] was the year the Mexitin arrived in Chapoltepec.

109. Cf. 18 : 9 below.

Mazatzin, a ruler of Chichimecs, was ruling at Chapoltepec at that time. And the priest of the Mexitin was a certain Tzippantzin.

12 : 45   Well, Mazatzin had a daughter named Xochipapalotl. And while the Mexitin were in the territory[110] of this ruler, this Mazatzin, they started to make fun of his daughter. Many times[111] they carried her off while she was asleep.[112] And with this they made much fun of the Chichimecs.

12 : 49   Annoyed, Mazatzin left them there and went away, taking his subjects with him, and they came and settled in Otlazpan, etc.

12 : 51   Now, when the Mexitin arrived at Chapoltepec, the ruler of Colhuacan was Cuahuitonal. The Tetzcoca say that Huemac, the one who fled Tollan, died at this time. That story is not valid, according to what was said—the narrative about it, the truth about it.[113]

12 : 55   2 Reed. 3 Flint. 4 House. 5 Rabbit.

12 : 56   6 Reed [1199]. In that year the Colhuacan ruler Cuahuitonal died. Then Mazatzin was inaugurated in Colhuacan.

12 : 57   7 Flint. 8 House. 9 Rabbit. 10 Reed. 11 Flint. 12 House. 13 Rabbit. 1 Reed. 2 Flint. 3 House. 4 Rabbit. 5 Reed. 6 Flint. 7 House. 8 Rabbit. 9 Reed. 10 Flint. 11 House. 12 Rabbit. 13 Reed. 1 Flint. 2 House.

13 : 2   3 Rabbit [1222]. In that year the Colhuacan ruler Mazatzin died. Then Cuetzaltzin[114] was inaugurated in Colhuacan.

13 : 4   The Tlahuaca landowners, or founders, were: Cuauhtlotlinteuctli and Ihuitzin and Tlilcoatzin and Chalchiuhtzin and Chahuaquetzin. These people were indeed Chichimecs. They were driven out of Xicco, these Chalca of Tlahuacan, and so they are known as Cuitlahuaca, the nobles of Tizic.[115]

13 : 8   4 Reed. 5 Flint. 6 House. 7 Rabbit. 8 Reed.

13 : 9   9 Flint [1228]. In 9 Flint the Tlaxcalteca were besieged, and those who did it were the Huexotzinca when Miccacalcatl was ruler and the Acolhuaque when Acolmiztli was ruler.[116]

13 : 12   11 Rabbit [1230]. In 11 Rabbit Coatomatzin was inaugurated in Cuitlahuac Tizic.

13 : 13   12 Reed. 13 Flint.

1 House [1233]. That was when the Chalca who had been driven out

---

110. For *yntlan* read *ytlan*.

111. Read *miecpa*.

112. If the verb were *concochmanaya*, as Lehmann observes, the translation would be "they laid her while she was asleep."

113. Anticlimactic word order reversed in the translation.

114. The spelling should probably be Quetzaltzin (per Velázquez) or Cuezaltzin (per Lehmann). Sources vary on the name of Mazatzin's successor (see García Granados, *Diccionario*: Quetzaltzin).

115. Marginal gloss: origin of the Cuitlahuaca.

116. Marginal gloss: war between Tlaxcallan and Huexotzinco and the Acolhuaque.

came to Cuitlahuac Tizic. Those who came were the Tlaltecayohuaque, the Mihuaque, the Acxoteca.[117]

13 : 15   2 Rabbit.

13 : 16   3 Reed [1235]. At that time the Colhuacan ruler Cuetzaltzin died. Then Chalchiuhtlatonac was inaugurated in Colhuacan. At that time the Chololteca were destroyed. Their pyramid was wrecked.[118] Huexotzinco's Miccacalcatl was the one who did it, etc.[119]

13 : 19   4 Flint [1236]. This was when Coatomatzin, the ruler of Cuitlahuac Tizic, died.

13 : 20   5 House.

6 Rabbit [1238] was when the Chalca prince Miahuatonaltzin Teuctli went to be inaugurated at Cuitlahuac.

13 : 22   7 Reed.

8 Flint [1240]. In that year the Mexitin, when they had already caused much annoyance,[120] were surrounded in battle at Chapoltepec.

13 : 24   And those who made war on them were the Colhuaque, Azcapotzalco, the Xochimilca, and the Coyohuaque. This was when Chalchiuhtlatonac ruled in Colhuacan, and Iztac Teuctli ruled in Xaltocan. And at this time they came and notified Quinatzin, the ruler of Cuauhtitlan, that his subjects were to make war.

13 : 28   But he would not consent. He refused. Immediately he sent messengers to assure the Mexitin that the Cuauhtitlancalque would not be hostile.

13 : 30   Cimatecatzintli went in the lead, bringing them quail, turkey eggs, and little snakes. These were the greeting gifts of the Cuauhtitlancalque.

[Cuauhtitlan genealogy: A.D. 1240 and later]

13 : 32   Well, the Mexitin had long been friends of the Cuauhtitlan Chichimecs. They had been friends since they had been in Tollan, Atlitlalaquiyan, Tequixquiac, Apazco, Citlaltepec, and Tzompanco, and from the time the Mexitin had spent a year in Cuauhtitlan, and from the time they had been in Coatitlan, etc. They were always friends.

13 : 37   Now, as soon as the ruler Quinatzin knew that the Mexitin had been defeated and carried off as prisoners,[121] he gave the command that if the Xaltocameca could be found, they were to rescue their captives, who were to be forcibly relinquished. And so it was done.

117. Marginal gloss: destruction of Chalco.
118. Lit., they wrecked their temple, i.e., one wrecked their temple. See GN sec. 4.2.
119. Marginal gloss: the Chololteca conquered by Miccacalcatl.
120. Read *tlaàmà*. Cf. line 16 : 36.
121. Anticlimatic word order reversed in the translation.

13 : 40   When the ruler Quinatzin had rescued them by force, a daughter of the Mexitin named Chimalaxochtzin was [found to be] a captive of the Xaltocameca. She was a daughter of the one called Huitzilihuitzin, who had been made ruler and was governing at Chapoltepec.

13 : 44   Now, Huitzilihuitl had become a prisoner in Colhuacan. And this Huitzilihuitzin, so they say, was the son of Tlahuizpotoncatzin, one of the Xaltocameca princes, though some say he was the son of the Tzompanco prince Nezahualtemocatzin, etc.

13 : 47   Now, when the Mexitin were carried off as prisoners, the seat [of Cuauhtitlan] was in Techichco.

13 : 48   Well, the ruler Quinatzin gave the order to save them and to go after the Xaltocameca, who had gone to fight at Chapoltepec, and to take back their captives by force,[122] and so it was done, [and] there at Iltitlan, in a canal, they were bathing that young woman, the prisoner, whose name was Chimalaxoch.[123]

13 : 52   Then, when the Cuauhtitlancalque were about to fire on the Xaltocameca, they gave up their captive. And when she had been given up, she was brought before the ruler Quinatzin in Tepetlapan.[124]

13 : 54   When the ruler saw her, he fell in love with her. Then he wanted to go to her and cohabit with her.

14 : 2   But she refused, telling him, "Not yet, my lord, for I am fasting. That which you desire may be done later, for I am a sweeper, a woman in service.[125] The vow I make is for just two years, finished in two more years, my lord. Please give the word to have them prepare for me a little altar of beaten earth, so that I can make offerings to my god,[126] offer up my sacred cup, and do my fasting."

14 : 7   So the ruler Quinatzin gave the order for an earth altar to be made, there at Tequixquinahuac Huitznahuac Huixtompan.

14 : 9   When the earth altar was finished, they left the young woman there, and she fasted. And when she had done her fasting, the ruler Quinatzin took her as his wife.

14 : 12   And then the young woman gave birth, and she said, "Let the ruler hear that a child has been born. Let him give it a name."

14 : 14   And the ruler was informed. Then he gave his child a name, saying, "His name will be Tlatzanatztoc [He Rattles the Reeds]."

14 : 16   Hearing this, his mother said, "It is because the ruler sired him in the woods and fields, in his hunting grounds, his shooting lands," etc.

---

122. Lit., gave the order for them [the Mexitin] to be saved, and also for the Xaltocameca to be chased . . . and for their captives to be relinquished by force.
123. Prisoners who were to be sacrificed were first bathed. See FC 2 : 130, 155.
124. Tepetlapan is in Techichco. See lines 12 : 32–33.
125. For sweeping as a religious obligation see FC 2 : 186, 3 : 1–2.
126. Read *noteouh*.

14 : 18 And as soon as his child had been born, the ruler Quinatzin gave the command, laid down his judgment, notifying all the Chichimec nobles, saying that the Xaltocameca were no longer to be their friends. They must never offer their friendship again, must never come to their aid.

14 : 22 And it became true. That is what happened. One day when the Xalto-cameca were traveling through the woods, they shot at them and brought them to a halt. And this was the beginning of the Xaltocameca war, in which the Cuauhtitlancalque fought against them. And they called the Xaltocameca "black shirts," the same as the Nonoalca and the Cozcateca.

14 : 28 Now, that woman, that daughter of the Mexitin, gave birth to a second child. But this time she did not send word to the ruler Quinatzin, [asking,] "What shall its name be?" She simply gave it a name on her own.[127] She called the child Tezcatl Teuctli [Mirror Lord]—the name of her god, Tezcatlipoca [Smoking Mirror].

14 : 32 When she had been taken prisoner, this young woman had been carry-ing a mirror bundled up in a precious cloth.[128] And this was the reason for the name Tezcatl Teuctli. She did not care for the name of her first-born, Tlatzanatztoc [He Rattles the Reeds]. And so she herself named her second child Tezcatl Teuctli, and it was he who became ruler of Cuauhtitlan, etc.

14 : 38 And when the ruler Quinatzin's firstborn, the one named Tlatzanatztoc, was grown, his father—who was ruler of Cuauhtitlan—set him up as keeper of the fields at Tepotzotlan. And that's where Tlatzanatztoc had his children:

14 : 42 The first was Xaltemoctzin, who was taken to Matlatzinco. He died in battle.

The second was Quinatzin, whose children will be listed below.

14 : 43 The third was a female, who came and settled in a spot called Chimal-pan, which is now a marketplace. It was alongside the palace house, where a pond was.

14 : 46 Already these three are the grandchildren of Quinatzin. But that young woman who was the sister of the Mexitin conceived again, and she gave birth to Teozatzin, her third child. Her fourth child was Tochtzin. The fifth was a female. And these were the children of Quinatzin.

14 : 50 Now, the above-mentioned grandson Quinatzin, the son of Tlatzanatz-toc, became a father, and the children he sired were: first, Ihuitltemoctzin; second, Chahuacuetzin; third, Cuauhizomoca; fourth, Cuecuenotl.

14 : 53 And Ihuitltemoctzin became a father. He had a son whom he named Quinatzin, who founded the dynasty of Tepotzotlan. His father, the above-mentioned Ihuitltemoctzin, petitioned on his behalf when he [the father]

127. Read *yneyxcahuil*.
128. Lit., green cloth or turquoiselike cloth. Recall Tezcatlipoca's wrapped mirror, men-tioned in line 5:31.

was taken to Chalco to be killed in battle. On behalf of his son he petitioned that he might be worthy of a little land, that Moteuczomatzin might grant it to him.

15 : 4   He was notified accordingly. And it was just for this purpose that he went to war and was killed—so that the descendants of the elder Quinatzin might rejoice, that they might obtain nobility, lordship, sovereignty, along with the lands they occupied thanks to their ancestor, for their father was keeper of fields,[129] etc.

15 : 8   A high priest of Tenayocan, who came to make a report, having escaped captivity in Chalco, gave the elder Moteuczomatzin the news, etc.

15 : 10   And so the elder Moteuczomatzin, who was ruler, looked with favor on Ihuitltemoctzin.[130] And then Quinatzin was inaugurated, thus founding the dynasty of Tepotzotlan.

15 : 13   Now, Quinatzin became a father, and the children he had were:

15 : 14   First, a daughter, Tzicuiltzin.

15 : 15   Second, Cuauhquece.

Third, Nanahuatzin, whom Quinatzin put to death for cuckolding him.

15 : 16   Fourth, Petlauhtocatzin.

Fifth, Acatentehuatzin.

15 : 17   Sixth, Aztatzontzin.

Seventh, Totec Yatetzin.

Tocuiltzin, eighth.

15 : 18   [And] numerous ladies.

The daughter Tzicuiltzin, who is named above, was the mother of Don Francisco Carlos Xoconochtzin.

15 : 20   Then Aztatzontzin was placed in office, and the one who put him in office was the ruler of Tenochtitlan, Moteuczomatzin by name.[131] It was he who gave the order, who made the decision that [Aztatzontzin] was to be ruler of the Cuauhtitlan nation. Well, his father, Quinatzin, on his own initiative, had already explored the matter with [Moteuczomatzin].[132]

15 : 24   At the time, Achicatzin Tlilpotoncatzin, son[133] of Ayactlacatzin, was prince in Cuauhtitlan. And in Cuauhtitlan there was a military chief: at that time the *tlacateccatl* Tehuitzin of Tepetlapan governed the nation.[134] When Aztatzontzin was inaugurated, there had been a military chief for eight years.

129. Cf. 14 : 40.

130. An Ihuitl Temoc is named among the honored war dead in FC bk. 6, ch. 3.

131. This refers to the younger Moteuczomatzin. See lines 59 : 38 and 59 : 52–54.

132. Lit., had already investigated it in the presence of [Moteuczomatzin]. The translation follows Velázquez.

133. For *ypil*ⁿ read *ypiltzin*.

134. "Para este negocio de ejecutar la justicia había dos personas principales, uno que era noble y persona del palacio, y otro capitán y valiente" (HG bk. 6, ch. 14, parag. 54). See Concordance: tlacochcalcatl.

15 : 28   And while Aztatzontzin was ruler of Cuauhtitlan, he became a father and sired children. He had:

15 : 30   First, Quecehuacatzin, whose mother was the daughter of Ticoctzin, *tlacochcalcatl* of Cuauhyacac.

15 : 31   Second, Catlacatzin, whose mother was a freed woman.

15 : 32   Third, Pablo Tlillotlinahual, whom he had with a woman from Tequixquinahuac. He [Pablo] is [now] a joint parent-in-law with Alonso Cimatzin.

15 : 33   Fourth. He had this one with a woman from someone else's house, a sister of Don Luis de la Vega.

15 : 34   Fifth. Another one with the sister of Don Luis. Tzipalle was the name.

15 : 35   Sixth. He had one called Don Pedro Macuilxochitzin with Doña María, a lady of Huitzilopochco.

15 : 37   Seventh. He sired Ayactlacatzin, born to the lady Moceltzin, who was a daughter of Moteuczomatzin.

15 : 39   Eighth. Another born to Moteuczomatzin's daughter. Don Juan Xaltemoctzin is the name.

15 : 40   Ninth. Another born to Moteuczomatzin's daughter. The name is Don Diego Quinatzin.

15 : 41   Tenth, a female named Tiacapantzin, whose mother was a young slave living in the bird house.[135] This lady went off with strangers when the rulers' daughters were requisitioned. The Marqués[136] was the one who requisitioned them when he first arrived in Tenochtitlan. And this lady, they say, lives in Cuetlaxcoac and has had children.

15 : 46   Eleventh. With a native of Tollantzinco he had[137] [a daughter], who is reported to be a lady of Momoztlatlan.

15 : 47   Twelfth and thirteenth. He had these, reportedly, with a girl from Apazco. Two females sired by him.

15 : 49   Fourteenth. With a lady from Azcapotzalco he had another female.

15 : 50   Fifteenth. With a slave from Tetlanman he had another female.

15 : 51   Sixteenth. He had this one with a slave who was a maker of fermented atole. Now, this child was mistreated[138] in Tetzcoco by the mother of Xaltemoctzin. And when he learned of it, Aztatzontzin gave the command[139] for the boy to be kept at Iztacalco, and he was kept by stewards.

135. Or, following Lehmann, "whose mother was Tlacotzintli of Totocalco." Velázquez would seem justified in rendering *tlacotzintli* as "young slave," since the nonapocopated form of the word implies a common noun. For Tenochtitlan the bird house (*totocalli* or *totocalco*) has been variously described as an aviary, a metalworkers' shop, a zoo, or the ruler's wardrobe (FC 8:45, 12:47). The paragraphing in CF bk. 8, ch. 14, implies that it was one of two places where slaves were kept.

136. Cortés.

137. Lehmann reads *quichihuilico*.

138. Lit., she injured him concubine-wise. The exact meaning is not clear.

139. Following Velázquez I read *itencopat*, the preterite form of a hypothetical verb *itencopati*, from *itencopa* (by his command). Such verbs are treated by Carochi (CAR 462 or

51

15 : 54   Seventeenth. He had this one with a native of Tlaltecayohuacan.

16 : 1   Eighteenth, Xonetzin. He had this Xonetzin with a freed woman who was a beverage maker.

16 : 3   Now, Quinatzin, the above-mentioned father of Aztatzontzin, was ruler in Tepotzotlan. Indeed, it was he who had founded the Tepotzotlan dynasty.[140] And this Quinatzin died just when the Spaniards, the Castillians, arrived. He was just eighty when he died, during Tecuilhuitl [June or July] when the Spaniards came out, when the Castillians came out to Tepotzotlan.[141] At that time the ruler Quinatzin had lived for eighty years.[142]

16 : 9   And upon the death of the Tepotzotlan ruler, Quinatzin, father of Aztatzontzin, the above-mentioned Don Pedro Macuilxochitzin, son of Aztatzontzin, was inaugurated as ruler of Tepotzotlan. He went and ruled in Tepotzotlan, but his palace house was in Tollantzinco.

16 : 14   And when Don Pedro Macuilxochitzin died, the son of Don Pedro Macuilxochitzin, named Don Diego Necuametzin, was inaugurated as ruler.

16 : 16   And when Don Diego Necuametzin, the son, died, the Huitzilopochco lady, Doña María, who had been the mistress of Aztatzontzin and the mother of Macuilxochitzin, married Don Luis de Manuel Malomitl, son of Xayocuitlahua. And when they got married, it was eighteen years after the Spaniards arrived, in the year 5 Flint, which was A.D. 1536. And when that occurred, Don Luis de Manuel became ruler, all because of the lady Doña María.

16 : 24   And just now it was 103 years since the Tepotzotlan dynasty was founded—now, [when this] was written, in A.D. 1563, at the end of the month of February.

16 : 27   Well, Don Luis de Manuel ruled for twenty-six [years].[143] Then Don Francisco Carlos Xoconochtzin was inaugurated as ruler of Tepotzotlan, and the year he was inaugurated was A.D. 1561. The summation of the years has already been given above. He was succeeded by Don Pedro de San Augustin, 1570.[144]

CAROC 59–59v) and Andrews (AND 360–62). Compare line 17:32, where the copyist wrote *ytencopat*, then struck the final letter, making *ytencopa*.

140. Marginal gloss: gobernador of Tepotzotlan.

141. Lehmann's note: "According to Nicolás León, *Compendio de la historia general de México* (Mexico 1902), p. 249, the Spaniards arrived in Tepotzotlan on July 3 [A.D. 1520], which agrees very well with the time given here."

142. Lit., At that time Quinatzin, who was ruler, was provided with eighty.

143. Follows Lehmann. Velázquez reads the figure as 25.

144. This paragraph must be an insertion, added no earlier than 1570. Although line 16:26 gives the time of writing as 1563, line 50:54 implies the date 1544 or 1545. See line 31:42 for the year 1570 given as the time of writing.

[The Mexica in captivity: A.D. 1240–86]

16 : 32 Here is related the Cuauhtitlancalque elders' narrative, along with their telling of how the Mexitin, having been surrounded in battle, were defeated at Chapoltepec.

16 : 34 It is told and related that when these Mexitin had been at Chapoltepec for forty-seven years, causing a great many upsets and disturbances by playing tricks on people, stealing things, snatching wives and daughters, and playing many other tricks, the Tepaneca of Tlacopan, Azcapotzalco, [and] Coyohuacan, [as well as the people of] Colhuacan, became angry. Then they got together and decided that the Mexitin were to be taken by siege.[145]

16 : 41 "Let the Mexitin be defeated," said the Tepaneca. "What are they doing, they who have come to settle in our midst? Let's carry them off as prisoners. So that it may be accomplished, first we'll have to draw out their men and send them on their way. To make it work, we'll have a sham battle[146] in Colhuacan. We'll send them ahead, and when they've left, we'll steal the women."

16 : 47 The Colhuaque agreed to it. So that's what happened.

16 : 48 Then they went and called the Mexica to war, to go on ahead and fight in Colhuacan. They said to them, "You're to make the first attack in a raid for captives on Colhuacan.[147] We're off to war!"

16 : 51 Then the Mexica went to battle. The Colhuaque, well prepared, came out to meet them.

16 : 52 And as for the Tepaneca, they went and attacked the women at Chapoltepec, demolished them, carried them off. And when they had defeated them,[148] then they raped them, gratuitously, for already the Mexitin were being destroyed—already [the Mexitin and] the Colhuaque were engaged in battle. Here are the words of a stanza, heard in a song:[149]

17 : 5 With [our] shields turned backward,[150] that's how we Mexica, aho! were destroyed at Chapoltepec, beside the rock.[151] Princes were carried off

145. Lit., the Mexitin were to be destroyed right in the middle.
146. Read *çannen tiyaotizque*.
147. Lit., You are to go attack first in order that you will capture people in Colhuacan. Read *anhuetzitihui*.
148. Lit., And when they had routed them. Read *oquinmomoyauhque*.
149. Lit., Here are stanza-words that are a song's means of being heard.
150. In other words, we fled with our shields on our backs (see NED: chimalli 1). Note that the song does not quite accord with the author's story.
151. The translation follows Lehmann, who reads *tetla[n]* = beside the rock, not *tetla* = place of rocks, assuming that the reference is to the rock of Chapoltepec. Cf. NED: Chapoltepetitlan, Tepantonco.

to the four directions. In misery went the ruler Huitzilihuitl, oh! a banner in his hand: he was stretched out in Colhuacan.[152]

17:9 And at that time the Xaltocameca went and fought there.

And it was said that because the Cuauhtitlancalque were old friends of the Mexitin they went as a group and consoled the Mexitin when they were conquered. This was in the year 8 Flint.

17:11 And it is said that they were in Contitlan for four years—in 9 House and in 10 Rabbit.

17:13 In 11 Reed [1243] the Colhuacan ruler Chalchiuhtlatonac sought them out at a time when the Xochimilca were threatening him. And so the Mexica were called together and assembled,[153] even those who were just women, if they passed for men. All were sought out.

17:17 Then they went and made conquests in Xochimilco. It was to get clippings that they gave chase.[154] When they were hunting for prisoners, it was only ears that they were stacking up in their bag so that it would be known how many they were capturing. And they were only clipping an ear from one side.

17:20 After that, the Mexitin were allowed to settle in Tizacapan. And this was in 12 Flint.

17:21 13 House.

1 Rabbit [1246]. This was when the Mexitin once again started to annoy people.[155] Was it not Necoc,[156] the Devil, who did it? Little children were requested; Colhuaque and Mexitin were the contestants, blowing sand at each other. And when they [the children] had been won [by the Mexitin], they were sacrificed; their breasts were cut open.

17:25 And there was more of this.

Therefore the Colhuaque declared war a second time against the Mexica.[157] And then the Mexitin ran away.

17:28 9 House [1241]. The Mexitin are at Contitlan.

10 Rabbit [1242]. The Mexitin at Contitlan. It is told and related that this is when the war with Xaltocan got started, again at Chapoltepec, after

---

152. The sacrificial victim carried a banner and was stretched over a stone so that his heart could be excised. (The verb *tecoc*, "he was stretched out," could also be translated "he was cut," as in lines 81:35 and 81:36.)

153. Anticlimactic word order reversed in the translation.

154. Lit., For cut things they chased people (?). Read *ipampa* instead of *ipan*.

155. For *peuhque yyo* read *peuhque yn*. In the manuscript the 'o' of *yyo* is actually a solid blob, which might have been meant as an 'n'. The extra 'y' is perhaps a copyist's slip.

156. In many of the old manuscripts, as perhaps here, the 'c' and the ambiguously curled 'l' are easily confused. Hence the copyist may have seen *necoc* and written *necol*. In fact Velázquez here reads *necoc*, though his translation of the passage does not agree with mine.

157. Lit., declared war a second time for the purpose of fighting the Mexica. Read *yc oppa yaotlatoque*.

the defeat of the Mexitin. And it was by command[158] of Quinatzin, who was then ruler of Cuauhtitlan, that the Xaltocan war began.

17:32   It was he who decided on it, because the Mexitin and the Colhuaque did not yet have any power at that time. Although they were angry,[159] they had no power. They never made decisions about killing people. And it was the same with the Azcapotzalca. They did not yet have any power at the time the Xaltocan war began. As yet the nations were unallied.[160]

17:38   11 Reed [1243] was when the Mexica were sought out.

12 Flint.

13 House [1245] was the year the Mexitin were settled at Atizapan[161] by command of the Colhuacan ruler Chalchiuhtlatonac, after they had succeeded in battle, after they had made conquests in Xochimilco. For the Xochimilca were enemies of the Colhuaque.

17:43   1 Rabbit [1246] was when the Colhuaque and the Mexitin fought each other.

2 Reed [1247]. This was when Tezcatl Teuctli was inaugurated as ruler at the place called Tequixquinahuac Huixtompan. He succeeded his father, the elder Quinatzin.

17:46   And as for those who talk much, one of them has said that Tlatzanatztoc and the elder Xaltemoctzin were sons of Tezcatl Teuctli. And according to what he says about him, Xaltemoctzin ruled for nineteen years and was killed by the Tepaneca. This genealogical information cannot be accurate, for the truth about how they are arranged [genealogically] has already been told [above].

17:50   In the time of 3 Flint [1248] the ruler Miahuatamaltzin died, and Acayoltzin came to be inaugurated as ruler of Cuitlahuac Tizic.

17:52   4 House. 5 Rabbit. 6 Reed.

7 Flint [1252]. This was when the Colhuacan ruler Chalchiuhtlatonactzin died. Then Cuauhtlix succeeded him and was inaugurated as ruler in Colhuacan.

17:54   8 House. 9 Rabbit. 10 Reed.

11 Flint [1256]. This was when Acayoltzin died, and Atzatzamoltzin came to be inaugurated as ruler of Cuitlahuac Tizic.

18:2   12 House [1257] was when the Chalca were destroyed. Those who destroyed them were the Huexotzinca, [whose] ruler was Xayacamachan, the Tlaxcalteca, the Totomihuaque, Tepeyacac, [and] Cuauhtinchan. Quehuatl was ruler in Cholollan.

---

158. The copyist wrote *ytencopat*, then corrected it to *ytencopa*. Cf. line 15:53.
159. The text is unclear. Read *cocoleque*?
160. Lit., As yet the nations [or peoples] were all alone.
161. Atizapan is another name for Tizacapan. The passage at hand merely retells the story given above in lines 17:13–27.

18 : 4 13 Rabbit.

1 Reed [1259] was when the Colhuacan ruler Cuauhtlixtli died. Then Yohuallatonac was inaugurated, succeeding him as ruler.

18 : 6 It was in 1 Reed that the Cuauhquecholteca were destroyed. The Huexotzinca, the Tlaxcalteca, the Totomihuaque, the Tepeyacahuaque, the Cuauhteca, Cuauhtinchan, and the Chololteca surrounded them.

18 : 8 It was also in 1 Reed that the Chalco ruler Tlalli Teuctli died. Then Toquihua Teuctli[162] was inaugurated and ruled in Chalco.

18 : 10 2 Flint [1260]. In that year the Cuahuaque Otomi arrived. They came and settled in Chichimecacuicoyan at the time when Tochtzin Teuctli, son of Tezcatl Teuctli, was prince and governor there. He allowed them to settle in his territory. But they were with him for only fifteen years. Then he sent them to live in a place called Tlacopantonco Xolotliatlauhyoc, in Tepotzotlan.

18 : 16 3 House. 4 Rabbit. 5 Reed. 6 Flint. 7 House. [8 Rabbit.] 9 Reed.

10 Flint [1268] is when the warehouse in Cuauhtitlan was established.

18 : 17 11 House [1269]. In that year the Colhuacan ruler called Yohuallatonac died. Then Tziuhtecatzin was inaugurated and ruled in Colhuacan.

12 Rabbit. 13 Reed.

18 : 20 1 Flint [1272] is when the Cuitlahuac ruler Atzatzamoltzin died and Totepeuh Teuctli was inaugurated. The Chalca dynasty in Cuitlahuac Tizic began at this time.

18 : 22 2 House [1273]. In that year the Mexitin were driven out. And so they came and settled in Tlalcocomocco. It was by command of the Colhuaque, when Tziuhtecatzin was ruling in Colhuacan.

18 : 25 Afterward, Colhuaque went to conquer the Mexica. But these Colhuaque only fell into the hands of their enemy, who went and adorned them [as sacrificial victims], and then those Mexitin extracted the hearts of the Colhuaque, sparing none.

18 : 28 3 Rabbit [1274]. In that year Tezcatzin Teuctli drove out the Otomi, sending them to Tepotzotlan, to the place called Tlacopantonco Xolotliatlauhyoc. And from there the Otomi dispersed. Some went to Cincoc. Some went to Huitziltepec and Xoloc, and some withdrew—back this way—to Cuauhtlaapan Tianquizzolco.

18 : 34 4 Reed. 5 Flint. 6 House. 7 Rabbit. 8 Reed. 9 Flint. 10 House.

18 : 35 11 Rabbit [1282]. In that year Tziuhtecatzin of Colhuacan died. Then Xihuitltemoctzin was inaugurated and ruled in Colhuacan.

18 : 37 12 Reed.

13 Flint [1286]. The Colhuaque say that Tezozomoctli of Azcapotzalco was born at this time.

18 : 38 1 House.

162. Marginal gloss: tochquihua teuctli.

2 Rabbit. In that year the Cuauhtitlan ruler Tezcatl Teuctli died. He had ruled for thirty-nine years.

[Cuauhtitlan's war against Xaltocan: A.D. 1287–97 and later]

18 : 40   3 Reed [1287]. In that year the Cuauhtitlan ruler Huactzin was inaugurated. His residence was in Techichco, and that's where he ruled.

18 : 42   The time of 3 Reed was when the Huehueteca were destroyed. They were conquered by the Huexotzinca, the Tlaxcalteca, the Totomihuaque, Cholollan, the people of Cuauhtinchan, and Tepeyacac.

18 : 45   4 Flint. 5 House. 6 Rabbit.

7 Reed [1291] was when Totepeuh, ruler of Cuitlahuac Tizic, died. Then Epcoatzin was inaugurated.

18 : 47   8 Flint [1292], say the Colhuaque, is when Ixtlilxochitzin the elder was born in Tetzcoco.

18 : 48   9 House.

10 Rabbit [1294]. The Cuitlahuaca say that Tezozomoctli of Azcapotzalco was born at this time.

18 : 49   11 Reed. 12 Flint.

13 House [1297]. This was the year—when the capital was at Techichco, in the time of the ruler Huactli—that his Chichimec captains were driven out and came away. The first was Maxtla; second, Xochipan; third, Mecellotl; fourth, Acatzin; fifth, Tlacuatzin; sixth, Tzohuitzin; seventh, Cuauhticatzin. These were the ones who came, and they settled in Tecoactonco.

19 : 1   Now, when these Chichimecs came and settled in that place, a man had already died there, a Chichimec named Tecoatl, who had been there first. Encountered were the Chichimecs Huauhquil and Telpoch, who were at Zacatlaltitlan, which is now called Tlatilco. They were there already when the Chichimecs who had parted company came and settled in Tecoactonco.

19 : 7   And then they withdrew. Soon they settled at a second place, called Xallan. They made Xallan their home and stayed there awhile.

19 : 9   And then they withdrew to a third place, Tlalcozpan, where the house of Don Juan Yollocamachaltzin stands today. Those who had [previously] come to settle there were simply driven out. Well, the one who was there, at Izquitlan, was a Chichimec named Ixahuatzin, [along with] Yaocotzitzitli [and] Xiyatl. And those who had withdrawn to Tlalcozpan were Tzonhuitzin and Cuauhticatzin.[163]

163. Two of the Chichimec captains named in lines 18 : 52–53 above.

19 : 14   Now, when they had been in that place for a while, they noticed the Xaltocameca, who were always courting danger to go quail hunting at Quail Hill. Indeed the quail-hunting area belonged to the Xaltocameca. It was their quail hill.

19 : 17   Then they conferred with each other, saying, "Who are these so-called Xaltocameca? Let's chase them away. They're going to bother us. They're bad people, they're vicious, they're the ones who made war against the Mexitin. And in fact our ruler gave the command that the Xaltocameca were never to be our friends." [164]

19 : 21   So then, right at that spot, [165] they provoked them, intending to make war on them, until finally they exerted their full force against them.

19 : 22   Now, they had been coming [there] during the reign of Quinatzin, and in the reign of Tezcatl Teuctli they were just snatching whatever they saw that belonged to them. They were just making fun of them.

19 : 25   Well, they kept remembering how those late rulers had commanded them, that these were to be their enemies. And it was during the time of the ruler Huactzin that the Xaltocan war began in such a way that it really did begin in earnest. [166]

19 : 28   For it is told and related that the territory, the boundaries, of the Xaltocameca came straight out to:

19 : 30   Acaltecoyan
Ocozacayocan
Coyomilpan
Cueppopan
Ixayoctonco
Tlilhuatonicac
Ixayoc
Citlaliniteopan
Cotzxipetzco
Zoltepec [Quail Hill]
Tepemaxalco
Cuitlachtepetl
Temacpalco
Cuauhxomolco
Huilacapichtepec
Otlayo
Cuauhtepetl
Tezonyocan

164. The command had been issued by Quinatzin. See 14 : 18–22.
165. Read *yc niman ye ōcan ȳyn*.
166. The earlier beginnings of this war were described in lines 14 : 22–28.

Tlacochcalco
Tehuepanco
Ecatepec
Chiucnauhtlan
Tecanman
Malinallocan
Tonanitlan
Papahuacan
Ichpochco
Tzompanco

19 : 36 Their boundaries came together with those of Xaltenco at Acalte-coyan.[167] And then the war started.[168] At that time the Chichimecs got together there in Tlalcozpan in order to fight them on all fronts.

19 : 39 There was a Chichimec of Xochicaltitlan named Pitzallotl. He was a very big man, and he brought the Xaltocameca to a halt. At the same time, they were halted by Chichimecs who were in Tehuiloyocan—Totoomitl, Tla-huitol, and other Chichimecs. And after a long while, they forced the Xal-tocameca to give up their boundary, and so the war was pushed back to Tlaltepan.

19 : 44 Then the boundary was pushed back to Tlamacazcatepec, which is now Tenexotli [Lime Road], and straight on back to Iztaccoac [and] Tamazo-lac. There it lasted a good while.

19 : 47 They kept a frontier with them at Iyehuacan, Teloloiyacac, [and] Tepan-ahuilloyan. There the war lasted fifteen years, so it is said.

19 : 49 Well, it was fifteen years that went by. And then again the Chichimecs forced the Xaltocameca to give up their boundary.

19 : 51 So then the war reached the place called Tezcacoac. It was to that place that the war was carried.

20 : 1 Then the Xaltocameca boundaries were set up at Tezcacoac, which has [just] been mentioned, [also at] Tlatlacualloyan, Tepanahuilloyan, Teno-paltitlan, Acocotlan, Teziuhtecatitlan, Nextlalpan, Atizapan, Teopanzolco, Iltitlan, Coacalco, Cuauhtepec.

20 : 5 And the boundaries stood there for nine years. And all that while the war went on, the war of the Cuauhtitlan Chichimecs. And then again they chased the Xaltocameca, until finally the war—the war of the Chichimecs—was carried to the place called Acpaxapocan. At last the war cooled off a little. At this time the Chichimec Huactzin was ruler of Cuauhtitlan.

20 : 11 Then, when the fighting had been carried to Acpaxapocan, the Chichi-

167. Lit., They [the Xaltocameca] come together with Xaltenco at Acaltecoyan.
168. Alternate translation: And there the war started.

mecs made war only from time to time. And also, the Xaltocameca no longer dared to attack them, because they were afraid of these Cuauhtitlan Chichimecs.

20 : 15 Now, when the war was in Acpaxapocan, many times the god of the Xaltocameca spoke to them in person, the so-called Acpaxapo [Water-weed Mirror], that came forth and appeared in the water there. It was a large serpent, and it had the face of a woman. And its hair was long like women's hair.

20 : 19 And it would let them know, would tell them, what was going to happen to them: whether they were to take prisoners, whether they were to die, whether they were to become prisoners [themselves]. And it would tell them whenever the Chichimecs were going to sally forth, so that the Xaltocameca could come out to meet them.

20 : 24 Well, the Chichimecs realized this, [and] whenever the Xaltocameca came to make payment, came to make offerings to Acpaxapo, the Chichimecs were waiting for them. There they were, and that's where the boundary was.

20 : 28 And finally, when the Colhuaque had arrived [in the region] and had come forth, they too made war at Acpaxapocan, by command of princes who were Chichimecs. Totomatlatzin and Cuauhtzoncaltzin were the ones who had authority over them.[169]

20 : 31 And so the Colhuaque took captives in that place. And with these they held their first dedication ceremony, offering three Xaltocameca. It was when the Colhuaque had newly prepared an earth altar for their gods—as will be told below, under the year 11 Reed,[170] two years before the death of the ruler Huactli. There will be heard the story of the arrival of the devils, or sorcerers, when the idolatry of the Cuauhtitlan Chichimecs got started.

20 : 38 And finally, when the elder Xaltemoctzin was ruler of Cuauhtitlan, in the year 7 Reed, the Xaltocameca were destroyed. The whole time that the war lasted, while the Cuauhtitlan Chichimecs were fighting against them, adds up to a hundred years altogether. It began when the Mexitin were defeated at Chapoltepec, for it is said that this was when the ire of the Cuauhtitlan Chichimecs was instilled.

20 : 45 And when the Xaltocameca were destroyed, it was in Tecanman that they went to their destruction.

20 : 46 When they were already terrified, they sent to Metztitlan to say they would go be servants there.

20 : 48 And they sent to Tlaxallan to say they would be servants there.

169. Lit., Totomatlatzin and Cuauhtzoncaltzin were their fathers.
170. See 24 : 25ff., especially 24 : 53.

20 : 49   Well, eventually they were asked why and for what reason they wai to be servants.

20 : 50   They answered, saying, "It's because our enemies the Cuauhtitlan Chichimecs are tormenting us, and we're about to perish in their hands. It was a long time ago that they provoked us and made war against us. The war began in the time of our fathers."

21 : 4   "We'll have to take a look at them," they said. "Fetch them. What are these people like who've been bothering you?"

21 : 5   Then, with their captives, the Xaltocameca entered Metztitlan and Tlaxcallan. Of which more is to be heard under the year 7 Reed, during the reign of the elder Xaltemoctzin, the *tecpanecatl*.[171]

21 : 8   Also at this time, when the Xaltocameca nation had been destroyed, the ruler Xaltemoctzin the elder stationed boundary keepers. He stationed them at Tzompanco, Citlaltepec, Huehuetocan, and Otlazpan.

21 : 11   By now the boundaries had been pushed back, enlarging the Cuauhtitlan nation. And so these boundaries, these frontiers of the Cuauhtitlan nation are named herewith.

21 : 14   First, where we begin the Mexica road, at a place called Nepopohualco. Then:

21 : 15   Otontepec
Cuauhtepec
Tlacoc
Tehuepanco
Ecatepec
Tezoyocan
Acalhuacan[172]
Epcoac
Tenanitlan
Axochtli
Toltecatzacualli
Chiconcuauhtliiteocal
Tlamamatlatl
Cihuatlicpac
Atehuilacachco
Ocelotlixtacan
Cuauhquemecan
Cuauhtlalpan

171. Xaltemoctzin's special title is given as *atecpanecatl teuctli* at 30 : 32. Huemac of Tollan was styled *atecpanecatl* (8 : 40). For further usages see NED: atecpanecatl, tecpanecatl.

172. Velázquez reads Acolhuacan. MEX 80 treats the two forms as synonymous (*Acalhuacan, anozo Aculhuacan* = Acalhuacan, or Acolhuacan).

Papahuacan
Tlatlachpanaloyan
Miccaapan
Xilotzinco
Huitzocuitlapillan
Atlacomolco
Cuezcomahuacan
Tenexcalco
Huixachcuauhyo-[173]
Macuexhuacan
Temamatlac
Tlatzallan
Acatzintitlan
Pachyocan
Nochtonco
Tatapaco
Hueitepec
Mazamican
Nopaltepec
Ozomatepec
Cuahuacatzinco
Cuicuitzcacalco
Chalchiuhtechcatitlan
Atecomoyan
Nacazhueyocan
Xoxomalpan
Chapolmalloyan
Ichpochtetitlan
Oztotlaquetzallocan
Ahuazhuatlan
Tecaxic
Tecoac
Zoltepec
Tepetlmaxalco
Tepetitlan

21 : 27   Which joins the above-mentioned Nepopohualco.

21 : 28   These are the boundaries of the Cuauhtitlan nation; and in order to grow larger in all directions, the Cuauhtitlan Chichimecs, by means of war, did indeed set them up in Xaltocan, as has been told.

173. Suffix missing?

21 : 31   And it was the same in Hueipochtlan and Xilotzinco. The same in Tlatzallan and Acatzintlan.

21 : 32   There was a battle there at Huecatlan Atlauhco, when Tollan people
confronted the nation.

21 : 34   It was the same in Chiapan. By means of war it was possible to set up a
boundary.

21 : 35   And it was the same in Cuahuacan. By means of war it [the boundary]
was pushed back during the time that Cozauhquixochitl was ruling in
Cuahuacan.

21 : 36   And even more famous than the Xaltocameca war was the war with the
Tepaneca. The Cuauhtitlan Chichimecs faced them with great courage.

21 : 39   And likewise, Xochilhuitl captives from Ecatepec were required in
Cuauhtitlan.[174]

21 : 40   Through the courage of the Cuauhtitlancalque, their boundaries, as
named above, were made good in all directions.

21 : 42   And upon the arrival of the Castillians, when the Marqués del Valle
came, the Cuauhtitlan nation was destroyed, broken up, so that Tepotzotlan, Otlazpan, Citlaltepec, and Tzompanco were detached. And Toltitlan
was also detached from the territory, etc.

[The fall of Colhuacan: A.D. 1298–1348]

21 : 46   1 Rabbit [1298].

2 Reed [1299]. This was when the Cuauhquecholteca were defeated for
the second time. They were surrounded again, just as was told above.[175]

21 : 48   3 Flint [1300] was when the Colhuacan ruler Xihuitltemoctzin died.
Then Coxcox Teuctli was inaugurated and ruled in Colhuacan.

21 : 50   4 House.

5 Rabbit [1302] was when Epcoatzin, ruler of Tizic Cuitlahuac, died.
Quetzalmichin Teuctli was inaugurated.

21 : 51   6 Reed [1303]. In that year it happened one day that the ruler of
Cuauhtitlan, who was Huactzin, went hunting, and he met a young
woman at the place called Tepolco. But he did not know whether this
young woman was a lady.

22 : 1   Finally he asked her. He said, "Who are you? Whose daughter are you?
Where do you come from?"

---

174. Lit., And also thus, with regard to Ecatepec, for [the feast of] Xochilhuitl, they
wanted to conquer people with regard to Cuauhtitlan. (For "tribute captives" brought from
enemy borders as part of Xochilhuitl celebrations, see FFCC bk. 1, ch. 14. See also lines
49 : 34–38 below.)
175. See line 18 : 6.

63

22 : 2   She answered him, saying, "My lord, I live in Colhuacan, and my father is the king, Coxcox Teuctli."

22 : 3   "And what does he call you?" he asked. "What is your name?"

22 : 4   "My name is Itztolpanxochi," she replied.

22 : 5   Well, when Huactli heard this, he took her home with him and made her his wife. And Huactli had children with her. The first was called Cuauhtliipantemoc. The second was Iztactototl. They were born the grandchildren of the Colhuacan ruler, Coxcoxtzin Teuctli.

22 : 9   7 Flint. 8 House. 9 Rabbit. 10 Reed. 11 Flint. 12 House. 13 Rabbit. 1 Reed. 2 Flint.

22 : 11   3 House [1313]. This was when Quetzalmichin Teuctli died. Then Cuauhtlotli Teuctli was inaugurated and ruled in Cuitlahuac Tizic.

22 : 12   4 Rabbit. 5 Reed. 6 Flint.

22 : 13   7 House [1317]. This was when Cuauhtlotli Teuctli died. Then Mamatzin Teuctli was inaugurated and ruled in Cuitlahuac Tizic.

22 : 14   8 Rabbit [1318]. This was the year that Mexico Tenochtitlan got started. As yet the Mexitin built only a few straw huts. There was only a wilderness of sedges all around when they made their settlement.

22 : 17   9 Reed.

10 Flint [1320]. In that year the Cuauhtitlan ruler Huactli gave the order for his son Iztactototl to lead a war party[176] at Xaltocan Acpaxapocan. He summoned his messengers and said to them, "Go tell my captains Acatzin, Tlacuatzin, Xochipan, and Mecellotl, who are in charge there at Acahuacan Tepeyacac. Give them this message: 'You are no longer in power here at Cuahuacan. Let that boy Iztactototzin be surrounded someplace or other. But he mustn't be thrown to the enemy, he mustn't be captured. Let them give heed to this. I beseech all my captains.'"[177]

22 : 27   Then the message was brought to the Chichimecs who were in charge at Tepeyacac. And when they had heard it, they said, "Our ruler has favored us. Let us do what we can."

22 : 30   And right away these Chichimecs sent to Coacalco, taking a message to the Tepaneca. They had just[178] come to settle there, in Coacalco, where a certain Xochmitl was governing,[179] and when Xochmitl heard the Chichimecs' command that they were to [go] with them [and] accompany the ruler's son Iztactototl into battle, then he authorized his Tepanec charges to go to war with this son of the ruler Huactzin.

---

176. Lit., gave the order for them to accompany his son Iztactototl into battle. See GLOS: yaoquixtia:te.

177. Lit., 'You are very much no longer in power here at Cuahuacan. Let them cause people to surround the very young man Iztactototzin somewhere there. Let it not be: let them not throw him in alien hands, let them not cause him to arrive in alien hands. They do very much know something. Indeed I beseech all my captains.'

178. Read *quin huel*.

179. Word order reversed in the translation.

22 : 36   And it was done. They followed the ruler's son Iztactototl to Acpaxa-pocan, where the Xaltocameca were in the habit of making payment.

22 : 38   Now, when they had appeared, they came forth and made the payment, though indeed it was as they usually came, always dressed for war. Immediately Iztactototl made a take, and as soon as he had gotten his prisoner, there was a battle. And on account of it the Chichimecs Acatzin and Tlacuatzin died, along with eight of the Tepaneca that Xochmitl had sent from Coacalco.

And it was all by himself that Iztactototl had taken the prisoner.[180]

22 : 43   When he had gotten his prisoner, the news was brought to the ruler Huactli, and they told him how ten had died because of it.

22 : 45   This upset him, and he gave orders for the war to be intensified, for the Chichimecs to fight hard and not let the Xaltocameca go free.

22 : 47   Now, when Iztactototl had gotten his prisoner, he sent word to his mother. And then she said to him, "Go see your grandfather, Coxcox Teuctli, the ruler of Colhuacan. Give him greetings and show him that you have taken a prisoner in Xaltocan."

22 : 51   And Iztactototl heeded his mother, for she was a princess of Colhuacan.

22 : 52   Then he went with his prisoner to inspire his grandfather, and his Chichimec captains went along as his guards. When he got there, he presented himself, offered greetings,[181] and explained that he was his grandson.

23 : 2   "O lord, O ruler," he said, "I have come from Cuauhtitlan to bring you greetings, for I have heard what perhaps is true, that you may have lost a daughter, the departed Itztolpanxochi." He continued: "She is my mother, and she has told me that it was you who sired her. And so today I have come before you to bring you inspiration. My father, Huactzin, had a war in Xaltocan. And I went there and took a prisoner."

23 : 8   He said to him, "Welcome, my child. It is true that I lost a daughter, from whom you have sprung. Sit down, for you are my grandson. Such as I am, I am old and must die. Here in Colhuacan it is you who will be ruler. You will be ruler of the Colhuaque."

23 : 13   And to Iztactototl he was a little like an oracle the way he spoke. And after hearing this speech, he said nothing.

23 : 15   Finally the ruler Coxcox Teuctli withdrew. From within his chamber he sent back a messenger to inform him that he was never to come again, and he was told that he would definitely become ruler, succeeding his grandfather.

23 : 18   Well, after he had heard these words, he laughed and said, "Whose ruler would I be? For the Colhuacan nation is not to endure. It is to be destroyed and broken up. But I say give this message to the king, my grand-

180. Novice warriors usually took prisoners with the help of others. See note to line 37 : 5 below.
181. Anticlimactic word order reversed in the translation.

father: Probably it will not happen in his lifetime, and when it does, some could go to our capital and become our followers there. For our land is so big that from there to Cuauhtepetl here, takes a whole day, so wide is the expanse. And the ruler is my father, Huactzin."

23 : 25   Then they took the message to the ruler Coxcox Teuctli. When he heard it, he was angry and insulted. He said, "That little boy, that baby, what is he saying? Ask him what it is that would happen to our nation and who would destroy us. Is this a death that is not native? How would it rise against us? Pox, bloody diarrhea, coughing sickness, fever, and consumption are here, of course. And of course we know that the sun might be eaten or the earth might shake or we might have to perform sacrifices.[182] How is our nation to be destroyed and broken up? What is the boy saying? Let him tell it plainly."

23 : 34   And then the messengers came back. In anger and amazement they questioned him.

23 : 35   And he answered them. "What is the king worried about?" he said. "Give him this message: It is not by war that the nation will be destroyed, no one will bother him, no one will make fun of him anymore.[183] The way it will happen is that lords and nobles will simply become agitated and rebel, and their vassals will be scattered in foreign lands. The nation will become deserted. And that is why I say, when you are destroyed, go to our capital, which lies beyond Cuauhtepetl here. The ruler, I say, is my father. He will be waiting for you, and he will give you land."

23 : 45   They took the message to the ruler, and with that he fell silent, etc.

23 : 46   11 House. 12 Rabbit. 13 Reed.

    1 Flint [1324]. This was when the Colhuacan ruler Coxcoxtli died. Then Acamapichtli was inaugurated and ruled in Colhuacan.

23 : 48   2 House [1325]. According to what the Cuitlahuaca know, this was when the elder Ixtlilxochitl of Tetzcoco was born.

23 : 49   3 Rabbit. 4 Reed. 5 Flint. 6 House. 7 Rabbit.

23 : 50   8 Reed [1331]. Cuitlahuaca say that at this time Tezozomoctli was inaugurated as ruler in Tlalhuacpan.[184]

23 : 51   9 Flint. 10 House. 11 Rabbit. 12 Reed.

23 : 52   13 Flint [1336]. This was the year that Achitometl killed Acamapichtli, who was ruler of Colhuacan. And having killed him, Achitometl was inaugurated as ruler. This was also when the ruler Achitometl spoke craftily

182. During solar eclipses prisoners were sacrificed (FC 7:37–38). But although the text means eclipses and earthquakes in a literal sense, according to Sahagún the expression *teotl qualo tlallolini* has the figurative meaning "Something terrifying comes to pass, perhaps war, perhaps the death of the ruler" (FFCC 1:82).

183. Word order reversed in the translation.

184. Tlalhuacpan [the Dry Lands] refers to the realm of the Tepaneca, whose seat was Azcapotzalco. See NED: Tlalhuacpan.

to the Mexitin.[185] Also it was when the elder Tezozomoctli was inaugurated as ruler in Azcapotzalco.

24 : 5 1 House [1337] was when the ruler of Cuitlahuac Tizic, Mamatzin Teuctli, died. Then Pichatzin Teuctli was inaugurated.

24 : 7 2 Rabbit.

3 Reed [1339] was when the Cuauhquecholteca were again defeated, and it was the Huexotzinca who defeated them, campaigning against them unaided.[186] This was when Xayacamachan was ruling in Huexotzinco.

24 : 9 The year 3 Reed is when the Chalco ruler Tozquihua died. Then a lord named Xipemetztli was inaugurated as ruler.

24 : 11 And it was in 3 Reed that Tezozomoctli of Tlalhuacpan[187] started his war in Techichco, which was filled with Chalca[188]—the people of Techichco were counted as Chalco. That's where the Chalca boundary, or frontier, was, there in Colhuacan. And this war of Tezozomoctli's lasted thirty-seven years. As yet the Tepanecatl was acting on his own when he set out for Techichco Colhuacan. As yet the Mexitin were not included.

24 : 19 4 Flint. 5 House. 6 Rabbit.

24 : 20 7 Reed [1343] was when the Totomihuaque were defeated. The Huexotzinca campaigned against them unaided, in the time that Xayacamachan was ruler.

24 : 22 8 Flint. 9 House.

10 Rabbit [1346]. This 10 Rabbit is when Ilancueitl and the ladies who accompanied her went to Coatlichan to get Acamapichtli,[189] who had been sent there to be brought up.

24 : 25 11 Reed [1347]. That was the year it came to pass that the Colhuaque were destroyed, were scattered and dispersed in foreign lands, when the people went off in all directions.

24 : 28 When the Colhuaque had been destroyed, their temple and their city sprouted grass.

24 : 30 In the year 12 [Flint: 1348] Achitometl, who had been ruler of Colhuacan, met his death. As soon as he died, the Colhuaque were destroyed.

24 : 32 These Colhuaque were not conquered: the way they were destroyed is that they just agitated each other. That's how they were destroyed.

185. After their defeat at Chapoltepec, when the Mexica begged Achitometl for a place to settle, he craftily sent them to Tizaapan, which was known to be infested with snakes. The story is told in DHIST ch. 4. Notice, however, that this account does not fit in with the information concerning the Mexica and Tizaapan (also called Tizacapan or Atizapan) given above in lines 17:20 and 17:39.

186. Read *quinmixcahuique*, as in line 24:21.

187. The same as Tezozomoctli of Azcapotzalco (see 24:4–5; see also 23:51 and accompanying note).

188. For *chalcayaoyotl* read *chalcayotl*, as in line 27:30.

189. Son of the Acamapichtli who is assassinated in line 24:1 above. He is to become the first ruler of Tenochtitlan (lines 26:39–42).

24 : 33 And that's when the Colhuaque, accompanied by the Mexicatzinca, came here to Cuauhtitlan. It was said that the Colhuacan nation was dispersed when Achitometl died.

[The founding of the city of Cuauhtitlan: A.D. 1348 and later]

24 : 37 Now, when the Colhuaque were newly arrived here in Cuauhtitlan, it was during [the fifteen "months"] called:

24 : 38
 1. Huei Tecuilhuitl
 2. Tlaxochimaco
 3. Xocotl Huetzi
 4. Ochpaniztli
 5. Teotl Eco
 6. Tepeilhuitl
 7. Quecholli
 8. Panquetzaliztli
 9. Atemoztli
 10. Tititl
 11. Izcalli
 12. Cuahuitl Ehua
 13. Tlacaxipehualiztli
 14. Tozoztontli
 15. Huei Tozoztli

24 : 41 Thus the Colhuaque stayed for 300 days [for fifteen twenty-day "months," mid-July through mid-May].

24 : 42 And also at this time, when the Colhuaque had started making themselves an earth altar, the incoming elders Cuauhnochtli, Atempanecatl, Xiloxochcatl, Mexicatl, and Tetec Tlamacazqui[190] set up their gods, known as Toci and Chiucnauhozomatli and Xochiquetzal.

24 : 47 Now, when these Colhuaque had built their earth altar, they petitioned the Chichimec princes called Totomatlatzin and Cuauhtzoncaltzin, who governed in Chichimecacuicoyan, sending them a message, telling them, "We have made our settlement at the waterside where you allowed us to settle, there in your territory. But what can we take?[191] For we are asking,

190. At least some of these names may be titles. See Concordance: cuauhnochtli, atempanecatl, tlamacazqui.
191. Lit., But how many portions are there? (reading *quezquican* for *quexcan*).

68

please won't you help us out with something like one little rabbit, a little snake, with which we might have just a bit of a dedication ceremony for the little earth altar we have made for our gods?"

25 : 2 And when the Chichimecs heard this, they got together and said, "Ah, that's where they're supposed to be. We believe that where they've come to settle they'll eventually be swept away by the water. Indeed, when we allowed them to settle there, we said, 'Here's your rampart,' for these are the people who made war on the Mexitin and chased them away.[192] Now, what are we going to tell them? Should we give them this rabbit, this snake that they're asking for? They would get used to hunting in our gardens.[193] That's impossible. But there's this: we have a war going on nearby in Xaltocan. Let's tell them to go get captives there, so that they can become worthy of receiving our daughters and our lands."[194]

25 : 12 And then the Chichimecs told this to the Colhuaque. Indeed, the Chichimecs said, "What would a snake or a rabbit be? Indeed, we have a war nearby. Go there, to Xaltocan. Is it far? Whoever takes captives wins our daughters. We'll present them to you along with our lands. Give heed to this. It's how you'll have your dedication ceremony."

25 : 18 And then the Colhuaque went off and made war in Xaltocan. And when the Colhuaque had gotten three captives, the Chichimecs took a great liking to the Colhuaque, and they all became friends. So the Chichimecs gave them their daughters. Also they were given land.

25 : 24 When it was Toxcatl,[195] the Colhuaque came and celebrated the feast in Cuauhtitlan for the first time. They came and made human sacrifices.

25 : 25 As yet the Chichimecs were not doing this, not making human sacrifices before their gods. Although they were taking captives and would eat them, they just killed them. It wasn't before their gods. They did not use them for dedication ceremonies, and as yet they had no temples.

25 : 29 It was at this time that the Colhuaque and the Chichimecs began to build themselves temples. It was then that the town that there is today got started and had its beginning.

25 : 32 And that's why the town lies in an out-of-the-way spot, because the Chichimecs had been driving the Colhuaque to desperation, thinking, when they settled the Colhuaque there, that eventually they would be flooded and would become weary and would perhaps go off somewhere. [But] it was not possible. In that very spot the town of Cuauhtitlan grew up where it is today.

25 : 37 Well, when the Colhuaque were finally settled, the river was still there,

192. Anticlimactic word order reversed in the translation.
193. Lit., There is this [that] establishes itself: in our gardens they would shoot things.
194. Lit., so that eventually they obtain that we give them our daughters and our lands.
195. Toxcatl follows Huei Tozoztli (see line 24:41 above).

and when the water would come, it would spread out. Later, however, the river was relocated, because a hundred households were swept away. Those who perished were Toltitlancalque. And so the waterway was relocated when Ayactlacatzin came in as ruler. It was he who relocated the waterway.[196]

25 : 43   And finally, as for those Chichimecs who had no temples, what they had were just arrows that they set up in beds of hay. They would make an earth altar and set up white plume-banners there, and each one would dress himself as Mixcoatl. Thus they remembered what the devil Itzpapalotl taught them. They always remembered it during [the feast] called Quecholli.

25 : 49   And as for the above-mentioned Colhuaque who went off in all directions, this was when they were scattered and dispersed in alien lands, some going to Azcapotzalco, Coatlichan, Huexotla, and Cuauhtitlan.

[The massacre of the Chichimecs: A.D. 1349 and later]

25 : 53   13 [House: 1349]. This was the year that Huactli, who had been ruler of Cuauhtitlan, died. Then a stand-in, or substitute, came to be inaugurated in his place. Soon the Colhuaque got themselves a ruler: they wanted to install [Iztactototl,] son of the ruler Huactli, since they knew he was the grandson of the above-mentioned Coxcox Teuctli, who had been ruler of Colhuacan. At this time they sheltered him[197] where the house of the devil Mixcoatl was. As yet Mixcoatl had the ruler Iztactototl with him in his calpulli temple.[198]

26 : 5   But eventually the Colhuaque supported him with great honor, honored the ruler Iztactototl. And they made many arrangements.

26 : 8   And furthermore, they introduced all the different manufactures, ceramic ware, matting, pots, bowls, and all the rest.

26 : 11   And it was they who built the town of Cuauhtitlan. And they provided it with lands, for the Chichimecs just kept being pushed back.

26 : 13   And it was they who brought all the idolatry. They brought their many gods.

196. This account of the flood and its aftermath is contradicted by lines 48:15–26 below.

197. Lit., they straw-housed him. In other words, they put him up in rude quarters in the manner of the Chichimecs. Rulers' straw-houses are mentioned in lines 4:19, 8:17, etc.

198. Or: As yet the ruler Iztactototl had [the idol] Mixcoatl with him in his calpulli temple. *Calpolco,* lit., calpulli place, is glossed by Sahagún as "una de las casas de oración que tenían en los barrios que ellos llamaban *calpulli,* que quiere decir iglesia del barrio o parroquia" (HG bk. 1, ch. 19, parag. 17 and FFCC 1:43:4: calpulco; see also FC 9:63:10).

26 : 14   And when they had become quite mingled with the Chichimecs, then they began to make milpa. And at last, peacefully, they began to mark off the boundaries of fields, laying out their calpulli lands.

26 : 17   And in later times, when all the people had become god worshippers, when Itzcoatzin was ruling in Tenochtitlan, still there were many Chichimecs. And then the Colhuaque went to Mexico to lodge charges against them, because they refused to worship the gods, refused to observe the so-called arrow fast.[199] In those days the arrow fast was customary.

26 : 24   On account of it, they were captured.[200] Indeed, they went as prisoners to Mexico. And those Chichimecs were these: a certain Xiuhcac from Toltepec, which is now called Xiuhcacco; then Pitzallotl's[201] grandchildren in Tlalcozpan Hueitoctitlan; then Cocotl from Cocotitlan, and Pipilo, who was also from there, toward Tzictla;[202] and others besides.

26 : 30   Those people went to their death in Mexico. So then they were stripped of their lands, which therefore are known today as Acxoteca lands,[203] Mexica lands. And it was the same with their other servant communities.

26 : 33   Indeed, Maxtlaton of Xallan was likewise killed, and his lands too are now known as Acxotlan lands, Mexica lands.

26 : 34   It was the same with all of Zoltepec and Cuauhtepec, and others as well that were Mexica lands.

26 : 36   And during this time the Chichimecs, who were being killed off, who were gradually disappearing and going to their destruction,[204] slipped away little by little and settled in Motozahuican and Tlachco.

[Colhuacan restored: A.D. 1349–77]

26 : 39   13 House [1349]. At this time Acamapichtli was brought to Tenochtitlan, when the woman Ilancueitl went and got him in Tetzcoco.[205]

26 : 41   1 Rabbit [1350]. It was in 1 Rabbit that the Tenochca got themselves a ruler, when Acamapichtli was inaugurated in Tenochtitlan. Now, it is

199. "Arrow fast" possibly refers to a ceremony performed in Mexico in connection with the worship of Huitzilopochtli. Men who fasted for the occasion cut special reeds and fashioned them into arrows, which were then bundled and offered to the god (FC bk. 2, ch. 33, and HG).

200. Read *anoque*.

201. Pitzallotl was the big Chichimec who stopped the Xaltocameca (line 19 : 39).

202. On the suffix *-copahuic*, see NED: -huic.

203. Acxotlan was one of the calpulli districts, or wards, of Mexico (FC 9 : 12 : 26, 9 : 63 : 11).

204. Anticlimactic word order reversed in the translation.

205. According to line 24 : 24 he was brought from Coatlichan. Varying sources make Ilancueitl the mother, stepmother, or wife of Acamapichtli. See García Granados, *Diccionario*, vol. 1, pp. 4–11.

26 : 45
told and related that his wife, Ilancueitl, was the one who put him in office. Here began the Mexica dynasty.

The time of 1 Rabbit was when the Totomihuaque were finally defeated. It was the Huexotzinca who defeated them.

26 : 46
The time of 1 Rabbit was when Tlahuacan Chalca were driven out.²⁰⁶ Departing from Xicco, they withdrew to what is now Chalco. And they were in Xicco for 212 years, during which time the rulers were Petlacalli Teuctli, Tezozomoctli, Mamatzin Teuctli,²⁰⁷ and other princes. Also Chalchiuhtzin, also Ecatzin.

26 : 51
2 Reed [1351] was when the Mixteca were defeated. The people of Teohuacan defeated them in Mixtlan when Ozomateuctli was ruler.

26 : 53
3 Flint. 4 House. 5 Rabbit. 6 Reed.

26 : 54
7 Flint [1356]. At this time Tepaneca who are known today as Toltitlancalque came to settle.²⁰⁸ Right there at the roadside, where they live today, they used to give people lodging and a hot supper. And they had just been provided with a ruler. Later it will be told and reported how their dynasty got started.

27 : 4
8 House. 9 Rabbit. 10 Reed. 11 Flint. 12 House.

27 : 5
13 Rabbit [1362]. In that year the Totomihuaque were dispersed. They left their country forever. It was the Huexotzinca who conquered them, during the reign of Tenocelotzin, son of Xayacamachan.

27 : 9
1 Reed [1363]. This was when the elder Ixtlilxochitl was inaugurated as ruler of Tetzcoco.

27 : 10
2 Flint [1364] was the year the Chalco ruler Xipemetztli died. Yecatl Teuctli was then inaugurated. And then he went to Tenochtitlan, where he sired a son named Cuapochtli.

27 : 13
3 House. 4 Rabbit.

27 : 14
5 Reed [1367] was the year the Cuauhtitlan ruler Iztactototzin died. He had ruled for nineteen years.²⁰⁹

27 : 16
6 Flint [1368]. At this time the Cuauhtitlan nation was inherited by the lady Ehuatlicuetzin, who had been Iztactototzin's wife. And she, too, lived at the temple of Mixcoatl, which had been the royal residence of Iztactototzin.

27 : 19
7 House. 8 Rabbit. 9 Reed.

206. Both Lehmann and Velázquez have it that these Tlahuacan Chalca merely separated or split off (from a larger group?).

207. A small superscript numeral precedes each of these first three names. Difficult to read, the numerals seem to be 1, 3, and 2, respectively.

208. Marginal gloss: The Tepaneca settled Toltitlan.

209. Marginal gloss: Not valid Colhuacan Acamapich Nauhyotzin. [This could mean that the glossator does not recognize Acamapichtli and Nauhyotzin as belonging to Colhuacan. Better-known are the Acamapichtli of Tenochtitlan and the Nauhyotzin of Tollan. See Concordance for locations in this codex.]

27 : 20   10 Flint [1372]. In that year the Chichimecs killed the lady Ehuatli-cuetzin. They went and shot her at a place called Callacoayan. The Chichimecs were angry because the Colhuaque had made her a whore.

27 : 23   11 House [1373] was when the Cuauhtitlan ruler Temetzacocuitzin was inaugurated, and he resided there at the temple of the devil Mixcoatl.

27 : 25   12 Rabbit. 13 Reed.

1 Flint [1376] is when the Mexitin and the Chalca began skirmishing.[210] As yet they were not taking prisoners or killing each other. It was as if they were just having fun. This is what is called a flower war.[211] It was in Techichco Colhuacan, this game of the Mexitin and the Chalca. And it went on for nine years, at the time when Colhuacan[212] was full[213] of Chalca.

27 : 31   2 House [1377]. This year Ilancueitl has become sad, for Colhuacan lies deserted. The city is sprouting grass. It lies in darkness. For thirty-one years it has had no ruler, only a military chief.

27 : 34   From the time that Achitometl killed Acamapichtli it began to be as if there were just a military ruler. Even though Achitometl had been inaugurated as king, there was nothing left to provide consolation. And when Achitometl died, the nation broke apart. The Colhuaque separated, as has been reported.

27 : 38   And this Ilancueitl, who had come to Mexico, was now saddened. She was troubled and felt pity for the nation of Colhuacan. Then she summoned the princes there in Mexico and sent them to Colhuacan.[214]

27 : 42   They went off, setting out from Mexico. The first was named Nauhyotzin, the second was named Mimichtzin, the third was named Xochitonal, the fourth was named Tlaltolcaltzin.

27 : 44   And then the above-mentioned Nauhyotzin was installed as ruler in Colhuacan.

[Cuauhtitlan's glory: A.D. 1378–1406]

27 : 45   3 Rabbit [1378]. In that year the Cuauhtitlan ruler Temetzacocuitzin died. He had ruled for only six years.

27 : 47   4 Reed [1379]. In that year Tlacateotzin was inaugurated as ruler. His

210. Read *moyayaotlaya.*

211. According to Chimalpain, only commoners (*macehualtin*) were killed in the Chalca-Mexica flower war; princes (*pipiltin*) were not killed (ZCHIM 1:79). Variant descriptions of flower war are given in TEZ ch. 96 and Pomar, pp. 41–42.

212. Colhuacan country? As we will be told in the next paragraph, Colhuacan city lies deserted or at least has suffered a decline.

213. Read *tentimanca.* Cf. 24:13.

214. Marginal gloss: Ilancueitl again rallies Colhuacan and installs lord.

straw-house was in the same place, where the temple of Mixcoatl was. There he lived as ruler, taking care of the Cuauhtitlan nation.

27 : 50   5 Flint. 6 House. 7 Rabbit.

27 : 51   8 Reed [1383]. In that year Ilancueitl died in Mexico.

27 : 52   9 Flint [1384]. Cuitlahuaca say that the Mexica dynasty began at this time, when Acamapichtli was inaugurated.

27 : 53   10 House [1385]. In that year the Mexitin and the Chalca finally provoked each other in earnest. It was said that the war began in Techichco, the war of the Mexica [and the] Tepaneca. At that time the flower war was broken off. And this Chalca War lasted seventy-two years altogether. It was in Amaquemecan that it cooled, at the time the war with Huexotzinco began, at the time the Chalca came and joined ranks [with Mexico],[215] during the reign of the elder Moteuczomatzin of Tenochtitlan.

28 : 3   In the year 10 House the Chalco ruler Yecatl Teuctli died. Then Xapaztli Teuctli was inaugurated, and he ruled for twenty-eight years. In his time it happened that the war spread to Chalco Atenco, the war of the Mexitin and the Tepaneca [and the] Cuauhtitlancalque.

28 : 7   Now, at this time, when there was war in Chalco, when the Chalca War was just eighty days old, the Cuauhtitlan princes Xaltemoctzin and Iquehuacatzin took captives. And Iquehuacatzin's captive was named Xaxama.

28 : 11   And at the same time the princes were taking captives the Cuauhtitlan Chichimecs were planning where their temple would be, the one that has stood there to this day. And then the captives, the princes' captives, were used as heart offerings.

28 : 15   Now, the way this house of the devil was built it had five levels,[216] and as it was only slowly that it grew larger and was provided with a facing, it took ten years all in all. Later, when the elder Xaltemoctzin was ruler, he made his temple [still] larger. What year that was will be told [below].

28 : 19   11 Rabbit. 12 Reed. 13 Flint.

1 House [1389]. In this year the Cuauhtitlan ruler Tlacateotzin died. He had ruled for eleven years.

28 : 21   2 Rabbit [1390] was when the elder Xaltemoctzin came to be inaugurated as Cuauhtitlan's ruler. His straw-house was at the Zacacalco [Straw House Place], which is now the monastery. But when he went hunting for captives in Chalco, before he was ruler, he lived at Cimapan Teopan.

28 : 25   In that same year Xiuhtepeca, Iyauhtepeca, and Tetelpan people came as immigrants from Cuauhnahuac. The names of these incoming Cuauhnahuaca were Quiauhtzin, Coatzin, Xiuhtlatonactzin, and Moteizcocopipina. And they came to live in Mexico. Their greeting gift was a turquoise

---

215. See 52 : 13–33 below.

216. "Five levels" evidently refers to the wedding-cake style of Mexican pyramid architecture.

crown. [Well,] it was like a turquoise crown. It isn't known what was on it, perhaps jade, or else turquoise. Also there were necklaces, ten neckpieces. Also a jade weaver's reed. Also a kind of snake-arm, with something like a hand where the head is. Also a jade spindle. Also a turquoise hand. Also two jadestones.

28 : 34   3 Reed.

4 Flint [1392]. At this time the ruler of Cuitlahuac Tizic, called Pichatzin Teuctli, [and others as well] were assassinated by command of the ruler who handed down the judgment—Tezozomoctzin, ruler of Azcapotzalco. Those who went to perform the assassinations were Tepaneca.

28 : 38   And those of Pichatzin's nobles who died were: first, Coyotliyacamiuh; second, Tzopallotzin; third, Hueiacatzin; fourth, Cuamamaztzin; fifth, Tlahuahuanqui; sixth, Xiuhtlapoca.

28 : 41   Anahuacatl, ruler of Tecpan, also met his death in Cuitlahuac at this time.[217] He had just fled to a chinampa when the Tecpaneca Cuitlahuaca went in and killed him—not the Tepaneca sent by[218] Azcapotzalco's Tezozomoctli.

28 : 44   5 House [1393] was when Tepolitzmaitl was inaugurated as ruler in Cuitlahuac Tizic. It was Tezozomoctli of Azcapotzalco who put him in office.

28 : 47   6 Rabbit.

7 Reed [1395]. In that year the Xaltocameca were destroyed at Tecanman, and so they entered Metztitlan and Tlaxcallan.[219] This was when they immigrated with their captives. It has already been told. It was reported along with the defeat of the Mexitin at Chapoltepec.[220] And those who had been made their captives were the Cuauhtitlancalque asked about in Metztitlan and Tlaxcallan when they were to be spoken of as to what these enemies of theirs were like and how they had been captured.[221]

28 : 53   Now, the defeat and exodus[222] of the Xaltocameca occurred during the rule of the elder Xaltemoctzin of Cuauhtitlan. And at this time Pantictzin Teuctli, Tlaltochtli, Teuctlacozauhqui, and Cincuani were ruling in Xaltocan.

217. Marginal gloss: Tezozomoc of Azcapotzalco ordered the killing of Pichatzin of Cuitlahuac Tizic. And the one from Tecpan, Anahuacatl. And others.

218. Read *yn tepaneca yn ytitlanhuan*.

219. Marginal gloss: Here they all evacuated Xaltocan and went to Tlaxcallan and to Metztitlan.

220. See lines 20:43 and 21:5–8.

221. A difficult sentence, which is clarified by the information given above in lines 20:49–21:5. In other words: the captives whom the Xaltocameca brought with them to Metztitlan and Tlaxcallan were the Cuauhtitlan natives of whom we have already heard; it will be recalled that the citizens of Metztitlan and Tlaxcallan asked the arriving Xaltocameca to describe, or speak about, the people of Cuauhtitlan, who had been enemies to the Xaltocameca, and to explain how these particular captives had been taken.

222. Anticlimactic word order reversed in the translation.

29 : 4 Well, the war began when the Mexitin were surrounded at Chapoltepec. The Cuauhtitlancalque were angry that the Xaltocameca went to war with the others there at Chapoltepec, because the Cuauhtitlancalque were friends of the Mexitin.

29 : 9 And it was also at this time that the Xaltocameca were destroyed at Tecanman.[223]

29 : 10 Now, the so-called Huitznahua Xaltocameca, along with the Ixayoctonca, as well as Totollan, Tlapallan, Tlilhuacan, and Ixayoc, came looking for lands where they could settle. Chalchiuh came as their leader from Ixayoctonco. And the ruler Xaltemoctzin received them gladly.

29 : 15 And in that very same year, 7 Reed, the ruler Xaltemoctzin gave orders for his boundary keepers to be sent off and stationed in Tzompanco, Citlaltepec, Huehuetocan, and Otlazpan.

29 : 18 To Tzompanco, the *tlacateuctli* Coyozacatzin went as leader, went to be governor.

29 : 19 To Citlaltepec, Itzcuintzin went as leader, went as governor.

29 : 20 To Huehuetocan, Cuauhchichitzin Tlacateuctzin went as governor, newly installed, having previously gone as governor to Otlazpan.

29 : 22 At this time Chalchiuhtzin was governing in Hueipochtlan. Pantli was ruling in Xilotzinco.

29 : 24 And when it had finally been accomplished that the boundaries were extended, then the ruler Xaltemoctzin began to increase the size of his temple, which stood in Cuauhtitlan.

29 : 27 At the same time that the elder Xaltemoctzin started on his temple, he used it to lay out the city of Cuauhtitlan in four quarters.[224] It was from this that he patterned it, building it to the four directions from the corners of his temple. Thus the city of Cuauhtitlan has four parts.

29 : 31 He built Tequixquinahuac at one corner by having Tepoxacco and Tzompanco bring workers there.

29 : 33 He built Chalmecapan at one corner, having [workers] brought by Cuauhtlaapan and Citlaltepec.

29 : 35 He built Nepantla at one corner, having them brought by Tepotzotlan and Huehuetocan.

29 : 37 He built Atempan at one corner, having them brought by Coyotepec and Otlazpan.

29 : 38 And in five years[225] the elder Xaltemoctzin's temple reached the top and was finished.

29 : 39 8 Flint. 9 House.

223. The author seems to forget that he has already reported this in lines 28:47–48.
224. Lit., When the elder Xaltemoctzin started his temple, at the same time it is from this that he established the city of Cuauhtitlan as four places.
225. Read *macuilxiuhtica*.

29 : 40 10 Rabbit [1398].[226] In that year the people of Cuauhtinchan were defeated while Teuctlacozauhqui was ruling.[227] Those who conquered them were the Mexitin, when Acamapichtli was ruler in Tenochtitlan and Cuauhtlatoatzin was ruler in Tlatilolco. With that the kingdom of Cuauhtinchan was permanently destroyed.

29 : 44 At this time the dynasty of Oztoticpac got started. Cuetzpalin Teuctli was the one who started it.

29 : 46 11 Reed [1399] is when the elder Xaltemoctzin's temple was finished. Its dedication ceremony was celebrated with people from Cuauhtinchan.[228] The Cuauhtitlancalque had gone there to get captives.

29 : 48 12 Flint. 13 House.

1 Rabbit [1402]. In that year Nezahualcoyotzin of Tetzcoco was born. His day sign was 1 Deer, so say the Cuitlahuaca.

29 : 50 2 Reed [1403]. A year-bundle feast was celebrated.

29 : 51 The stories of the Cuitlahuaca say that at this time Acamapichtli died and Huitzilihuitl was inaugurated.

29 : 52 3 Flint [1404]. In this year the one called Ayactlacatzin was born, who was to be made ruler in Cuauhtitlan. He was born in the place called Cuauhtlaapan Tianquizzolco. His mother's name was Xochicozcatl. His father's name was Xaltetl. And his grandfather, the father of his mother, was Cuauhixtli.[229] His great-grandfather was the steward Tozantzin, steward to the elder Xaltemoctzin.

30 : 5 The reason he was named Ayactlacatl [Nobody] is that he was born in the sweating room when no one was present.[230] His second princely name was Xaquin Teuctli, which means 'ant'. His actual ruler's name was Ayactlacatl. He was a very rich man. Four times a year he would entertain and provide regalement.[231] And he was a true soldier and warrior. The Cuauhtitlancalque simply asked him to become their ruler.

30 : 11 When he was inaugurated, he was already a warrior, already a captor, having gone to get prisoners in Cuahuacan. And when he had gotten his prisoner etc., he returned to Cuahuacan to live there. [But] those of Cuauhtlaapan went and fetched him, for he was a son of their people, etc.

226. Marginal gloss: The Turk proceeded and stopped in this year, on the day of the Holy Trinity. Great victory. [Cf. gloss at 51 : 15.]

227. Marginal gloss: Teuctlacozauhqui, lord of Cuauhtinchan. War that the Mexica waged against them.

228. As sacrificial victims. Cf. 20 : 32, 25 : 18, 25 : 29.

229. Probably the text should read either *inantzin yta quauhixtli* or *inantzin yta ytoca quauhixtli.*

230. Prenatal care and obstetrics were attended to by midwives, who practiced in the sweat bath, or sweating room (FC 6 : 151–52, 6 : 155–56, 6 : 167, 11 : 191).

231. For *concuia* read *cuicuicaia* or *cuicuicac*, as in line 30 : 15. In Tenochtitlan the custom of entertaining with music and regaling people with food was observed by rich merchants (FC bk. 9, ch. 7) and others of high status (see FC 2 : 68 : 2–11, 2 : 137 : 18–28).

They went and established him at Cinpallanalco, and they built him a residence there. In that place, too, he often entertained and provided regalement. It was from there that the Cuauhtitlancalque fetched him in order to make him their ruler. And all his years were ninety, during the time that he was growing up and when he was ruler, during the time that he lived and ruled.

30 : 19   This was also the year that the Tenochtitlan ruler Acamapichtli died. Then Huitzilihuitl was inaugurated and ruled in Tenochtitlan. He was the second to be made ruler of the Tenochca.

30 : 22   At the same time, Chimalpopocatzin was installed as *tlacateccatl*. [With] a daughter of the Cuauhnahuac people, before he was ruler, Chimalpopocatzin, who was the younger brother of Huitzilihuitl, had a son, Itzcoatzin. And the grandfather of Itzcoatzin was Acamapichtli. And Chimalpopocatzin sired the elder Moteuczomatzin, whose female forebears were requisitioned in Colhuacan by Ilancueitl. The female forebears of the Mexica rulers were women from that place.

30 : 29   4 House.

5 Rabbit [1406]. In this year Tezozomoctli of Cuitlahuac Tizic was born.

[Origins of the Tepaneca War: the rise of Toltitlan: A.D. 1407–8 and later]

30 : 31   6 Reed [1407].

7 Flint [1408]. In this year the Tepaneca put to death the elder Xaltemoctzin *atecpanecatl teuctli*, who was ruler of Cuauhtitlan. He was hanged by judgment of Tezozomoctli, ruler of Azcapotzalco. They summoned him craftily, came and invited him to a feast in Tepanohuayan, and they took along many of his nobles and lords. And when all was ready, Tezozomoctli of Azcapotzalco killed the ruler of Cuauhtitlan.

30 : 36   After that, none of the Chichimec princes in Cuauhtitlan dared to be ruler. For nine years Cuauhtitlan lay in darkness. No one was ruler. There was only a military chief.

30 : 40   At this time the Toltitlancalque became enormously proud, making war on the Cuauhtitlan nation. The Azcapotzalca, who were Tepaneca, incited them all the more. This was by command of Tezozomoctli, ruler of Azcapotzalco. Thus they joined forces against the Cuauhtitlan nation, because Toltitlancalque are Tepaneca. And so it was all the more that the Tepaneca took it upon themselves to come make war in Cuauhtitlan.

30 : 48   And this was when a dynasty got started in Toltitlan, the dynasty of the Toltitlancalque.

30 : 49   The first to rule, the one who started the dynasty, was called Cuauhtzin Teuctli.

30 : 50 The second to rule in Toltitlan was called Xopantzin.

30 : 51 The third to rule in Toltitlan was called Tepanonoc. As for this Tepanonoc, it was he above all who took it upon himself to incite them against the Cuauhtitlan nation. It was he who widened the war, as will be heard under the year in which the Tepaneca War was waged.

31 : 4 The fourth to rule in Toltitlan was called Epcoatl. He was the son of Azcapotzalco's Tezozomoctli, who came to Toltitlan to install him as ruler, who indeed is the one, moreover, who came and widened the conflict with the Cuauhtitlan nation, the war. Here is the one who intensified, who heightened the fury. For this Tezozomoctli, this ruler of Azcapotzalco, desired in his heart to make one of his children the ruler of Cuauhtitlan.

31 : 11 But the Chichimec princes would not consent. They disregarded the very jealous Tezozomoctli, whose son was not received as ruler of Cuauhtitlan, for indeed he had killed the late ruler, the elder Xaltemoctzin.

31 : 15 And so, during the time of this Epcoatl, who was ruler of Toltitlan, it befell him that after his father, Tezozomoctli, had died, then indeed in his time the Tepaneca of Toltitlan were destroyed. The story of that battle will be told presently. It will be heard under the year in which the Tepaneca nation was destroyed,[232] when the Toltitlan ruler Epcoatl died. During his time the people moved away. He died in battle.

31 : 21 Now, when war and destruction had passed, when the Toltitlancalque and the Tepaneca had disbanded, there was no ruler in Toltitlan for twenty years, and only gradually did the Toltitlancalque, returning, come back to settle in their country.

31 : 25 And subsequently, after the passage of the twenty years, a certain Ocelotlapan was inaugurated as ruler. And when he died, Acolmiztli, succeeding him, was inaugurated. Only forty days did he rule. He was assassinated.

31 : 29 When he was dead, Citlalcoatl succeeded him and was inaugurated as ruler. It was in his time that the Spaniards arrived. He was shorn like an *otomitl*[233] on account of the war in Mexico.

31 : 31 Then Yohualtonatiuh was inaugurated. It was in his time that the Spaniards arrived.[234] Both Citlalcoatl and Yohualtonatiuh died of the smallpox.

31 : 34 Then Don Hernando Matlalihuitzin was inaugurated as ruler. Then they got rid of him, and Don Antonio Acolmizton was installed as his successor.

31 : 36 And at the death of Don Antonio Acolmizton, the son,[235] then Don Pedro Tlacateuctzin was installed as his successor.

232. See line 45 : 28 et seq.

233. Refers to the hair style of a high-ranking warrior. See Concordance: tlaotonxintli.

234. For *ançico* read *ahçico*. This probably refers to the Spaniards' arrival in Cuauhtitlan territory (see line 16 : 6), whereas the preceding paragraph must refer to their arrival in Mexico in 1519.

235. Presumably the son of his predecessor. Compare the similar usage in line 16 : 17.

31 : 39   Upon his death Don Gerónimo de los Angeles was installed as his successor.

31 : 40   Upon his death Don Gabriel de Tápia Mazacihuatl was installed as his successor.

31 : 42   Now is the year 1570. This was written in August.

[Origins of the Tepaneca War: the tyranny of Tezozomoctli: A.D. 1409–28]

31 : 43   8 House. 9 Rabbit. 10 Reed. 11 Flint.

31 : 44   12 House [1413]. This was the year the Colhuacan ruler Nauhyotzin died. He was killed by Tezozomoctli, ruler of Azcapotzalco. Then a certain Acoltzin was inaugurated as ruler and ruled in Colhuacan.

31 : 47   13 Rabbit [1414]. In that year the Chalco ruler whose name was Ixapaztli Teuctli died. Then Cuauhnextli Teuctli was inaugurated as Chalco's ruler.

31 : 50   1 [Reed: 1415]. In that year, for the first time, the Mexitin made war in Tepanohuayan. At that time they appropriated what was still only a small amount of eagle land.[236] As yet this was their only possession.

32 : 3   In that same year the Cuitlahuac ruler Tepolitzmaitl died. He had ruled for twenty-three years. Then Tezozomoctli was inaugurated as ruler of Cuitlahuac Tizic.

32 : 6   2 Flint.

3 House [1417]. In that year the Tenochtitlan ruler Huitzilihuitl died. And at that time Chimalpopocatzin was inaugurated as ruler of Tenochtitlan. Tetzcoca say it truthfully.[237] Colhuaque say it in their year count.

32 : 11   The year 3 House was the ninth year that there was no ruler in Cuauhtitlan.

32 : 12   And it was also in that year that the Amaquemecan ruler called Cacamatzin met his death, when there was war in Chalco. They came and treacherously abandoned him to the Cuitlahuaca,[238] who by this time were confronting them,[239] for they too were fighting there at Chalco Atenco, since the war had been pushed back.[240]

32 : 18   4 Rabbit [1418]. In that year Tezozomoctli was inaugurated as ruler of

236. Land taken in battle? See GLOS: ²cuauhtlalli.

237. For a change. Tetzcoca traditions are rejected by the author in lines 4:31 and 12:53, and by a glossator at line 8:38.

238. Lit., abandoned him in the presence of and with the knowledge of the Cuitlahuaca. See GLOS: -ixpan/-matian.

239. Lit., the Cuitlahuaca were confronting it (i.e., Chalco, the Chalca nation). Cf. 32:27.

240. Pushed back from Techichco to Chalco Atenco. See line 28:6. For more on the Cuitlahuaca see 32:26–29.

Cuauhtitlan. He came from Tlatilolco and was the son of Cuauhtlatoatzin. He came and founded a dynasty at Huexocalco, came there to build his palace house.

32 : 23 And at this time the name of the ruler of Tlatilolco was Tlacateotzin. These people were more boastful than Tenochtitlan.

32 : 26 In that same year, 4 Rabbit, the Chalca were driven out when the Tlahuaca[241] encountered them, indeed confronted them.[242] For incoming Tlecuilque, Tlilhuaque, and Pochteca had joined their ranks,[243] had joined Cuitlahuac.

32 : 30 5 Reed [1419]. In that year the elder Ixtlilxochitzin, ruler of Tetzcoco, died. He did not take sick. The Tepaneca executed him, and it was Tezozomoctli, ruler of Azcapotzalco, who handed down the sentence. Ixtlilxochitzin's nephew, the *tlacateccatl* Cihuacuecuenotzin, also died at this time.

32 : 35 Cihuacuecuenotl died because he would have mounted a war party in Otompan. By dint of arrows and shields he would have freed his uncle, Ixtlilxochitzin. But when the people of Otompan heard that Cihuacuecuenotl was rallying them to war, they immediately became angry and said, "What is Cihuacuecuenotl saying? What a scoundrel! Would anyone[244] want to make war on his own father?"

32 : 41 With that they stoned Cihuacuecuenotl there in Otompan, for he was the son[245] of Azcapotzalco's Tezozomoctli.

32 : 44 And Ixtlilxochitzin of Tetzcoco died, too.

6 Flint. 7 House. 8 Rabbit. 9 [Reed]. 10 Flint.

32 : 45 11 House [1425]. In the year 11 House the Azcapotzalco ruler Tezozomoctli apportioned tribute labor, apportioned vassals. As for the Tetzcocatl, as well as Coatlichan, he accordingly took both towns to serve as vassals for himself, counting them as his own.

32 : 48 And he apportioned the Cuitlahuaca Tizica to Tlatilolco.

33 : 1 And as for the Cuitlahuaca Teopancalca, Atenchicalcan, and Tecpan, he apportioned all three to Tenochtitlan, to whom he allotted them as vassals.

33 : 4 And when Azcapotzalco's Tezozomoctli had handed down his judgment and made the arrangement, then Tenochtitlan, Tlatilolco, and Azcapotzalco were served by those places for seven years.

33 : 7 12 Rabbit.

13 Reed [1427]. In that year the Azcapotzalco ruler Tezozomoctli died. Cuitlahuaca say that he ruled for 131 years. When he finally died, many a sigh was heaved, now that he was gone.[246] For while he was still alive, still

241. I.e., the Cuitlahuaca. See 13 : 4–8.
242. Lit., encountered it . . . confronted it (i.e., Chalco, the Chalca nation). Cf. 32 : 16.
243. Lit., had entered among them (*yntlan hualcallacque*). GLOS: calaqui 3.
244. Following Lehmann, read *aççin* as a contraction of *ac ce in*. GLOS: *ac ce*.
245. Grandson per 36 : 12.
246. Lit., When he died, finally, many [were] their sighs here [i.e., now] in his absence, [which] were made. GLOS: ihiyotl, nican, -tepotzco, tlamantli.

ruling, while it was still in his time, he kept setting up his children as rulers of cities, sending them off to rule in distant parts:

33 : 14   He installed the first, named Quetzalmaquiztli, as ruler of Coatlichan.

33 : 15   He installed the second, named Cuauhpiyo, as ruler of Huexotla.

33 : 16   He installed the third, named Teyollocoa, as ruler of Acolman.

33 : 17   He installed the fourth, named Epcoatl, as ruler of Toltitlan.

33 : 18   He installed the fifth, named Quetzalcuixin, as ruler of Mexicatzinco.

33 : 19   As his successor he installed the sixth, Quetzalayatzin, as ruler of Azcapotzalco. Thus he commanded him, saying, "If I should die, you would be my successor. You would be ruler here in Azcapotzalco."

33 : 22   He installed the seventh, named Maxtla, as ruler of Coyohuacan.[247]

33 : 23   He installed the eighth, named Tepanquizqui, as ruler of Xochimilco.

33 : 24   Now, when Tezozomoctli, ruler of Azcapotzalco, was dead, then his son named Maxtlaton, who was supposed to have ruled in Coyohuacan, came and made himself ruler of Azcapotzalco, usurping the rulership of his younger brother, Quetzalayatzin.

33 : 30   1 Flint. This was when the Tenochtitlan ruler Chimalpopocatzin was assassinated by the Tepaneca. The Azcapotzalco ruler Maxtlaton handed down the sentence.

33 : 32   The way Chimalpopocatzin met his death is that he was dragged. They brought him through the streets.

33 : 33   And as to [why] he was punished with death, it is said that he gave advice to Quetzalayatzin, whose older brother was Maxtlaton. He said to him, "Friend, why has your older brother Maxtla taken your kingdom away from you? Really, you are the ruler. Your father put all of you in office before he died.[248] So kill this older brother of yours, this Maxtla. He is ruling your kingdom. The way to kill him is to set up a pavilion and invite him to a feast. That's where you will kill him."

33 : 40   Well, these words were repeated to Maxtlaton, who then sentenced Chimalpopocatzin to be killed. It was in Tenochtitlan that he met his death.

33 : 42   Now, when the Tepaneca assassins came, people were in the process of carving stone. As they arrived, the Tenochca were about to enlarge the temple of Huitzilopochtli.

33 : 45   And at this time Teuctlahuacatzin, *tlacochcalcatl* of Tenochtitlan, committed suicide. It was because he was filled with fear when the ruler Chimalpopocatzin was killed, thinking that perhaps they were going to make war on the Tenochca, who would perhaps be defeated. And so he sacrificed himself by swallowing poison.[249] And when this became known,

247. The copyist's *colhuacan* is evidently a slip. Cf. 33 : 26. See also García Granados, *Diccionario* 1 : 429–37.

248. Lit., Your father went away having put you (plural) in office. See NED: yauh 4; cf. line 46 : 45 below.

249. Cf. 42 : 1–2 ("committed suicide by swallowing poison").

when it was found out, then the Tenochca princes and nobles were angry. And because of it, the Mexica called a meeting. They came together and held council and pronounced and decreed that none of his sons, his nephews, or his grandsons would gain honor and nobility. Rather they would belong to them as vassals forever. And that is what happened. For even though his descendants were able warriors and fighters, none gained nobility and honor.[250]

34 : 5　　And at this time the Tlatilolco ruler Tlacateotzin made up a story[251] that the Mexica Tenochca were going to be attacked. And for this he was put to death. It was the Azcapotzalco ruler, the above-mentioned Maxtlaton, who handed down the sentence.

34 : 10　　And it also happened at this time that Maxtlaton, ruler of Azcapotzalco, caused Nezahualcoyotzin of Tetzcoco, son of the elder Ixtlilxochitzin, to go into exile, and he went to live in Atlancatepec, Tliliuhquitepec, Tlax-callan, and Huexotzinco. And that is where Nezahualcoyotzin sired his children: the first, called Tlecoyotl; also Tliliuhquitepetl; also Tlahuexolotl.

34 : 17　　As for Tenochtitlan, well, at this time in Tenochtitlan, challenged by enemies, Itzcoatzin was inaugurated as ruler. And at the time he was in-augurated, it was the elder Moteuczomatzin who was supposed to have been made ruler. [But] it is told and related that he did not want it.

34 : 21　　He refused, saying, "I will be ruler later. Let it be my dear beloved uncle Itzcoatl. I wish to serve as his guarantor, putting the Mexica Tenochca in a state of readiness for the sake of their livelihood, and I will establish their authority. I do not wish to be ruler. Therefore install me as *tlacateccatl*. For now, let my dear uncle[252] Itzcoatl be ruler. I will be going to war, and I will provide him with lands at the expense of those nations that sur-round us.[253]

34 : 29　　Also in that year, 1 Flint [1428], the Chalco ruler Cuauhnextli died. Then Caltzin Teuctli, also called Temiztzin—which was one of his names—came to be inaugurated as ruler, and he ruled in Chalco.

[Origins of the Tepaneca War: the exile of Nezahualcoyotl]

34 : 33　　Here is told the story of Tezozomoctli of Azcapotzalco and how he ruled.

---

250. Cf. the parallel passage, 66 : 19–23.

251. Lit., imagined, invented, and declared. The statement is reiterated in lines 66 : 4–6 below and rephrased in lines 66 : 32–33. Note that the oracle of Cuitlahuac is put to death for making a similar prophecy in lines 61 : 52–62 : 11.

252. Father per 36 : 22–24.

253. For similar phraseology regarding the nations that surrounded Mexico see FC 8 : 57 : 23.

34 : 34   What it tells is how rulers hated each other and made war, how the Tepaneca were destroyed, how assassinations got started. It was the Tepaneca who were warred against when the hatred set in.

34 : 38   Here it will be told, and now you will hear, how it all came about, long ago, when Tepaneca were destroyed in the war that was made against them.

34 : 41   This Tezozomoctli, who got to be ruler of Azcapotzalco, had children. [The first] born was named Tepanquizqui. And the second one that he had was Quetzalmazatl, and the third was named Cuauhpiyotzin. The fourth born[254] was Epcoatzin. The fifth born, Chalchiuhtlatonactzin. The sixth, Teyollocoatzin. The seventh, Quetzalcuixin. The eighth was named Quetzalayatzin. The ninth, Maxtlatzin.

34 : 48   And then the aforementioned Chalchiuhtlatonactzin got married, taking a daughter of Coxcoxtzin from Tetzcoco. It was Techotlalatzin's sister, Cuauhcihuatzin, that Chalchiuhtlatonac took as his wife. Then Cihuacuecuenotzin was born.

35 : 2   At Cihuacuecuenotzin's birth, his elder kinsmen[255] grew angry, hating their newborn nephew. Enraged, they took him off and abandoned him in Mazahuacan, secretly leaving him to die. And when Cihuacuecuenotzin's mother found out about it, she fled to Tetzcoco, and there she stayed. And while she was living there, she got married, taking a man named Zacancatlyaomitl as her husband.

35 : 9   Now, when Tezozomoctli found out that his daughter-in-law was married in Tetzcoco and that Zacancatlyaotl was the one who had taken her, he was furious. He summoned[256] his captain Tecolotzin and a few others, who came along too, and he said to them:

35 : 14   "Tecolotzin, Chachatzin, Teuctzin, Cihuaxochitzin! From what I know and hear—and this is what I have found out—Zacancatlyaomitl of Huexotla has laid the former wife of your comrade Chalchiuhtlatonactzin. He has slept with her. My princes, hear me! As I stand before you,[257] my anger is aroused, I am insulted.

35 : 19   "And would [I let] one of my own princes, my own lords lie with her? What good will it do[258] that [ruler] who gives all the commands?[259] Is

---

254. For *tlacatl* read *tlacat* (was born).

255. Lit., his elder brothers. Perhaps the text means Chalchiuhtlatonactzin's elder brothers.

256. Read *connotz*.

257. For *can iz ancate* read *ca in iz ancate*, lit., indeed here you are.

258. What good will it do . . . ?, lit., Why has he done this?

259. *Centlatolhua* (complete command owner, i.e., the king—a term I have not found elsewhere). Lehmann, followed by Velázquez, reads *çentlacolhua* (half owner—whatever that may mean). In my view Lehmann's reading is untextual. The somewhat odd formation of the second 't' is repeated in line 35:34, where it appears as the third character in *yxtlilxochitzin*.

he not [to be] our shield slave, our arrow slave? Let Ixtlilxochitl command no more! Those Tepaneca whom I authorize are to go kill him in Chicocuauhyocan."

35 : 26   So it became true. It happened. He met his death in a pavilion.

Well now, when they saw[260] the Tepaneca assassins coming, they put Ixtlilxochitzin's sons in a cave in the woods, and therefore they did not die. These were Nezahualcoyotzin and his older brother Tzontecochatzin. And the ones who hid them were, first of all, Huahuantzin, also Xiconocatzin and Cuicuitzcatzin. And so[261] there were three.

35 : 33   That night, when Ixtlilxochitzin was dead, the rescuers, the ones who had hidden them—Huahuantzin, Xiconotcatzin, and Cuicuitzcatzin—brought them out from the cave and took them to Chiauhtzinco by way of Tetzihuactla. Then they led them to Cuamincan and hid them among the crags. And there they slept a little.

35 : 40   Then they hurried them on, bringing them to Teponazco, and in a gorge they hid those princes, Nezahualcoyotl and Tzontecochatzin. And then, in the white light of dawn, they brought them to Otonquilpan.

35 : 44   Then Coyohua comes along to supervise, and he takes the princes to Acalhuacan,[262] leaving them in the care of Huahuantzin and Xiconocatzin. Then in Acalhuacan,[263] at midnight, they bring them out and are looking around, and Coyohua finds some people in a boat. It seems they've been sent by Itzcoatzin.

36 : 3   Then Coyohua called out to them. He said, "Hey, brother."[264]

36 : 4   They don't hear him. So he shouts. He says, "Hey, brothers! Is it you?"

36 : 6   Then they called back, they said, "Yes, brother. And are you Coyohua?"[265]

36 : 8   He said, "Yes, brothers, it is I."

Then they asked, "Brothers, did the children die?"

36 : 10   One of them told what had happened: "My prince Ixtlilxochitzin has become a slave.[266] And, in Otompan, it is the same with Cihuacuecuenotzin, the grandson of Tezozomoctli." And when he was able to see them in the midnight darkness, he said to them, "The children are over there. Let me go get them."

260. *Oquinhualytonque*, corrected by Velázquez to *oquinhualytaque* (they saw them hither).

261. For *ipa* read *ipā*. GLOS: ipan.

262. Lit., *came and left them in Acalhuacan.*

263. Notice that the text seems to have *acolhuacan*, but *acalhuacan* in line 35:45 above. Lehmann and Velázquez read both names as *acolhuacan*, i.e., the region governed by Tetzcoco. But *acalhuacan* (boat town), perhaps designating a particular place where boats were docked, seems more in keeping here. See note to the translation at 21:16.

264. Coyohua uses the term *iccauhtli* (younger brother) in addressing the envoys, who in turn address him as *tiachacauh* (elder brother).

265. Lit., "Yes, it is we, brother. Are you Coyohua?"

266. He has become a slave in the other world, i.e., he has died. See NED: tlācohti 2.

36 : 15   "Good. Bring them along," they said. "Itzcoatzin sent us here to look for them."²⁶⁷

36 : 17   Then they went and got them and put them in the boat.

36 : 18   And then they took them away.²⁶⁸ The reason they had made such an effort to search for them is that these were the grandchildren of Itzcoatzin. All the searchers were sons of Itzcoatzin, therefore uncles of Nezahualcoyotzin.

36 : 22   And here are the sons of Itzcoatzin: first, Cahualtzin, and Moteuczomatzin the elder, Tecallapohuatzin, Citlalcoatzin, Cuitlahuatzin, Tzompantzin, Cuauhtlatoatzin, Tzacatzin the elder, Tepolomitzin, Tochihuitzin. These were the ten sons of Itzcoatzin.

36 : 28   Then all the children's uncles came back to Itzcoatzin.

36 : 30   Then Tzontecochatzin is being taken care of by Xiconocatzin, Cuicuitzcatzin, and Coyohua. And so Nezahualcoyotzin is fooling around. And so he falls into the water there.

36 : 33   Well, tradition has it that sorcerers²⁶⁹ came and seized him and carried him to the summit of Poyauhtecatl, there to perform a sacrament. And it used to be told that in that place they anointed him with flood and blaze,²⁷⁰ charging him: "You shall be the one. We ordain your fate, and by your hand a nation shall be destroyed."

36 : 40   After that, the sorcerers carried him off, bringing him back to exactly where they had gotten him. And then Nezahualcoyotzin emerged.

37 : 1   And when Itzcoatzin saw him, he marveled greatly and was astonished that Nezahualcoyotzin had reappeared.

37 : 3   Now, the way Nezahualcoyotl grew, he was already getting bigger and stronger. And so, at Zacatlan, then, he took a captive with the help of others and became a man. He was the second.²⁷¹ Then he wanted to come into Tenochtitlan, and he did.

37 : 7   Then he also went to Azcapotzalco in order to present his partial captive to Tezozomoctli. Coyohua led the way for Nezahualcoyotzin. Well, this Coyohua was not from Tetzcoco. He was from another place, called Teopiazco, and he went along to lead the way for Nezahualcoyotzin. And when they've arrived in Azcapotzalco, and they've entered and announced themselves,²⁷² then he addresses Tezozomoctli, he says to him:

267. Marginal gloss: prophesies about Nezahualcoyotl [evidently refers to lines 36 : 33–39].

268. Lit., Then they [the envoys of Itzcoatzin] came conducting them.

269. Lit., those who are sorcerers.

270. The figurative expression "flood and blaze" means the spirit of battle or war itself. NED: teoātl/tlachinōlli.

271. A creditable performance. When novice warriors helped take a captive, as many as six might participate. The principal captor would receive the victim's torso and right leg. The second received the left leg, while the others had to divide up the arms. FC bk. 8, ch. 21.

272. Entered and announced themselves, lit., entered and said something.

37 : 14 "O child, my son![273] O Tezozomoctzin! A poor orphan comes before you to make a gift. He goes about here at your doorstep, here in Mexico.[274] That's where he is sustained."

37 : 18 Then Tezozomoctli answers. He says to Coyohua, "Well now, Coyohua, what is this? Nezahualcoyotl lives, Coyohua?"

37 : 20 "The poor orphan lives right here in Tenochtitlan, O child."

37 : 22 "And what is this, Coyohua?" said Tezozomoctli. "He has brought me a gift?"

37 : 23 But they gave him nothing.

Just so did Nezahualcoyotzin come, and then he went.

37 : 25 Then he volunteered for the war in Chalco. And there Nezahualcoyotl took a prisoner. He captured a woman named Cilimiyauhtzin. Then, with his prisoner, he went and sat before Tezozomoctli. Coyohua came along, too, and when he got there, he addressed Tezozomoctli, uttering all the things by which sorcerers[275] are addressed.

37 : 31 Then Tezozomoctli answered him, saying, "Coyohua! What is this? Is Nezahualcoyotl alive?"

37 : 33 Then he called for his captain, [who came accompanied by others,][276] and he said to them, "Tecolotzin! Teuctzin! Cihuaxochitzin! Who put the arrow and the shield in the hands of this Nezahualcoyotl? Is this his due, his lot, his charge? Rather deer and rabbit are the proper game for this Nezahualcoyotl, this little Chichimec. And who is at fault? Is it not Itzcoatl who is at fault? He marries his daughters off in Acolhuacan. Would we go and set up a daughter of ours in Acolhuacan? Isn't the Acolhua our arrow slave, our shield slave?" Such were the words of Tezozomoctli, with which they were being briefed.

37 : 44 And as for Nezahualcoyotl, who had come to give Tezozomoctli his captive, he was there, but he did not hear what was being said about him.[277]

37 : 46 Meanwhile, Cougar Arm, Fuzzy Face, Big Dart, Man-eater, and Mudhead came[278] to deposit tribute, and Nezahualcoyotl was rewarded with what they brought. All he got was a tilma.

38 : 1 Then Nezahualcoyotzin went back to Mexico. He was not there long before Itzcoatzin gave him a command, saying, "Nezahualcoyotzin! The

273. The ruler Topiltzin is similarly addressed in the passage beginning with line 5 : 39 above.

274. Now part of Mexico City, Azcapotzalco is only 8 km from the former center of Tenochtitlan.

275. Read *tlacatecollo*.

276. See 35 : 12–14.

277. Lit., he did not hear what about him they were being briefed.

278. Lit., went. (The names of the tribute payers, here translated, are Acolmiztli, Ixtomi, Hueiimiuh, Tecuani, and Cuatlalatl.)

Sun and Tlalteuctli have taken pity on you. So proceed to Acolhuacan. Govern your nation."

38 : 7   And it was then that Nezahualcoyotzin went to Tetzcoco and was inaugurated. And he lived there.[279]

38 : 8   Now, afterward—after a long time—Tezozomoctli remembered Coyohua, and he issued an order, saying, "Have Coyohua fetched. Have him come."

38 : 11   Then Coyohua was fetched, and he came before Tezozomoctli, and when he had arrived in his presence, he said to him, "Come here, Coyohua." Then he said, "Listen, Coyohua. Here is why you have been called. Who is this truly bad one that I have dreamed about? An eagle is standing on top of me. A jaguar is standing on top of me. A wolf is standing on top of me. A rattlesnake is lying on top of me. My dream terrifies me.

38 : 19   "And I say, Coyohua! don't let Nezahualcoyotl destroy me. Don't let him look for his father, Ixtlilxochitl, and his uncle, Cihuacuecuenotl. Don't let him turn the flood and blaze[280] against my sons who are lords and rulers.

38 : 24   "And this I say: Listen! here is the command that I give. For my sons who are lords and nobles are to be found all around, and they will support you. Now, this Nezahualcoyotl is quite a little landowner, owns quite a few cultivated fields. His lands are quite something. Be his successor.

38 : 29   "I am well aware that you are very close to him, you who are bringing him up and educating him. But there's this: go to my sons who are lords and nobles, who will give you support. And hear this: you will have lands, you will plant by the *mecatl*.[281] You will have two or three storekeepers. And here's this—a dart. Let it pierce his neck. At daybreak give him a scrubbing at the waterside.[282] Perhaps he has accidentally choked in his sleep.[283] And I want to hear about it from you. Now go!"

38 : 36   And when Coyohua left, he went and spoke to Nezahualcoyotzin. He said, "Tezozomoctli summoned me to Azcapotzalco. O my child! O Nezahualcoyotzin! I'm supposed to kill you. Here is the dart that he gave me, that I'm supposed to stick in your neck. I'm to strangle you, and I'm

---

279. This report—indeed, the entire passage at hand—seems to contradict the tradition that Nezahualcoyotl spent his exile years in the Huexotzinco region and was not installed as ruler of Tetzcoco until 1433. On the exile in Huexotzinco, see 44:29 below; on Nezahualcoyotl's inauguration, see 47:39 and 48:31.

280. I.e., make war on my sons. Cf. 36:36.

281. A certain measure of land (GLOS: mecatl 2). Or a cord for measuring land (GLOS: mecatl 1).

282. Sahagún mentions corpses disposed of at daybreak (*in oallatvi*) and corpses solicitously bathed (not scrubbed), sometimes at the waterside (*atenco*). See FC 2:121:22, 4:45:9, 6:161:15, 7:17:28. Following Lehmann, the translation here depends upon reading the element *-ate-* as *-aten-*. Velázquez reads *-ate-* (testicles), translating *xicatexaxaquallo* "estrégale los compañones."

283. For *ca nen* read *ça nen*. GLOS: zannen.

to give you a scrubbing at the waterside. These are the words of Tezo-zomoctli, his command to me. You are not the only one who feels it, soldier!"

38 : 44   Then Coyohua said to him, "Have no fear, Nezahualcoyotzin, for I am Coyohua![284] Be glad. Rejoice. Am I not going to turn it back on this Tezozomoctli? For I am Coyohua!"

38 : 46   And at this time Coyohua made his first return trip to Azcapotzalco. And for this purpose, once again, Tezozomoctli sent[285] to have him fetched.

39 : 1   Even a second time were Tezozomoctli's messengers sent forth. And when they arrived, they said, "Well, now, Coyohua. We've been sent by Tezozomoctzin. How are you doing? About that command he gave you, how are things going? Did it get done?"

39 : 4   And then he said, "Well, fellow! I haven't been able to get near him.[286] He's always with those little captains of his."

39 : 7   Then they also said this: "Coyohua, let the ones who are with him take him out for some recreation, and when he crosses a bridge, let them give him a kick. He'll have fallen into the water by accident. Let them take him up to a rooftop for some recreation, and let them knock him over. He'll have accidentally fallen from the roof."

39 : 11   Then Coyohua answers. He says, "All right, fellow. Let's try it. Perhaps we'll be able to do it. I'll tell them to give it a try. You won't be informed about it until they've been able to do it."

39 : 15   Then Coyohua went away. He went to speak with Nezahualcoyotzin. "Nezahualcoyotzin!" he said. "Listen to the words of Tezozomoctli. He has given me another command. You're supposed to be kicked into the water. And thrown from a roof. You will have been broken to pieces by accident. Alas, these are the words of Tezozomoctli."

39 : 20   But once again Tezozomoctli's orders were defeated.

39 : 22   And for a third time this Tezozomoctli of Azcapotzalco summoned Co-yohua. When he had summoned him, he said to him, "Come, Coyohua. Pay close attention. I told you you would plant your gardens by the *mecatl* and you would have storekeepers. And my sons who are lords and rulers would give you support. I told you this many times."

39 : 27   And then Coyohua says to Tezozomoctli, "Well then, my child, well then, my dear. Let me bring him in, because I just haven't been able to do it. Kill him here yourself. That way you will have no doubt about it. I tried everything for you,[287] but I just haven't been able to do it."

---

284. Evidently a play on words. The name Coyohua literally means "coyote owner"; and Nezahualcoyotl is "fasting coyote" (see NED: nezahualli).

285. Read *huallaihua* as in line 54 : 3 below.

286. Lit., Indeed he just does not arrive beside me anywhere yet.

287. GLOS: nolhuilia:te.

39 : 32   "What's this?"[288] said Tezozomoctli. "Tecolotzin! Chachatzin! Teuctzin! Cihuaxochitzin! Let's have him here! Let it be done, let it be carried out as Coyohua has said."

39 : 35   And then Tezozomoctli said, "When Chichimecs are coming in to deliver their tribute—after Tepaneca have killed him—they must fetch him and carry him off.[289] Perhaps he will have been [killed by being] knocked down somewhere.[290]

39 : 38   Then Coyohua said, "Very well, O child. But the way to do it is for Nezahualcoyotl to be missing from his prison cage,[291] and meanwhile perhaps your Chichimec friends[292] will address you: 'Hey! Yonder your Tepaneca friends are killing him!' But your Chichimecs won't be coming to fetch him after he has been killed."

39 : 43   Well then, Coyohua went off to speak craftily to Nezahualcoyotl in order to fetch him, having previously inspected a cage with a hole in it, where he would come be imprisoned. And when he had been fetched—after he had come to speak with him—then, accompanying him, he took him in. Then he went to greet Tezozomoctli. Arriving with him, he went to greet Tezozomoctli.

39 : 48   And he went and put Nezahualcoyotzin where he was supposed to die.

39 : 49   Well, then the Chichimecs who were to come in where he was, did come in. And at nightfall, when they had gone, Coyohua took leave of Nezahualcoyotl, saying, "My son! Nezahualcoyotzin! When the time comes, I know how to set you free."[293]

[The Tepaneca War: the sack of Cuauhtitlan: A.D. 1429–30]

40 : 1   2 House [1429]. In that year, in a time of enemy confrontation, Xiuhcozcatzin came, sent here by Itzcoatzin.

40 : 3   3 Rabbit [1430]. In that year the war grew much wider with declara-

---

288. Read *tleço tel*. Cf. 37:9, 37:22, 37:32.

289. The proper understanding of this passage, down through line 39:53, depends upon knowing that felons were customarily jailed in the warehouse, where items of tribute were deposited. See FC 8:44:1–10.

290. From a rooftop, for example. Cf. 39:9–11 above.

291. Lit., But the way it is to be done is that Nezahualcoyotl will no longer be settled in the cage.

292. Lit., uncles, here and in lines 39:41 and 39:42. The term is evidently figurative, perhaps ironic. I take it to be equivalent to such English expressions as "friends," "gents," "guys," "people." For comparable "uncles" in the Cantares Mexicanos see NED: tlahtli.

293. Lit., Still I know how, in time, to come conduct you (see MOL: iua:nite = dar de mano al preso). Notice that the story seems incomplete. Perhaps the copyist overlooked the continuation, or never received it. There is no rupture in the manuscript as it has come down to us. In fact the blank space following the last word indicates a *finis*.

tions of war against the Tepaneca. At first there were victories in Cuauhtitlan. This at the time when Maxtlaton was ruling Tepanohuayan[294] and Epcoatl was ruling in Toltitlan. And Cuauhtitlan was being ruled by Tezozomoctli of Tlatilolco, the son of Tlacateotl. And at that time, challenged by enemies, Itzcoatzin was ruling Tenochtitlan. And Telitl was ruling Tenayocan.

40 : 11 Now, in Cuauhtitlan, especially, they were going out to meet the Tepaneca, to make war against them, because they had been greatly provoked. Indeed, Tezozomoctli had assassinated Xaltemoctzin, who had been Cuauhtitlan's ruler. And furthermore, Tezozomoctli had wanted one of his sons to be ruler of Cuauhtitlan, and the Cuauhtitlancalque would not agree to it. This intensified the hatred and the fury.

40 : 18 Thus the war began. For twenty-two years they kept attacking each other. And they hurt each other badly.

40 : 20 Then at a later time the Cuauhtitlancalque were severely attacked, and the market was planted with magueys, and it was moved to Azcapotzalco. And so there was no more slave market in Cuauhtitlan,[295] since it had been moved to Azcapotzalco—and slaves were still being sold there when the Castillians arrived.

40 : 26 And from time to time during the war, Cuauhtitlancalque were being scattered afar. Retreating, they were escaping to Cocotitlan and Xonacapacoyan, and it often happened that people escaped to Tehuiloyocan. There Cuauhtitlancalque were being mistreated and abused. Furthermore, some of them were being laughed at, women were being violated, etc.

40 : 33 And furthermore, it often happened that Cuauhtitlancalque who wanted to take refuge in Tzompanco, in Citlaltepec, and in Otlazpan were mistreated there. Then because of it the Cuauhtitlan rulers were completely insulted.

40 : 37 And really the only place where Cuauhtitlancalque were treated kindly was Huehuetocan, and on many occasions they took refuge there.

40 : 39 Indeed, during this Tepaneca War all who surrounded the city of Cuauhtitlan began to change sides, namely the Toltitlancalque, the Tepozteca, the Cuauhtlaapan people, the Cuahuaque, the Tepotzoteca, the Coyotepeca, the Otlazpaneca, the Citlaltepeca, and the Tzompanca. And then Tollan and Apazco, the whole Great Land.[296] Also Xilotepec and Chiapan. And then, those who as a group are known as the Tepaneca. They all attacked the city of Cuauhtitlan.

---

294. Tepanohuayan is Tepaneca country, of which the capital is Azcapotzalco. Concordance: Tepanohuayan.

295. Lit., Thus there (*oncanon*) in Cuauhtitlan one was no longer selling humans.

296. Lit., thus the whole Great Land. Alternate translation: the first [original?] Great Land. The reference is to the northern plains, original home of the Chichimecs who settled in the Valley of Mexico.

40 : 48   Well, the ruler Maxtlaton presented gifts to the *tlacateccatl* and the *tla-cochcalcatl* of each of the cities that have been mentioned. He gave them shields and emblems, rallying them to battle, so that they would make war on the city of Cuauhtitlan.[297]

41 : 3   And it became true. It happened.

41 : 4   Now, at this time Cuauhtitlan's ruler was the Tezozomoc who had come from Tlatilolco. And it was during his reign that the Tepaneca succeeded in capturing the city of Cuauhtitlan. This was when they finally came and broke up the soil in the marketplace of the Cuauhtitlancalque and planted it with magueys and set fire to their temple.

41 : 9   And when the Tepaneca had captured the city of Cuauhtitlan and a great many prisoners had been taken, they were brought to Azcapotzalco. And indeed there were many Cuauhtitlancalque who were sacrificed. And ultimately many who did not die became captive servants.

41 : 15   When the city of Cuauhtitlan had been captured, the Cuauhtitlancalque performed eighty days of tribute labor in Tepanohuayan.

41 : 17   And as for the tribute goods, the manufactured goods,[298] they only went twice to deposit them. The first time was when the city was captured. The second time was after the eighty days had passed. What they delivered in tribute were little widths of cloth a forearm in length, counted as streamers.[299] Etc.

41 : 22   Well now, this was when the city of Cuauhtitlan was captured and when the ruler Tezozomoctli[300] took refuge at Cincoc Huehuetocan. And when the city was destroyed, the Cuauhtitlancalque went and informed him, went and brought him the news. And when he heard that the city of Cuauhtitlan had been destroyed—had been captured—he did not quite believe it.

41 : 28   At this time he had a servant with him named Coatequitl, also a Tehui-lacatzin. Then he sent them back here to find out for certain how it had happened.

41 : 31   They set out from Cincoc.

Then they saw that people had indeed died, and many prisoners had been carried off, and Tepaneca and Toltitlancalque were living in the palace at Huexocalco.[301]

---

297. Before a campaign rulers would give valuable shields and emblems to military leaders in exchange for their loyalty. See FC 2:115:14–19, 8:52:15, 8:64:31, 8:65: 10–11, 12:45:27 et seq.

298. According to Sahagún (FC 8:53:36–38), "when a city had been captured and destroyed, then the tribute was established according to what was manufactured there" (auh in jcoac oaxioac altepetl in ovmpoliuh, njman icoac motlalia, in tequjtl, in tlacalaqujlli itech mana [see GLOS: ana:tla 1] in tlein vmpa muchioa).

299. Small banners used as sacrificial offerings. GLOS: tetehuitl.

300. Tezozomoctli of Cuauhtitlan. See 41:4–5 above.

301. Tezozomoctli's palace. See 32:22 above.

41 : 34   And the ruler Tezozomoctli's messengers went immediately to give him the news, that the city of Cuauhtitlan had in fact been captured.

41 : 37   And when the ruler Tezozomoctli heard this, he wept, he grieved, and he dismissed the Cuauhtitlancalque who had been keeping him company.

41 : 39   This was in the time of 3 Rabbit. Then the Cuauhtitlan ruler Tezozomoctli took to the road. Then he traveled, and his servants Coatequitl and Tehuilacatzin went with him. Along the way he dispatched Coatequitl, saying, "It would somewhat behoove me to reach people in Mexico. Tell it to our granduncles, our elder brothers."302 In this way he sent him off, deceitfully.

41 : 45   And when he got to Atzompan, he took leave of Tehuilacatzin, telling him, "Please, come back and meet our grandfather303 Coatequitl here in Atzompan, [and the two of] you are to come to me."

41 : 48   Tehuilacatzin took to the road, leaving the ruler Tezozomoctli all alone. And in that year and in that place—in Atzompan—the ruler Tezozomoctli, Cuauhtitlan's ruler, committed suicide by swallowing poison.

42 : 3   He killed himself because the Cuauhtitlan nation had bodily traveled off during his reign. And the reason he was filled with such great fear, the reason he committed suicide, is that absolutely everything was burned. Their temple, with its thatched roof, had been set on fire.

42 : 7   Never before had this happened. For the first time they had all been quite successfully brought under a single command in order to lay siege to the city of Cuauhtitlan.304 Indeed, the Tepaneca and the men of Cuauhtlaapan came courting danger at Chiancuac, and they lighted a fire at the straw house.305 And the Tepotzoteca lighted a fire at Tlacocouhcan. Indeed they destroyed the city, and Tezozomoctli imagined that Cuauhtitlan would never rise again,306 for his enemies had surrounded the whole town. This is why Tezozomoctli committed suicide, as told above.

[The Tepaneca War: Cuauhtitlan joins with Mexico: A.D. 1430]

42 : 18   Afterward, when the Cuauhtitlancalque had somewhat regained their composure, they got themselves a [new] ruler. Very prudently they in-

302. Our superiors (GLOS: achcauhtli, colli). But "our grandfather" in line 41:47 below, is a subordinate.

303. A term meaning "grandfather" is used by Topiltzin Quetzalcoatl in addressing subordinates (lines 5:35, 5:38, etc.).

304. Lit., For the first time very ably did they command them all so that in battle they surrounded the city of Cuauhtitlan.

305. The ruler's residence? See GLOS: zacacalli, zacacaltitlan.

306. Lit., never be again.

stalled a Chichimec prince named Tecocoatzin. In the palace at Huexocalco they accommodated him in a manner befitting a ruler, and there he
observed his ruler's fast. And furthermore, they did not notify Maxtlaton,
the ruler of Azcapotzalco. The only ones who knew of it were the Mexica
Tenochca, and it was they who gave the approval.

42 : 26   And while he was observing his ruler's fast, he was adorned as a Huexotzincatl.[307] That's how he fasted. And he would put on his eagle tail feathers, along with the leather braid[308] that he would tie on his head; also his
amapatlachtli earplugs; also his eagle labret; his curved lip pin, carried on
his back;[309] his fine, white *cuappayahualolli* necklace; also the white loin-
cloth that they put on him; and his braided leather [foot] bands with the
jingles;[310] also his sapodilla staff.

42 : 34   And as for his nobles and captains, each one was adorned the same way.
They all carried harpoon staffs,[311] macana staffs. They looked like Hue-
xotzinca, and they went around in the palace talking to each other as
Huexotzinca.

42 : 39   Now, the reason it was done this way is that there had been an official
pronouncement, an official decision, as to how the Tepanecatl was to be
warred against. It was not without cause that the Cuauhtitlan Chichimecs
appeared this way, adorning themselves as Huexotzinca. The Mexica were
privy to it, and some of the Acolhuaque knew about it too.

42 : 44   And furthermore, the Tepaneca had caused much suffering, for they had
assassinated people's rulers on a great many occasions. Tezozomoctli was
the one—as well as his son Maxtlaton—who had condemned many rulers
to death.

42 : 48   It was Tezozomoctli who, by his command, had killed the Colhuacan
ruler Nauhyotzin.

42 : 50   And he had also killed the Tetzcoco ruler Ixtlilxochitzin the elder.

43 : 1   And he had killed Pichacatzin Teuctli, ruler of Cuitlahuac Tizic.

43 : 3   And he had killed the ruler of Tlatilolco, Tlacateotzin.

43 : 4   And he had killed the Cuauhtitlan ruler Xaltemoctzin the elder.

43 : 5   And he had killed the former ruler of Tenochtitlan, Chimalpopocatzin.
Maxtlaton had handed down the sentence.

---

307. Identification with Huexotzinco, Mexico's traditional enemy, is repeatedly implied
in the Cantares Mexicanos. See Bierhorst, *Cantares Mexicanos*, pp. 29–30, 40, 452, 466,
490, 511. For a guide to text references see NED: Huexōtzincatl, Huexōtzinco.

308. Leather braid is associated with Huexotzinco in CM fol. 73, l. 28.

309. Describing the rulers' dance attire, Sahagún (HG bk. 8, ch. 9, parags. 2–3) refers
to various lip ornaments that were carried (*traían*) but not worn (*que ya no las usan*).

310. Bands of leather braid (*tecuecuextli*) hung with little golden bells were worn on the
arm or on the instep (TEZ ch. 99, p. 407; NED: tēcuecuextli).

311. Unusual harpoon arrows (*chichiqujlli*) were carried by the Huexotzinca warriors
who entered Tenochtitlan with Cortés (FC bk. 12, ch. 16).

43 : 7   And he had killed the Tlatilolco ruler Cuauhtlatoatzin. Maxtlaton had handed down the sentence.

43 : 9   And he had put to flight the Tetzcoco ruler Nezahualcoyotzin, along with many of his nobles.

43 : 11   Their lords had suffered with them, as has been told in the year-count entries.

[The Tepaneca War: embassies to Huexotzinco: A.D. 1430]

43 : 13   Now, while this ruler Tecocoatzin is holding office challenged by enemies, Itzcoatzin of Tenochtitlan is also a ruler challenged by enemies. And when these rulers had decided to make war against the Tepaneca, then emissaries, messengers, were sent to Huexotzinco for the Tepanecatl to tell of their scorn, etc., and he told how they were to come treat their neighbors the Mexica, the Cuauhtitlancalque, and the Acolhuaque as a mere reed, a mere pebble.[312] Etc.

43 : 23   Now, at this time the ruler of Huexotzinco was Tenocelotzin. And the council house was at Chiauhtzinco, for it is said that this was the way things were in Huexotzinco: they kept moving the seat of government, rotating it among three places.[313]

43 : 28   Well, it was first to Huexotzinco that the ruler of Azcapotzalco, Maxtlaton, sent emissaries asking for aid in battle. They carried many jade necklaces, along with shields, emblems, etc.[314] Also they went to ask Chalco, also Chiapan. Everywhere they went they left jade necklaces, etc.

43 : 34   And it is told and related that the ruler of Huexotzinco received their request gladly. And they were stationed there to await Huexotzinca who were to come lead them. And these messengers, Maxtlaton's messengers, were under the leadership of a certain Chalchiuh.

43 : 40   And then the Cuauhtitlan ruler Tecocoatzin also sent emissaries to Huexotzinco, beseeching the ruler Tenocelotzin. And he used his high officials as his emissaries.[315]

---

312. Ambiguous pronouns make this a difficult passage to read. Evidently the ones who sent emissaries were the Tepaneca, who spoke for their ruler, the Tepanecatl. For other references to the "Tepanecatl" see 24:18 and 42:40 above. For more on the embassy to Huexotzinco see 43:28 et seq. below.

313. Lit., the rulership kept being moved, it appeared in three places the way it was moved.

314. On the shield and the emblem as a military covenant see note to the translation at 41:3 above.

315. Lit., And his elder brothers became his emissaries. The four officials named in the list that follows represent the four quarters of Cuauhtitlan town (cf. 29:27–38 above).

43 : 43   These Cuauhtitlancalque that he sent to Huexotzinco were: first, Chicanitzin, the lord priest of Tequixquinahuac; second, Tziuhcoatzin of Nepantla; third, Coatzin of Chalmecapan; fourth, the *tlacochcalcatl* Callaxochitl of Atempan Huauhtlan.

43 : 48   Well, these were the emissaries who arrived in Huexotzinco, the
Cuauhtitlan ruler's emissaries as named and mentioned above.[316] And at
last, tearfully they submitted their petition. But their greeting gift was not
very precious. So they were treated as nothing. And ultimately they were
put in jail to be sacrificed.[317] Etc.

44 : 5   Now, while this was going on[318] and calls to arms were being issued,
the ruler Tecocoatzin ordered all the relatives [of] the captive servants in
Azcapotzalco to go tell them that they should gently slip away.[319] They
were to merrily tell the slaveowners they would be going to their homes
for a little while. And so it happened. It became true. All the captives were
fetched. And finally, as for those who were not given permission, they all
got together[320] and fled as a group.[321]

44 : 12   Then Maxtlaton sent for the captive slaves to be returned. But in the
palace at Huexocalco they beat each and every one of the envoys on the
rump as a punishment.[322] In the courtroom they bent them over a pole—
they were upon it, curled around. As many messengers as there were, all
were mistreated in this manner, by being beaten on the rump.

44 : 19   On account of it, the Tepaneca, at last, were greatly annoyed, etc.

44 : 20   Next, the Tlatilolca sent emissaries to Huexotzinco to beseech the ruler
Tenocelotzin, and these Mexica Tlatilolca told and revealed how the Tepaneca had made fun of everybody and had become overproud and assassinated many rulers. Furthermore, the jades and bracelets that they carried
were extremely precious. Also the shield and the emblem were their greeting gifts, etc.

44 : 29   And when they realized that Nezahualcoyotzin was living there, having
been put to flight by Maxtlaton's father, Tezozomoctli, they summoned
him to speak in company with them before the Huexotzinca. And Nezahualcoyotzin spoke even more plainly. He told it from the beginning: how
Tezozomoctli had always deceived people, and how his son Maxtlaton was

---

316. Read *omoteneuhque*.
317. Lit., they were jailed in order that they would die.
318. Lit., while already there is this. GLOS: nemi.
319. These were Cuauhtitlancalque who had been enslaved by the Tepaneca. See line
41 : 11 above.
320. Read çazçen. GLOS: zan cen.
321. Lit., And finally, when they very much were together, all as a group fled, with regard
to those who were not given permission.
322. Follows Lehmann. Following Velázquez: they drove a stake into the anus of each
and every one of the envoys. See GLOS: tzincuauhtetzotzona:te.

ready to do[323] just the same, etc. Then at last, the crimes of the Tepaneca could be clearly seen.

44 : 38 Then the Cuauhtitlancalque were summoned—the ones who have been mentioned by name.[324] They, too, provided verification, swearing on their ancestry, for which the Cuauhtitlancalque were famed,[325] and on their [sacred] arrows and on their god Mixcoatl.[326]

44 : 43 They told everything. They even told how the Tepaneca were not related to them, because they carried the stone sling.[327] And furthermore, they said they did not recognize them because their one god was Cuecuex.[328] They were different.

44 : 47 It was finally decided that some Tepaneca should be sacrificed there[329]— in public and at the foot of the Huexotzinca god, who was Camaxtle.[330] On the eagle bowl[331] before him, knives were laid. And with these, [the Tepaneca] were cut open.

45 : 1 Now, these Tlatilolca emissaries who had gone to Huexotzinco were all Amaxaccalque. The first was Cuachayatzin; also there were Atepocatzin, Tecatlatoatzin, and Callatlaxcaltzin; and Nezahualcoyotzin called them together to tell them they should go spread the word in Tliliuhquitepec, Atlancatepec, and Tlaxcallan; and it was done: they went and exposed the effrontery of the Tepaneca. Thus it became true. Thus it happened. Nezahualcoyotzin went along as their leader.

45 : 9 And so an agreement was reached for the Huexotzinca, the Tlaxcalteca, and the Tliliuhquitepeca to come to battle, for Nezahualcoyotzin was well acquainted with the Tliliuhquitepeca, the people of Atlancatepec, the Tlaxcalteca, and the Huexotzinca. And so his avowal that the Tepaneca were to be warred against was given much credence. It was because of this that a pact was made.

---

323. Lit., to be.

324. See lines 43 : 40–44 : 5.

325. Lit., They, too, verified things, and they addressed people by means of the Cuauhtitlancalque being known for ancestry.

326. For the arrows and the god, see lines 25 : 43–49, 26 : 4–5.

327. Sahagún mentions that the non-Nahuatl-speaking Matlatzinca used the *tematlatl* (stone sling, or sling for hurling stones), unlike the Chichimecs, whose weapon was the bow (FC bk. 10, ch. 29, sec. entitled "The Quaquata, the Matlatzinca, the Toloque").

328. Cuecuex is associated with the Tepaneca in the eleventh of the twenty songs preserved in the appendix to bk. 2 of Sahagún's *Historia*. By contrast, "the Chichimecs . . . had just one god, Mixcoatl" (in chichimeca . . . çan ce in jnteouh catca, itoca Mixcoatl) (FC 6 : 34 : 31–32).

329. For *oppa mictilloque* read *ompa mictilloque*, as in line 45 : 24 below.

330. Muñoz Camargo relates that as a relic of early Chichimec days, ashes of "Camaxtli Mixcohuatl" were kept in Huexotzinco (*Historia* bk. 1, ch. 7). See also line 50 : 50 (*camaxtle mixcohuatl*); and note that the god of the Huexotzinca is named as Mixcoatl in line 57 : 20.

331. Presumably the same as *cuauhxicalli* (eagle receptacle), described by Durán as a kind of operating table, where the hearts of live victims were excised (DHIST chs. 32–33).

45 : 15   It was said that the Cuauhtitlancalque, the Acolhuaque, and the Mexica had to be marked, so that none of them would be misidentified and killed. It was said that they had to muddy their faces and tie a grass string around the head, so that they could be found and their friends who had come to help them could recognize them.

45 : 21   Well, when it had been decided that the Huexotzinca, the Tlaxcalteca, etc. would be coming along, the Tlatilolca and the Cuauhtitlancalque were sent back first.

45 : 24   As said previously, Tepaneca were sacrificed there [in Huexotzinco]—they were cut open.

45 : 25   After that, Itzcoatzin's emissaries set out. His call to arms was made in haste,[332] for it had already been decided and announced that the Tepaneca were to be defeated.

[The Tepaneca War: Nezahualcoyotl's campaign: A.D. 1430]

45 : 28   It was in the time of 3 Rabbit that Nezahualcoyotzin came forth, accompanied by Huexotzinca, Tlaxcalteca, and also Chalca. It was then that Nezahualcoyotzin sought out the sons of Tezozomoctli in all the places where they were ruling; and conquests were made in all those places.

45 : 33   The way Nezahualcoyotzin came, the way he approached, is that he took to the road in Chalco. Then, to begin with, he came leading the way toward Tetzcoco, and the very first conquest was in Coatlichan. At that time Quetzalmaquiztli was ruling there, and he met his death.

45 : 37   The second place was Huexotla. At that time Cuauhpiyo was ruling there, and he was killed.

45 : 38   Then there were conquests in a third place, Acolman. At that time Teyolcocoatzin was ruling there.

45 : 40   And Toltitlan was the fourth place where conquests were made. At that time Epcoatl was the ruler. When Nezahualcoyotzin arrived there, on a day 1 Flint, with the Huexotzinca, the Tlaxcalteca, and the Chalca, it was the Toltitlancalque who took to the road. And at this time a daughter of [Cuauhtitlan's] ruler Tecocoatzin was seized and taken into captivity. She had become a lady of Toltitlan. She had become the wife of the ruler Epcoatl.

45 : 47   Now, this lady, before the war began, was privy to the joint resolution that Tepaneca were to be destroyed. Moreover, she was accurately report-

---

332. The call to arms was made only [by] his act of hurrying [lit., running]. The analysis follows Velázquez. See GLOS: -totocaca.

ing what the Toltitlancalque were saying. Whenever they talked war, she sent word to the ruler Tecocoatzin. And for this reason, when the battle had begun, she was very definitely on the watch. Indeed, she climbed to the top of Toltitlan's house of the Devil. And then this lady all by herself set fire to the thatched roof of the Devil house and burned it up, etc.[333]

46 : 6   And the way she was captured is that when prisoners were taken, she, too, was made a prisoner and taken into captivity along with others. It was the Chalca who seized her.

46 : 8   Well, they were carrying her off, and she said to the captors, "Who is the gentleman standing here?"—he was wearing a quetzal-feather warbonnet.

46 : 11   "That's the ruler Tenocelotzin," she was told.

46 : 12   "Let me greet him," she asked. Then she greeted him and said, "O lord, I am your sister,[334] for my father is the king and ruler Tecocoatzin of Cuauhtitlan. He came and left me here, having suffered torment, having agonized in heart and flesh, etc."

46 : 17   The ruler Tenocelotl of Huexotzinco gave the command for her to be set free. And it was done.

46 : 19   Well, then the Toltitlan nation goes away. They're banished[335] to Cuitlachtepec and Temacpalco, at the time when Telitl is ruling in Tenayocan. They're herded. They're driven onward.

46 : 21   And then they were taken to Azcapotzalco, at the time when Maxtlaton was ruling there.

46 : 23   And a sixth place, Coyohuacan, was laid waste.

46 : 24   A seventh place was laid waste—Xochimilco. Tepanquizqui was ruling there at the time.

46 : 25   And all the places that were laid waste were ruled by sons of Tezozomoctli, the former ruler of Azcapotzalco. And well did the ruler Nezahualcoyotzin contrive it,[336] taking his revenge against them, for Tezozomoctli had killed his father, the elder Ixtlilxochitl.

46 : 31   And so, the war was waged. Those rulers who declared it and waged it were Itzcoatzin, Tecocoatzin of Cuauhtitlan, Nezahualcoyotzin of Tetzcoco, and Tenocelotzin of Huexotzinco.

46 : 33   Along the way,[337] the Colhuacan ruler Acoltzin died in battle. The Tepaneca killed him.

46 : 35   And it was in Xochimilco that the war cooled off. The Tepaneca remained there for only a day until they were taken to Tonanixillan, also to

---

333. Anticlimactic word order reversed in the translation.
334. I.e., ally. GLOS: hueltiuhtli.
335. Lit., they [impersonal] go and banish them. See GN sec. 4.2.
336. GLOS: imati:tla
337. Lit., At this time therein, i.e., at this time during [the war]. GLOS: oncan.

Atltepachiuhcan and Cuauhximalpan, where they spent four years. These were the Tepaneca of Toltitlan, Tenayocan, Azcapotzalco, Tlacopan, and Coyohuacan, along with some of the Xochimilca, etc.

46 : 40 And, also, from the time that the war began, there were a few who died among the Tetzcoca [and those of] Coatlichan, Huexotla, and Acolman.

46 : 43 And by this time Cuauhtitlan's system of fourfold servant communities had broken down.[338] Now destroyed was the arrangement made by the elder Xaltemoctzin before he died: [339]

[1.] Tequixquinahuac. Its servant community had been Tepoxacco and Tzompanco.

[2.] Chalmecapan. Its servant community had been Cuauhtlaapan and Citlaltepec.

46 : 47 [3.] Nepantla. Its servant community had been Tepotzotlan and Huehuetocan.

46 : 48 [4.] Atempan. Its servant community had been Coyotepec and Otlazpan.

46 : 49 When the war had finally passed, Cuauhtitlan's ruler thought back on it. This was the time when Ayactlacatzin ruled, after the death of Tecocoatzin. He thought back. And he did so in anger, seeking revenge for the siege of Cuauhtitlan. Then he apportioned lands, handing them out, giving them as grants. Then the Cuauhtitlan nation was provided with lands. It was on account of the war that the grants came to be made, etc.

47 : 9 Now, Tzompanco and Citlaltepec were lands that he apportioned, allotting them to himself alone. At the temple of the Citlaltepeca the ruler Ayactlacatzin personally assigned these lands to himself. And the emissaries who came to mark the boundaries were Tenochca and Tlatilolca.

47 : 13 Then Otlazpan was marked off. And after that, Tepoxacco and Tehuiloyocan were marked off.

47 : 15 Finally, communal lands were created,[340] and boundaries were marked off in all the places that had been conquered.

47 : 17 But no boundaries were marked off in Huehuetocan, because the Huehuetocameca had been kind to the Cuauhtitlancalque when they had fled there during the war. They had helped them very much. Indeed, they had treated the Cuauhtitlancalque as members of their household.

47 : 22 Here is what is understood from a song on the defeat of the Tepaneca: 3 Rabbit was the second time the Mexicatl confronted the Tepanecatl. Twelve years earlier the Tepaneca had performed tribute labor in Tenochtitlan, having been conquered in 1 Reed, at which time the Mexitin put

338. Lit., And by this time Cuauhtitlan was broken [as to] the way the towns had been in four places that had been being made its servant communities. Cf. 56 : 11 below.

339. The quartering of Cuauhtitlan is described in lines 29 : 27–38 above, and mentioned again in line 56 : 11 below.

340. Lit., began to be created.

47 : 30

together what was still just a small piece of eagle land. But in 3 Rabbit the Mexitin increased their eagle land in Tepanohuayan.[341]

The Colhuaque provide verification of this report.

47 : 31

But Colhuaque also say that the Xochimilca were defeated in 4 Rabbit,[342] defeated by Nezahualcoyotzin at the time he was inaugurated as ruler.

47 : 35

Well, it was told and recounted that 3 Rabbit [1430] was the year the Tepaneca were conquered. This was also when the Cuauhnahuaca and the Xaltocameca were conquered—conquered by Nezahualcoyotzin, Itzcoatzin, and Cuauhtitlan's Tecocoatzin.

[After the Tepaneca War: A.D. 1431]

47 : 39

4 Reed [1431]. This was the year Nezahualcoyotzin was inaugurated as ruler in Mexico.[343]

47 : 41

And in that same year, during Izcalli, while the Cuauhtitlancalque were celebrating the feast and people were coming in from towns everywhere, Toltitlancalque[344] went to Cuahuacan to speak with the Cuahuacan ruler Xochitlcozauhqui. They told him the Cuauhtitlancalque might be conquered, because they were off guard, celebrating their feast.

47 : 46

And the Cuahuacan ruler received their petition favorably and declared war against the Cuauhtitlancalque. Then they took to the road and came to fight in Cuauhtitlan.

47 : 49

Well, none other then the Toltitlancalque of Ahuacatitlan came and reported this to Cuauhtitlan's ruler, Tecocoatzin—came and warned him. Immediately he put these Toltitlancalque under guard. They were not to leave. If what they said were to be found false, they were to be killed.

48 : 1

And in no time at all it did prove true: the Cuahuaque Tepaneca came to make war. Very cleverly a trap was laid for them, so that all who came here to do battle were made prisoners. Then, during the feast, they were shot with arrows. It was thanks to them that the feast was celebrated.

48 : 5

After that, the ruler of Cuauhtitlan established lands for the Ahuacatitlan people. He gave them a homeland that would provide for their sustenance,[345] etc. Also, an order was handed down that no future attempt

341. On "eagle land" and the conquest of the Tepaneca see 31:50–32:3 above. See also 66:1 (Azcapotzalco) and 66:12–13 below.

342. Should be 4 Reed, per 47:39.

343. The ceremony took place in Mexico, but Nezahualcoyotl was being inaugurated as ruler of Tetzcoco (IXT 1:543–44). Cf. 48:31 below.

344. This refers to the exiled Toltitlancalque. They are not repatriated until line 48:42 below.

345. Lit., a homeland by means of which they would live there.

must ever be made to incite these people against the Cuauhtitlan nation.[346]

48:10   The year 4 Reed. At this time the ruler Itzcoatzin of Tenochtitlan declared war. As yet he could not proceed openly, for he had been inaugurated as a ruler challenged by enemies.

48:12   Well, the ones he called to battle were the Cuitlahuaca, whom he wished to conquer. Campaigning against them all by himself, the Tenochcatl waged war for three years. But he did not succeed. He simply gave up.

48:15   And in that same year, 4 Reed, in the town of Cuauhtitlan the river turned and changed course, so that it flowed into the *temilco* next to Huexocalco,[347] passing through the heart of the city.

48:17   And after this change, it often happened that things were swept away, and often houses were destroyed as the stream overflowed. And, finally, when the river changed course, a hundred empty houses were destroyed in Toltitlan. When all these houses were swept away, there was no one there—in accordance with the wishes of the Cuauhtitlancalque. For the Tepaneca of Toltitlan now lived in Cuauhximalpan.[348]

48:23   And then, after the ruler Tecocoatzin had expressed his grief, he ordered that the stream be dug up where the river—which is there today—had turned. The digging went on for two years. After that, the stream was diverted.

[Mexico's glory begins: A.D. 1432–39]

48:27   5 Flint [1432]. In that year the Tenochtitlan ruler Itzcoatzin was able to come out into the open,[349] for he ruled everywhere, over rulers from town to town. Here, finally, began the glory of the Mexicatl Tenochcatl, etc.

48:31   6 House [1433]. In that year the ruler Nezahualcoyotzin went and established himself in Tetzcoco, leaving Tenochtitlan. Itzcoatzin had installed him as ruler, though his inauguration in Tenochtitlan had been under enemy challenge. Only in that year did he go off to govern the city of Tetzcoco.

48:36   The year 6 House was when the Tepaneca were sent back from Tonanitlan and Cuauhximalpan and Atltepachiuhcan, where they had spent four years. First they came and humbled themselves, beseeching the ruler Te-

346. Lit., And they [impersonal] were ordered that never again were they [impersonal] to want to incite them against the Cuauhtitlan nation. For *ỳca* read *yca*.

347. Temilco (lit., people's gardens?) was the name of a body of water in Citlaltepec where Mexican priests came to gather special reeds (FC 2:11 and 74). The significance of the Cuauhtitlan *temilco* is not apparent; its location, however, is "next to Huexocalco," site of the ruler's palace (see 32:22, 41:34, etc.).

348. They had been relocated after the Tepaneca war. See lines 46:35–40 above. For a differing account of the flood, see lines 25:37–43.

349. He was no longer challenged by enemies. See 48:10–12.

cocoatzin and the Cuauhtitlan nobles and princes: then they were given permission to come settle in their home town, Toltitlan. And they were all admonished that if they ever rose up against the Cuauhtitlan nation again, they would not be pitied, etc. And with that, they went off to be settled in Toltitlan.

48 : 45 And then the ruler Tecocoatzin apportioned laborers to the Toltitlancalque so that they could divert the river at a place called Tepolnexco. They went and diverted it with logs. The timbers filled the streambed standing upright, not crosswise, following the course of the stream, filling it up. And so finally the stream that had turned was closed off and relocated. Thus the river today passes into Citlaltepec.

48 : 51 In the year 6 House the Cuauhtitlan ruler Tecocoatzin died, having ruled for only four years. Cuauhtla-Huexocalco is where he ruled.[350]

48 : 54 7 Rabbit [1434]. In that year the people were seven-rabbited: there was famine.[351]

49 : 1 And in that same year the Cuauhtitlan ruler called Ayactlacatzin, or Xaquin Teuctli, was inaugurated, and he ruled in Cuauhtla-Huexocalco. How he was born and why he was named Ayactlacatl has been told above.[352]

49 : 4 The year 7 Rabbit was when Itzcoatzin of Tenochtitlan again declared war on the Cuitlahuaca. He called out the Tetzcoca, and for two years he just waited for these Tetzcoca, who were not turning up.[353] And when many a Mexicatl had already died, the Tetzcoca set out and came along to Mexico, at which time Tezozomoctzin was ruler of Cuitlahuac—which had the same ear-stream insignia. The ear streams of the Cuitlahuaca and the Tetzcoca were exactly alike.[354]

49 : 12 8 Reed [1435]. In that year there was an influx of Cuitlahuaca who wished to be counted as Mexica.[355]

49 : 14 In the year 8 Reed, moreover, the river was finally diverted, so that it passed into Citlaltepec.[356] The water course, or waterway, was completely reclaimed.[357] It was seven years before the waterway was all good again and the settlements were dried out. Today where the waterway had been[358] is called Aitictli [In Waters' Midst]. Now it is milpa.

350. The name Ayactlacatzin, evidently an old marginal gloss, has been copied into the text at this juncture. It belongs with line 49 : 2.

351. Cf. 9 : 3 above.

352. 30 : 5.

353. GLOS: tlatzto:te, NED: quetza:mo 3–5.

354. GLOS: ananacaztli (flowing plumagelike ear decorations), namiqui:mo.

355. Lit., In that year Cuitlahuaca came entering in order to be regarded as those who are counted as Mexica. GLOS: toca:mo.

356. In the text this statement is preceded by the disconnected word *atl* (water), no doubt an old gloss. Cf. 48 : 53.

357. For *omoçenyectillin* read *ommocenyectili* or *ommocenyectilia*.

358. For *ỳcaca* read *ỳcacan*.

49 : 19   The year 8 Reed was when those who are today called Xaltocameca were formed into a settlement: Acolman people, Colhuaque, Tenochca, and Otomi. Just a mixture of people. But a dynasty was not established until the Spaniards got there.[359]

49 : 22   By this time [8 Reed] the [old] dynasty was completely lost, because the Xaltocameca had been destroyed. It was the Cuauhtitlancalque who had conquered them, and as a result they had emigrated to Metztitlan and Tlaxcallan. And when the Xaltocameca had been destroyed, Xaltocan was deserted and no one lived there for thirty-one years. Well, they had finally been pushed back to just Tecanman, for it was there that the Xaltocameca had been destroyed, etc.[360]

49 : 29   The year 8 Reed was also when the Tenochca and the Tlatilolca came to survey the Mexica lands in Toltepec and Tepeyacac.[361] Also they surveyed what were called the Tlatilolca waters in Cuachilco, which had a boundary in common with Tlachcuicalco and Tozquenitlal.

49 : 34   In that year, on Xochilhuitl, on [a day] 7 Flower, a place for dancing was set up;[362] and the Ecatepeca went to Itzcoatzin to ask for protection, explaining that the Cuauhtitlancalque, having taken up arms, wanted them [as sacrificial victims].[363]

49 : 36   Itzcoatzin granted their request and sent eighty recruits to come stand guard, etc., and it was along the Lime Road that they came to watch for Cuauhtitlancalque.

49 : 39   9 Flint.

    10 House [1437]. This was the year the war spread, the war of the Mexica: it reached Chalco Atenco [and] Tlacochcalco. It took forty-three years for the Chalca War to reach those parts.

49 : 42   11 Rabbit. 12 Reed.

[The reign of Moteuczomatzin the elder: A.D. 1440–68]

13 Flint [1440]. This was the year the Tenochtitlan ruler Itzcoatzin died. Then the elder Moteuczomatzin, Ilhuicaminatzin, was inaugurated as ruler of Tenochtitlan.

49 : 46   And in this same year, eleven years after the death of the Colhuacan ruler called Acoltzin, Xilomantzin was inaugurated as ruler of Colhuacan.

---

359. Lit., until the Spaniards got to it [the settlement] when they came [to America].
360. The events are set forth in lines 20:45–21:8 and 28:47–53 above.
361. These are evidently the confiscated Chichimec lands (see 26:24–36 above).
362. The extraneous "7 dias" (7 days) appearing in the text at this point is probably another old gloss (cf. 48:53 and 49:13 above).
363. Cuauhtitlan's plans for a Xochilhuitl celebration are mentioned above in lines 21:39–40.

It was at the end of the year 13 Flint that he was inaugurated.

49 : 50   1 House [1441]. In that year Cuitlahuaca were engaged in combat, making war on one another: the Atenchicalque were just feuding among themselves, attacking one another. At this time Acolmiztli was ruler there. On a day 4 Dog, while the war in Chalco was going on, it happened that Tizica Cuitlahuaca went off to join the battle. This was when Tezozomoctli was ruler. So [364] the Atenchicalcatl observed him and said, "Ah, the Tizicatl has gone off to join the battle in Chalco. When he comes back, I will have conquered his women and children." Then Acolmiztli began his siege. He made war, attacking the Tizica, who were only children and old people.

50 : 3   Well, when the Tizica, who had gone to battle in Chalco, came back, Atenchicalque had moved into their territory and settled down.

50 : 4   Then Tezozomoctli sent messengers to Atenchicalcan, saying, "Ask Acolmiztli why he would treacherously ruin me like this. Consequently we can offer ourselves in five days. Let him put on his regalia, for I, the Tizicatl, adorn myself."

50 : 8   So the message was brought to the Atenchicalque. But then, two days later, the Atenchicalque were attacked during the night, and on the morning of 6 Grass they withdrew to Itztapalapan—old women, old men, children, and young men. There they spent the next day, 7 Reed.

50 : 13   Then they went to inform Moteuczomatzin the elder, telling him that they had left their country. It was a certain Cuauhtlatoa who gave the information, saying, "Esteemed child, O ruler, our neighbor the Tizicatl has conquered us. Today is the second day that your subjects have stayed in Itztapalapan. My esteemed child, today they have run out of their accustomed food,[365] for in their haste they left behind all their corn. And are you going to abandon them now? Here we are, the Atenchicalque, and we give our nation to you."

50 : 22   Then Moteuczomatzin called for his sons: to begin with, Citlalcoatzin, the *tlacochcalcatl*, also Iquehuacatzin, the *tlacateccatl*. And he said to them, "Come, you lords, you princes. Here is an Atenchicalcatl giving us his nation. Now, if we were to tell Acolhuacan about this, we would get little of it indeed. So let it be just for us Mexica, together with the Tlatilolca, as well as our Four Lords: Mexicatzinco, Colhuacan, Itztapalapan, [and Huitzilopochco].[366] Let us go by ourselves to lead the Atenchicalque back to their homeland."

364. For *iça* read *ica*.

365. Lit., Today is the second day that your subject has stayed in Itztapalapan; my esteemed child, today what he usually eats is indeed no longer anything. For *caoctley* read *ca aoctley*.

366. The Four Lords are thus listed in FC bk. 12, ch. 14 (*nauhtecutli*). See also lines 63 : 51–52 below.

50 : 31   The day of this conference was 8 Jaguar, and it was on the day 9 Eagle that the Atenchicalque reentered their homeland, at which time they went and burned the temple of the Cuitlahuaca, which was a house of the devil Mixcoatl. And on this occasion Yaocuixtli of Mexicatzinco was the first to rush to the top of the Mixcoatl, seizing the ashes of Itzpapalotl—what was called the bundle, etc. [The ashes] were contained in two [lengths of] quetzal bamboo.[367]

50 : 37   Then Tenochtitlan's Citlalcoatzin and Iquehuatzin and Axicyotzin and Tenamaztzin spoke to Tezozomoctli: "O Tezozomoctzin," they said, "Mixcoatl the younger[368] was burned, for you failed to pick up your shield and arrows. Now, there's this: Where did you put Mixcoatl?[369] We must take him away. Give him to us."

50 : 43   But Tezozomoctli, ruler of Tizic, said, "If I gave up Mixcoatl, what would befall my children in times yet to come?"

50 : 45   Therefore they arranged for an image of the devil Teuhcatl to be brought forth. This was a god of Tizic, kept there in a place called Tepixtloco. And this is what the Mexica brought back with them. It was this that stayed in Tenochtitlan, at the place known as Mixcoatepec. It was not really the image of the so-called Camaxtle Mixcoatl. It was just the one named Teohcatl [*sic*]. It had the same costume as Mixcoatl, and this is what the Mexica took it for, thinking it was he. Thus the Mexica were deceived. This happened 104 years ago.

51 : 1   1 House [1441] is when the people of Oztoticpac were defeated, at which time Cuetzpalli was ruler there. Those who defeated them were the Huexotzinca, when Tenocelotl was ruler in Huexotzinco, and also the Tepeyacahuaque, when Chiauhcoatl was ruler in Tepeyacac.

51 : 6   2 Rabbit.

    3 Reed [1443]. The Chalco ruler Caltzin Teuctli, or Temiztzin, died at this time. Then Tlaltzin Teuctli was inaugurated, and he ruled for twenty-four years.

51 : 8   And this was when the Xaltocameca came and sat before Ayactlacatzin so that laborers could be apportioned to the Mexica—they were to perform labor, etc.

---

367. Lit., Two were the quetzal bamboos by means of which they were contained. Within the sacred bundle of Huexotzinco, by contrast, the ashes of the god Camaxtle were contained in a single length of bamboo ("dentro de un cofrecillo de palo hallaron . . . las cenizas" [Muñoz Camargo, *Historia* bk. 2, ch. 8]). On the origin of the Itzpapalotl bundle, with its ashes, see lines 1:15–21 above; in lines 80:10–19 below, the bundle is said to have contained a flint. Compare the ash-bundle phantom mentioned in line 81:51 below (described in FC bk. 5, ch. 12).

368. The White Mixcoatl. See 1:14 above.

369. The statue is meant. In the preceding lines "Mixcoatl," or "Mixcoatl the younger," evidently refers to the temple.

51 : 11   4 Flint. 5 House.

6 Rabbit [1446]. This was when Xilomantzin[370] of Colhuacan made land arrangements.[371]

51 : 12   7 Reed.[372] 8 Flint. 9 House. 10 Rabbit.

51 : 13   11 Reed [1451]. In this year snow fell knee deep. It fell for five days.

51 : 15   12 Flint.[373] 13 House.

1 Rabbit [1454]. At this time the people were one-rabbited,[374] while the Chalca War was being fought at Cuauhtenampan; and so it came to an end, because no one was being attacked anymore. And for three years there was hunger. The corn had stopped growing.

51 : 20   And the year 1 Rabbit was also when Nezahualcoyotzin planned where his temple would be in Tetzcotzinco. He came and took up residence in order to consider it, and when he had looked upon it carefully, he began the temple. It was finished in thirteen years, built to the top in the year 1 Reed—where a report of it will be set forth.[375]

51 : 26   2 Reed [1455]. At this time[376] Nezahualcoyotzin laid the foundation for his temple. Also, a year-bundle feast was celebrated. And in this second year of hunger, the famine became much worse.

51 : 29   3 Flint [1456]. At this time it happened that amaranth was just all that was being eaten. People were dying. This was the third year of the famine. Painted [in the picture writing] are [what look] like people being eaten by vultures and coyotes.

51 : 33   4 House.

5 Rabbit [1458]. In this year the elder Moteuczomatzin declared war, and consequently all went to Coaixtlahuacan to fight the battles and make the conquests. At this time the great ruler Atonal was ruling there, occupying himself with tribute collection from everywhere in the coastlands.

51 : 37   Now, it is said that this Atonal was a remaining descendant of the Toltecs who had lived in Toltitlan Tamazolac,[377] from which place they had set out at the time of the Toltec migration, when they had been disbanded.

370. Lehmann convincingly argues that the original manuscript must have had *Xilo-Mātzjn*, which appeared to the copyist as *XVMotzjn* (the lost 'o' masquerading as a calligraphic flourish), leading him to write *xomotzin*. We know from lines 49:47 and 57:2 that Xilomantzin was ruler of Colhuacan at this time.

371. An obscure statement. Word for word the reading is "This was when X of Colhuacan arranged [or established] things for their land." GLOS: tlalia:tla 3.

372. Marginal gloss: In 7 Reed on the 2d of January, Granada was won, and the Jews left Castile by way of Sagunto. [The retaking of Granada from the Moors and the expulsion of the Jews occurred in 1492, not 1447 as implied here.]

373. Marginal gloss: In 12 Flint the great Turk, Mohammed, took Constantinople, and the Emperor Frederick died. [In fact Constantinople fell in 1453; Frederick died in 1493.]

374. I.e., there was famine in a year 1 Rabbit. Cf. 9:3 and 48:54 above.

375. See 53:44 below.

376. For the untranslated *yancuican* see GLOS.

377. See 10:40–43 above.

51 : 40   And it is said that when Atonal met his death,[378] his wife was fetched. She was very large. They took her back to Mexico Tenochtitlan. And the ruler Moteuczoma wanted to go to her and cohabit with her. She simply fainted. Well, he did not cohabit with her.

51 : 44   And it is said that between this[379] woman's legs there was polished jade on her private parts, etc.

51 : 46   Then the ruler, the elder Moteuczoma, sent her back to gather in the tribute goods from all over. She became a kind of female tribute collector. By this time the city of Coaixtlahuacan had been captured. Then for the first time gold, quetzal plumes, rubber, cacao, and other wealth began coming in; then the Mexica began to feel cheered, thanks to the tribute goods.

52 : 1   The year 5 Rabbit is when those who were defeated by the Tepeyacac people emigrated to Matlatzinco. It was when Chiauhcoatl was ruler of Tepeyacac, and the Cuauhtinchan rulers were Xochicozcatl, Tlazolteotl, Tecanmecatl, and Yaopan.[380]

52 : 5   6 Reed.

7 Flint [1460]. In that year[381] the elder Moteuczomatzin, ruler of Mexico, installed Quinatzin in Tepotzotlan; and so began the Tepotzotlan dynasty. Here there was no official determination on the part of the Cuauhtitlan ruler, Ayactlacatzin.[382]

52 : 10   8 House [1461]. All went to battle, all went to make conquests in Atezcahuacan. And Huitzilteuhcatzin of Colhuacan died at this time.

52 : 13   9 Rabbit [1462]. At the end of the year, as yet only secretly, Chalca were coming to offer themselves, that they might join ranks with Mexico.

52 : 15   10 Reed [1463]. In that year Chalca came before the elder Moteuczomatzin, ruler of Mexico, to notify him and let him hear that they would be going in with Mexico. Those who came were: first, Necuametl, and second, Tepoztli the elder. And, secondly, they went before Nezahualcoyotzin, ruler of Tetzcoco. Thus they went to give their report in both places, as if to test [the intentions of] those who had surrounded their country, Chalco.

52 : 23   They came to the rulers Moteuczomatzin and Nezahualcoyotzin, saying, "Esteemed child, O lord,[383] ruler, now Chalco and the war are through.

378. Because he refused to serve Moteuczoma. See lines 66:45–50 below.
379. For *inic çihuatl* read *ini çihuatl.*
380. The parallel passage in HTCH (fol. 44v [Ms. 54–58, side 45]) makes it clear that the emigrants to Matlatzinco were the Cuauhtinchan people, following their defeat by Chiauhcoatl of Tepeyacac.
381. For the untranslated *yancuican* see GLOS.
382. This matter regarding Tepotzotlan, which was within Cuauhtitlan's purview, had already been arranged by Quinatzin's father. See lines 14:53–15:13 above.
383. Read *totecue.* GLOS: teuctli.

Assign us a kingdom. What does your heart require? [384] The war is through, and with it the realm." [385]

52 : 28   Moteuczomatzin replied, "The boundaries should be just at Cocotitlan and Nepopohualco and Oztoticpac. So at last you have come to your senses? Indeed the realm is through. Now all you have to do is fetch the people." [386]

52 : 33   And Nezahualcoyotzin told them, "What you have said is good. Now, go. Go round up the people. Let the vassals be gathered in. Don't let them go with Huexotzinco."

52 : 36   Then he asked a question, saying, "Is the elder Tepoz *pilli*?" [387]

52 : 37   "No," replied the elder Tepoz, "I am not *pilli*. Necuametl is *pilli*." Then in accordance with a command of Moteuczomatzin, he said, "Let Necuametl be dispatched as the emissary."

52 : 40   Well, it was when Moteuczomatzin had already given them their orders that Nezahualcoyotzin said, "Already the king has told you, 'You've come to your senses? Indeed it is through.' Now round up the vassals."

52 : 44   And when Moteuczomatzin presented them with gifts, [388] what he gave were:

52 : 45   plume tassels [389]
a neckpiece, a jade necklace, for each one

52 : 46   eagle tail feathers for each one
gold armbands for each one

52 : 47   a gold-skin collar [390] for each one

52 : 48   gold legbands for each one
a load of twenty tilmas

53 : 1   And Nezahualcoyotzin, ruler of Tetzcoco, gave them:

53 : 2   gold earplugs for each one
gold armbands for each one

53 : 3   a gold-skin collar for each one
two loads of twenty tilmas each

384. NED: qu-en 6.
385. Read *ca ye onnalquiça* as in line 52:26.
386. GLOS: ana:tla, zan oc.
387. *Pilli* means prince, or member of the noble class.
388. Gifts of obligation? See note to line 41:3 above.
389. The *quetzallalpiloni* consisted of "dos borlas hechas de plumas ricas, guarnecidas con oro muy curiosas . . . atadas a los cabellos, de la coronjlla de la cabeça q̃ colgauan hasta el pescueço, por la parte de las sienes" (CF bk. 8, ch. 9). Cf. NED: tlalpil-oni.
390. I.e., a broad, thin ornament of beaten gold, worn around the neck (CF bk. 9, ch. 15).

53 : 4   Then Necuametl and Tepoztli the elder went back to Chalco.

53 : 7   11 Flint [1464]. The son of Tetzcoco's Nezahualcoyotzin, called Nezahualpiltzintli, was born at this time. And this was also when the young
corn plants were blown away by the wind, and trees were uprooted.

53 : 10   12 House [1465]. It was in this year that the Chalca actually joined
ranks [with Mexico]. At this time it came about that the Chalco ruler
Tlaltzin Teuctli died. Upon his death no one was made ruler. And it was
after he had died that the war cooled off, and shields and arrows were
laid aside. It was in Amaquemecan that the war [finally] cooled. This
was when military rule began in Chalco. For twenty-one years there was
military rule.

53 : 17   And as for their tribute goods, they delivered them[391] to the place called
Tlaltecahuacan. Xocuetzin, who went to [assume] his seat at Tlailotlacan,
and Cuauhtzipitl were assigned the vassals, etc.

53 : 21   The war now shifted: it was carried to Huexotzinco.

53 : 22   Some say that Tetzcoco's Nezahualpilli was born at this time.

53 : 23   And the year 12 House was when conquests were made at Huehuetlan.

53 : 24   And in this same year, in Tenochtitlan Mexico, a communal task force
was put together in order to begin building the Chapoltepec aqueduct
leading into Tenochtitlan.

53 : 28   Now, the ruler of Tenochtitlan at this time was the elder Moteuczomatzin. But it was the ruler of Tetzcoco, Nezahualcoyotzin, who spoke in
favor of the aqueduct.

53 : 32   13 Rabbit [1467]. In that year Nezahualcoyotzin went and guided the
water, so that it flowed for the first time into Tenochtitlan. And they came
and quickened it with Tepeyacahuaque, sacrificing them to the water.[392]
[Up until] then, people were still going to Chapoltepec to draw water.

53 : 37   Well, this was the time—this was the year—that the Tepeyacahuaque
were conquered. It was when Chiauhcoatl was ruler of Tepeyacac. And
the one who conquered them was Axayacatzin, before he was ruler [of
Mexico].

53 : 40   In Coatepec, Quetzaltototl was military chief; in Tecalco the ruler was
Mozauhqui; and in Cuauhtinchan, Xochicozcatl was ruling when they
were defeated at Tepeyacac and at all the [other] places just named.

53 : 44   1 Reed. It was in the year 1 Reed that Nezahualcoyotzin's temple was
built to the top.[393] And when it was topped, he went to implore the elder
Moteuczomatzin to grant some Tzompanca, some Xilotzinca, and some
Citlaltepeca. These he requested [as sacrificial victims] for his dedication

---

391. For *concaquia* read *concalaquia*. Cf. 37:47, 39:36, 41:20.
392. Lit., And they came and increased it by means of Tepeyacahuaque, who came and
died before the water.
393. Construction of the temple is briefly discussed in lines 51:20–27 above.

ceremony.[394] And the Tenochtitlan ruler was obliging. He granted them, etc.

54 : 2   Then word was brought to the Cuauhtitlan ruler—Moteuczomatzin sent the messenger—and in this way he was informed that Tzompanca were to be placed under guard. Cuauhtitlancalque were to perform the task in Toltitlan, in Cuitlachtepec, etc.[395] This was being done as a favor by the ruler of Tenochtitlan.

54 : 7   And it became true. The Tzompanca were placed under guard. At the time, Teyahualoatzin was governing there.

54 : 9   And in Xilotzinco, it was when Pantli was ruling.

54 : 10   And when Nezahualcoyotzin had issued the call to arms, and the Tetzcoca Acolhuaque had come forth to make war, children and young women appeared who had climbed to the top of Citlaltepetl [Hill of the Star] and had taken it upon themselves to be eagles and jaguars[396] in order to fight the war.

54 : 14   This is how it was done: they had everybody backpack all the prickly pears and magueys in that place, and they put them on their shields as emblems, cleverly tying them onto the wood.[397] They were formidable. And during the night they liberated[398] the Tzompanca and the Xilotzinca.

54 : 18   When morning came, the Acolhuaque had been turned back[399] and were in the water at Citlaltepec.[400] They were attacked, then routed. And the Tzompanca and the Xilotzinca went out to engage them, chased after them, and caught them in a rabbit ravine. Seeing this, many of the Acolhuaque were terrified, for the ravine was on fire, and the flames were rising toward them.

54 : 25   At last the Acolhuaque were destroyed. Corpses filled the rabbit ravine, and in fact the brave warriors[401] of the Acolhuaque were finished off.

54 : 28   By this time all the Totonaque and Cuexteca had come along, wearing no breechcloths, exposing their crotches.[402] They had come to make war in Tzompanco, where at first they displayed the egret banner that guided them and served as their sign. [But] finally they were chased away.

394. Lit., Tzompanca, Xilotzinca, Citlaltepeca, whom he went to request, by means of whom [as sacrificial victims] he would ceremonially dedicate something. For *ica* read *inca*.

395. GLOS: chihua:mo, tequipan.

396. Warriors.

397. Lit., the wood of them, i.e., the wood of the shields.

398. Lit., took them from people [who were guarding them]. Cf. 54:4–9 above.

399. In place of "had been turned back," Lehmann and Velázquez give "had strayed off course." See GLOS: ixcuepa:mo.

400. Forcing the enemy into water was a favorite tactic (see MEX 58; FC 12:83:25, 12:87:30, 12:117–18; CM fols. 6v:29 and 54v:7). For another "morning after" battle scene, see lines 50:9–13 above.

401. Cf. *vei tiacauh cenca oquichtli* (a great warrior, a very brave one) (FC 12:87:25).

402. Nothing unusual for Cuexteca, whose nudity was proverbial (see FC bk. 3, chs. 5–6; bk. 10, ch. 29, sec. entitled "Cuexteca").

54 : 33   The war cooled off in Otompan and Papahuacan.

54 : 34   By that time eagle lands⁴⁰³ had been created, and the lands' boundaries had been marked off at Tizayocan. Indeed, Tizayocan is where the eagle lands were. Today they are Acolhuacan lands. The place used to be an established battleground. Indeed, it is still there, covered with vegetation.⁴⁰⁴ Cuauhtitlan, Toltitlan, and Cuitlachtepec were the ones who got the eagle lands, etc.

54 : 40   This was the year the Chalca dedicated their temple. They came to notify Moteuczomatzin, saying, "O esteemed child, let the Tlacochcalca come back and dedicate the pyramid they left so hurriedly."

54 : 43   And the elder Moteuczomatzin said, "So be it. It is well. Let it be done."

[The reign of Axayacatzin: A.D. 1469–80]

54 : 46   2 Flint.

3 House [1469]. In that year the elder Moteuczomatzin died. It was when the above-mentioned year 2 Flint had drawn to a close. He had ruled for twenty-nine years.

55 : 1   Then, during that [year], Axayacatzin was inaugurated as ruler. And it was he who conquered the Tlatlauhquitepeca.

55 : 3   Also in that year Cuappotonqui, who became ruler of Teopancalcan, was born in Cuitlahuac.

55 : 6   4 Rabbit [1470]. All went to war in Cuaxoxocan.

5 Reed [1471]. In that year eagle lands⁴⁰⁵ were marked off in Matlatzinco. Those who governed, who went to take charge, were Cuauhtitlancalque [from] Tequixquinahuac [and] Chalmecapan, [as well as] Nepantla's Tziuhcoatl [and] Atempan's Tepecomecatl.⁴⁰⁶

55 : 11   6 Flint [1472]. This was the second year that lands were marked off in Matlatzinco. Also, Nezahualcoyotzin of Tetzcoco died at this time. Then Nezahualpiltzintli was inaugurated as Tetzcoco's ruler. And in this same year Cuappotonqui was inaugurated as ruler of Cuitlahuac Teopancalcan.⁴⁰⁷

55 : 16   7 House [1473]. In this year the Tenochca and the Tlatilolca fought each other. It was when Axayacatzin was ruler. And at this time Moquihuixtli was ruling in Tlatilolco. The story of it is here set forth:

---

403. Lands reserved for battle? GLOS: ²cuauhtlalli.
404. Cf. 24:29 ("their temple and their city sprouted grass"). GLOS: xoxotitimani.
405. GLOS: ²cuauhtlalli.
406. Representing the four boroughs of Cuauhtitlan. See lines 29:31–38 and 43:43–48 above.
407. According to lines 55:3–5, Cuappotonqui had been born three years earlier.

55 : 19   When there was no war [as yet], Moquihuixtli was doing many bad things with women.

55 : 21   At this time the daughter of the Tenochtitlan ruler Axayacatzin was Moquihuixtli's wife. And this lady was telling Tenochtitlan everything. All Moquihuix's secret war talk she was passing on to Axayacatzin.

55 : 26   Well, at this time Moquihuixtli was scandalizing the people in many ways. He was fattening all his women until they were huge.[408] And as for the lady who was Axayacatzin's daughter, he would thrust his forearm into her crotch and feel inside her body.

55 : 31   Now, it is told that this lady's vulva spoke out and said to him, "Why are you grieving, Moquihuix? Why have you left the city?[409] There can be no future, there can be no dawn."[410]

55 : 33   And then, it had come about that he had settled his concubines[411] inside the palace.

55 : 35   And, to give himself pleasure, he would bathe the concubines with a slippery [pad of] nopal.[412]

55 : 36   Well, he would undress his women, so that they could be rubbed with oil,[413] and he cohabited with each one. Etc.

55 : 38   When many scandalous things had occurred, Moquihuixtli sent a messenger[414] to Cuauhtitlan to solicit aid. He petitioned the ruler Ayactlacatzin, who refused the request.

55 : 42   Now then, the Tenochtitlan ruler, Axayacatzin, also sent a messenger petitioning[415] the ruler Ayactlacatzin for aid, and he granted the request, saying, "The king must not worry. It will come true. It will be done as the king asks, for he prays[416] to our gods as well as his own gods."

55 : 48   Then the Tlatilolco ruler Moquihuix issued an order, saying, "If I, the Tlatilolcatl, am not conquered, then you will pillage the Cuauhtitlan-

408. Compare the sensuality of Huemac and the temptation of Moteuczomatzin (see lines 8:45–55 and 51:40–44 above). In a variant of the story at hand, Moquihuixtli slighted his wife who was Axayacatzin's daughter because "she was just a thin little thing, she was not fleshy" (*zan pitzactzintli catca amo nacayo*) (MEX 117).

409. Not an observation but a prophecy, foretelling the downfall of Tlatilolco. Compare the variant passages in TEZ ch. 63 and DHIST ch. 43.

410. Durán's variant has the lady's privates saying, "What will have become of me by this time tomorrow?" (¿Qué será de mí mañana a estas horas?) (DHIST ch. 63, parag. 20).

411. Lit., his mounds, or mounds of Venus, i.e., women as sex objects. GLOS: tepetl.

412. In the more decorous *Crónica mexicana* version the queen's servants bathe her in a tub, and it is while she is in the bath that the prophecy issues from her *natura* (private parts) (TEZ ch. 63).

413. Lit., Well, he would undress his women, so that the women would come be rubbed with oil (-*ox*-) on their torsos (-*tlac*-).

414. For *huallayhuan* read *huallayhua*, as in line 55:42.

415. Read *quihuallatlauhti*.

416. Read *quinhuallatlauhtia*.

calque." He made his promise to Tollan, Apazco, Xilotepec, Chiapan, and Cuahuacan, saying, "When we have defeated our enemy, the Tenochcatl, I will give you the city of Cuauhtitlan. All you have to do is surround it. And as soon as I have destroyed the Tenochcatl, you will pillage the Cuauhtitlancalque."

56:4 And so it was done. The Otomi got together and assembled on the heights of Macuexhuacan in order to pillage the city of Cuauhtitlan. All the nations mentioned above came to settle in, placing the city under observation, etc.

56:8 And then the king, the ruler Axayacatzin, charged and commissioned those who were to aid the city of Tenochtitlan.

56:11 Then people were mustered from the four quarters of Cuauhtitlan town,[417] the fighters, the great marksmen, the strong warriors who were to go off in squadrons of forty each to aid the city of Tenochtitlan.

56:15 So it became true. It happened. It was for this that the people were mustered, and they jointly resolved to take to the road.[418]

56:16 They entered by night, going in by way of Chapoltepec Atlixyocan. Unsheathed[419] were the arrows, the bows of these Chichimecs. Etc.

56:18 When they arrived, the campaign was already in progress: the Tenochca had gone to capture Tezoncaltitlan.

56:20 Since the battle was begun, they set out to join in.[420] [But] when the Cuauhtitlancalque were noticed, Axayacatzin was skeptical. He did not think they were real warriors. As he looked them over, he grew discontent, etc.

56:23 After that, the Cuauhtitlancalque were adorned: they were given insignia, and in this way they were arrayed as Mixcoatl.[421] Also, they were given food and drink at the *apetlatl*,[422] in the courtyard of the Devil.

56:27 Well, then the war got started. It took place during Tecuilhuitontli [June or July], and it was on a day 5 Rain that the Tlatilolca were destroyed.

---

417. Lit., Then people were mustered [as to] the way that Cuauhtitlan town is in four places. Cf. 46:43 above.

418. For *atatacoz*, Lehmann sees *otatacoz*, which, in my view, is not translatable. It seems preferable to read this as an error for *otlatocoz* (people would take to the road). If the text is allowed to stand, the translation would be "The reason the people were mustered is that a joint decision was made to excavate the stream." See GLOS: atataca, and cf. 48:24–25 above.

419. For *petlaticayaya* read *petlauhticaya*.

420. Lit., They went for the purpose of coming along, since begun was the battle.

421. Cf. 25:47 above.

422. Also known as *itlaquaian vitzilobuchtli* (Huitzilopochtli's dining place), the *apetlatl* was a low platform at the base of the great pyramid, where victims were assembled for sacrifice (CF bk. 9, ch. 14; see also FC 2:107:29, FC 2:128:22). The custom of feeding warriors a soup made from the victims' dried blood, to give courage, is described in TORQ bk. 2, ch. 58, p. 177.

56 : 30　　At length, after the war had begun, the Cuauhtitlancalque, two by two, were put into canoes, and they were being rowed. And along the way some of them were fighting and skirmishing as they traveled. They just kept on without stopping. Nothing hindered them. The way they started out is that they shot first into the air, then toward the ground. It was all finished in the east. Etc.

56 : 37　　When the war was through, some of the Cuauhtitlancalque just came straight home. As they were setting out, what they snatched was perhaps a tilma or a stick of kindling.[423]

56 : 40　　But it also happened that many of the men became crazed. After the war they acted as though they did not know their own kinsmen, etc.

56 : 44　　And it is said that while the war between Mexico Tenochtitlan and Tlatilolco was in progress, the Devil played a trick on the Otomi who had surrounded the city of Cuauhtitlan. An arrow fell in their midst, and they heard the rattle of shields and people ululating. And with that, the Otomi scattered, etc.

57 : 1　　The year 7 House is also the time when Colhuacan's ruler Xilomantzin met his death. Axayacatzin indicted him.[424]

57 : 3　　When he was dead, Maxihuitzin, or Malihuitzin,[425] the son of Chimalpopocatzin, was inaugurated, and he went off to rule in Colhuacan.

57 : 5　　Now, at the time of Xilomantzin's death there were forty tribute collectors. Then Axayacatzin fetched them home.

57 : 7　　And as for this Malihuitzin, he ruled for only sixty-four days. Then Tlatolcaltzin was inaugurated as Colhuacan's ruler.

57 : 10　　8 Rabbit [1474]. At this time there was supposed to have been a war in Huexotla. This was also the time when the Matlatzinca dispersed.

57 : 12　　9 Reed.

　　10 Flint [1476]. Here there were conquests in Ocuillan. The Cuauhnahuaca were defeated.[426] Also, there was an eclipse of the sun.

57 : 14　　11 House [1477]. Here the Poctepeca were defeated.

　　This was also when Huexotzinca came to stay. Toltecatzin was Chiauhtzinco's ruler at this time, and he came before the ruler of Tenochtitlan, Axayacatzin. And what Toltecatzin brought with him were two of his wives.[427]

---

　　423. Lit., The manner in which they departed hitherward is that what they snatched was perhaps a tilma or a stick.
　　424. Xilomantzin was executed for conspiring with Moquihuix of Tlatilolco (TORQ bk. 2, ch. 58, p. 177: *Cacique de Culhuacan . . .* and p. 180: *mataron a Xiloman . . .* ; see also IXT and MEX).
　　425. An alternate name is given in the same manner in line 49 : 2 (cf. 30 : 6).
　　426. Lit., They [impersonal] defeated the Cuauhnahuaca. See GN sec. 4.2.
　　427. Evidently the wives are a "greeting gift." For other such gifts see 13 : 31, 21 : 5(?), 28 : 28, 44 : 2.

57 : 18   Well, the reason they had emigrated to Mexico is that a war had been stirred up in Huexotzinco. It was all because of an effort to move the image of Mixcoatl to Chiauhtzinco, and there was no [pyramid] temple there; all they had was a calpulli temple. So this is why they had come to Mexico.[428]

57 : 22   Now, when they were living in Mexico, the wives were ensconced in the kitchen quarters. And after a while, on command of the ruler Axayacatzin, the wives just[429] cooked for him and fed him,[430] etc.

57 : 26   12 Rabbit [1478]. This is when Matlatzinco, by a joint decision, was decimated: the ruler Axayacatzin conquered them at Xiquipilco. At this time Axayacatzin took captives there.

57 : 29   13 Reed [1479]. In that year Cuitlahuaca went to Tliliuhquitepec and met their death. And also, when Ixtotomahuatzin of Teopancalcan died, a son of Camaxtle named Calixto was inaugurated; he ruled for only eighty days, then Don Mateo Ixtliltzin was inaugurated.

57 : 34   1 Flint [1480]. This was when Tlazolyaotzin of Huexotla died. Then Cuitlahuatzin was inaugurated as ruler.

[The reign of Tizocicatzin: A.D. 1481–85]

57 : 36   2 House [1481] was when the ruler Axayacatzin died. Then Tizocicatzin was inaugurated as ruler of Tenochtitlan. Also, there was an eclipse of the sun.

57 : 39   3 Rabbit [1482]. At this time the Colhuacan ruler called Tlatolcaltzin died. Then his son, called Tezozomoctli, was inaugurated as ruler of Colhuacan.

57 : 42   4 Reed [1483]. At this time, in Tenochtitlan, the foundation was laid for the house of the devil Huitzilopochtli, started by the ruler Tizocicatzin.

57 : 44   This was also when Cuauhnahuaca met their death. They had been try-

---

428. According to Torquemada, Toltecatl and his followers were driven out by a band of dissolute priests, who scandalized the town and made war on the people with the aid of the god Camaxtle (TORQ bk. 2, ch. 66, p. 191). As stated in the Annals of Tlatilolco, "In the year 7 Reed [1498] the Huexotzinca began to be dissolute; the ruler Toltecatzin set out from Chiauhtzinco; this Toltecatzin came to live here in Mexico" (*chicomaca[tl] xiuitl yquac peuh motlaçolteuuia uexotzinca chiauhtzinco peuh Toltecatzin tlatoani ŷ toltecatzi mexico nica nemico*) (UAH sec. 282; cf. HTCH sec. 403).

429. The "just" is significant. We have seen what happens to rulers who succumb to sensuality (lines 8 : 39–56, 55 : 19–30) and how Moteuczomatzin the elder was spared by a lady's fainting spell (lines 51 : 40–44). Compare Axayacatzin's restraint with the rash behavior of Moteuczomatzin the younger, who, on the eve of the Spanish Conquest, takes a Huexotzinca woman by force (line 63 : 28 below).

430. Anticlimactic word order reversed in the translation.

57 : 46 ing to conquer the Huexotzinca, who went and adorned them [as sacrificial victims] in Atlixco.

57 : 46 And also at this time the Cuitlahuac ruler Tezozomoctli died. Then Xochiololtzin was inaugurated as ruler of Cuitlahuac Tizic.

57 : 49 5 Flint [1484]. Chiapan was captured.

57 : 50 6 House [1485]. This is when Cuappopocatzin of Coatlichan died. Then Xaquintzin was inaugurated.

[The reign of Ahuitzotzin: A.D. 1486–1502]

57 : 52 7 Rabbit [1486]. It was during this year that Tizocicatzin died. Then Ahuitzotzin was inaugurated, and he ruled in Tenochtitlan.

58 : 1 It was the year the Cozcacuauhtenanca were defeated. This was also when the Tlappaneca, the Tziuhcoaca, and the people of Mictlancuauhtla were defeated.

58 : 3 It was also the year a dynasty began in Chalco Tlacochcalco, starting with Itzcahuatzin, who was made lord at this time. Those who tolerated him there, since they had no ambition of being princes themselves, were the landholding Tlaltecayohuaque Chalca.

58 : 7 Now, the only ones who boasted of being princes were in San Juan, in Contlan, and in Tlailotlacan. And at this time, when already they were styling themselves princes, these Conteca, Mihuaque, and Tlailotlaque were chattering about Itzcahuatzin's rule. Then they came before Ahuitzotzin, ruler of Mexico. Those who came were the prince Tlacochtzin from the Mihuaque. And the prince Chichicuepotl from Tlilhuacan.

58 : 13 But from Tlaltecahuacan[431] no one came.

58 : 14 Already they had been abused again and again. And when they had beseeched Ahuitzotzin and had said to him, "Oh, how painful it is to beg for charity, etc."[432] and "Oh, that Itzcahua is taking away our farm lands. How painful it is to do the sweeping and lay the fire,"[433] then Ahuitzotzin sent them off, saying, "Take back your lands."

58 : 19 And when Itzcahua heard this, he was quick to anger. "I must see the ruler," he said.

58 : 20 Then he came before Ahuitzotzin, saying to him, "Sire, you sent home the Mihuaque, the Tlilhuaque, and the Tlailotlaque, giving them back their lands. But you had made me lord. Where is my estate? It is as though

431. Presumably the home borough of the tolerant Tlaltecayohuaque mentioned in line 58:6 above. See Concordance.
432. GLOS: chinamitl.
433. Women's work. GLOS: tlachpanaliztli/tletlaliliztli.

117

they themselves were the lord. Well, take a look at them. Really, it would
· seem that these Mihuaque, Tlilhuaque, and Tlailotlaque are claiming to be
princes, making themselves great," etc. Now, when Itzcahuatzin made this
trip to Mexico he had already been ruling for fourteen years.

58 : 28   Then the ruler Ahuitzotzin sent him on his way, telling him, "I have
heard your plea, and I give you permission. I leave them in your hands. It
is up to you. Give them a thrashing and hang them by the neck—these
people who are setting themselves up as princes."

58 : 32   So Itzcahua did just that. He executed the boastful princes.

58 : 33   Those self-styled princes were the only princes who died at this time,
etc. Many are the stories about it.[434]

58 : 35   8 Reed [1487]. This is when the house of Huitzilopochtli was dedicated
in Tenochtitlan. In four years it had been built to the top.[435] And it was
dedicated with prisoners who met their death. Here, all told, are the
nations:

58 : 38   The Tzapoteca dead were 16,000.
The Tlappaneca dead were 24,000.

58 : 39   The Huexotzinca dead were 16,000.

58 : 40   The Tziuhcoaca dead were 24,400.
And this includes Cozcacuauhtenanca and people from Mictlancuauhtla.

58 : 42   Thus all the prisoners add up to 80,400.

58 : 44   9 Flint [1488]. At this time Chiapaneca were defeated. And the dedication of the Tenochtitlan temple went into a second year. Also, Cozcacuauhtenanca were defeated. Also Tziuhcoac.

58 : 47   10 House [1489] was when Tzintemazatl made a quick foray to
Cuauhnahuac and fell into the hands of Xochimilca, who killed him there.

58 : 49   11 Rabbit [1490]. In that year Nezahualpilli took captives in Huexotzinco. Also, the Totolapaneca took captives.

58 : 50   And at that time the ruler Ahuitzotzin gave away forty prisoners in
Cuauhnahuac. The Cuauhnahuaca used them to dedicate their temple.

58 : 53   Also, there was an eclipse of the sun. Stars appeared.

58 : 54   12 Reed.
13 Flint [1492]. At this time the Xicochimalca were defeated. And there
was also an eclipse of the sun.

59 : 1   1 House [1493]. At this time Ayotochcuitlatlan and Xaltepec were
defeated.

59 : 2   And also there was an eclipse of the sun. Stars appeared.
And in the same year, Santo Domingo was routed, also Granada. And
the Jews fled.[436]

---

434. The only variant known to me is in Chimalpain (CHIM 230–31; ZCHIM 1 : 137).
435. See lines 57 : 42–43 above.
436. Compare the marginal gloss at line 51 : 12 above.

59 : 4   2 Rabbit.

3 Reed [1495]. In that year the Cuauhtitlan ruler Ayactlacatzin died. After[437] his death, no one was inaugurated as ruler in Cuauhtitlan. There was only a military chief. The *tlacateccatl* Tehuitzin of Tepetlapan was the one who governed.[438]

59 : 8   In the same year, there was war in Tliltepec. Many Tetzcoca went to their death in that place.

59 : 9   And in that year Tlacahuepantzin went to his death in Huexotzinco.

59 : 11   4 Flint [1496]. This was the year Xochtlan was decimated. Also, there was an eclipse of the sun.

59 : 13   5 House [1497] is when Tecuantepec was decimated. And Amaxtlan was decimated.

59 : 14   6 Rabbit [1498]. In that year the Huexotzinca came to Coatepec and were destroyed. It snowed there. Meanwhile the Cuitlahuaca were supposed to be holding Huexotzinco under guard, and they met death. It snowed in that place, too.

59 : 17   In the same year, Chiauhcoatl, Huitzilihuitl, and Maxtla met their death. They had cuckolded Nezahualpilli of Tetzcoco.

59 : 20   7 Reed [1499]. The [stream called] Acuecuexatl flowing from Coyohuacan appeared in that year. It was on a day 4 Jaguar that it came forth, so as to enter Tenochtitlan.[439] And on that very day the earth shook four times.

59 : 23   And it is said that this was when the Huexotzinco ruler Toltecatzin of Chiauhtzinco emigrated [to Mexico]—which was told above, which was mentioned twenty-three years back.[440]

59 : 26   8 Flint [1500]. At this time the Xaltepeca were soundly defeated at last.[441]

And at this time, too, the [waters of] Acuecuexatl finally came spreading out everywhere, reaching Cuitlahuac, Mizquic, Ayotzinco, and Xochimilco, at the same time flooding Tepetzinco [at] Tetzcoco Atenco. And they reached to Xalmimilolco, to Mazatzintamalco.

59 : 30   Very much did the waters overflow in Mexico.

59 : 31   9 House.

10 Rabbit [1502]. In that year the Cuitlahuaca dispersed on account of flood and famine, when the Acuecuexatl had completely overflowed their neighborhoods. Also at that time Mayehuatzin was inaugurated as ruler

437. For *iqua* read *iquac*.
438. At this time Cuauhtitlan also had a "prince," according to lines 15 : 24–28 above.
439. Though warned that it would cause flooding, Ahuitzotzin had the stream diverted in order to raise the level of the Lake of Mexico (DHIST chs. 48–49).
440. See lines 57 : 14–22. Torquemada places the event in the twelfth year of the reign of Ahuitzotzin (TORQ bk. 2, ch. 66, p. 191).
441. See line 59 : 1 above.

of Cuitlahuac Atenchicalcan. And at the same time it stopped raining altogether, so that we came up against 1 Rabbit,[442] and people suffered famine.

[The reign of Moteuczomatzin the younger: A.D. 1503–17]

59 : 37   11 Reed [1503].[443] Ahuitzotzin, ruler of Tenochtitlan, died at this time. Then the ruler Moteuczomatzin was inaugurated.

59 : 38   And at the same time, the Cuauhtitlan ruler Aztatzontzin was inaugurated. How this son of Quinatzin came to be inaugurated as ruler is that he scattered turquoises, which came down in Tepotzotlan.[444] Etc.

59 : 41   Also at this time, the house of the Devil in Tlalmanalco was built to the top.

59 : 43   12 Flint [1504]. In that year Spaniards were routed in Cuba.[445]

And in that same year, Tehuehueltzin of Cuauhnahuac died. Then Itzcoatzin, the father of Don Hernando, was inaugurated as ruler in Cuauhnahuac.

59 : 46   Also in that year, the Cuitlahuaca enlarged their temple of Mixcoatl.

59 : 47   On a day 13 Death there was an eclipse of the sun.

59 : 48   And also in that year, the ruler called Cuappotonqui died in Cuitlahuac Teopancalcan. Then Ixtotomahuatzin, father of Don Mateo Ixtliltzin, was inaugurated as ruler of Teopancalcan, on the day 13 Death.

59 : 52   13 House [1505]. In that year the Cuauhtitlan ruler Aztatzontzin searched out and tracked down[446] lands. So that Tlaxoxiuhco and Huexocalco steward lands and calpulli lands would provide him with tribute, he dispatched Tlacateuctzin Tzincopintzin, who was a native of Tollantzinco, impressing his words upon him, saying, "Don't let your gods be angry with you. Take the lands away from them," etc.

442. The calendrical sign 1 Rabbit was associated with hunger. See GLOS: aci ce tochtli itech, cetochhuia:mo.

443. Marginal gloss: At this time the Turk, Selim, began his rule [?]; he was crowned the day of the battle of Ravenna. [The battle of Ravenna, between French and Spanish forces, was fought in 1512, the same year Selim I became sultan of the Turks.]

444. The plainspoken author seems out of character. His fancy phrase might mean that Aztatzontzin had made an eloquent speech in Tepotzotlan (for eloquence compared to the scattering of jewels see FC 6:248–49). As we know from lines 15:20–24, it was the Tepotzotlan ruler Quinatzin who caused his son, Aztatzontzin, to be placed on the throne of Cuauhtitlan. Coincidentally (?), Tepotzotlan was the site of a famous turquoise mine (CF bk. 10, ch. 28, sec. 1).

445. GLOS: tepehui. Or, if the verb *pehua:te* (to conquer someone) is meant, the translation would be "Spaniards made conquests [or took prisoners] in Cuba." Possibly the statement is an old gloss, mistakenly incorporated by the copyist.

446. Anticlimactic word order reversed in the translation.

59 : 58   Also in that year, people went to the Totonaque. On account of the famine, they carried shelled corn from Totonacapan.

59 : 60   1 Rabbit [1506]. In that year Zozollan was decimated on a day 13 Reed.

60 : 1   At this time the aforementioned Ixtotomahuatzin of Cuitlahuac Teopancalcan was all aglow[447] that he had been made ruler. This was precisely the year people recovered from the famine, a famine that had caused torment for just three years.

60 : 5   2 Reed [1507] is when the year-bundle feast was celebrated:[448] it was on a day 8 Reed that the fire drill ignited at Huixachtlan.[449]

60 : 6   Also at this time, Cuitlahuatzin of Huexotla died.

60 : 7   And in the city of Cuauhtitlan a round-stone was set up, where striping could occur.[450] Well, when it had been set up, it was dedicated with just two prisoners from Cuauhtitlan, and also seven Atotonilca, who were prisoners of the Metztitlancalque.

60 : 11   As for the prisoners, reportedly when the Cuauhtitlancalque performed their dedication ceremony at the round-stone, there was first the *ticoc yahuacatl* Maxtlatzin, who had gotten a prisoner at Ecatepec. Second, there was the valiant warrior Itztoltzin, a native of Tollantzinco, who had gotten a prisoner in the coastlands: it was a child that he had captured. And someone was brought forth for this purpose by command of the ruler of Tepexic. It was a young man, whom they had gone to get by bartering: to fetch the prisoner they had gone and laid out a shield and a load of twenty blankets. Reportedly, when that *ticoctzin*, that valiant, took his captive at Ecatepec, the only one who died in battle was Yohualpaintzin.

60 : 19   At this time in Ecatepec a party of executioners had been impounded for eighty days in an executioners' barracks.[451] The taking of captives occurred when they were off on their official errand.[452]

60 : 21   The impoundment was during the time that Tolnahuacatzintli of Tenochtitlan was governing in Ecatepec, and in Cuauhtitlan the governing *tlacateccatl* was Macuextzin.[453]

---

447. For *omixtonac* read *onixtonac*.

448. Marginal gloss: year-bundle feast.

449. The new fire ceremony at Huixachtlan is described in FC bk. 7, chs. 9–10.

450. The round-stone was a kind of table, where prisoners were sacrificed; in a preliminary ritual the victims were "striped," or thrashed, by a fully armed warrior (FC 2:44:n17, 2:176:9–26, 2:190–91).

451. According to Sahagún, the executioners themselves were condemned to death if they failed in their mission: "Auja tambien otra sala del palacio, que llamaua achcauhcalli: en este lugar se juntauan, y residian los achcacauhti, que tenjan cargo de matar, a los que condenaua el señor . . . y si no cumplian lo que les mandaua el señor, luego les condenaua a muerte" (CF bk. 8, ch. 14, para. 4).

452. Lit., when they [impersonal] take captives is at the time they had gone along having been made official sent ones.

453. Since we know that Aztatzontzin was ruler of Cuauhtitlan (see lines 59:38 and 64:7), it would appear that the Cuauhtitlancalque were still under the dual leadership of a "prince," i.e., Aztatzontzin, and a *tlacateccatl*. See 15:24–28 and cf. 59:7–8.

60 : 24　　When the aforementioned *ticoc yahuacatl* Maxtlatzin got his captive at Ecatepec, it was following this impoundment in the executioners' barracks, which were located at a place called Nahuicallocan, or Macuilocotlan.

60 : 27　　And finally one day [the men in] the executioners' barracks went off to Xiuhtlan to perform the assassination.

60 : 28　　Both [he, Maxtlatzin, and] Tzonmolcatl of Tequixquinahuac were captive takers. It was just the two of them who assassinated the ruler, for they caught him in the woods at night, [where] the ruler was fleeing, surrounded by his nobles and ladies. It was after a full day and night of travel that they caught up with him. And by this time all the Mexica, the Tepaneca, the Acolhuaque, etc., had fallen behind.[454]

60 : 34　　Well, when they arrived in Mexico and reported to the ruler Moteuczomatzin, they were granted the haircut, the ear plugs, and the body paint—everything pertaining to the Mexica, as worn by the warrior braves of the Mexica.[455]

60 : 37　　But the ruler of Cuauhtitlan did not wish this. "Leave well enough alone," he said. "Let's not be hated, etc." All he gave them were their carmine-colored [hair] ribbons,[456] etc.

60 : 40　　In this year of 2 Reed, Teuctepec was decimated. Also Iztitlan was decimated.

60 : 41　　And there was an eclipse of the sun.

　　Also in this year they say that Aztatzontzin went to take prisoners in Huexotzinco. The prisoners were taken in Atlixco, at Atzomiatenanco. Aztatzontzin captured[457] one called Macuilxochitl. And his younger brother, named Totec Iyauhteuh,[458] captured the very sibling of Macuilxochitl, his very brother, who was called Tepetl. These were sons of the Chichimec lord of Atlixco, and they were princes, etc.

60 : 48　　3 Flint [1508]. In that year the cloud banner[459] appeared for the first time. It was seen in the east, where the sun comes up, at dawn.

60 : 50　　Also in that year Tzontemoctzin was inaugurated as ruler of Huexotla.

60 : 51　　Also in that year people went to take captives at Amilpan in Huexotzinco. All the women were captured on a day 13 Jaguar.

60 : 53　　Also at that time, during that year, the Mexica princes of Tenochtitlan

454. Lit., No longer was there one of the Mexica, the Tepaneca, the Acolhuaque, etc.

455. Lit., the way the warrior braves of the Mexica looked.

456. Warriors with carmine ribbons tied around their topknots are shown in Codex Mendoza. GLOS: cuia:tla, -tlacuiaya.

457. Read *çaçic*, as in the following line.

458. The name of Aztatzontzin's younger brother is written Totec Yatetzin in line 15 : 17 above. (The names may be regarded as identical, if it is kept in mind that *y* is often written for *iy*, the *uh* at the end of a syllable is occasionally dropped, and the terminal *-tzin* in personal names is optional.)

459. The cloud banner, much described in the old histories, was evidently the tail of a comet, said to have been "like a cloud." See GLOS: mixpamitl. See also lines 61 : 11 and 61 : 19.

and Tlatilolco were given lands in Tehuiloyocan, so that today these are communal lands.

60 : 55   The lands were apportioned when Moteuczomatzin was ruler of Tenochtitlan, and Aztatzontzin was ruler of Cuauhtitlan.

60 : 57   The way the land was given out is that it was in the hands of the stewards[460] of Acxotlan. The princes, the nobles, of Cuauhtitlan were not put in charge of it.

61 : 1   As for those who were given lands:
There was Tzihuacpopocatzin of Tlatilolco, whose grant was the Tehuiloyocan hill[s?], known today as Tlatilolca lands.

61 : 3   Secondly, there was Techotlalatzin, whose grant was in the irrigated fields called Atzacualpan [Place of Impounded Water]; [he was] the lord of Itztapalapan, etc.

61 : 4   Thirdly, there was Tochihuitzin of Mexicatzinco,[461] whose grant was of irrigated fields, also located in the Atzacualpan,[462] where the Coatzinca dwelled.

61 : 6   And then, reserved for the palace in Tezoncaltitlan, were the Macuiltzinco lands, where the sons of the *tlacochteuctli* of Tehuiloyocan dwelled, in Atzacualpan, there at Cuauhacaltitlan [Place of the Wooden Flume].

61 : 9   Thus were the aforementioned princes given lands.

61 : 11   4 House [1509].[463] In that year the cloud banner began to appear in the east.[464]

61 : 12   And in that same year, lands were again marked off in Chalco. For nine years the people worked the soil there and had food. In the tenth year it just came to an end.

61 : 16   5 Rabbit [1510]. At this time a son was born to Aztatzontzin. Doña Maria, a lady of Xochimilco, was the one who gave birth to him, and the child she bore was Don Pedro Macuilxochitl, who later ruled in Tepotzotlan.

61 : 18   Also at this time, at long last, people were terrified by the cloud banner appearing in the east. It seemed like fire. The people were extremely terrified.

61 : 21   And in this year all went to war at Icpatepec and Izquixochitepec. The destruction occurred on a day 2 Deer. Ixtotomahuatzin of Cuitlahuac took a captive there.[465]

61 : 25   6 Reed [1511] was the year the Tlachquiauhca were destroyed. This

---

460. For *calpixqui* read *calpixque*.
461. Like Itztapalapan (mentioned in the preceding sentence), Mexicatzinco was a member of the *nauhteuctli* (see GLOS), thus virtually a part of Mexico.
462. For *onçò mani* read *oncã mani*, as in lines 19 : 10, 25 : 9, 25 : 31.
463. Marginal gloss: the war of Oran [city in Algeria, held by the Spanish from 1509 to 1708].
464. But apparently not for the first time. See line 60 : 48 above.
465. Marginal gloss: Also Granada was won.

was also when a daughter of Moteuczomatzin's went to be married in Colhuacan.

61 : 28   7 Flint [1512]. At this time all went to war at Quimichtlan. Also in this year a daughter of the Tenochtitlan ruler Moteuczomatzin came to Cuauhtitlan to be married: he gave her to the ruler Aztatzontzin.

61 : 31   And at this time the Cuauhnahuac ruler Itzcoatzin died. When for three years no one had ruled, Yaocuixtli succeeded him and became ruler.

61 : 34   8 House [1513]. At this time Tezontlaltzin was inaugurated as ruler of Cuitlahuac Tecpan. Also at this time Cuitlahuaca went to their death in Huexotzinco. Those who died were Miztliima and Mexayacatl, brothers of the Teopancalcan ruler Ixtotomahuatzin.

61 : 37   Also, the daughter of Moteuczomatzin in Colhuacan gave birth at this time.

61 : 39   9 Rabbit [1514].[466] In this year all went off to [make war against] Iztactlalocan. And all went off to [make war against] Macuiloctlan. Cuitlahuac's Ixtotomahuatzin took a captive at Iztactlalocan.

61 : 42   10 Reed [1515]. Nezahualpiltzintli of Tetzcoco died at this time. Also, Yaocuixtli was inaugurated as ruler in Cuauhnahuac.

61 : 43   And, in the same year, the Centzontepeca were defeated on a day 7 Vulture. This was where Ixtotomahuatzin got his haircut.[467]

61 : 45   And, in the same year, some Huexotzinca emigrated to Mexico Tenochtitlan. These were Xayacamachan, Ixtehueyo, Miztliima, Tezcatlpopoca, Iyauhpotonqui, and a woman compatriot of theirs, etc.

61 : 48   And, in the same year, Don Diego Tizaatzin of Colhuacan was born.

61 : 50   11 Flint [1516]. In this year Cacamatzin was inaugurated as ruler of Tetzcoco.

61 : 52   12 House [1517]. In this year Moteuczoma put to death the skull rack lord of Cuitlahuac,[468] killing all his sons as well. Those who performed the executions were Cuitlahuaca under orders from Moteuczoma, ruler of Mexico.

61 : 55   The reason the skull rack lord met his death is that he had answered Moteuczoma—who had asked him how things ought to be done, saying, "As I see it, the house of Huitzilopochtli ought to be all gold, and the inside should be jade, with quetzal plumes, etc. Indeed,[469] it would require

466. Marginal gloss: On August 24th the Turk, Selim, conquered Sop[ ]. [Sophi?, i.e., Sofia?]

467. We have been told in lines 61:23 and 61:40 of at least two captives taken by Ixtotomahuatzin. According to Sahagún (bk. 8, ch. 21), the warrior who had taken four became a valiant (*tequihua*) and was granted the special haircut of that rank. See also 60:35 above.

468. An oracle, who predicted the arrival of the Spaniards (DHIST, TEZ, Concordance: tzompanteuctli). As we learn in lines 63:3–7 below, his name was Quetzalmazatzin.

469. GLOS: ca nozo.

tribute from all over Anahuac. It would be used for our god. Well, what do you think?"

62 : 2   At that, the skull rack lord answered him, saying, "O lord, O ruler, no! Understand that by so doing you would invite the destruction of your people. And you would offend our home, the heavens, for we are being watched here. You must realize, you must understand: that one is not to be our god, for there's the lord and master, the owner of creation. Indeed he is coming. He will arrive, etc."

62 : 9   Hearing this, Moteuczoma was enraged. He said to the skull rack lord, "Begone, and await my command." And that's how the skull rack lord and all his sons met their death.

[On the origin of the skull rack lords]

62 : 11   Reportedly, *tzompanteuctin* [lords of the skull rack] is another way of saying *nahualteuctin* [magician lords]. Here is their story—of how these skull rack lords originated, came to be, came into existence.[470] They have many accounts of how sorcerers, or devils, came to deceive people; and in these [accounts] they trace their ancestry to the one called Mixcoatl, also known as White Mixcoatl or Mixcoatl the younger.[471] In the story about him,[472] so it goes, they [the sorcerers] descended on Colhuacan, etc. Well, [Mixcoatl] circled nine times around Anahuac, and no place was pleasing to him. Then he came back;[473] and once there, he came traveling along, and at the wayside he went in.[474]

62 : 20   Then he:
           came to Tecoac,
62 : 21   came to Zacatzontitlan,
           came to Cuauhyacac,
62 : 22   came to Tetzcoco,
           came to Coatlichan,
           came to Chicualoapan,
62 : 23   came to Aticpac, on the far side of [Mount] Cuexomatl,
           came to Tepotoniloyan,
62 : 24   came to Teyayahualco,

---

470. GLOS: yauh/nemi.
471. Lit., Many are their accounts of how sorcerers, devils, came to deceive people; therein they are derived [or they derive themselves] from the one called Mixcoatl, the one named White Mixcoatl, Mixcoatl the younger. GLOS: -itolloca, oncan, ana:mo.
472. Read *oncā ytolloca* (cf. line 62:15: oncan).
473. Came back to the Valley of Mexico? Cf. 62:27 below.
474. Lit., when he went to the wayside, he went in. For *onallac* read *oncallac*. Cf. *ocalla-quico* in line 62:27.

came to Omeacac,
came to Itzcalpan.

62 : 25   And then he reached Atempan.

He came upon the place where the Comalteca were,[475] [and] the Maquizteca, at the time that Tecoma was ruling, and also Maquiztli. The Comalteca were in Chilpan.

62 : 27   Now, when he had made his entry here,[476] he came out into the lake, into the Cuitlahuac marshes. And when he got there, he bled himself. He was on rafts made of reed. And there a person, a vassal, was born. And thereafter, wherever [this person] went, the one who had become his father, whose name was Terror,[477] led the way for him; they were always together.[478]

62 : 32   And to this living person who had been created from his blood-leavings Mixcoatl at first gave the name Driblet. And when [Driblet] grew up, he took a wife.

62 : 34   And then, one named Raccoon was born. And when he grew up, he took a wife.

62 : 36   Then Spirit Guide was born.

These, the three sons of the devil Mixcoatl, sprang to life and were born from his own blood. As yet they were not very human. Daybreak had not yet come.[479]

62 : 39   And then, those who were born later were already human:

62 : 40   Then Zonelteuctli[480] was born.

Then Calli Teuctli [House Lord] was born.

62 : 41   Then Pilli Teuctli [Prince Lord] was born.

Then Malintzin, a female, was born, and she too was a skull rack lord.

62 : 42   And then Atzin Teuctli was born.

62 : 43   And then Quetzal Teuctli was born. And this Quetzal Teuctli was the very one who divided the magician lords into four groups, establishing Tizic, Teopancalcan, Tecpan, and Atenchicalcan. Then he, Quetzal Teuctli, ruled them as their lord.

62 : 47   And when he died, Malpantzin Teuctli was inaugurated.

---

475. Mixcoatl's visit to the Comalteca is briefly described in lines 80 : 17–21 below.

476. We are picking up the story left off in line 62 : 20.

477. Evidently the Cuitlahuaca god Mixcoatl was named Terror (*tetzauh*), just as the Mexica god Huitzilopochtli: "auh in Vitzilobuchtli: no mjtoaia tetzauitl" (And Huitzilopochtli was also called Terror) (FC 3 : 5 : 3).

478. Lit., And thereafter everywhere that he came in order to come forth, he came leading him, he who came along having become his father, whose name was Terror, who kept accompanying him.

479. Cf. lines 1 : 54–55: "During these years that the [early] Chichimecs lived . . . there was still darkness."

480. Should *çonelteuctli* be read as *conelteuctli*, i.e., *conetl teuctli* [Baby Lord]? On the replacement of *tl* by *l*, see GRAM sec. 3.7.

62 : 48   Upon his death, Quetzalmazatzin was inaugurated. This was the one who faced the Tenochca when Itcoatzin ruled.[481]

62 : 50   When Quetzalmazatzin died, Tlazolteotzin was inaugurated. Then he went and fetched the daughter of Moteuczomatzin the elder, called Yohuatzin.

63 : 1   And when Tlazolteotzin died, Maquizpantzin, the grandson of Moteuczomatzin, was inaugurated.

63 : 3   And upon his death, Quetzalmazatzin [the second] was inaugurated. It was with him that the lineage of the magician lords came to an end. This one, this Quetzalmazatzin, was [one of] two sons of Yohuatzin. Maquizpantzin was the older [of the two]. And the one who was put to death was the one called Quetzalmazatzin.[482]

63 : 7   Those whose names have been listed here are all the former Cuitlahuac residents, now passed away, who became skull rack lords.[483] The first of these to arrive, Mixcoatl, who was called White Mixcoatl or Mixcoatl the younger, made a circuit of the lands he claimed, in order to establish his boundaries.[484] He began with:

63 : 12   Techichco,
then the home of Chalchiuhtamazolin [Jade Toad],
then Pantitlan,

63 : 13   then Aticpac,
then at[?] Xochiquilazyo,

63 : 14   then at[?] Ocoyo,
then at[?] the *xiuhteteuctin* [fire lords],
then Techimalco,

63 : 15   then Tzitzintepec,
then Texcalyacac,
then Ayauhcontitlan,

63 : 16   then Amoxpan,
then Nahualliiapan,

63 : 17   then the abode of Iztaccoatl,
then Mizquic,
then Xictlan,

63 : 18   then Acuacualachco,
then Cuatizatepec,
then Texopeco,

481. On the war between Cuitlahuac and Tenochtitlan see lines 48 : 10 – 15 and 49 : 4 – 14 above.

482. Put to death by Moteuczomatzin the younger. See 61 : 52.

483. Lit., all who pass away having become skull rack lords who were Cuitlahuac residents. On the *-hui* of *mochiuhtihui* see NED: yauh 4.

484. Lit., in order to set up boundaries for himself he made a circuit of that which he appropriated to serve as land for himself.

63 : 19   then Cuacuicuilco,
          then Tetlpozteccan,
63 : 20   then Tlaltetelpan,
          then Moyotepec,
          then Techcuauhtitlan,
63 : 21   then Tennecuilco,
          then Teoztoc.
          There it comes [back] to join Techichco.

[The reign of Moteuczomatzin the younger, continued: A.D. 1517–18]

63 : 22   The year 12 House [1517] was also when they went and got Texo-cuauhtli Totec, who represented the Devil, and brought him to Mexico.

63 : 25   13 Rabbit [1518]. In that year the above-mentioned Huexotzinca who had emigrated to Mexico—Xayacamachan, Miztliima, Ixtehueyo, Yauhque-mepotonqui, and Tezcatlpopoca—turned toward home.

63 : 28   Well, Moteuczomatzin had taken their countrywoman and had made her his concubine.

63 : 29   Now, when it had been three years since they had come to Mexico and they were ready to go, they counseled together, and when they had decided on it, the one called Ixtehueyo said, "Indeed, we comrades[485] must flee. We must go tomorrow night."

63 : 32   Then the ruler [Moteuczomatzin] heard about it, etc., and he gave orders for them to be placed under surveillance when the time came for them to leave. Then they went off to be ambushed in Amaquemecan. Well, it was for this purpose, then, that they were being trailed, and they were assassinated there at Cuauhtechcac,[486] etc.

[Four eras]

63 : 36   At first the seats of rule were Tollan, Cuauhchinanco, Cuauhnahuac, Huaxtepec, Cuahuacan.

63 : 37   When it came to an end, there was still rulership in Azcapotzalco, Colhuacan, Coatlichan.

63 : 38   Then, when it came to an end, the rule was in Tenochtitlan Mexico, Tetzcoco Acolhuacan, Tlacopan Tepanohuayan.

63 : 40   Then the Spaniards arrived.

485. See GLOS: icniuhtli.
486. The pass between Iztactepetl and Popocatepetl (FC bk. 12, ch. 12), on the road from Amaquemecan to Huexotzinco.

[Realms, rulers, and tribute: ca. A.D. 1518]

63 : 41   1 Reed [1519]. In the year 1 Reed, at the time the Spaniards arrived, when they first came, in the year one thousand five hundred nineteen, A.D. 1519, the rulers of the nations were [as follows]:

63 : 44   In Tecamachalco, Acuechetzin was ruler.

In Tepeyacac, Ixcozauhqui was ruler.

63 : 45   In Cuauhquechollan, Calcozametl.

In Itzyocan, Nahuiacatl.

63 : 46   In Tenanco, Tlacayaotzin.

In Amaquemecan, Cacamatzin.

63 : 47   In Chalco, Itzcahuatzin.

In Huaxtepec, Tizapapalotzin.

63 : 48   In Cuauhnahuac, Yaomahuitzin.

In Mizquic, Chalcayaotzin.

63 : 49   In Xochimilco, Tlatolcaltzin.

Cuitlahuac:[487] in Aten[chicalcan], Mayehuatzin; in Tizic, Atlpopocatzin; in Teopancalcan, Ixtotomahuatzin; in Tecpan, Cempohualxochitzin.

63 : 51   [Mexico's Four Lords:][488] in Itztapalapan, Cuitlahuatzin; in Mexicatzinco, Tochihuitzin; in Colhuacan, Tezozomoctzin; in Huitzilopochco, Huitzilatzin.

63 : 52   In Coyohuacan, Cuappopocatzin.

63 : 53   In Tlacopan, Totoquihuatzin.

In Azcapotzalco, Teuhtlehuacatzin.

63 : 54   In Tenayocan, Moteuczomatzin.

In Ecatepec, Panitzin.

63 : 55   In Matlatzinco, Mazacoyotzin.

In Cempohuallan, Don Juan Tlacochcalcatl.

63 : 56   In Nauhtlan, Coatlpopoca.

In Tlaxcallan, Xicotencatl.

63 : 57   In Cholollan, Temetzin.

In Huexotzinco, Quecehuatl.

64 : 1   In Calpan, Teohua.

In Chiucnauhtlan, Tlaltecatl.

In Acolman, Coyoctzin.

64 : 2   In Teotihuacan, Mamalitzin.

In Otompan, Cuechimaltzin.

64 : 3   In Huexotla, Tzontemoctzin.

In Coatlichan, Xaquin Teuctli.

64 : 4   In Toltitlan, Citlalcoatl.

---

487. On the fourfold division of Cuitlahuac see lines 62:43–47 above.
488. On the Four Lords allied with Mexico see 50:29.

In Tepexic, Ayocuan.

In Tepotzotlan, Quinatzin.

64 : 5 In Apazco, Matlalihuitzin.

In Xippacoyan Tollan, Xochitzetzeltzin.

64 : 6 In Xilotepec, Imexayac.

In Chiapan, Acxoyatl.

64 : 7 In Xocotitlan, Ocelotzin.

In Cuauhtitlan, Aztatzontzin; its Four Lords[489] were Tzompanco, Citlaltepec, Huehuetocan, Otlazpan; its dependencies were Toltitlan, Tepexic, Tepotzotlan—these were its great land, its dominion, its estate.

64 : 10 Apazco controlled twenty towns, [also?] Tollan controlled [the?] twenty towns.[490] Apazco started the dynasty—there was Atlapopocatzin.[491] As for Don Juan Matlalihuitzin,[492] he had a sister in Tezcacoac who married Aztatzontzin [and] a daughter who was the wife of Pablo Yaotlamin. Those who ruled in Tollan were Iztauhyatli, Ixtlilcuechahuac, Don Pedro Tlacahuepantzin.

64 : 17 The rulers of Tetzcoco had this many years: Nezahualcoyotzin, forty-two years; Nezahualpiltzintli, forty-six years. Here are [towns] that were reserved for Tetzcoco: 1. Cuauhnahuac, 2. Atlpoyecan, 3. Miacatlan, 4. Mazatepec, 5. Tlaquiltenanco, 6. Zacatepec, 7. Olintepec, 8. Ocopetla-pan, 9. Huehuetlitzalan.

64 : 22 Names of "months" [in which tribute was deposited?]:

64 : 23 Tlacaxipehualiztli [the second "month"]:

400 arrowhead-serpent tilmas.[493]

400 black wide ones.

64 : 24 400 embroidered-serpent tilmas.

400 fine ones, bordered ones.

64 : 25 Etzalcualiztli [the sixth "month"]:

200 eye-spotted *cacamoliuhqui* skirts.[494]

64 : 26 Tecuilhuitl [the seventh "month"]:

100 flood-painted tilmas.[495]

100 breechcloths.

489. GLOS: nauhteuctli.

490. Twenty tribes associated with Tollan are listed in Kirchhoff et al., pp. 131–32. For discussion see Davies, pp. 302–12.

491. Ruler of Apazco (see García Granados, *Diccionario*).

492. Ruler of Apazco when the Spaniards arrived (?, see line 64 : 5 above).

493. Not included among the many decorated tilmas mentioned in FC bk. 8 (especially ch. 8). That source, however, does name the *itzmjxicalcoliuhquj* (arrowhead . . . ?) tilma and the *itzcoaio* (blade-serpent) tilma. See FC 8 : 74 : 9 and 8 : 47 : 11 (cf. TEZ ch. 87: mantas . . . de culebras *Ytzcoayo*).

494. GLOS: ixtecuicuiliuhqui, cacamoliuhqui.

495. Sahagún (FC bk. 8, ch. 8) names the *teuatl tlachinoltilmatli* (flood-and-blaze tilma). On "flood and blaze" see note to line 36 : 36 above.

64 : 27 Ochpaniztli [the eleventh "month"]:
400 arrowhead-serpent tilmas.
400 black wide ones.
400 arrowhead-serpent tilmas.
400 pitch-black-roundel flood [tilmas].[496]

64 : 29 Quecholli [the fourteenth "month"]:
100 flood-painted tilmas.
100 breechcloths.

64 : 30 Panquetzaliztli [the fifteenth "month"]:
200 *cacamoliuhqui* skirts and huipils [and?] their overdresses[?].

64 : 31 200 *cacamoliuhqui* tilmas.

64 : 32 Tetzcoco [and] all the realm [of] Nezahualcoyotzin and Nezahualpiltzintli: Huexotla, Coatlichan, Chimalhuacan, Otompan, Teotihuacan,
Tepetlaoztoc, Acolman, Tepechpan, Tezonyocan Tetzcoco, Chiauhtla Tetzcoco, Chiucnauhtlan, Tollantzinco, Cuauhchinanco, Xicotepec, Pantlan.

64 : 37 Those who paid tribute here [i.e., to Tetzcoco?]: Coatepec, Itztapallo-
can, Papalotlan Tetzcoco, Xaltocan, Ahuatepec, Oztoticpac, Axapochco,
Aztaquemecan, Tizayocan, Tlallanapan,[497] Tepepolco, Coyoac, Oztotl,
Tlatlauhyan,[498] Achichilacachocan, Tetliztacan, Tliltzapoapan, Tecpan,
Mollanco,[499] Tanchol, Xococapan, Tamazollan, Teocuauhtla, Chamollan,
Chicontepec, Teonochtlan, Teccizapan, Zozotetlan, Xochimilco, Ahu-
atlan, Cozcatecotlan, Ayacachtepec, Tecatlan, Xicallanco, Palzoquitlan,
Cuachicol, Tonallan, Tamaoc, Cozoquentlan, Tlapalichcatlan, Cihuatlan,
Tlacotepec, Tziuhcoac, Macuextlan, Tlapacoyan, Tlatlauhquitepec.

64 : 48 Tribute from towns everywhere was divided into three parts, for Mexico, for Tetzcoco, for Tlacopan. The tribute:

64 : 50 3200 [i.e., 8 X 400] Tochpaneca-style[500] tilmas, each eight fathoms
long.
400 [tilmas, as follows:] multicolored tilmas called *centzontilmatli*,[501]

496. Or, "pitch-black-swirl [tilmas] of the flood variety" (cf. the flood-painted tilmas of
line 64:26). Among the decorated tilmas made by the Cuexteca, Sahagún mentions "las que
dize ixnextlacujlolli, pintadas de remolinas, de agua enxeridos vnas, con otros" (CF bk. 10,
ch. 29, fol. 135v).

497. Several of these names are run together in the manuscript. My reading follows similar tribute rolls given in IXT 1:334, 1:436, 2:114; cf. IXT 1:382–84.

498. But the punctuation in the text implies that Oztotl Tlatlauhyan (cavern adoratory)
is a single place. Cf. Concordance: Oztotl.

499. The punctuation in the text implies Tecpan Mollanco, a single place. Elsa Ziehm
(personal communication) points out that Tecpan Molonco could mean "ruined palace." See
Concordance: Mollanco, Tecpan.

500. Tochpan is described as a "gran provincia" (IXT 2:107) on the "costa del mar del
norte" (IXT 2:15).

501. The varicolored *centzontilmatli* (myriad tilmas) were made by the Cuexteca
(CF bk. 10, ch. 29, sec. entitled "Cuexteca").

also cotton tilmas, also bordered [tilmas], also black wide ones—a hundred of each. [Thus] the first four hundred.

64 : 53   400 of the same, known as the second tribute, the second four hundred.

1600 [i.e., 4 X 400] skirts and huipils [and?] their overdresses[?], embroidered ones.

1200 [i.e., 3 X 400] [tilmas, as follows:] knot [tilmas],[502] multicolored ones, fine ones—four hundred of each of these.

65 : 1   1200 [i.e., 3 X 400] painted ones, ones with the jaguar head, ones with the *olintecciztli*.[503]

65 : 2   5 bales of feathers.[504]

5 bales of *axin*.[505]

65 : 3   20 Cuexteca slaves.

65 : 4   Those who worked for the Mexica:

65 : 5   ¶ Atecpan, Ixicayan, Tlapallitlan, Tozpantlan, Yeiitzcuintlan, Atlxoxouhcan, Itzmatla,[506] Cemacac, Ometlan, Tecolotlan, Mazaapan, Cuaxipetztenantlan, Tepetlapan, Coaapan, Cihuateotitlan,

65 : 8   ¶ Teteltitlan, Cuauhtzapotitlan, Chinamecan, Citlalpollan, Pantzontlan, Tlacoxochitla, Itzmatla, Teotitlan, Chiucnahuac, Ollan, Tizapan,

65 : 10   ¶ Tlatoloyan, Amatzcalapan, Ichcapetlacotla, Cuauhtlaacapan, Chiconcoac, Xochiquentlan, Iyactecuizotlan, Mazatlan, Tlazohuallan, Tochmilco, Cozcacuauhtlan, Tochpan,

65 : 13   ¶ Ahuitzilco, Moyotlan, Cuaxipetztecomatlan, Tetlpozteccan, Micquetlan,

65 : 14   ¶ Apachicuauhtla, Tecomaapan, Tetlmopaccan, Miahuaapan,

65 : 15   ¶ Totollocan, Miztontlan, Patoltetitlan, Ayotepec, Cuauhcalapan, Ocelotepec,

65 : 16   ¶ Eztecallan, Pollotlan, Coyochimalco, Xochimilco, Cuauhtzapotla, Tolapan, Quetzalcoatonco, Coatlachco, Cuauhcalco, Huiloc, Omacatlan, Tozpotonco, Pohuazanco, Papatlan,

65 : 19   ¶ Tlamacaztlan, Xochititlan, Mollanco, Xollan, Teuctonallan.

65 : 20   Here is how tribute from towns everywhere was divided:

502. A *tlalpilli* (knot) tilma, with its broad border enclosing a design of five large loops, or knots, is shown on fol. 5 of the Codex Magliabechiano (where it is evidently mislabeled—see Boone 173: tlalpilli).

503. Lit., movement conch, or movement snail. (Several tilmas with conch designs are illustrated in the Codex Mendoza tribute lists.)

504. Or, "5 X 8000 [= 40,000] feathers."

505. Possibly the author is thinking of the Spanish term *axi* (chilis), rather than the Nahuatl *axin* (a kind of unguent handled in lumps or balls). The Codex Mendoza tribute lists show bales of dried chilis ("cargas de axi seco") and, on fol. 52, bales of chilis placed next to bales of feathers—as here. GLOS: axin.

506. Note that the name is repeated in line 65:9.

65 : 21 '/. As for Tenochtitlan Mexico, here was its share:
100 eight-fathom [tilmas].
65 : 22 100 four-fathom [tilmas].
200 serpent tilmas.
200 cotton tilmas.
400 skirts and huipils are deposited [and] their overdresses[?].
65 : 23 400 twist-woven bands of fabric are deposited.[507]
400 bordered ones, [tilmas with] colored borders, are deposited.
65 : 24 400 breechcloths, fine ones, are deposited.
65 : 25 400 red-[painted palm-fiber] mats.
Coyote skins are deposited.[508]
100 ducks.[509]
100 loads of mosquito chilis.[510]
65 : 26 100 loads of cotton.
100 turkeys.
40 loads of rabbit [and] deer are deposited.
65 : 27 20 loads of sea salt—20.
10 female slaves.
65 : 28 '/. As for Nezahualpilli of Tetzcoco, his share was:
65 : 29 5 twenties of eight-fathom [tilmas] = 100.
5 twenties of four-fathom [tilmas] = 100.
10 twenties of serpent tilmas = 200.
65 : 30 10 twenties of fine [tilmas] = 200
400 skirts and huipils are deposited [and?] their overdresses[?].
65 : 31 400 twist-woven bands of fabric are deposited.
400 bordered ones, [tilmas with] colored borders, are deposited.
65 : 32 400 breechcloths, fine ones, are deposited.
400 red-[painted palm-fiber] mats.
[Coyote?] skins are deposited.[511]
65 : 33 100 ducks.
100 loads of mosquito chilis.
100 loads of cotton.
65 : 34 100 turkeys.

507. Lit., They deposit twist-[weave] border fabric-lengths. GLOS: cahuia:tla, ilacatz-iuhqui, tlatenzotl.
508. Do the skins go with the mats? Here the copyist has separated the two items with a bullet, but not in the parallel passage in line 65:33 below.
509. Possibly duck feathers are meant, or the ducks are to be used for their feathers. In a list of tribute items from the Cuexteca, Alvarado Tezozomoc includes "plumajes que llaman *Xomome* y *chiltecpin*" (plumages which they call ducks, and mosquito chilis) (TEZ ch. 65, p. 483). See following note.
510. This tiny chili, writes Hernández, "se llama *chiltecpin* del nombre de los mosquitos, a los que parece imitar en la pequeñez y en el color" (HERN 1:138).
511. Cf. line 65:25 above.

<table>
<tr><td></td><td>40 loads of rabbit [and] deer are deposited.</td></tr>
<tr><td>65 : 35</td><td>20 loads of sea salt—20.</td></tr>
<tr><td></td><td>10 female slaves.</td></tr>
<tr><td>65 : 36</td><td>·/. As for Totoquihuatzin of Tlacopan, his share was:</td></tr>
<tr><td>65 : 37</td><td>50 eight-fathom [tilmas].</td></tr>
</table>

65 : 35

65 : 36

65 : 37

40 loads of rabbit [and] deer are deposited.
20 loads of sea salt—20.
10 female slaves.
·/. As for Totoquihuatzin of Tlacopan, his share was:
50 eight-fathom [tilmas].
50 four-fathom [tilmas].
200 serpent tilmas, fine ones.
200 skirts and huipils.

65 : 38

200 coyote-colored cotton [tilmas], fine ones.
200 multicolored cotton tilmas.

65 : 39

10 fine breechcloths.[512]
5 skins—5 twenties [= 100].
5 red-[painted palm-fiber] mats—100 [i.e., 5 twenties].
60 cranes.

65 : 40

60 loads of mosquito chilis.
60 loads of cotton.
60 turkeys.
20 loads of sea salt.
20 [loads of?] rabbit [and] deer.[513]
10 female slaves.

65 : 42

[For?] Moteuczomatzin of Tenochtitlan, Nezahualpilli of Tetzcoco, and Totoquihuaztli of Tlacopan:

65 : 44

[From?] Quechollan, Tlacoapan, Chiltepec, Poctlan, Oxitlan, Ichcatlan, Tlecuauhtla, Zoyatepec, Tzinacaoztoc, Xalapan, Otlatitlan, Tochtepec:

65 : 46

cacao, 31 loads.
achiote, 400 [seeds?].
rubber, 5 loads.[514]

[A short history of the Mexica: A.D. 1350–1518]

65 : 48

Their ruler and governor was called Acamapich. And this Acamapich ruled for fifty-four years. And at the expense of others he appropriated—

512. Should be 10 twenties?
513. Cf. lines 65 : 26 and 65 : 34 above.
514. For *cs*, read *cargas* (loads), as in line 65 : 40. Following the five loads of rubber, the manuscript has a short string of symbols evidently representing items of tribute: a stack (of wood?) or bin (of grain?) accompanied by the numeral 10, another stack (or bin?) labeled CCCC (= 400), three vessels of produce (?), and a single round pot (or twenty-day sign?). The more carefully drawn tribute items in Codex Mendoza may be compared.

he conquered—four towns. The first was Mizquic, [then] Xochimilco, Cuauhnahuac, and Cuitlahuac.

65 : 52 Now, in those days good tilmas were not made, were not known.[515] People had to wear what are today called *ayates*.[516]

65 : 55 When Acamapichtzin died, Huitzilihuitzin was installed as ruler. And he ruled for ten years. And he pacified, appropriated, and reserved for himself eight towns. The first was Tollan, [then] Cuauhtitlan, Azcapotzalco, Chalco, Otompan, Acolhuacan, Tollantzinco, and Acolman.

66 : 3 And when Huitzilihuitzin died, Chimalpopocatzin succeeded him and ruled for thirteen years.

66 : 4 And during that time the Tlatilolco ruler, whose name was Tlacateotzin, made up a story that the Mexica Tenochca were going to be attacked.[517] And because of it, this Tlacateotzin was put to death. Maxtlaton, ruler of Azcapotzalco, handed down the sentence.

66 : 9 And he [Maxtlaton] was also ruler at the time five Mexica were put to death in Tlacochcalco—it was the Chalca who performed the executions—and they broke three canoes to show that they would make war on the Mexica. Well, they did not wish to serve them, they did not wish to go to them on command.[518]

66 : 13 And this frightened Chimalpopoca. And, what is more, he had consulted with Tezozomoctli's son Quetzalayatzin, had urged him to have Maxtlaton, the ruler of Azcapotzalco, put to death.

66 : 16 And when Maxtlaton heard about it, he sentenced Chimalpopocatzin to die. The Tepaneca dragged him through all the streets.[519]

66 : 19 This frightened those Tenochca who believed that they would be conquered. And because of it, the Mexica called a meeting, came together and held council, pronouncing and decreeing that none of the sons, nephews, or grandsons [of the cowardly ones] would gain honor. Rather they would belong to them as vassals.

66 : 23 And that is what happened. For even though their descendants were able warriors[520] and fighters, none gained nobility and honor.

66 : 27 Now, upon the death of Chimalpopocatzin, Itzcoatzin succeeded him and ruled for twelve years. And this Itzcoatzin retook the Chalca na-

515. Lit., And at this time, the making of, the knowledge of good tilmas was not yet possessed.

516. Lit., As yet there was only this: people wrapped themselves with what are today called *ayates* (maguey-fiber cloaks). GLOS: nemi, ayatl.

517. The same phraseology is used in lines 34:5–8 above.

518. Evidently Azcapotzalco is rebelling against Tenochtitlan. On the conquest of the Azcapotzalca (i.e., Tepanohuayan) see 31:50–32:3 and 66:1; on their servitude see 47:25–27. For *iyoc* see GLOS: ihiyotl.

519. The story of this unusual execution and its aftermath is more fully told in lines 33:24–34:10 above.

520. Read *yaoquiçaya*.

tion.[521] And he put to death the Tlatilolco ruler called Cuauhtlatoatzin— he, too, for declaring war, just as Tlacateotzin had been put to death for wanting the Mexica Tenochca to be conquered.

66 : 33 And then he took back, he regained, all the nations named here, the first one being Azcapotzalco, [then] Acolhuacan, Tlacopan, Atlacuihuayan, Teocalhuiyacan, Mizquic, Cuitlahuac, Xochimilco, Coyohuacan, Mixcoac, Tetzcoco,[522] Cuauhnahuac, Xiuhtepec, Cuezallan, Yohuallan, Tepecuacuilco, Tollan, Cuauhtitlan, Tecpan, Huitzitzilapan.

66 : 41 And when Itzcoatzin died, the elder Moteuczomatzin became ruler, and he was called, his name was, Ilhuicamina. He obtained lordship, sovereignty,[523] and ruled for twenty-nine years. He was the first to build, the first to erect, the aqueduct at Chapoltepec.[524]

66 : 45 And he put to death a king, the ruler of Coaixtlahuacan, who was called Atonal, after decreeing that he would destroy the Coaixtlahuacan nation. Then began four years during which he wore his hair the way those barbarians, those Mixteca, wear their hair.[525] And the reason the ruler of Coaixtlahuacan was put to death is that he refused to serve the Mexicatl.

66 : 51 Now, this ruler counted up for himself the additional nations here named, including the Chalca nation, which he took possession of and appropriated:

66 : 53 Chalco, Chiconquiyauhco, Mamalhuazyocan, Totolapan, Atltlatlauhyan, Cuetlaxtlan, Cuauhtochco, Coaixtlahuacan, Xiuhtepec, Cuauhnahuac, Quiauhtepec, Huaxtepec, Itzyocan, Yohualtepec, Tlachco, Tepecuacuilco, Tlalcozauhtitlan, Quiauhteopan, Xilotepec, Itzcuincuitlapilco, Tlapacoyan, Chapolicxitla, Tlatlauhquitepec, Yacapichtlan.

67 : 6 And when Moteuczoma died, Axayacatzin became ruler. And it was for nine years that he ruled. And he conquered the Tlatilolca, etc., along with other nations to be named herewith—as for Tlatilolco, it was when Moquihuix was ruling that the nation was defeated:

67 : 10 Tlatilolco, Xiquipilco, Tollocan, Tzinacantepec, Tlacotepec, Calimaya, Teotenanco, Tenantzinco, Xochiyacan, Ocuillan, Metepec, Oztoman, Capolloac, Atlappolco, Tlaximaloyan, Xalatlauhco, Cuappanohuayan, Ocoyacac, Tepeyacac, Tecalco, Cuezcomaixtlahuacan, Matlatlan, Oztoticpac, Tlaollan, Ahuilizapan, Tozcauhtlan, Tototlan, Cuetlaxtlan, Cuetzaloztoc, Mixtlan, Tzapotitlan, Micquetlan, Tochpan, Tenexticpac, Tapatel, Tamomox.

---

521. Lit., And this one, Itzcoatzin, again counted for himself the nation Chalco.

522. An error? Acolhuacan (i.e., Tetzcoco) has already been named in this list.

523. Such terminology can apply to an ordinary ruler, as in line 15:7; but here it probably reflects the increased power of Mexico (see lines 48:27–31).

524. Lit., the aqueduct that comes standing at Chapoltepec. Cf. NED: yahtihca.

525. Alternate translation: Then began four years during which they [the Mexica] wore their hair the way those barbarians, those Mixteca, wear their hair. (The people of Coaixtlahuacan were Mixteca; see DHIST ch. 22.)

67 : 19   And when Axayacatzin died, Tizocicatzin was inaugurated as ruler, and he ruled for just five years. And he counted up for himself all the nations that are written here:

67 : 22   Tecaxic, Tonalliimoquetzayan, Toxico, Ecatepec, Cillan, Matlatzinco, Mazatepec, Ecatlicuappanco, Tamapachco, Micquetlan, Tlappan, Yancuitlan, Xochiyetlan, Atezcahuacan.

67 : 26   And when Tizocicatzin died, Ahuitzotzin became ruler, and he ruled for fourteen years, and he captured the nations here named—counted up his realm—and the first was Tlappan, [then] Tziuhcoac, Mollanco, Tzapotlan, Xaltepec, Tototepec, Xochtlan, Amaxtlan, Chiapan, Cozcacuauhtenanco, Xollochiyuhyan, Cozohuipillan, Coyocac, Apancallecan, Xiuhtlan, Acatliyacac, Acapolco, Totollan, Tecpantepec, Nexpan, Iztactlalocan, Teocuitlatlan, Teopochtlan, Xicochimalco, Cuauhxayacatitlan, Coyolapan, Cuauhnacaztitlan, Cuetzalcuitlapillan, Izhuatlan, Cihuatlan, Huehuetlan, Huitztlan, Xolotlan, Mazatlan, Huipillan, Tecuantepec, Ayotochcuitlatlan, Cuauhtlan, Mizquitlan, Tlacotepec, Cuappilollan.

67 : 42   And when Ahuitzotzin died,[526] then Moteuczomatzin the second was installed as ruler. And he ruled for eighteen and a half years. And the nations that he captured, conquered, are named here, beginning with a place called Achiotlan, [then] Zozollan, Teuhtepec, Nocheztlan, Tototepec, Tlanitztlan, Zoltepec, Icpatepec, Izquixochitepec, Quiauhtepec, Chichihualtatacallan, Texotlan, Piyaztlan, Ollan, Huitztlan, Tzinacantlan, Tlatlayan, Yancuitlan, Xicotepec, Toztepec, Micquetlan, Huexolotlan, Tliltepec, Nopallan, Tlalcozauhtitlan, Texopan, Itzyoyocan, Caltepec, Panco, Teochiauhtzinco, Teochiapan, Tlachquiauhco, Malinaltepec, Quimichtepec, Centzontepec, Quetzaltepec, Cuezcomaixtlahuacan, Zacatepec, Xalapan, Xaltianquizco, Yolloxonecuillan, Itzcuintepec, Iztitlan.

68 : 9   And when Moteuczomatzin was ruling, the Spaniards came here for the first time. They first appeared, arrived, at the place called Chalchiuhcueyecan.

68 : 12   And when Moteuczomatzin's overseers, the Cuetlaxtlan people, whose leader was the Cuetlaxtecatl called Pinotl,[527] became aware of this and were able to find out about it, they started off to visit these Christians. When they saw them, they took them for gods. Later, however, they called them Christians.

68 : 19   The reason they said they were gods is that this is what they called their devils 4-Wind Sun,[528] Quetzalcoatl, etc.

---

526. For *onomic* read *onmic* as in line 67 : 6.

527. The translation follows Velázquez, though the text has *ytoca cuetlaxtecatl Pinotl* (the one called Cuetlaxtecatl Pinotl). Cf. FC bk. 12, ch. 2; TEZ ch. 106.

528. 4 Wind is the name of the second sun (see line 75 : 16 below), which was Quetzalcoatl himself, according to the *Historia de los mexicanos por sus pinturas*, ch. 4. For the prophecy of Quetzalcoatl's return and his identification with the Spaniards see FC bk. 12,

68 : 22   And it was at this time that the Christians learned, were told that Moteuczoma was the great ruler yonder in Mexico. And then the Christians
sent him their greeting gift—with which they greeted Moteuczomatzin—
and those who carried it were the ones who were the overseers there, who
were the caretakers of tribute. The first, whom we have mentioned, was
the Cuetlaxtecatl named Pinotl. The second was Tentlil. The third was
Cuitlapitoc.

68 : 32   And here are the greeting gifts the Christians presented to Moteuczomatzin:[529] one green cassock; and two capes, one black, one red; and a
pair of shoes; a knife; a hat; also a cap; also a piece of cloth; also a drinking
cup; also some beads.

---

chs. 2–4 and 16; FC bk. 8, ch. 7; CM fol. 56v; "Códice Vaticanus 3738" fol. 9v: CHIM
62; IXT 2:ch. 1, p. 8; TEZ ch. 107; DHIST 2:chs. 71 and 74. For the story at hand, see
especially FC bk. 12, ch. 2, and note that the Spaniards who met the Cuetlaxtlan people were
not Cortés and his men (as stated in TEZ and DHIST) but Grijalva's party, which arrived a
year earlier, in 1518. The point is discussed by Orozco y Berra in TEZ, p. 697.

529. Compare the similar list in TEZ ch. 108, p. 690: "sartales de cristalinas cuentas
azules . . . una camisa de ruan y unos calzones y alpargates, un sombrero, y de la manera de
traer las espadas y dagas se la pusieron con su talabarte. Al cabo le dieron una cajeta de
conserva y una bota de vino y bizcocho blanco." The parallel passage in CF bk. 12, ch. 2,
fol. 4v, mentions only "cuētas de vidro, vnas verdes, y otras amarillas" (*cozcatl, xoxoctic, coztic*).

Legend of the Suns

Contents

[Preamble]

^{75 : 1} Here are wisdom tales made long ago, of how the earth was established,[1] how everything was established, how whatever is known started, how all the suns that there were began.[2]

^{75 : 4} There are 2513 years today, on the 22nd day of May, 1558.

[The first sun]

^{75 : 6} This sun was 4 Jaguar: it was 676 years. These people, who lived in the first age, were eaten by jaguars in the time of the sun 4 Jaguar, and what they ate was 7 Straw.[3] That was their food.

^{75 : 8} And it was 676 years that they lived, and thirteen years that they were eaten by the man eaters, destroyed, and finished off. Then the sun was destroyed. And their year was 1 Reed.

^{75 : 13} And when they began to be eaten, it was on a day sign 4 Jaguar, right when they were being finished off, when they were being destroyed.

[The second sun]

^{75 : 16} This sun is named 4 Wind. These people, who lived in the second [age], were blown away by the wind in the time of the sun 4 Wind. And when they were blown away and destroyed,[4] they turned into monkeys. All their houses and trees were blown away. And the sun also was blown away.

---

1. For the textual *mamaca* read *momanca*.
2. Read *inic in tzintic in izquitetl in omanca tonatiuh*.
3. Here and in lines 75:20, 75:30, and 75:41 the ancient people's foods are designated by calendric names. Similarly, in the Ruiz de Alarcón *Treatise on Superstitions*, corn is called "7 Snake" and squash is "7 Eagle" (RUIZAL 125 and 126; for a guide to figurative names in Ruiz de Alarcón see RUIZA 301–17). Although the foods in our text remain unidentified, it may be conjectured that these early staples are wild seeds or primitive grains, becoming progressively more like corn—as in variants of the myth preserved in "Códice Vaticanus 3738," "Histoyre du Mechique," and "Historia de los mexicanos por sus pinturas" (for discussion see Moreno, "Los cinco soles," p. 205).
4. Anticlimactic word order reversed in the translation.

75 : 20   And what they ate was 12 Snake. That was their food.

75 : 21   It was 364 years that they lived, and only one day that they were blown by the wind, destroyed on a day sign 4 Wind. And their year was 1 Flint.

[The third sun]

75 : 25   This sun is 4 Rain. These people[5] lived in the third one,[6] in the time of the sun 4 Rain. And the way they were destroyed is that they were rained on by fire. They were changed into turkeys.

75 : 27   And the sun also burned. All their houses burned.

75 : 28   And it was 312 years that they lived. But when they were destroyed, it rained fire for only one day.

75 : 30   And what they ate was 7 Flint. That was their food. And their year was 1 Flint. And it was on a day sign 4 Rain. And when they died they were children. Therefore today they are called the baby children.

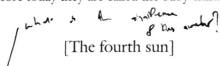

[The fourth sun]

75 : 34   This sun is named 4 Water. And for fifty-two years there was water.

75 : 35   These people lived in the fourth one,[7] in the time of the sun 4 Water. And it was 676 years that they lived. And they died by drowning. They turned into fish.

75 : 39   The skies came falling down. They were destroyed in only one day.

75 : 40   And what they ate was 4 Flower. That was their food.

75 : 41   And their year was 1 House. And it was on a day sign 4 Water that they were destroyed. All the mountains disappeared.

75 : 43   And the water lay for fifty-two years.

75 : 44   And when their years were complete,[8] then Titlacahuan gave a command to the one called Tata,[9] and to his wife, who was called Nene. He said to them, "Put aside your cares.[10] Hollow out a big cypress, and when it's Tozoztli [April] and the skies come falling down, get inside."

5. *Inic ei*, for *inique i*. Cf. line 75:35.

6. *Ic etlamanti nenca*. See following note.

7. *Ic nauhtlamanti nenca* (lived in the fourth one). The expected form is *ic nauhtlamantli nenca*. Lehmann writes *ic nauhtlamantinenca*.

8. That is, when they were to be destroyed (prior to the fifty-two years).

9. *Intoca nata*. Read *itoca tata*, following Velázquez, who points out that the form is *tata* at 76:6.

10. Lit., Don't care about anything anymore (GLOS: tlazotla:tla). Following Horcasitas, the free translation would be "Don't work anymore" ("An Analysis of the Deluge Legend in Mesoamerica," p. 195). In modern folkloric variants the man has been trying to clear his

75 : 49 And so they got inside. Then he sealed them in and said, "You must eat only one of these corn kernels.[11] Also your wife must eat only one." Well, when they had eaten it all up, they went aground.

75 : 51 It can be heard that the water is drying. The log has stopped moving. Then it opens. They see a fish. Then they drill fire and cook fish for themselves.

76 : 2 Then the gods Citlalinicue and Citlalatonac looked down and said, "Gods, who's doing the burning? Who's smoking the skies?"[12]

76 : 5 Then Titlacahuan, Tezcatlipoca, came down and scolded them. He said, "What are you doing, Tata? What are you people doing?"

76 : 7 Then he cut off their heads and stuck them on their rumps, and that way they were turned into dogs.[13]

[Origin of the new-fire ceremony]

76 : 8 Now, it was in a year 2 Reed that the skies were [again] smoked. This is how we ourselves exist, how the fire drill ignited.

76 : 10 When the sky was established was in a year 1 Rabbit.[14] [Yes,] this is how[15] the fire drill ignited, when fire appeared [for the new-fire ceremony].[16]

---

land, but the trees he cuts down keep rising up again; finally, in one version, a spirit appears to him, saying, "Don't work anymore, because the world is coming to an end." See Paredes, *Folktales of Mexico*, no. 1 (version told in Spanish by an Otomi of Nahua ancestry in Tlaxco, Puebla); other variants are summarized and discussed in Horcasitas, "An Analysis of the Deluge Legend." For still further variants see Bierhorst, *Mythology of Mexico and Central America*, p. 215.

11. In a modern Nahuatl variant from San Pedro Jícora the man, unaccompanied by a wife, loads the hollowed-out log with corn and other supplies, then seals himself in: *kuakin ya ukalak kuakin umutsákua kual kipepetx in puerta* (when he has entered, then he closes himself in; then he sealed the door thoroughly) (Ziehm, *Nahua-Texte* 1 : 136).

12. Why are the gods annoyed? In several of the versions discussed by Horcasitas (see note above) the survivors of the flood give offense because they kindle fire before being told to do so. In other variants the problem seems to be that the survivors have eaten forbidden meat; either the fish represents the inhabitants of the previous world (implying cannibalism) or it is said to be carrion (fit for animals, not humans). In a few of the variants Heaven is annoyed simply because someone has survived a destruction that was supposed to have been total.

13. Read *chichime*.

14. The author alludes to a story he has not told. Recall that the skies came falling down in line 39 : 39 above. Afterward, according to the variant in HMPP ch. 5, Tezcatlipoca and Quetzalcoatl changed themselves into a pair of tall trees and lifted the sky to its present position; when this occurred, "the year was Rabbit."

15. Read *izcatqui inic*.

16. The somewhat fuller statement in HMPP ch. 6 has it that Tezcatlipoca—in a year "Reed," the second year after the flood—originated the custom of drawing fire from the fire

76 : 12   Now, it was dark for twenty-five years.[17]

76 : 14   Well, it was in the year 1 Rabbit that the sky was established. And when it had been established, the dogs sent up smoke, as mentioned above. And after the fire drill had ignited—after Tezcatlipoca had drilled fire—he smoked the skies once more, and this was in a year 2 Reed.

[The restoration of life]

76 : 18   And then the gods talked to each other and said, "Who will there be? Sky has been established, Tlalteuctli has been established. Gods, who will there be?" They were sad. Citlalinicue, Citlalatonac, Apanteuctli, Tepan-quizqui, Tlallamanqui, Huictlolinqui, Quetzalcoatl, and Titlacahuan [were their names].

76 : 22   Then Quetzalcoatl went to the dead land, and when he came to the dead land lord, the dead land lady, he said to him, "I've come for the precious bones that you are keeping. I've come to get them."

76 : 25   Then he said, "To do what, Quetzalcoatl?"

76 : 26   And he answered him, "It's because the gods are sad. Who will there be on earth?"

76 : 27   The dead land lord replied, "Very well. Blow my conch horn and circle four times around my precious realm." But his conch horn was not hollow.

76 : 30   Then he summoned worms, who hollowed it out. Then bumblebees and honeybees went in. Then he blew on it, and the dead land lord heard him.

76 : 32   Then the dead land lord answered, "Very well, take them!" But he said to his messengers, the dead land people, "Spirits, go tell him he has to leave them here."

76 : 35   But Quetzalcoatl said, "No, I'm taking them forever."

76 : 36   And then his nagual said to him, "Tell them, 'I'll leave them [with you].'"

76 : 38   Then he said to them, he shouted to them,[18] "I'll leave them [with you]!" and he quickly ascended.

76 : 39   Then he takes the precious bones. The male bones are in one pile, the female bones are in another pile. Then Quetzalcoatl takes them, wraps them up, and comes carrying them off.

---

drill; "and when the flame had been drawn, it was the festival of making many and large fires." (For descriptions of the ceremony, held every fifty-two years, see FC 4 : 143–44 and FC bk. 7, ch. 9; and note the "year-bundle" feasts, always in 2 Reed, mentioned above in lines 11 : 25, 29 : 51, 51 : 27, and 60 : 5.)

17. This agrees with HMPP ch. 7, which explains that the sun was created in the twenty-sixth year after the flood.

18. Lit., to him.

76 : 42   Again, the dead land lord said to his messengers, "Spirits, Quetzalcoatl is really taking the precious bones away. Spirits, go dig him a pit." Then they went and dug it for him.

76 : 44   So he fell into the pit, stumbled and fell, and quail frightened him and he lost consciousness.

76 : 46   Then he spilled the precious bones, and the quail bit into them, nibbled them.

76 : 47   And when Quetzalcoatl came to, he cried. Then he said to his nagual, "My nagual, how will they be?"

76 : 49   And he said to him, "How will they be? They've been ruined. Let them go that way."[19]

76 : 50   Then he gathered them together, picked them up, wrapped them. Then he carried them to Tamoanchan. And when he had brought them, the one named Quilaztli, Cihuacoatl, ground them up. Then she put them into a jade bowl, and Quetzalcoatl bled his penis on them.

76 : 54   Then all the gods, who have been mentioned, did penance: Apanteuctli, Huictlolinqui, Tepanquizqui, Tlallamanac, Tzontemoc, and number six[20] is Quetzalcoatl.

77 : 2   Then they said, "Holy ones, humans, have been born."[21] It's because they did penance for us.

[The discovery of corn]

77 : 3   Again, they said, "Gods, what will they eat? Let food be looked for."

77 : 4   Then the ant went and got a kernel of corn out of Food Mountain, and Quetzalcoatl met the ant and said, "Where did you get it? Tell me."

77 : 6   But it won't tell him. He insists. Then it says, "Over there," and it shows him the way.

77 : 8   Then Quetzalcoatl changed into a black ant.

19. Hence the origin of mortality? (an interpretation offered in Bierhorst, *Four Masterworks*, p. 69; cf. RUIZAL 371). But according to the variant in "Histoyre du Mechique" (pp. 26–27), the bones were those of giants that had formerly inhabited the earth (cf. line 2:31 above); the accident, therefore, explains why people today are small, compared to the giants. Mendieta's version (bk. 2, ch. 1; adapted in Clavijero, bk. 6, ch. 2) has it that the accident resulted in broken bones of different sizes, thus explaining why some people are tall and others are short. An incantation for treating fractures evidently alludes to this myth, saying, " . . . Lord Quail! What are you doing with this Dead Land bone that you've splintered, that you've shattered? . . . " (. . . tecuçoline . . . tlen tic-aitia in mictlanomitl: in oticpoztec, in oticxamani. . . .) (RUIZ 163, RUIZA 267–68).

20. Lit., someone's six, a peculiar but seemingly feasible solution proposed by Velázquez. Lehmann reads *techiquaçeca* as a proper name.

21. The translation follows Garibay, *Literatura de los aztecas*, p. 20 ("¡Dioses nacieron: son los hombres!"). Lehmann has "Gods and men have been born." Velázquez's "Born are the vassals of the gods" and Garibay's "Men have been born of gods" (*Epica náhuatl*, p. 27) seem incorrect.

77:9   It shows him the way, and he goes inside. Then they carry it out together.

77:10   The red ant, it seems, showed Quetzalcoatl the way.

77:11   Outside he lays down the kernels, then he carries them to Tamoanchan. Then the gods chew them and put them on our lips.

77:13   That's how we grew strong.

77:14   Then they said, "What will we do with Food Mountain?" Then Quetzalcoatl went and tried to carry it, tied it with ropes, but he couldn't lift it.

77:16   Then Oxomoco counted it out,[22] and Oxomoco's wife, Cipactonal, also counted its fate. The woman is Cipactonal.[23]

77:18   Then Oxomoco and Cipactonal said, "Nanahuatl will strike Food Mountain," for they had counted it out.

77:20   Then all the tlalocs are summoned, blue tlalocs, white tlalocs, yellow tlalocs, red tlalocs.

77:22   Then Nanahuatl strikes it,[24] and the foods are stolen by the tlalocs.[25]

77:24   The white, black, and yellow [corn], the red corn, the beans, the amaranth, the chia, the fish amaranth, all the foods were stolen.

[The fifth sun]

77:27   This sun is named 4 Movement. We who live[26] today [have] this one, it's our sun, though what's here is [merely] its signification, because the sun [itself] fell into the fire, the spirit oven, at Teotihuacan.

77:30   It's the same as the sun of Topiltzin, Quetzalcoatl of Tollan. And before it was the sun, its name was Nanahuatl, whose home was yonder in Tamoanchan.

77:32   Eagle, jaguar, falcon, wolf.[27] 6 Wind, 6 Flower: both are names of the sun.

22. Lit., Then Oxomoco counted things out for it, i.e., Oxomoco counted corn kernels to divine the future of Food Mountain (MOL: tlapouia:nite = echar fuertes a otro el hechizero o agorero con mayz).

23. The author emphasizes his disagreement with the tradition that Cipactonal is the male, Oxomoco the female (FC 4:4:6: Oxomoco cioatl . . . auh in Cipactonal oqujchtli).

24. With lightning. In a modern Nahua variant of this myth, Nanahuatl (called Nanawatzin) is the captain of the thunderbolts. See Taggart, *Nahuat Myth and Social Structure*, p. 90; see also NED: nānāhuatl 3. For a full list of Middle American variants of the Hidden Corn myth, see Bierhorst, *Mythology of Mexico and Central America*, p. 215.

25. The translation agrees with both Lehmann and Velázquez but seemingly violates Carochi's rule against naming the agent of a passive verb. See GN sec. 2.2.

26. For *tonneimi* read *tonnemi*.

27. These four animals figure in the myth that is about to be told (see 77:48–52 below). In the text a small circle with rays, like a miniature sun, appears between the words for "eagle" and "jaguar."

77 : 34   Now, here is what is called the spirit oven. For four years it burned.

77 : 35   Well then, Tonacateuctli and Xiuhteuctli summoned Nanahuatl. They said to him, "You are the one who must keep the sky and the earth."

77 : 37   And then he was very sad. He said, "What are they saying? There are gods, and I am a worthless invalid!"

77 : 38   They also summoned 4 Flint, the moon. The ones who summoned him were Tlalocanteuctli and Nappateuctli.

77 : 40   And so Nanahuatl fasts. He takes his spines and his needles. Then he gives thorns to the moon, and they do penance.[28]

77 : 42   Then Nanahuatl bathes first. Afterward the moon bathes.

77 : 43   His needles are plumes, his spines are jade. He uses jade as incense.

77 : 44   And when four days have gone by, they feather Nanahuatl, and they chalk him.[29] Then he goes off to fall in the fire, and 4 Flint meanwhile sings and dances for him like a woman.

77 : 47   So Nanahuatl went off to fall in the fire. But the moon only went to fall in the ashes.

77 : 48   And so he went off. And he was able to grab the eagle and carry it along.[30]

77 : 49   But he could not carry the jaguar. It just stood next to the fire and jumped over it.[31] That's how it became spotted. At that time the falcon became smoke-colored. At that time the wolf was singed. These three were unable to go with him.

77 : 53   Well, when he got to the sky, Tonacateuctli and Tonacacihuatl bathed him. Then they sat him in a *quechol* chair. Then they adorned his head with a red border.

77 : 55   Then he tarries in the sky for four days. And then he appears on 4 Movement.

78 : 1   But he spent four days without moving, just staying in place.

Then the gods say, "Why doesn't he move?" Then they send the blade falcon, who goes and tells the sun that it has come to question him. It tells him, "The gods are saying, 'Ask him why he doesn't move.'"

78 : 4   Then the sun said, "Why? Because I'm asking for their blood, their color,[32] their precious substance."[33]

---

28. That is, they puncture themselves with the needles, or thorns, in order to draw sacrificial blood. Cf. 4:38 and 6:52 above.

29. Sacrificial victims were customarily smeared with chalk and crowned with feathers (see NED: tīzatl/ihhuitl).

30. Hence the origin of the eagle's dark plumage. See the variant at FC 7:6:12.

31. Anticlimactic word order reversed in the translation.

32. In Mendieta's variant (bk. 2, ch. 2) the sun refuses to move until the gods sacrifice themselves ("hasta haberlos muerto y destruido á ellos").

33. For *intlacoca* I read *intlaçoca[uh]*. Lehmann reads *inin tlacoca* and translates the whole phrase, "I'm asking for the noble blood of those who did the damage."

78 : 6 Then the gods hold council. And then Tlahuizcalpanteuctli grows angry. He says, "Well, why is this? I'll shoot him! He must not stay put!"

78 : 8 Then he shoots him. But he failed to hit him.

78 : 9 Meanwhile the sun is shooting at Tlahuizcalpanteuctli, and he succeeds in hitting him because his arrows are like shafts of flame. And then the nine layers[34] covered up his face.

78 : 11 This Tlahuizcalpanteuctli is the frost.

78 : 12 Then all the gods get together: Titlacahuan, Huitzilopochtli, and the women Xochiquetzal, Yapalliicue, Nochpalliicue. And there[35] in Teotihuacan they all died a sacrificial death. So then the sun went into the sky.

78 : 16 And then goes the moon, who had fallen only in the ashes. And when he got to the edge of the sky, Papaztac came and broke his face with a rabbit pot.[36]

78 : 18 And then at a crossroads he met the *tzitzimime*, the *coleletin*, and they said to him, "Come here." They detained him for a long while, dressing him all in rags.

78 : 21 And so it was the sun of 4 Movement that appeared at that time. And at that time, too, he established nightfall.

[How the sun was given a drink]

78 : 24 Now, Mixcoatl[37] lived for thirty-nine years, and his wife was named Chimalman.

78 : 26 And Topiltzin had fifty-six years.[38] It was in 1 Reed, certainly, that he traveled, that he went away, that he left his city, Tollan. And it was 4 Rabbit when he died, in Tlapallan.

78 : 30 It was in a year 1 Flint that the Mixcoa were born. The way it happened,

34. "Nine layers" refers to the heavens in line 4:46 above. But it may also refer to the underworld (see NED: chiucnāuhixtlāhuatl).

35. Read *in ye oncan*.

36. Hence the origin of the supposed rabbit image on the face of the moon. In Sahagún's variant of the myth, one of the gods strikes the moon not with a "rabbit pot" but with a rabbit per se (FC 7:7:28). The rabbit pot, *tochtecomatl*, is mentioned by Sahagún in a quite different context: it was used as the vessel in a wine-drinking ceremony, in which the singer-participants were called *centzontotochtin*, four hundred rabbits, a group of spirits associated with wine (FC 2:194:3, cf. FFCC 1:24:7).

37. Labeled pictographs in the manuscript at this point show Mixcoatl and Chimalman and their son Topiltzin, also the town of Tollan, the mountain Xicococ, and four houses named *cohuacalli* (serpent house), *teocuitlacalli* (gold house), *chalchiuhcalli* (jade house), and *xiuhcalli* (turquoise house). Two additional glyphs, both simple squares, are labeled *ce tecpatl* (1 Flint) and *ce Acatl* (1 Reed). Immediately above the *ce Acatl* glyph are the words *52 años* (52 years).

38. Topiltzin, also called Ce Acatl or Quetzalcoatl, was the son of Mixcoatl and Chimalman (see 80:43–51 below).

Iztacchalchiuhtlicue gave birth to four hundred Mixcoa, then she went into a cave. And when they had gotten into the cave, their mother delivered again, and five more Mixcoa were born. The first is named Cuauhtliicoauh, the second is named Mixcoatl, the third is a female named Cuitlachcihuatl, the fourth is named Tlotepe, the fifth is named Apanteuctli.

78 : 38 And when they were born, they entered the water,[39] put themselves in the water, spent four days in water. And when they came out, Mecitli suckled them. This Mecitli is Tlalteuctli. And so we today who are Mexica are not really Mexica but Mecitin.

79 : 2 And then the sun commands the four hundred Mixcoa: he gives them darts and says to them, "Here is how you will give me a drink, how you will serve me"—also a shield. And the darts are precious darts. They have quetzal wings, egret wings, troupial wings, *teoquechol* wings, roseate spoonbill wings, cotinga wings. "And the one who is your mother is Tlalteuctli."

79 : 6 But they did not do as they were commanded. They just shot birds, they just played. At that point [the darts] were called bird darts.

79 : 7 And when they catch a jaguar, they do not give it to the sun. And then, when they get the jaguar, they feather themselves. And while they're feathered, they sleep with women.

79 : 10 Then they tipple on pulque and get completely drunk, completely intoxicated.

79 : 11 And then the sun commands the five who were born last: he gives them thorn darts, gives them a spirit shield, and says, "My children, pay attention. You must now destroy the four hundred Mixcoa, the ones who fail to say, 'Mother! Father!'"

79 : 15 Then they put themselves in a mesquite, and seeing them there, they say, "Who are these people that are just like us?" Then they made war on each other.

79 : 17 Then Cuauhtliicoauh went into the tree, and Mixcoatl went into the earth, and Tlotepe went into a mountain. Then Apanteuctli stood in water, and their sister, Cuetlachcihuatl, stood in a ball court.[40]

79 : 20 Then they surrounded them. None of them were in the mesquite anymore, they were in hiding, and the tree cracks and splits open on top of them, and Cuauhtliicoauh comes out from inside the tree.

79 : 24 And then there's a shaking of the earth, and out comes Mixcoatl, who had gone into the ground.

---

39. A newborn infant, bathed by the midwife, was said to "enter" the water (FC 6: 176:24).

40. The narrator seems to be punning on Cuauhtli and tree (*quahuitl*), Tlotepe and mountain (*tepetl*), Apanteuctli and *apan* (water place), Cuetlachcihuatl and *tlachco* (ball court).

79 : 25   And the mountain breaks apart, collapses,[41] and out comes Tlotepe.

79 : 26   Then the water churns, and out comes Apanteuctli.

79 : 27   And then they conquered them, destroyed them, and served the sun and gave it a drink.

79 : 29   And the few who remained came and spoke to them in order to appease them, and said, "We have annoyed you. Go to Chicomoztoc. It's your cave. Enter. It's your home. Can it still be our cave? You've ruined our cave, our home. We'll just settle at the cave's edge."

[Xiuhnel and Mimich]

79 : 34   Then two deer descend [from the sky],[42] each with two heads. And two of the Mixcoa, one named Xiuhnel, the other named Mimich, go hunting in the desert lands.

79 : 37   Xiuhnel and Mimich chase the deer, trying to shoot them, chasing them all night, all day, finally wearing them out in the evening.

79 : 40   Then they tell each other, "Come on, you build your shelter there. I'll build mine over here. Hah! Those bad ones are coming now."

79 : 41   And then the ones who had been deer passed by, now changed into women. "Xiuhneltzin! Mimichtzin!" they cried.[43] "Where are you? Come here. Come drink, come eat."

79 : 44   Hearing this, they said to each other, "Come on, don't speak to them."

79 : 46   But Xiuhnel did speak to them. He said, "Come here, sister."

79 : 47   And she answered him, "Xiuhneltzin, won't you have a drink?" And Xiuhnel drinks the blood, and then he lies next to her.

79 : 49   But when he had lain with her,[44] then she turned over on top of him and bit him, breaking open his chest.

79 : 50   Then Mimich says, "Alas, my elder brother is eaten."

79 : 51   But the other woman is calling to him. "Man-child," she says, "won't you eat?" Mimich doesn't answer. Then he uses the fire drill and makes fire. And when Mimich had made it, he rushed into it. And the woman ran after him, into the fire.

80 : 1   All night she ran after him, still running after him when it was noon. And finally, at noon, a pot cactus descended [from the sky].[45] The woman fell on top of it and got stuck.

41. Read *huitomi*.

42. The variant in HMPP (ch. 8) reads, "hubo un gran ruido en el cielo y cayó un venado de dos cabezas."

43. Read *tzatzitihui*, lit., they go shouting.

44. Lit., But when he had laid her.

45. Cf. line 79 : 35 above.

.nd when he saw that the ogress lay fallen, he shot her repeatedly, then
.ned around and came back.

80 : 5　He . . . ,[46] comes crying because his elder brother has been eaten.

[Origin of the sacred bundle]

80 : 7　Then those spirits, the *xiuhteteuctin* [fire lords], hear him, and they go
to get the woman, Itzpapalotl. Mimich leads the way. And when they get
her, they burn her.

80 : 10　And then they all shined forth: first, the blue flint shined. Second, the
white flint shined. They took the white one and wrapped it up. Third,
the yellow flint shined. They didn't take it, they just looked at it. Fourth,
the red flint shined. And again they didn't take it. Fifth, the black flint
shined. Again they didn't take it.

80 : 16　But Mixcoatl made the white flint his spirit power, and when they had
wrapped it up, he backpacked it.[47]

80 : 17　Then he goes off to make conquests in a place called Comallan, back-
packing the flint. It's his spirit power, Itzpapalotl. And when the Comalteca heard about it, they came out to meet Mixcoatl, and they laid down
food for him, just to appease him.

80 : 21　And then he went to Tecanman, and they also appeased him. They said,
"How goes it with the gentleman?[48] Let him be welcome. Well now, get
him some pulque.[49] I wouldn't hack him to pieces here!"[50]

80 : 24　And then he went to Cocyama and made conquests. And when he had
conquered in Cocyama, he went to Huehuetocan and conquered again.

46. The text has *tlamatzayantihuitz tlatzonilpitihui[t]z tlamachiotitihuitz*, lit., he comes
parting [or separating] something, comes tying something with regard to his hair, comes
marking [or designing] something. According to Velázquez, Xiuhnel is separating himself
from the woman, also binding and styling his hair. According to Lehmann, he has parted his
hair, has swept his tresses into a chieftain's coif, and is sporting designs on his flesh. Gingerich's interpretation (in "Three Nahuatl Hymns," p. 218) essentially agrees with Lehmann:
"[He comes] parting and tying his hair, painting his face." Garibay (in *Epica náhuatl*, p. 22)
gives: "va lentamente apartándose, va trenzando sus cabellos, va haciendo el afeite de pintura
de su cuerpo" (he goes slowly withdrawing [from the woman], goes braiding his hair, goes
applying cosmetic paint to his body). For me the passage is inscrutable. See GLOS: machi-
yotia:tla, matzayana:tla, tzonilpia:tla.

47. The variant story given in lines 1:15–19 above implies that the bundle contained the
"ashes" of Itzpapalotl. See also line 50:36.

48. Lit., What does the noble one do? (using the honorific form of ayi:tla, to do something). Cf. NED: chīhua:tla 2, where similar phrases carry the meaning "What ill befalls?"
or "What mishap occurs?"

49. Lit., "Get his thorns," or "Get thorns for him."

50. Following Velázquez, I read *ma nican niquitzo[l]tili*, assuming a playful allusion to
the "thorns" (i. e., pulque) of the preceding sentence. Lehmann reads *ma nican niquitzotili*,
which might be given in English as "Let me not cause him to become filthy here!"

And when he had made conquests in Huehuetocan, he went to Pochtlan and conquered once more.

[Mixcoatl and Chimalman]

80 : 29 And then Mixcoatl goes off to make conquests in Huitznahuac. Meeting the woman Chimalman, he lays down his shield and positions his darts and his dart thrower. She just stands there naked, no skirt, no blouse. And having sighted her, Mixcoatl shoots her repeatedly.

80 : 33 He shot one at her and it just went over her. She ducked.

80 : 34 The second time he shot at her,[51] it went by on one side. She just dodged.

80 : 35 The third time he shot at her, she caught it in her hand.

The fourth time he shot at her, she made it pass between her legs.

80 : 36 And when Mixcoatl had shot at her the fourth time, he turned around and went away. And the woman ran and hid in a cave, she went into a gorge.[52]

80 : 38 And again Mixcoatl adorned himself and got darts. And then he went and looked for her again, but he couldn't find her.

80 : 40 Then he killed some of the Huitznahua women, and the Huitznahua women said, "Let's go down and get her."

80 : 42 They said to her, "Mixcoatl is looking for you. Because of you, he's killing your sisters."

80 : 43 And so they fetched her, and she came to Huitznahuac. And Mixcoatl went again and met her, and again she stands there, exposing her crotch. And he lays down his shield and his darts. And again he shoots at her.

80 : 46 Again a dart went over her, and one passed by her side, and she caught one in her hand, and one went between her legs.

80 : 48 After that he took hold of her, and he lay beside this woman from Huitznahuac, this Chimalman. And with that she became pregnant.

[The deeds of Ce Acatl]

80 : 50 Now, when he was being born he gave his mother great pain for four days. And so, he was born, this Ce Acatl.

80 : 51 And no sooner has he been born than his mother dies. And Ce Acatl is brought up by Quilaztli, Cihuacoatl. When he has grown a little, he goes

51. Lit., he hurled it at her. GLOS: tlaxilia:te-tla.
52. Read *oztotl atlauhcan*.

off with his father to make conquests. And he learned war by taking captives in a place called Xihuacan.

81 : 3   Now, Ce Acatl's uncles, who are of the four hundred Mixcoa,[53] absolutely hated his father, and they killed him.

81 : 5   And when they had killed him, they went and put him in the sand.

81 : 6   So Ce Acatl looks for his father, asking, "Where's my father?"

81 : 7   Then the king vulture says to him, "They've killed your father. It's over yonder that he lies, that they've buried him."

81 : 9   So he went and dug him up and put him in his temple, Mixcoatepetl.

81 : 10   Now, his uncles, the ones who killed his father, are called Apanecatl, Zolton, and Cuilton, and they say, "How will he dedicate his temple?[54] If there's only a rabbit, if there's only a snake, we would be angry. A jaguar, an eagle, a wolf would be good."[55] And so they told him this.

81 : 14   Ce Acatl said—he told them—"All right. It shall be."

81 : 15   Then he called the jaguar, the eagle, and the wolf. He said to them, "Come, uncles. They say I must use you to dedicate my temple.[56] But you will not die. Rather you will eat the ones I use to dedicate my temple— they're those uncles of mine." And so it was without any real purpose that ropes were tied around their necks.

81 : 20   Then Ce Acatl summoned gophers. He said to them, "Uncles, come! We must dig a hole in our temple." And the gophers scratched away. They dug a hole inside it, and with that Ce Acatl entered his temple and came out at the top.

81 : 24   Now, while the uncles are saying, "We're the ones who'll drill the fire on top," they're rejoicing, having seen the jaguar, the eagle, and the wolf all in misery. And when they've recovered their presence of mind, already Ce Acatl is drilling the fire.

81 : 28   Then his uncles are furious, and off they go, Apanecatl in the lead, climbing quickly.

81 : 30   But Ce Acatl rose up and broke his head with a burnished pot, and he came tumbling down.

81 : 32   Then he seizes[57] Zolton and Cuilton. Then the animals blow [on the fire]. Then they sacrifice them.

81 : 34   They cover them with hot pepper, cut up their flesh a little. And after they've tortured them, they cut open their breasts.

---

53. Evidently among the "few who remained" after the massacre. See line 79:29 above.
54. A presumed copyist's error duplicates *in iteocal* (his temple).
55. An attempt to frustrate the hero. According to the variant in "Histoyre du Mechique" (ch. 10), his antagonists are confident he will be unable to capture these animals.
56. Read *noteocal*.
57. Read *quintzitzquia*.

81 : 37   And then Ce Acatl makes more conquests, in a place called Ayotlan.

81 : 38   When he had conquered, he went on to Chalco, to Xicco, and conquered again.

81 : 39   And having conquered, he went on to Cuixcoc, and again he conquered.

81 : 40   He went to Zacanco, conquered again, then to Tzonmolco, conquered again.

81 : 41   To Mazatzonco, conquered again. To Tzapotlan, conquered again.

81 : 43   Then he went to Acallan, crossed over the water, and conquered again,[58] and that's how he got to Tlapallan.

81 : 44   There he took sick. He was sick for five days, then he died.

81 : 46   Well, when he was dead, they set him on fire, and he burned up.

[The stinking corpse]

81 : 47   Now, in Tollan the people were no more.[59]

Huemac was ruler. The second was called Necuametl, the third was Tlaltecatzin, the fourth was called Huitzilpopoca. The four were left behind by Topiltzin when he went away. And the ruler of Nonoalco was called Huetzin. . . . [60]

81 : 51   Now then, an omen came to him: he saw an ash-bundle man,[61] a giant. And it was the very one who was eating people.

81 : 52   Then the Toltecs say, "O Toltecs, who is it that's eating people?"

81 : 53   Then they snared it,[62] they captured it. And what they captured was a beardless boy.[63]

81 : 55   Then they kill it. And when they've killed it, they look inside it: it has no heart, no innards, no blood.

82 : 2   Then it stinks. And whoever smells it dies from it, as well as whoever does not smell it, who [simply] passes by. And so a great many people are dying.

82 : 4   Then they try to drag it away, but it cannot be moved. And when the

---

58. A presumed copyist's error duplicates *no*.

59. For clarity the author might have added: "And here is how it came about."

60. A blot in the manuscript obscures what may be a title or other designation following the name Huetzin.

61. See note to the translation at 50 : 37.

62. For *quipia* I read *quilpia* (see GRAM sec. 5. 2). Evidently Lehmann has the same idea, translating "Da nehmen sie fest."

63. Read *amotlanetentzotzonyotia*? Lit., a boy who does not provide himself with something to serve as one's lip hairs. A doubtful translation, possible only if the element *ne* is taken as a replacement for *te* (as it seems to be in CAROC 80v:27, 30). Following Velázquez, one might read *amo tlane tentzotzoyotia*, who has no teeth and has filthy lips.

rope breaks, those who fall down die on the spot. And when it moves, all those who come in contact with it die. It eats them all.

82 : 7   Well, now that it could be moved, all the young men, old men, children, and young women fixed it up. They tied it with eight ropes. Then they dragged it off.

82 : 10   When they got it to Itzocan, it rose up. And those who were dragging it failed to let go of the ropes and were simply left hanging. Well, as for anyone who had grabbed a rope and just held on to it,[64] it carried him aloft.

[The fall of Tollan]

82 : 14   Then Huemac played ball. He played with the tlalocs, and the tlalocs said to him, "What do we win?"

82 : 15   Huemac said, "My jades, my quetzal plumes."

82 : 16   And then to Huemac they said, "Likewise, you win our jades, our quetzal plumes."

82 : 18   So they played ball. Huemac won.

Then the tlalocs were about to switch it, about to give Huemac an ear of green corn; and instead of their quetzal plumes, the shuck[65] in which the green ear grows.

82 : 21   But he did not take it. He said, "Is this what I won? Wasn't it jades? Wasn't it quetzal plumes? Well, bring it here!"

82 : 23   So the tlalocs said, "All right. Give him the jades, the quetzal plumes. Fetch those jades of ours, those quetzal plumes!" Then they fetched them, then they went away.

82 : 25   Then they said, "Very well. But we are definitely hiding our 'jades.' The Toltecs will have to suffer. And for four years."

82 : 27   So then it snowed, the snow fell knee deep, and the crops were destroyed. It was in Tecuilhuitl [June or July] that it snowed.

82 : 29   Except that in Tollan, where there was intense heat, all the trees, the prickly pears, and the magueys dried up, and all the stones broke apart and were shattered by the heat.

82 : 31   And when the Toltecs are suffering, when they're dying of hunger, then they're sacrificed. Well, perchance if anyone is keeping a little something for himself, then he buys a little turkey, makes himself a tamale, and eats.

82 : 35   Well then, a little old woman selling banners settles herself at Chapoltepecuitlapilco, and whoever buys a banner goes and dies on the stone of sacrifice.

---

64. Anticlimactic word order reversed in the translation.
65. Read *toquizhuatl*.

82 : 37   And when the four years of hunger had passed, the tlalocs appeared in Chapoltepec, where the water is. And milk corn—food—is rising to the surface. And there's a Toltec who is nearby, and he picks up the food, and he feeds on it.

82 : 42   And then a tlaloc spirit came out of the water and said to him, "Hey, fellow! Do you recognize this?"

82 : 44   And the Toltec said, "O lord,[66] I do indeed. It's been a long time since we lost it."

82 : 45   "Very well," he replied. "Now stay here and let me tell the master." And he went back into the water. He wasn't gone long.

82 : 46   Then he reappeared carrying an armload of green corn,[67] and he said, "Hey, fellow! Here it is. Give it to Huemac. Now, the gods are asking for the daughter[68] of Tozcuecuex,[69] for [one of] the Mexitin, for they want to eat her[70]—for the Toltecs are to go on eating very little, the Toltecs are to be destroyed. There are to be Mexica. And they [the Mexica] are going to give her to them at Jade Whirlpool, at Banner Place."[71]

82 : 53   Then he went to inform Huemac, telling him how the tlaloc had told him what had to be.

83 : 1   Then Huemac was sad. He wept and said, "Perhaps it is so. Perhaps the Toltecs are to pass away. Perhaps Tollan is to be destroyed."

83 : 3   Then he sent, he dispatched, to Xicococ two of his messengers, someone named Chiconcoatl, also Cuetlachcoatl, to go and ask the Mexitin for their daughter Quetzalxotzin, who was not yet grown, who was still a child.

83 : 7   So they went to Xicococ and told them, "Huemac sends us. He says, 'The tlalocs have appeared, asking the Mexica for a daughter of theirs.'"

83 : 9   Then the Mexica fasted. They mourned her for four days. And when the four days were up, they took her to Banner Place. Her father went with her.

83 : 12   Then they sacrificed her.

    And in that place the tlalocs appeared again, to Tozcuecuex, saying to

---

66. Read *totecuyo*, i.e., *toteucyo*.

67. The ink here is too faded for the word to be legible in the Velázquez facsimile, but both Velázquez and Lehmann read *elotl* or *ellotl*.

68. Facsimile unclear. The reading follows León y Gama (see following note).

69. Tozcuecuex was the leader of the wandering Mexica, or Mexitin, shortly before their arrival at Chapoltepec (UAH secs. 1–2, 123–26, 136; cf. CHIM 134, 273); when the Mexica were stricken by famine and disease, Tozcuecuex sacrificed his own daughter (UAH secs. 124–25). Here, in a fuller version of the story, we learn that the gods' request was conveyed to the Mexica by the Toltecs.

70. Or, they would eat her. For the future tense with conditional meaning see GRAM sec. 6.4.

71. The famous whirlpool in the Lake of Mexico, where human victims, jewels, and banners spattered with liquid rubber were offered to the rain gods and other spirits (FC bk. 2, chs. 20 and 25; TEZ ch. 80).

him, "Tozcuecuex, do not be sad. Your daughter is really with you. Open your tobacco flask."[72]

83 : 15   And there they placed his daughter's heart, together with all the different foods, and they said to him, "Here is what the Mexica are to eat, for the Toltecs are to be destroyed."

83 : 18   And then it becomes cloudy.[73] Then it rains, it pours. For four days it rained. Every day and every night the water is being absorbed. Then all kinds of plants sprout up, all the herbs and grasses. But their coming into existence was superfluous when the corn sprouted.

83 : 22   Well, Toltecs did the planting, and when we arrived in a month or two, already the corn was grown, already it was formed.

83 : 24   Now, when the corn was formed, it was in the time of the year sign 2 Reed. And it was in 1 Flint that the Toltecs were destroyed. That's when Huemac went into Cincalco.

83 : 27   Then some groups turned back, and some went on, dispersing everywhere.

83 : 29   Now then, the Mexica are coming.
And setting out at this time are 1. Tezcacoatl Huemac, 2. Chiconcoatl, 3. Coatlayauhqui, 4. Cuitlachcoatl. There are thirteen years. It's 1 Reed.

83 : 32   Well, he [Topiltzin?] left these people in command, these four whose names were—the first man, named Coatlayauhqui; the second, named Cuiltachcoatl; and the third, named Chiconcoatl; and the fourth, named Tezcacoatl, who is Huemac. And it's thirteen years that they were in command, that they were traveling.

[History of the Mexica]

83 : 38   Now, it's fifty-eight years since they came from Colhuacan, from Aztlan, since the Mexitin departed. It's 1 Flint.

83 : 40   Now, here's when they were at Chapoltepec, still in the time of Huitzilihuitl. For forty years they were there. It's 13 Rabbit.

83 : 42   Now, here's when they were in Colhuacan, in Tizaapan. It's twenty-five years.

83 : 44   Well, when the Toltecs went away in 1 Flint, that's when the Mexica set out from Xicococ. It was thirty-seven years until they arrived at Chapoltepec. And there at Chapoltepec they spent forty years.

---

72. Read *miyetecon*.
73. The following sentence is preceded by the letter 'o', which could be the interjection Oh! or a copyist's error.

83 : 47   Then the Colhuaque hired them as mercenaries, the Xaltocameca having gone and hired them out, and the Mexica came and gathered there in their territory[74] and said to them, "I'll sleep right here in your territory. I'm going over there." Then they slept in their territory there.

83 : 51   It seems that it was only in this manner that they went and guarded them.

Well, then the Colhuaque set out, and they met them and said, "You have entered the homeland of the Colhua and the Xaltocamecatl and the Cuauhtitlancalqui, and the Acolhua and the Tenayo and the Azcapotzalcatl, as well as Cuahuacan and Mazahuacan, also the Xiquipilcatl and the Matlatzincatl and the Ocuiltecatl and the Cuitlahuacatl, the Xochimilcatl, and others."

84 : 4   The Colhuaque were in command there. They're the ones who captured Huitzilihuitl. Then Mexica women and children were stolen. And the other Mexica, escaping, went and gathered themselves at Acocolco, where they spent six days.

84 : 9   And this is when they landed here in Tenochtitlan, which was still just a place of bulrushes, just a place of reeds, where they suffered hardships for fifty years, and they had no ruler. As yet the Mexica just minded their own business.

84 : 12   There are fifty-one [years]. It's 2 House. Colhuacan. Tenayocan. Well, here are the Mexica conquests that were made: Colhuacan and Tenayocan, just two.

84 : 15   [Marginal numeral:] 1

Now, it was at this time that King Acamapichtli became ruler, and he ruled for twenty-one years. Twenty.[75] 1 Flint.[76] Xochimilco. Cuitlahuac. Cuauhnahuac. Mizquic. Well, here are the conquests that he made: Xochimilco and Cuitlahuac and Mizquic and Cuauhnahuac—Acamapich made conquests in four places.

84 : 21   [Marginal numeral:] 2

Now, here's when Acamapichtli's son, named Huitzilihuitl, was ruler, and it was for twenty-one years that he ruled. 9 House. Xaltocan. Acolman. Otompan. Chalco. Tetzcoco. Tollantzinco. Cuauhtitlan. Toltitlan. Well, here are the conquests that were made. Eight were the nations that Huitzilihuitl conquered.

---

74. Read *oncan itlan.*

75. This should be "twenty-one," to agree with the statement just made. Cf. the reiterated numbers in lines 84:27–28 and 84:31–32 below.

76. In other words, Acamapichtli acceded to the throne in 1 Flint (A.D. 1376) and ruled for twenty-one years. Here and in the following paragraphs the date marks the beginning of the king's reign.

84 : 26 [Marginal numeral:] 3

Now, here's when Huitzilihuitl's son, named Chimalpopocatzin, was ruler. It was ten years that he ruled. Chalco. Tequixquiac. Ten years.[77] 4 Rabbit. Well, here are his conquests. Two were the nations that Chimalpopocatzin conquered.

84 : 30 [Marginal numeral:] 4

Now, here's when Acamapichtli's son named Itzcohuatzin was ruler. And it was thirteen years that he ruled. Thirteen. 1 Flint. Now, all the places where Itzcoatzin's conquests were made: Azcapotzalco, Tlacopan, Atlacuihuayan, Coyohuacan, Mixcoac, Cuauhximalpan, Cuahuacan, Teocalhuiyacan, Tecpan, Huitzitzilapan, Cuauhnahuac, Tetzcoco, Cuauhtitlan, Xochimilco, Cuitlahuac, Mizquic, Tlatilolco, Itztepec, Xiuhtepec, Tzacualpan, Chalco, Yohuallan, Tepecuacuilco, Cuezallan.

84 : 38 [Marginal numeral:] 5

Now, here's when Huitzilihuitl's son known as Ilhuicaminatzin, the elder Moteuczomatzin, was ruler. And as for how long he ruled, twenty-nine years is what it was. Twenty-nine. 1 House. Now, here are the conquests made by the elder Moteuczomatzin: Coaixtlahuacan, Chalco, Chiconquiyauhco, Tepoztlan, Iyauhtepec, Atlatlauhcan, Totolapan, Huaxtepec, Tecpatepec, Yohualtepec, Xiuhtepec, Quiauhteopan, Tlalcozauhtitlan,Tlachco, Cuauhnahuac, Tepecuacuilco, Coatlan, Xilotepec, Itzcuincuitlapilco, Tlapacoyan, Chapolicxitla, Tlatlauhquitepec, Yacapichtlan, Cuauhtochco, Cuetlaxtlan.

84 : 48 [Marginal numeral:] 6

Now, here's when the one named Axayacatzin ruled, who was the grandson[78] of the two rulers Moteuczomatzin the elder and Itzcoatzin.[79] Twelve years is how long he ruled. Twelve. 4 Rabbit. Now, all the places of Axayatzin's conquests: Tlatilolco, Matlatzinco, Xiquipilco, Tzinacantepec, Tlacotepec, Tenantzinco, Xochiyacan, Teotenanco, Calimaya, Metepec, Ocoyacac, Capolloac, Atlappolco, Cua. . . .[80]

---

77. Velázquez reads the ambiguously formed figure as 20 but concedes that it ought to be 10. Lehmann reads 10.

78. But *ixhuiuhtli* may also mean cousin, brother's son, or sister's daughter (MOLS: primo . . .).

79. Implausibly the text combines two traditions regarding the lineage of Axayacatzin. There is no consensus on this king's relationship to other rulers (see García Granados, *Diccionario biográfico* 1 : 69–80). Various traditions make Axayacatzin the brother of his two successors, Tizocicatzin and Ahuitzotzin (ibid., 2 : 282–86). Hence these two are also called grandsons of Moteuczomatzin the elder and Itzcoatzin (see below).

80. The catchword *qua* in the lower right corner of side 84 (i.e., folio 43v) indicates that the long-lost remainder of the manuscript began with a page starting *qua*[ ], evidently for *quappanohuayan* (compare the list of Axayacatzin's conquests on side 67). The missing text is preserved on sides 121 and 122 of the León y Gama copy, which, as established by Tschohl in his "Das Ende," completes the Legend of the Suns.

121 : 1   Cuappanohuayan, Xalatlauhco, Tecalco, Tepeyacac, Oztoman, Tlaximalloyan, Ocuillan, Cuezcomatliyacac, Matlatlan, Oztoticpac, Tlaollan, Ahuilizapan, Tetzapotitlan, Mixtlan, Cuezaloztoc, Cuetlaxtlan, Poxcauhtlan, Miquetlan, Tenexticpac, Tochpan, Tampatel, Cuauhtlan, Tamooc.[81]

121 : 6   [Marginal numeral:] 7

Now, here's when [Tizocicatzin], the grandson of the two rulers Moteuczomatzin the elder and Itzcoatzin, ruled. Five years is how long he ruled. Five. 3 Rabbit. Now, all the places that this Tizocicatzin conquered: Tonalliimoquetzayan, Ecatepec, Toxico, Matlatzinco, Mazahuacan, Atezcahuacan, Cillan, Tlapan, Yancuitlan, Tamapachco, Coatlicuauhpechco, Xochiyetlan, Miquetlan.

121 : 13   [Marginal numeral:] 8

Now, here is when [Ahuitzotzin], the grandson of the two rulers Moteuczomatzin the elder and Itzcoatzin, ruled. Sixteen years is how long he ruled. Sixteen. 8 Reed. And here are the conquests that he made: Tlapan, Tziuhcohuac, Molanco, Tzapotlan, Xaltepec, Tototepec, Xalapan, Apancallecan, Xihuacan, Acapolco, Xollochiuhcan, Cozohuipillecan, Acatepec, Cozcacuauhtenanco, Amaztlan, Xochtlan, Coyocac, Chiapan, Tecpatepec, Huexolotlan, Teocuitlatlan, Xiuhteuczatlan, Xicochimalco, Tecuantepec, Coyollapan, Huehuetlan, Huipillan, Cahuallan, Iztatlan, Nantzintlan,[82] Comitlan, Izhuatlan, Cuauhxayacatitlan, Iztactlallocan, Huitztlan, Xollotlan, Cuauhnacaztlan, Mazatlan, Mapachtepec, Cuezalcuitlapillan, Cuauhtlan, Tlacotepec, Mizquitlan, Cuauhpilollan, Ayotochcuitlatlan.

121 : 27   Now, here is when the one named Moteuczomatzin, son of Axayacatzin, was ruler. How long he ruled was sixteen years. Sixteen. 11 Reed. And all the places that this Moteuczomatzin made conquests were: Achiotlan, Zozollan, Nocheztlan, Teuctepec, Huilotepec, Tlaniztlan, Zollan, Tzinacantlan, Huitztlan, Oxitlan, Piyaztlan, Texotlan, Chichihualtatacallan, Iztactlallocan, Icpatepec, Tlatlatepec, Amatlan, Pipioltepec, Zacuantepec, Nopallan, Tecozauhtlan, Hueiapan, Quimichtepec, Malinaltepec, Tlachquiauhco, Teochiapan, Teoatzinco, Pantepec, Caltepec, Tecpatlan, Centzontepec, Quetzaltepec, Cuezcomaixtlahuacan, Zacatepec, Xallapan, Xaltianquizco, Yolloxonecuilco, Comaltepec, Atepec, Huexolotlan, Tliltepec, Iztitlan, Miquiztlan, Itzcuintepec.

---

81. The non-Nahuatl-sounding *Tamooc* is corroborated by the phonically similar, if not identical, *tamuoc* in the Codex Mendoza conquest list for Axayacatzin. However, the Anales de Cuauhtitlan has *tamaoc* (see Concordance), raising the possibility that León y Gama may have miscopied; the 'a' and the 'o' are sometimes indistinguishable in the Codex Chimalpopoca (compare note 1 above).

82. The León y Gama text has *Nautzintlan*, presumably another of León y Gama's scribal errors (see preceding note). Codex Mendoza has *nantzintlan*.

122 : 6   This is when the Marqués arrived, in the year 1 Reed, forty-two years ago from now.[83] This one, the one who made war, was the second one to enter Mexico.[84] 1 Reed. Forty-two. 11 Reed. 12 Flint. 13 House. 1 Rabbit. 2 Reed. 3 Flint. 4 House.[85]

83. As elsewhere, the particle *ye* is here translated "ago." See GLOS: [2]YE 3.

84. Lit., this one, the one who lays out his dagger, is the second one who enters Mexico. For *ye tocomana ic omei in callaquico mexico* read *ye[h] tacamana ic ome i[n] in calaquico mexico.* In writing the nonsensical "tocomana," León y Gama may again have confused the 'a' and the 'o' (see note 81 above). As for "second one," Cortés (here called the Marqués) is so designated presumably because he was preceded by Juan de Grijalva, whose arrival a year earlier is described in the Annals of Cuauhtitlan: "And when Moteuczomatzin was ruling, the Spaniards came here for the first time . . ." (see line 69:9 et seq. and note 528). Of course, Grijalva did not reach Mexico City, as here implied—if my reading is the right one. The noun *taca* (dagger) and the transitive verb *mana* in the sense of to lay out or offer something as an act of war are independently attested usages (see NED), but the term *tacamana*, though grammatically acceptable, is not elsewhere attested to my knowledge.

85. Tschohl ("Das Ende," p. 252) reads 4 House as the date 1561. And in fact, if the scribe is writing forty-two years after Cortés' arrival in 1 Reed (A.D. 1519), the year would have to be 4 House (1561). It is unclear, however, why the sequence of years given here should begin with 11 Reed (1555). In any event, this final paragraph, at least, must have been added after the main composition, which is dated 1558 in line 75:5 above.

Concordance to Proper Nouns
and Titles

All personal names in the Codex Chimalpopoca, whether of supernaturals or mortals, as well as all group names and place names (both real and mythical), are entered in this Concordance with a complete list of occurrences. References to the Codex are by side and line number: for example, 45:12 (side 45, line 12).

The asterisk (*) identifies a hypothetical or unattested form. Quotation marks enclose an attested form (such as "CHIAPPAN") that appears to have been misspelled in the paleograph. Abbreviations are as follows:

abbrev., abbreviation
apoc., apocopated
assoc., associated
cf., compare
g.n., group name (e.g. Chichimecatl, Españoles, Mexicatl)
lit., literally
p.n., personal name (male unless "female" is specified)
pc.n., place name, geographical name
pl., plural
sing., singular
Span., Spanish
syn., synonym
var., variant, variants

ACA, var. ACAPOL, p.n. Ruler of Chalco. 9:26 (acapol), 11:31 (aca).
    Cf. ACATZIN.
ACAHUACAN, pc.n. 22:22 (acahuacan tepeyacac).
ACALHUACAN, pc.n. 21:16 (= ACOLHUACAN?, see note to translation),
    35:45, 35:48 (?, see note to translation).
ACALLAN, pc.n. 81:43.
ACALTECOYAN, pc.n. 19:30,36.
ACAMAPICHTLI, apoc. var. ACAMAPICH (84:19), p.n.
    1. Ruler of Colhuacan. 23:47, 24:1, 27:35.
    2. Ruler of Tenochtitlan. 24:25, 26:39, 26:42 (acamapixtli), 27:53, 29:43,51,
       30:20,26, 65:48,49,55, 84:15,19,21,30.
ACAPOL, see ACA.
ACAPOLCO, pc.n. 67:34, 121:17.

ACATENTEHUATZIN, p.n. 15:17.

ACATEPEC, pc.n. 121:18.

ACATITLAN, pc.n. 10:44.

ACATL, p.n. 12:1,20. Cf. ACA, ACATZIN.

ACATLIYACAC, pc.n. 67:34.

ACATZIN, p.n. A Chichimec captain. 18:52, 22:22,41. Cf. ACA, HUEIACATZIN

ACATZINTITLAN, pc.n. 21:22 (tlatzallan acatzintlan), 21:32 (tlatzallan acatzintlan).

ACAYOLTZIN, p.n. 17:51, 17:54 (açayoltzin).

ACHCAUHTLI, lit., elder brother (sometimes used as a title, see GLOS: achcauhtli 5).

ACHICATZIN TLILPOTONCATZIN, p.n. 15:24.

ACHICHILACACHOCAN (Clavijero per SIM, IXT 1:384: Achichilacazyocan), pc.n. 64:40 (achichillacachyocan).

ACHIOTLAN, pc.n. 67:46 (achiyotlan), 121:30.

ACHITOMETL, p.n.
  1. An early ruler of Colhuacan. 12:28,36.
  2. A later ruler of Colhuacan. 23:52, 24:2,3,30,35, 27:34,36,37.

ACOCOLCO, pc.n. 84:7.

ACOCOTLAN, pc.n. 20:3 (acocotla).

ACOLHUA, pl. ACOLHUAQUE, g.n. 13:11, 37:42, 42:44, 43:23, 45:17, 54:11 (tetzcoca acolhuaque), 54:19,24,26,28, 60:34, 84:1.

ACOLHUACAN, var. ACOLIHUACAN (50:27, NED), pc.n. 3:42, 35:48 (?, see note to translation), 37:40,41, 38:5, 50:27, 54:36, 63:39 (tetzcoco acolhuacan), 66:2,36. See ACALHUACAN.

ACOLHUAQUE, see ACOLHUA.

ACOLMAN, pc.n. 33:17, 45:39, 46:41, 49:20 (acolman tlaca), 64:1,34, 66:2, 84:22.

ACOLMIZTLI, p.n.
  1. Ruler of the Acolhuaque. 13:12.
  2. Ruler of Toltitlan. 31:28.
  3. Ruler of the Atenchicalque Cuitlahuaca. 49:52, 50:1,6.
  4. Cougar Arm, a Chichimec. 37:47.
  5. See ANTONIO ACOLMIZTON.

ACOLMIZTON, see ANTONIO ACOLMIZTON.

ACOLNAHUAC, pc.n. 12:39 (popotlan acolnahuac).

ACOLTZIN, p.n. 31:47, 46:34, 49:48.

ACPAXAPO (Water-weed Mirror), p.n., god of the Xaltocameca. 20:18,27.

ACPAXAPOCAN, pc.n. 20:9,11,15,29, 22:20 (xaltocan acpaxapocan), 22:37.

ACUACUALACHCO, pc.n. 63:18.

ACUECHETZIN, p.n. 63:44.

ACUECUEXATL, name of a spring in Coyohuacan (FC 8:2:3, FC 11:250:2, UAH sec. 282, DHIST chs. 48–49). 59:20,27,33.

ACXOCUAUHTLI, p.n.
1. 10:17.
2. 11:49.

ACXOTECA, g.n., pl.
1. Chalca group that came to Cuitlahuac Tizic. 13:15.
2. Pertaining to AXCOTLAN (the calpulli in Mexico). 26:31 (axcotecatlalli).

ACXOTLAN, pc.n., calpulli district in Mexico (cf. AXCOTECA 2). 26:34 (axcotlan tlalli), 60:58 (stewards of Acxotlan).

ACXOYATL, p.n. 64:7.

AGUSTIN, see PEDRO DE SAN AUGUSTIN.

AHUACATITLAN, pc.n. (refers to a part of TOLTITLAN). 47:50, 48:6 (ahuacatitlan chaneque).

AHUATEPEC, pc.n. 64:38.

AHUATLAN, pc.n. 64:43.

AHUAZHUATLAN, pc.n. 21:26 (ahuazhuatla).

AHUILIZAPAN, pc.n. 67:16, 121:3.

AHUITZILCO, pc.n. 65:13.

AHUITZOTZIN, p.n. 57:53, 58:11,14,18,21,29,51, 59:37, 67:27,42.

AITICTLI (In Waters' Midst, cf. NED ātlihtic), pc.n. 49:18.

ALONSO CIMATZIN, p.n. 15:33.

AMAQUEMECAN, pc.n. 27:57, 32:13, 53:15, 63:34,46.

AMATLAN, pc.n. 121:33.

AMATZCALAPAN, pc.n. 65:10.

AMAXACCALQUE, g.n., pl. (pertaining to Amaxac, a district in Tlatilolco; see FC bk. 12, chs. 37–40). 45:2.

AMAXTLAN, pc.n. 59:13, 67:32 (conquered by Ahuitzotzin). Cf. AMAZTLAN.

AMAZTLAN, pc.n. 121:19 (conquered by Ahuitzotzin). Cf. AMAXTLAN.

AMILPAN, pc.n. 60:51 (amillpan). See GLOS: amilpan.

AMIMITL, p.n. 3:32.

AMOCHCO (At-the-Water-Weed), pc.n. 4:37, 7:22. Cf. NED.

AMOXPAN, pc.n. 63:16.

ANAHUAC, the world. See GLOS: anahuac, anahuacatlalli, anahuatl.

ANAHUACATL, p.n. 28:41.

ANAHUACATLALLI, see GLOS.

ANGELES, see GERONIMO DE LOS ANGELES.

ANTONIO ACOLMIZTON, p.n. Don antonio acolmizton, 31:36,37.

APACHICUAUHTLA, pc.n. 65:14.

APANCALLECAN, pc.n. 67:33, 121:17.

APANECATL, p.n. 81:11,30.

APANTEUCTLI, p.n.

1. A spirit or deity. 76:21,55.
2. One of the MIXCOA. 78:38, 79:19,27.

APAZCO, pc.n. 13:35, 15:48, 40:45, 55:51, 64:5,10,12.

ATECOMOYAN, pc.n. 21:25.

ATECPAN, pc.n.
   1. Water Shrine ("palace" is the usual translation of TECPAN, but cf. TEC-CALLI). 4:37, 7:22.
   2. Town controlled by Mexico. 65:5.

ATECPANECATL, an official title (ytlatocatoca) assumed by Huemac when he became ruler of Tollan (see NED). 8:40. Cf. ATECPANECATL TEUCTLI, TECPANECATL.

ATECPANECATL TEUCTLI, title held by XALTEMOCTZIN 3. 30:32. Cf. TECPANECATL 1.

ATEHUILACACHCO, pc.n. 21:18.

ATEMPAN, pc.n.
   1. One of the four quarters of Cuauhtitlan town. 29:37, 43:47 (atempan huauhtlan), 46:48, 55:10.
   2. Place visited by Mixcoatl. 62:25.

ATEMPANECATL
   1. An official title (FC 2:100:18, FC 9:34:23, García Granados *Diccionario* 1:58–59, for discussion see FC 9:47:n.10).
   2. P.n. (?). 24:46.

ATENCHICALCAN, pc.n. 33:2, 50:5, 62:46, 63:49 (aten[chicalcan]). See also CUITLAHUAC ATENCHICALCAN.

ATENCHICALCATL or ATENCHICALQUI (50:10,26), pl. ATENCHICAL-QUE (a division of the CUITLAHUACA), g.n. 49:51, 49:55 (sing.), 50:4–33 passim.

ATENCO, see CHALCO ATENCO, TETZCOCO ATENCO.

ATEPEC, pc.n. 122:4.

ATEPOCATLALPAN, pc.n. 10:40.

ATEPOCATZIN, p.n. 45:3.

ATEZCAHUACAN, pc.n. 52:10, 67:25, 121:10.

ATICPAC, pc.n.
   1. Place where Moteuczoma II was reared (García Granados, *Diccionario*).
   2. = 1 (?). 62:23 (aticpac cuexomatl ytepotzco).
   3. = 1 (?). 63:13.

ATIZAPAN, see TIZAAPAN.

ATLACOMOLCO, pc.n. 21:21.

ATLACUIHUAYAN, pc.n. 66:36, 84:33.

ATLAN, pc.n. (FC). 9:15 (izquitlan atla[n]). See also GLOS: atlan.

ATLANCATEPEC, pc.n., town in Tlaxcallan (Clavijero per SIM, Gibson *Tlaxcala*: atlangátepec). 34:14, 45:6, 45:12 (atlancatepec tlaca).

ATLAPOPOCATZIN, p.n., ruler of Apazco. 64:12. Cf. ATLPOPOCATZIN.

ATLAPPOLCO, pc.n. 67:13, 84:53 (atlapolco).

ATLATLAUHCAN, pc.n. 84:43.

ATLAUHCO, pc.n. 21:33 (huecatlan atlauhco).

ATLITLALAQUIYAN, pc.n. 12:16 (atlytlallacyan), 13:34 (atlitlalacyan).

ATLIXCO, pc.n. 57:45, 60:43,47.

ATLIXYOCAN, pc.n. 56:17 (chapoltepec atlixyocan).

ATLPOPOCATZIN, p.n. Ruler of Tizic. 63:50. Cf. ATLAPOPOCATZIN.

ATLPOYECAN, pc.n. 64:19.

ATLTEPACHIUHCAN, pc.n. 46:37, 48:37.

ATLTLATLAUHYAN, pc.n. 66:54.

ATLXOXOUHCAN, pc.n. 65:6.

ATONAL, p.n.
1. Ruler of Toltecs at Tamazolac. 10:42.
2. Ruler of Coaixtlahuacan, descendant of the Tamazolac Toltecs. 51:36,37,41, 66:46.

ATOTONILCA, g.n., pl. 60:10.

ATZACUALPAN (Place of Impounded Water), pc.n. 61:3,5,8.

ATZATZAMOLTZIN, p.n. 18:1,21.

ATZIN TEUCTLI, p.n. 62:43.

ATZOMIATENANCO, pc.n. 60:43 (atlixco àtzomiatenanco).

ATZOMPAN, pc.n.
1. 10:34.
2. = 1 (?). 41:45,47, 42:1.

AUGUSTIN, see PEDRO DE SAN AUGUSTIN.

AXAPOCHCO (IXT 2:35, IXT 2:40, etc.), pc.n. 64:38.

AXAYACATZIN, p.n. 53:39, 55:2,17,22,25,29,42, 56:9,22, 57:2–36 passim, 67:7,19, 84:49,51, 121:27.

AXCAHUA/TLATQUIHUA, master/possessor, i.e., omnipotent god. Key word: lord and master.
1. Refers to a pre-Conquest deity (FFCC ch. 20: axcaoa . . . tlatqujoa).
2. Refers to the God of Christianity (CAROC 55: cemāxcāhuàcātzintli, cen-tlatquihuàcātzintli = dueño y señor de toda quanta hazienda ay). 62:7.

AXICYOTZIN, p.n. 50:39.

AXOCHTLI, pc.n. 21:17.

AÏACACHTEPEC, pc.n. 64:44.

AYACTLACATL (Nobody) or AYACTLACATZIN, p.n.
1. Ruler of Cuauhtitlan. 15:25, 25:42, 29:53, 30:5–7 (how he got his name), 47:2,12, 48:53, 49:2,3, 51:9, 52:9, 55:41,43, 59:5. Syn. XA-QUIN TEUCTLI.
2. Son of AZTATZONTZIN. 15:38.

AYAHUALOLCO, pc.n. 11:18 (covatolco ayahualolco).

AYAUHCONTITLAN, pc.n. 63:16.

AYAUHCOYOTZIN, p.n. 4:29, 8:10.

AYOCUAN, p.n. 64:4.

AYOTEPEC, pc.n. 65:15.

AYOTLAN, pc.n. 11:1, 81:37.

AYOTOCHCUITLATLAN, pc.n. 59:1, 67:40, 121:26.

AYOTZINCO, pc.n. 59:28.

AZAYOLTZIN (?, see ACAYOLTZIN).

AZCAPOTZALCATL, pl. AZCAPOTZALCA (17:36), g.n. 17:36, 30:43, 84:1.

AZCAPOTZALCO, pc.n. 10:45, 13:24, 15:49, 16:39, 18:38,49, 24:4, 25:51, 28:37,44,46, 30:34,36,44, 31:5,9,45, 32:32,43,46, 33:5,6,8,21,22,25, 28,31, 34:9,12,33,41, 37:7,12, 38:38,47, 39:23, 40:22,24, 41:12, 42:23, 43:29, 44:7, 46:22,27,39, 63:38,53, 66:1,8,16,35, 84:33.

AZTAMAMAL, p.n. 10:20.

AZTAQUEMECAN, pc.n. 64:38.

AZTATZONTZIN, p.n. 15:17,20,28,28, 16:4,10,12,18, 59:39,53, 60:42,44, 57, 61:16,31, 64:7,13.

AZTAXOCH, p.n. 10:20.

AZTLAN, pc.n. 11:23, 83:38.

CACAMATZIN, p.n.
  1. Ruler of Amaquemecan. 32:14, 63:47.
  2. Ruler of Tetzcoco. 61:50.

CAHUALLAN, pc.n. 121:21.

CAHUALTZIN, p.n. 36:23.

CALCOZAMETL, p.n. 63:45.

CALIMAYA (UAH sec. 61, cf. FC 8:2:12: callimaia, ZCHIM 1:27: calliyman-yan), pc.n. 67:11 (callimayan), 84:53 (calliimayan).

CALIXTO, Span., Calixto, p.n. 57:31 (Calisto).

CALLACOAYAN, pc.n. 27:21.

CALLATLAXCALTZIN, p.n. 45:3.

CALLAXOCHITL, p.n. 43:47.

CALLIIMANYAN, see CALIMAYA.

CALLI TEUCTLI (House Lord), p.n. 62:41.

CALPAN, pc.n. 64:1.

CALTEPEC, pc.n. 68:3, 122:1.

CALTZIN TEUCTLI, p.n. 34:31, 51:6. Syn. TEMIZTZIN.

CAMAXTLE, p.n.
  1. God of the Huexotzinca and Tlaxcalteca (Muñoz Camargo bk. 1, chs. 4 and 7). Note: Like CF, CM, HTCH, and UAH, AC gives "camaxtle," not "camaxtli." 44:49 (see note to the translation). See also CAMAXTLE MIXCOATL

2. = 1 (?). 57:31 (ytelpoch camaxtle).

CAMAXTLE MIXCOATL, name assigned by historians to the Chichimec god known variously as CAMAXTLE or MIXCOATL (Muñoz Camargo, bk. 1, ch. 7: camaxtli mixcohuatl; cf. HMPP ch. 8: Camasale, or por otro nombre, Mixcoatl). 50:50 (camaxtle mixcohuatl).

CAPOLLOAC, pc.n. 67:13, 84:53.

CARLOS, Span., p.n., see FRANCISCO CARLOS XOCONOCHTZIN.

CASTILLAN TLACA, see CAXTILTECA.

CASTILTECA, see CAXTILTECA.

CATLACATZIN, p.n. 15:31.

CAXTILTECA, vars. CASTILTECA (21:42), CASTILLAN TLACA (40:25), Span., i.e., Castillians, pl., g.n. 16:6,8. 21:42, 40:25.

CE ACATL, p.n. 4:1 (topiltzin tlamacazqui çe acatl quetzalcohuatl), 4:34 (yn topiltzin yn çe acatl quetzalcoatl), 5:40 (nopiltzin çe acatl quetzalcohuatl), 10:1, 80:51,52, 81:3–37 passim. See also QUETZALCOATL 2, TO-PILTZIN. See GLOS: ce acatl.

CE COATL, p.n. 10:8.

CEMACAC, pc.n. 65:6.

CEMPOHUALLAN, pc.n. 63:55.

CEMPOHUALXOCHITZIN, p.n. 63:50.

CENTZONTEPEC, pc.n. 68:5, 122:2.

CENTZONTEPECA, g.n., pl. 61:44.

CHACHATZIN, p.n. 35:14, 39:33.

CHAHUACUETZIN, p.n. 14:52.

CHAHUAQUETZIN, p.n. 13:6.

CHALCA, see CHALCATL.

CHALCAITOA:MO, to be called or known as a Chalcatl. 12:2.

CHALCA MIHUAQUE, g.n., pl. 12:6. See also MIHUAQUE.

CHALCAPOL, p.n. 9:27.

CHALCA TENANCA, g.n., pl. 12:4. See TENANCO.

CHALCATL, pl. CHALCA, g.n. 9:25, 12:2,9, 13:14, 13:21 (chalcapilli), 18:2, 18:21 (chalcatlatocayotl), 24:15, 27:26,30,54, 28:2, 32:26, 45:30, 43, 46:8, 52:14,15, 53:11, 54:40, 58:7 (tlaltecayohuaque chalca), 66:11; chalcayaoyotl = the Chalca War, 27:56, 28:9, 49:41, 51:17. See also CHALCA MIHUAQUE, CHALCA TENANCA, CHALCA TLACOCH-CALCA, CHALCA TLAHUACAN, CHALCAYOTL, CHALCO.

CHALCA TLACOCHCALCA, g.n., pl. 12:24. See also CHALCO TLACOCH-CALCO, TLACOCHCALCA.

CHALCA TLAHUACAN, i.e., the Chalca of Tlahuacan, the Tlahuacan Chalca. 12:8, 13:7, 26:47.

CHALCAYAOTZIN, p.n. 63:48.

CHALCAYOTL, Chalca people or Chalca nation. 24:14 (see note to the translation), 27:30.

CHALCHIUH, p.n. Cf. CHALCHIUHTZIN.
1. 29:13.
2. 43:39.

CHALCHIUHCOLIUHYAN (Jade Whirlpool), name of a whirlpool in the Lake of Mexico, also called PANTITLAN (see TEZ ch. 80). 82:52.

CHALCHIUHCUEYECAN (Bernal Díaz, ch. 160: un rio que se dice Chalcho-cueca; TEZ ch. 32, p. 331: Chalchincuecan, que ahora es San Juan de Ulùa, y la Veracruz; TORQ bk. 4, ch. 16, p. 386: chalchicoeca; TORQ bk. 4, ch. 58, p. 473: chalchiuhquaecan; Cortés, 2d letter: chalchilmeca; Lienzo de Jacutácato per GKC 319: Chalchicueyehcan), pc.n. 68:12.

CHALCHIUHTAMAZOLIN (Jade Toad), p.n.(?). 63:12.

CHALCHIUHTECHCATITLAN, pc.n. 21:24.

CHALCHIUHTLATONAC or CHALCHIUHTLATONACTZIN, p.n.
1. Ruler of Colhuacan. 13:17,25, 17:14,40,53.
2. Son of TEZOZOMOCTLI 1. 34:45,48, 35:1,15.

CHALCHIUHTZIN, p.n. Cf. CHALCHIUH.
1. One of the Tlahuaca founders. 13:6.
2. A ruler of the Tlahuacan Chalca in Xicco (= 1?). 26:51.
3. Governor of Hueipochtlan. 29:23.

CHALCO, pc.n. 11:30, 12:1,19, 15:2,10, 18:9,10, 24:10, 24:14 (chalco pouhque), 26:48 (chalco axcan = present-day Chalco); 27:11, 28:3,8,24, 31:48,50, 32:15, 34:30,33, 37:25, 43:32, 45:34, 49:53,55, 50:3, 51:6, 52:23,26, 53:6,11,16, 61:13, 63:47 (refers to Chalco Tlacochcalco, cf. 58:5), 66:2,30,52,53, 81:38, 84:23,27,37,42. See also CHALCATL.

CHALCO ATENCO, pc.n. 28:6, 32:17, 49:40.

CHALCO TLACOCHCALCO, pc.n., see TLACOCHCALCO 2. See also CHALCA TLACOCHCALCA.

CHALCOTZIN, p.n. 9:26.

CHALMECAPAN, pc.n. (one of the four quarters of Cuauhtitlan town). 29:33, 43:46, 46:46, 55:9.

CHAMOLLAN, pc.n. 64:42.

CHAPOLICXITLA, pc.n. 67:5, 84:46.

CHAPOLMALLOYAN, pc.n. 21:26.

CHAPOLTEPEC, pc.n. 10:49, 11:7,13, 12:42,43,52, 13:23,43,50, 16:33,35, 17:1,6,30, 20:43, 28:50, 29:6,7, 53:27 (aqueduct), 53:36, 56:17 (cha-poltepec atlixyocan), 66:45, 82:39, 83:40,46,47.

CHAPOLTEPECUITLAPILCO, pc.n. (FC 3:27:22). 82:35.

CHAYACAMACHAN, see XAYACAMACHAN.

CHIANCUAC, pc.n. (within the city of Cuauhtitlan). 42:11.

CHIAPAN, pc.n. (CF bk. 8, ch. 1, fol. 2; NED). Chiappan, 21:34, 43:33; chi-yappan, 40:46, 55:52, 57:49, 67:32; chiyappā, 64:6; Chiyapan, 121:19. Cf. TEOCHIAPAN.

CHIAPANECA, g.n., pl. 58:44 (chiappaneca).

"CHIAPPAN," see CHIAPAN.

CHIAUHCOATL, p.n.

1. Ruler of Tepeyacac. 51:4, 52:3, 53:38.
2. One who cuckolded Nezahualpilli. 59:17.

CHIAUHTLA, pc.n. 64:35 (chiauhtla tetzcoco).

CHIAUHTZINCO, pc.n. Cf. TEOCHIAUHTZINCO.

1. Where Nezahualcoyotl hid. 35:38.
2. = 1 (?), a town of Huexotzinco. 43:25 (seat of Huexotzinco government), 57:15,20, 59:24.
3. A name for the other world (?, NED).

CHICANITZIN, p.n. 43:45.

CHICHICUEPOTL, p.n. 58:13.

CHICHIHUALTATACALLAN, pc.n. 67:48, 121:32.

CHICHIMECACIHUATL, female p.n. 3:33.

CHICHIMECACUICOYAN, pc.n. 18:11, 24:50.

CHICHIMECATEUCTLI, title used by certain kings (NED: chīchīmēcatl tēuctli). 60:47 (of Atlixco).

CHICHIMECATL, pl. CHICHIMECA, g.n. Key word: Chichimec (sing.), Chichimecs (pl.).

1. An aborigine of the central highlands, a barbarian (for extended discussion see FC bk. 10, ch. 29, pp. 170–75). Note: This category is often difficult to distinguish from 2, below. 12:43,49, 39:35,41,43,50.
2. A rude tribesman of the northern part of the central highlands or one who claims ancestry from such tribesmen (see NED, FC 9:83:24, FC 10: 196–97, FC 11:256, DHIST ch. 59, p. 449, parag. 9). 1:9,10,24,55, 3:15,29,32, 3:34 (chichimecapilli), 3:38.
3. = 2, especially those who settled Tetzcoco. 1:38 (inchichimecayeliz), 37:38 (chichimecatontli = little Chichimec).
4. = 2, especially those who settled Cuauhtitlan. 1:45, 3:3, 3:13 (chichimecatlatocayotl), 3:16(?), 8:18 (chichimecatlatoque), 9:16, 14:20, 18:51 (iachcahuan yn chichimeca = his Chichimec captains), 19:2,3,4,6,12,38,39, 41,42,50, 20:9, 20:10 (chichimecatl vactzin = Huactzin the Chichimec), 20:12,23,24,27,30, 22:28,30,33,41,46,53, 24:49 (chichimecapipiltin), 25: 3–43 passim, 26:12,15,20,25,36, 27:21,22, 30:38 (chichimecapipiltin), 31:12 (idem), 42:21 (chichimecapilli), 56:18; chichimeca cuauhtitlancalque, see CUAUHTITLANCALQUI.
5. = 2, refers to the Cuitlahuaca. 13:7.
6. = 2, refers to the Chalca Mihuaque. 12:6 (huitznahua chichimeca).
7. = 2?, refers to the Colhuaque. 2:11.

CHICHIMECATL TEUCTLI, see CHICHIMECATEUCTLI.

CHICOCUAUHYOCAN, pc.n. 35:25.

CHICOMOZTOC, pc.n. 1:24,42, 79:31.

CHICONCOAC, pc.n. 65:11.

CHICONCOATL, p.n. 83:5,30,34

CHICONCUAUHTLIITEOCAL, pc.n. 21:17.

CHICONQUIYAUHCO, pc.n. 66:53, 84:42.

CHICONTEPEC, pc.n. 64:42.

CHICONTONATIUH, p.n. 1:38, 2:13 (written "7 tonatiuh"), 2:52 (idem).

CHICUALOAPAN, pc.n. 62:22.

CHILPAN, pc.n. 62:27.

CHILTEPEC, pc.n. 65:44.

CHIMALAXOCH or CHIMALAXOCHTZIN, p.n. 13:42,52.

CHIMALCOTITLAN, pc.n. 12:3.

CHIMALHUACAN, pc.n. 64:33.

CHIMALMAN, female p.n., 4:2 (chimanan), 78:26, 80:30,49.

CHIMALPAN, pc.n. 14:44.

CHIMALPOPOCATZIN, p.n. 30:23,24,26, 32:8, 33:31,33,41,47, 43:6, 57:4, 66:3,14,17,27, 84:26,29.

"CHIMANAN," see CHIMALMAN.

CHINAMECAN, pc.n. 65:8.

CHIQUIUHTEPETLAPAN, pc.n. 12:34 (chiquiuhtepetlapan tecpayocan).

CHIUCNAHUAC, pc.n. 65:9 (chiucnauhuac).

CHIUCNAUHIXTLAHUATL (Nine Fields), pc.n., refers to the underworld (NED). 1:11.

CHIUCNAUHNEPANIUHQUI (Nine Layers), i.e., the heavens (or the underworld?). 4:46 (refers to sky), 78:11.

CHIUCNAUHOZOMATLI, p.n., a supernatural. 24:45.

CHIUCNAUHTILIHUICAN (Nine Hills), pc.n., refers to the underworld (?, cf. FC 3:41:9 and HG bk. 3, app. ch. 1, parag. 15: chicue tiliuhcan = ocho collados). 1:11.

CHIUCNAUHTLAN, pc.n. 19:34 (chicunauhtlā), 64:1,35.

CHIYAPAN, see CHIAPAN.

CHOLOLLAN, pc.n. 10:52, 12:26, 18:4,44, 63:57.

CHOLOLTECA, g.n., pl. 13:18, 18:8.

CHRITIANOTIN, see XPIANOTIN.

CIHUACOATL, female p.n., a supernatural. 76:52, 81:1.

CIHUACUECUENOTL or CIHUACUECUENOTZIN, p.n.

    1. Rebel son (grandson per 36:12) of TEZOZOMOCTLI 1. 32:34 (çihua-quequenotzin), 32:35,39,40,42, 36:12, 38:22.

    2. Infant grandson of TEZOZOMOCTLI 1. 35:2,2,6.

CIHUATEOTITLAN, pc.n. 65:7.

CIHUATLAN, pc.n. 64:46, 67:38.

CIHUATLICPAC, pc.n. 21:18 (cihuatlyicpac).

CIHUAXOCHITZIN, p.n. 35:14, 37:35, 39:33.

CILIMIYAUHTZIN, female p.n. 37:27.

CILLAN, pc.n. 67:23, 121:10.

CIMA, p.n.

    1. 12:5.

    2. See ALONSO CIMATZIN.

CIMAPAN, pc.n.

    1. 11:29 (cimapan tehuiloyocan).

    2. = 1 (?). 28:24 (cimapan teopā).

CIMATECATZINTLI, p.n. 13:30.

CIMATZIN, see ALONSO CIMATZIN. Cf. CIMA.

CINCALCO, pc.n. 11:7, 83:27.

CINCOC, pc.n.

    1. 10:7,7, 18:32.

    2. = 1 (?). 41:24 (cincoc huehuetocan), 41:31.

CINCUANI, p.n. 29:4.

CINPALLANALCO, pc.n. 30:14.

CIPACTONAL, female p.n. (but male p.n. per FC 4:4:6), a mythical character.
    1:27,28, 77:17,18,19.

CITLALATONAC, p.n., a spirit or deity. 4:44, 76:3,20.

CITLALCOATL or CITLALCOATZIN (36:24), p.n.

    1. Ruler of Toltitlan. 31:29,33, 64:4.

    2. Son of ITZCOATL 1. 36:24.

    3. Son of MOTEUCZOMA 2. 50:23,38.

CITLALINICUE, female p.n., a spirit or deity. 4:44 (çitlali ycue), 76:3,20.

CITLALINITEOPAN, pc.n. 19:31.

CITLALPOLLAN, pc.n. 65:8.

CITLALTEPEC, pc.n. 29:20, 48:50, 49:15 (çitlaltepecpa = to Citlaltepec),
    54:19, 64:8 (as one of Cuauhtitlan's Four Lords); coupled with TZOM-
    PANCO, 12:21, 13:35, 21:11,45, 29:18, 40:34, 47:9; coupled with
    CUAUHTLAAPAN, 29:35, 46:47. Cf. CITLALTEPETL.

CITLALTEPECA, g.n., pl. 40:44, 47:10, 53:47.

CITLALTEPETL (Hill of the Star). 54:12 (at CITLALTEPEC, cf. 54:19).

COAAPAN, pc.n. 65:7.

COACALCO, pc.n. 20:4, 22:31,33,42.

COACUEYE or COACUE (8:45), female p.n.

    1. One of the early Chichimec women. 3:33.

    2. Goddess, called "my mother" in song sung by Topiltzin Quetzalcoatl. 7:4.

    3. Wife of Huemac. 8:43,45.

COACUEYECAN, pc.n. 8:44.

COAIXTLAHUACAN, pc.n. 11:1, 51:35,50, 66:46,47,49, 67:1, 84:42.

COATEPEC, pc.n. 11:43, 53:40, 59:15, 64:37.

COATEQUITL, p.n. 41:29,41,42,47. See also GLOS: coatequitl.

COATITLAN, pc.n. 12:23, 13:36.

COATL.
1. Female p.n. 3:32.
2. See COATZIN.
3. As common noun, see GLOS.

COATLACHCO, pc.n. 65:17.

COATLAN, pc.n. 84:45.

COATLAYAUHQUI, p.n. 83:31,33.

COATLICHAN, pc.n. 24:24, 25:52, 32:47, 33:15, 45:35, 46:41, 57:50, 62:22, 63:38, 64:3,33.

COATLICUAUHPECHCO, pc.n. 121:11.

COATLIYOPAN, pc.n. 10:39.

COATLPOPOCA, p.n. 63:56.

COATLYAYAUHCAN, pc.n. 11:39.

COATOLCO, pc.n. 11:18 (covatolco ayahualolco).

COATOMATZIN, p.n. 13:13,20.

COATZIN, p.n.
1. 28:27.
2. 43:46.
3. Cf. COATL 1.

COATZINCATL, g.n. 61:6.

COCOTITLAN, p.n. 26:28, 40:29, 52:29.

COCOTL, p.n. 26:28.

COCYAMA, pc.n. 80:24 (cocyamaa), 80:25 (cocyama).

COHUIXCO, pc.n. 3:39.

COLELETLI, see TZITZIMITL/COLELETLI.

COLHUA or COLHUACATL (50:29), pl. COLHUAQUE, g.n., inhabitants of COLHUACAN 4. 2:11 (chichimeca colhuaque), 11:4,19,51, 12:13,41, 13:24, 16:47,52, 17:4,23,26,34,42,43, 18:24,25,26,28,37,47; 23:13, 25:50, 32:11 (their year count), 47:30,31 (their traditions as source), 49:20, 50:29, 83:48,52,53, 84:4; refers to the exiled Colhuaque of Chichimeca-cuicoyan who founded Cuauhtitlan town, 20:29,32,34, 24:27–48 passim, 25:13–55 passim, 26:6,20, 27:23,38.

COLHUACAN, pc.n.
1. Ancient homeland of the Mexica (FC 10:196:7: Colhoaca Mexico, cf. HMPP ch. 9: Culhuacán). 83:38 (in colhuacan in aztlan).
2. Name applied to TOLLAN. 4:32 (tollan colhuacan).
3. Reference unclear. 62:17 (in mythic times Mixcoatl and other devils "descended on Colhuacan").
4. Town and nation immediately south of Mexico. 10:50, 11:16,20,26,44,47, 48, 12:15,16,27,28,36,37,52,56,57, 13:3,4,16,17,24,44, 16:40 (grouped

with Tepaneca), 16:45,49,50, 17:8,13,40,52,54, 18:4,18,19,25,36,36, 21: 48,49, 22:3,8,50,52, 23:12,19,46,47, 24:1,16, 24:19 (techichco colhuacan), 24:30,36, 26:3, 27:28 (techichco colhuacan), 27:31,32,40,41,45, 30:28, 31:44,47, 42:49, 46:34, 49:46,48, 51:12, 52:12, 57:1,5,9,39,41, 61:27,38,49, 63:38,51, 83:42, 84:12,13. See COLHUACANTI.

COLHUACANTI, to reach Colhuacan (see GN sec. 2.4). 12:11.

COLHUAQUE, see COLHUA.

COMALLAN, pc.n. 80:18.

COMALTECATL, pl. COMALTECA, g.n. 62:26,27, 80:19.

COMALTEPEC, pc.n. 122:3.

COMITLAN, pc.n. 121:22.

*CONELTEUCTLI, p.n. (?, see note to the translation at 62:40).

CONTECA, g.n., pl., inhabitants of CONTLAN, q.v. 58:9.

CONTITLAN, pc.n. 17:12,28,28.

CONTLAN, pc.n., one of the original boroughs of TLALMANALCO (?, the Conteca were one of five groups that settled Tlalmanalco per CHIM 165, ZCHIM 1:40). 58:7.

COPILCO, pc.n. 11:1.

COTZXIPETZCO, pc.n. 19:31.

COXCOXTLI, vars. COXCOX TEUCTLI, COXCOXTZIN, COXCOXTZIN TEUCTLI (22:9), p.n.
  1. Ruler of Colhuacan. 21:49, 22:3,9,49, 23:15,26,47, 26:3.
  2. Ruler of Tetzcoco. 34:49.

COYOAC (IXT 2:114), pc.n. 64:39 (coyohuac).

COYOCAC, pc.n. 67:33, 121:19.

COYOCHIMALCO, pc.n. 65:16.

COYOCTZIN, p.n. 64:2.

COYOHUA, p.n. 35:45, 36:1,3,7,31, 37:9–32 passim, 38:10–19, 38:37–48 passim, 39:2–52 passim.

COYOHUACAN, pc.n. 16:39, 33:23 (copyist has erroneously written "colhuacan"), 33:26 (coyoacan), 46:23,40, 59:21, 63:52, 66:37, 84:33.

COYOHUAQUE, g.n., pl. 13:25.

COYOLAPAN, pc.n. 67:37, 121:21 (Coyollapan).

COYOMILPAN, pc.n. 19:30.

COYOTEPEC, pc.n. 29:37, 46:49.

COYOTEPECA, g.n. 40:43.

COYOTLINAHUAL, p.n., god of featherworkers (HG bk. 9, ch. 18). 5:53,54, 6:2,10.

COYOTLIYACAMIUH, p.n. 28:39.

COYOTZIN, p.n. 10:47.

COYOZACATZIN, p.n. 29:19.

COZAUHQUIXOCHITL, p.n. 21:36.

COZCACUAUHTENANCA, g.n., pl. 58:1,41,46, 121:18.

COZCACUAUHTENANCO, pc.n. 67:32.

COZCACUAUHTLAN, pc.n. 65:12.

COZCATECA, g.n. 14:28.

COZCATECOTLAN (should be Cozcateuctlan?—the third town on fol. 54 of Cod. Mendoza is "Cozcatecutlan"), pc.n. 64:44.

COZCATLAN, pc.n. 10:52.

COZOHUIPILECAN, pc.n. 121:18 (Cozohuipillecan, conquered by Ahuitzotzin). Cf. COZOHUIPILLAN.

COZOHUIPILLAN, pc.n. 67:33 (conquered by Ahuitzotzin). Cf. COZOHUIPILECAN.

COZOQUENTLAN, pc.n. 64:45.

CUACHAYATZIN, p.n. 45:2.

CUACHICOL, pc.n. 64:45.

CUACHILCO, pc.n. 49:32.

CUACUICUILCO, pc.n. 63:19.

CUAHUACAN, pc.n. 21:35,36, 22:24, 30:12,13, 47:44,44,47, 55:52, 63:37, 84:2,34.

CUAHUACATZINCO, pc.n. 21:24.

CUAHUAQUE, g.n., pl. 40:43, 48:2 (cuahuaque tepaneca).

CUAHUAQUE OTOMI, g.n., pl. 18:11. See also CUAHUAQUE, OTOMITL.

CUAHUICOL, p.n. 3:31.

CUAHUITLICACAN, pc.n. 11:28.

CUAHUITONAL, p.n. 12:37,53,56.

CUAMAMAZTZIN, p.n. 28:40.

CUAMINCAN, pc.n. 35:39.

CUAPOCHTLI, p.n. 27:13.

CUAPPANOHUAYAN, pc.n. 67:14, 121:1.

CUAPPILOLLAN, pc.n. 67:41.

CUAPPIYO, see CUAUHPIYO.

CUAPPOPOCATZIN, p.n.
   1. Ruler of Coatlichan. 57:50.
   2. Ruler of Coyohuacan. 63:53.

CUAPPOTONQUI, p.n. 55:4,15, 59:49.

CUATIZATEPEC, pc.n. 63:18.

CUATLALATL (Mudhead), p.n. 37:48.

CUAUHACALTITLAN (Place of the Wooden Flume), pc.n. 61:9.

CUAUHCALAPAN, pc.n. 65:15.

CUAUHCALCO, pc.n. 65:17.

CUAUHCHICHITZIN TLACATEUCTZIN, p.n. 29:21.

CUAUHCHINANCO, pc.n. 63:36, 64:36.

CUAUHCIHUATZIN, female p.n. 34:50.

CUAUHIXTLI, p.n. 30:3.

CUAUHIZOMOCA (should be Coaizomoca?, see GLOS: izomoca), p.n. 14:53.

CUAUHNACAZTITLAN, pc.n. Conquered by Ahuitzotzin, 67:37, 121:24 (Cuauhnacaztlan).

CUAUHNACAZTLAN, see CUAUHNACAZTITLAN.

CUAUHNAHUAC, pc.n. 30:23 (los de quauhnahuac), 58:47,52, 59:44,45, 61:32,43, 63:36,48, 64:19, 65:51, 66:38, 67:1, 84:17,19,35,45.

CUAUHNAHUACA, g.n., pl. 28:25 (quauhnahuacan), 28:26, 47:36, 57:13, 44, 58:52.

CUAUHNENE, female p.n. 10:11.

CUAUHNENEC, pc.n. 10:10,12.

CUAUHNEXTLI or CUAUHNEXTLI TEUCTLI, p.n. 31:49, 34:31.

CUAUHNOCHTLI

  1. An official title (for discussion see FC 9:47:n10).

  2. P.n. (García Granados *Diccionario*).

  3. P.n. (?). 24:46.

CUAUHPILOLLAN, pc.n. 121:25.

CUAUHPIYO or CUAUHPIYOTZIN, p.n. 33:16 (quappiyo), 34:44 (quauhpiyotzin), 45:37 (quappiyō).

CUAUHQUECE, p.n. 15:15.

CUAUHQUECHOLLAN, pc.n. 3:40, 63:45.

CUAUHQUECHOLTECA, g.n., pl. 18:6, 21:47, 24:7.

CUAUHQUEMECAN, pc.n. 21:19.

CUAUHTECA, g.n., pl. 18:8.

CUAUHTECHCAC, pc.n. 63:35.

CUAUHTENAMPAN, pc.n. 51:16.

CUAUHTENCO, pc.n. 10:51 (tlapechuacan quauhtenco), 11:19 (idem).

CUAUHTEPEC, pc.n. 20:5, 21:15, 26:35. Cf. CUAUHTEPETL.

CUAUHTEPETL, pc.n. Cf. CUAUHTEPEC.

  1. Place held by Xaltocan before the war with Cuauhtitlan. 19:33.

  2. Place near Colhuacan, held by Cuauhtitlan (= 1, above?). 23:23,43.

CUAUHTEXPETLATZIN, p.n. 11:17,20,26,44,47.

CUAUHTICATZIN, p.n. 18:53, 19:14.

CUAUHTINCHAN, pc.n. 18:3,8,44, 29:44, 52:3, 53:41; quauhtinchan tlaca, 29:40,47.

CUAUHTITLAN, pc.n.

  1. The nation or country. 1:39, 1:51 (altepetl quauhtitlan = country of Cuauhtitlan), 2:13,53,56, 3:13,48, 4:12,28,29, 8:9,13,21,25,34,35, 9:11, 13, 10:40 (huehue quauhtitlan = old Cuauhtitlan), 12:19 (nican quauhtitlan), 12:30, 13:27,35, 14:36,39, 15:22,24,25,29, 17:31, 18:17,39,41, 20:10,39, 21:12,14,29,40,44,52, 22:18, 23:3, 24:34, 24:37 (nican . . . quauhtitlan), 25:24,52,53, 27:15,17,23,46,50, 28:9,20,21, 29:2, 30:32, 35,37,39,42,45,47, 31:1,7 (altepetl quauhtitlan), 31:11,14, 32:12,19.

  2. The town. 26:11 (altepetl quauhtitlan), 29:27 (where the temple stood),

29:29,31 (has four quarters), 40:24 (where slave market was), 40:41, 48, 41:6,10,15,23,27,36, 42:9,15, 46:43 (its servant communities), 48:15, 56:1,7,12,46 (altepetl quauhtitlan), 60:7. See also CUAUHTI-TLANCALCAYOTL.

3. Nation or town. 29:53, 40:5,7,11,13,16, 41:3,4,40, 42:3, 43:4,40,49, 46:15,32, 47:1,5,38,49,51, 48:7,9,43,51, 49:1, 52:8, 54:2,38, 55:40, 59:4,6,39,52, 60:9,23,38,57, 61:1,30, 64:7, 66:1,39, 84:23,35.

CUAUHTITLANCALCAYOTL, that which pertains to Cuauhtitlan; the Cuauh-titlan nation or people. 25:36 (altepetl quauhtitlancalcayotl = the town of Cuauhtitlan?), 42:4 (people of Cuauhtitlan), 47:7 (altepetl quauhtitlancal-cayotl = nation of Cuauhtitlan).

CUAUHTITLANCALQUI (81:53), pl. CUAUHTITLANCALQUE, g.n. 13: 30,32,53, 14:26, 16:32 (quauhtitlancalque huehuetque), 17:10, 21:41, 28:7,51, 29:6,8,48, 30:10,16, 40:17–38 passim, 41:7,13,16,26,38, 42: 18, 43:22,43, 44:38,41, 45:16,23, 47:19,21,42,45,48, 48:21,40, 49:24, 36,38, 54:5, 55:8,50, 56:4,21,24,32,39, 60:12, 83:53; chichimeca cuauh-titlancalque or cuauhtitlancalque chichimeca, 1:41,44,52, 3:12, 13:33 (yn chichimeca yn quauhtitlancalque), 20:7,14,38,41,45, 21:1,30,39, 28:12, 42:42. See also CHICHIMECATL 4.

CUAUHTLAACAPAN, pc.n. 65:10.

CUAUHTLAAPAN, pc.n. 8:27 (tianquizçolco quauhtlaapan), 8:36, 18:33 (quauhtlaapan tianquizçolco), 29:34, 30:1 (quauhapan tianquizçolco), 46: 47; quauhtlaapan tlaca, 30:13, 40:43, 42:10.

CUAUHTLA-HUEXOCALCO, see HUEXOCALCO.

CUAUHTLALPAN, pc.n. 21:19. Cf. GLOS: cuauhtlalli.

CUAUHTLAN, pc.n. 67:40, 121:5,25.

CUAUHTLATOA (50:16) or CUAUHTLATOATZIN, p.n. (cf. GLOS: cuauhtlatoa).

1. Ruler of Tlatilolco. 29:43, 32:21, 43:8, 66:31.

2. Son of ITZCOATL 1. 36:25.

3. Emissary to Mexico from Cuitlahuac Tizic. 50:16.

CUAUHTLI, p.n. (cf. GLOS: cuauhtli).

1. P.n., high priest who succeeded Huemac as "Quetzalcoatl" of Tollan. 8: 47,56.

2. P.n. 10:19.

3. P.n. 10:35.

4. See CUAUHTZIN TEUCTLI.

CUAUHTLIICOAUH, p.n. 78:35, 79:17,23.

CUAUHTLIIPANTEMOC, p.n. 22:7.

CUAUHTLIXTLI or CUAUHTLIX, p.n. 17:53, 18:5.

CUAUHTLIZTAC, p.n. 10:34.

CUAUHTLOTLI TEUCTLI, or CUAUHTLOTLINTEUCTLI (13:5), p.n.

1. A founder of Cuitlahuac Tizic. 13:5.
2. A later ruler of Cuitlahuac Tizic. 22:11,13.

CUAUHTOCHCO, pc.n. 66:54, 84:47.

CUAUHTZAPOTLA, pc.n. 65:16.

CUAUHTZAPOTITLAN, pc.n. 65:8.

CUAUHTZIN TEUCTLI, p.n. 30:50.

CUAUHTZIPITL, p.n. 53:19.

CUAUHTZONCALTZIN, p.n. 20:31, 24:51.

CUAUHXAYACATITLAN, pc.n. 67:36, 121:23.

CUAUHXIMALPAN, pc.n. 46:38, 48:22,37, 84:34.

CUAUHXOMOLCO, pc.n. 19:33.

CUAUHYACAC, pc.n. 15:30, 62:21.

CUAXIPETZTECOMATLAN, pc.n. 65:13.

CUAXIPETZTENANTLAN, pc.n. 65:7.

CUAXOXOCAN, pc.n. = CUAXOXOUHCAN (?). 55:6.

CUAXOXOUHCAN, pc.n. 3:1,45,47. Cf. CUAXOXOCAN.

CUBA, pc.n. 59:43.

CUECHIMALTZIN, p.n. 64:2.

CUECUENOTL, p.n. 14:53.

CUECUEX, p.n., god of the Tepaneca. 44:46 (see note to the accompanying translation).

CUEPPOPAN, pc.n. 19:30.

CUETLACHCIHUATL, see CUITLACHCIHUATL

CUETLACHCOATL, see CUITLACHCOATL.

CUETLAXCOAC, pc.n. 15:46.

CUETLAXTECATL, g.n. 68:15,30.

CUETLAXTLAN, pc.n. 66:54, 67:16, 68:14 (cuetlaxtlan tlaca), 84:47, 121:4.

CUETZALCUITLAPILLAN, pc.n. 67:37.

CUETZALOZTOC, pc.n. 67:17.

CUETZALTZIN, (should be Quetzaltzin or Cuezaltzin?), p.n. 13:4,16.

CUETZPALLI or CUETZPALIN TEUCTLI, p.n.

1. First ruler of Oztoticpac. 29:45 (cuetzpalin teuctli).
2. Later ruler of Oztoticpac. 51:2 (cuetzpalli).

CUEXOMATL, pc.n., a mountain on the northern frontier between Mexica lands and Acolhua lands (IXT 2:84). 62:23.

CUEXTECATL, pl. CUEXTECA, g.n. 9:43, 54:29, 65:3. See CUEXTECATLICHOCAYAN.

CUEXTECATLICHOCAYAN (Place Where the Cuexteca Weep), pc.n. (perhaps a nonce name). 9:33.

CUEXTLAN, pc.n. 3:42, 4:23, 9:32 (cuextlanpa = from Cuextlan), 9:34.

CUEZALLAN, pc.n. 66:39, 84:37.

CUEZALCUITLAPILLAN, pc.n. 121:24.

CUEZALOZTOC, pc.n. 121:4.

CUEZALTZIN (?), see CUETZALTZIN.

CUEZCOMAHUACAN, pc.n. 21:21.

CUEZCOMAIXTLAHUACAN, pc.n. 67:15, 68:6, 122:2.

CUEZCOMATLIYACAC, pc.n. 121:2.

-CUICOYAN, see CHICHIMECACUICOYAN.

CUICUITZCACALCO, pc.n. 21:24.

CUICUITZCATZIN, p.n. 35:33,37, 36:31.

CUILTON, p.n. 81:11,33.

CUITLACHCIHUATL or CUETLACHCIHUATL, p.n. 78:36, 79:20.

CUITLACHCOATL or CUETLACHCOATL, p.n. 83:5,31,34.

CUITLACHTEPEC or CUITLACHTEPETL, p.n. Coupled with TEMAC-
PALCO, 19:32, 46:20; assoc. with TOLTITLAN, 54:6,38.

CUITLAHUAC

1. Pc.n. Note: Cuitlahuac was divided into four communities, TIZIC, TEO-
PANCALCAN, TECPAN, and ATENCHICALCAN (see 62:44–46). 13:
21, 18:20, 28:41, 32:3,29, 49:9, 55:5, 57:46 (refers to CUITLAHUAC
TIZIC), 59:28, 61:24,41 (refers to CUITLAHUAC TEOPANCALCAN),
61:52, 62:28, 63:9,49, 65:52, 66:37, 84:16,18,36.

2. P.n., see CUITLAHUATZIN.

CUITLAHUAC ATENCHICALCAN, pc.n. 59:34. See also ATENCHI-
CALCAN.

CUITLAHUACATL, pl. CUITLAHUACA, g.n. 13:8, 18:48, 23:48,50,
27:52, 28:43 (tecpaneca cuitlahuaca), 29:50,52, 32:15,16, 33:1 (cuitlahuaca tiçica), 33:2 (cuitlahuaca teopancalca), 33:9, 48:12, 49:5,11,12,
49:50 (cuitlahuaca . . . atenchicalque), 49:54 (tiçica cuitlahuaca), 50:34
(refers to the Tizica), 57:29, 59:16,31,46, 61:35,54, 84:3. See also
TLAHUACA.

CUITLAHUAC TECPAN, pc.n. 61:34; tecpaneca cuitlahuaca, see CUITLA-
HUACATL. See also TECPAN 2.

CUITLAHUAC TEOPANCALCAN, pc.n. 55:15, 59:48, 60:2; cuitlahuaca
teopancalca, see CUITLAHUACATL. See also TEOPANCALCAN.

CUITLAHUAC TIZIC, pc.n. 13:13,14,20, 17:51, 18:1,22,45, 21:5 (tiçic cuitlahuac), 22:12,14, 24:5, 28:35,45, 30:30, 32:6, 43:2, 57:48 (cuitlahuac
tizic); cuitlahuaca tiçica, see CUITLAHUACATL. See also TIZIC.

CUITLAHUATZIN, var. CUITLAHUAC (FC bk. 8, ch. 1), p.n.

1. Son of ITZCOATL 1. 36:25.

2. Ruler of Huexotla. 57:35, 60:7.

3. Ruler of Itztapalapan. 63:51.

CUITLAPITOC, p.n. 68:31.

CUIXCOC, pc.n. 81:39.

DIABLO (Devil), see GLOS.
DIEGO QUINATZIN, p.n. 15:41 (Don Diego quinatzin).
DIEGO NECUAMETZIN, p.n. 16:16,17 (Don diego necuametzin).
DIEGO TIZAATZIN, p.n. 61:49 (Don Diego tiçaatzin).
DOMINGO, see SANTO DOMINGO.

ECATEPEC, pc.n. 19:34, 21:16, 60:18, 63:54, 67:23; ècatepec, 12:23, 21:
    39, 60:13,19,22,25, 121:9 (Yecatepec).
ECATEPECA, g.n., pl. 49:35 (ècatepeca).
ECATLICUAPPANCO, pc.n. 67:24.
ECATZIN, p.n., a ruler of Tlahuacan Chalca in Xicco. 26:51. Cf. YECATL
    TEUCTLI.
EHUATLICUETZIN, p.n. 27:17,20.
EPCOAC, pc.n. 21:17 (epcohuac).
EPCOATL or EPCOATZIN, p.n.
    1. Ruler of Cuitlahuac Tizic (epcoatzin). 18:46, 21:50.
    2. Ruler of Toltitlan (epcoatl). 31:5,16,20, 33:18, 34:45, 40:7, 45:41,47.
ESPAÑOLES, g.n., pl. 16:6,7,21, 31:30,32, 49:22, 59:43, 63:40,42, 68:10.
    See also CAXTILTECA.
EZCOATZIN, p.n. 11:29,36.
EZTECALLAN, pc.n. 65:16.
EZTLAQUENCATZIN or EZTLAQUENTZIN, p.n., a ruler of Cuauhtitlan.
    9:21, 11:25.
EZTLAQUENQUI, p.n., a spirit or deity. 4:45.

FRANCISCO CARLOS XOCONOCHTZIN, p.n. 15:19, 16:28.

GABRIEL DE TAPIA MAZACIHUATL, p.n. 31:41 (Don gabriel de tapia
    maçacihuatl).
GERONIMO DE LOS ANGELES, p.n. 31:40 (Don geronimo de los angeles).
GRANADA, pc.n. 59:3. See also marginal glosses at 51:12 and 61:24.

HERNANDO, p.n. 59:45 (Don hernando [of Cuauhnahuac]).
HERNANDO MATLALIHUITZIN, p.n. 31:34 (Don Hernando Matlali-
    huitzin).
HUACTLI or HUACTZIN, p.n.
    1. Early ruler of Cuauhtitlan. Vactli, 3:15,18,28, 4:12,20.
    2. Later ruler of Cuauhtitlan. Vactli *or* vactzin, 18:41,50, 19:27, 20:11 (chi-
    chimecatl vactzin), 20:36, 21:53, 22:5,7,19,36,44, 23:8,25, 25:54, 26:2.
HUAHUANTZIN, p.n. 35:32,36,46.
HUAUHQUIL, p.n. 19:3.

HUAUHTLAN., pc.n. 43:48 (atempan huauhtlan).

HUAXTEPEC, pc.n. 63:37,47, 67:2, 84:43.

HUECATLAN, pc.n. 21:33 (huecatlan atlauhco).

HUECOMPAN (At the Great Pot Cactus), pc.n. 10:22 (hueyconpan). Cf. GLOS: huei comitl.

HUEHUE CUAUHTITLAN (Old Cuauhtitlan), pc.n. 10:40 (in or near TAMAZOLAC).

HUEHUETECA, g.n., pl. 18:43.

HUEHUETEOTL (Old Spirit), epithet of XIUHTEUCTLI. 1:6.

HUEHUETLAN, pc.n. 53:24, 67:38, 121:21.

HUEHUETLITZALAN, pc.n. 64:21.

HUEHUETOCAMECA, g.n. 47:18.

HUEHUETOCAN, pc.n. 1:41 (macuexhuacan huehuetocan), 21:11, 29:18, 20,36, 40:38, 41:24 (cincoc huehuetocan), 46:48, 47:17, 64:8 (one of Cuauhtitlan's Four Lords), 80:26,27.

HUEIACATZIN, p.n. 28:39. Cf. ACATZIN.

HUEIAPAN, pc.n. 121:34.

HUEIIMIUH (Big Dart), p.n. 37:47.

HUEIPOCHTLAN, pc.n. 21:31, 29:23.

HUEITEPEC, pc.n. 21:23.

HUEITOCTITLAN, pc.n. 26:27 (tlalcozpan hueitoctitlan).

HUEMAC, p.n. 8:40, 8:40 gloss (huemac atecpanecatl), 8:50,54, 9:6, 10:2, 6,8,11, 11:6,12, 12:54, 81:48, 82:14,15,17,18,19,49,53, 83:2,8,27. See also TEZCACOATL.

HUETL, p.n., = HUETZIN (?). 10:19.

HUETZIN, p.n.
  1. Ruler of Tollan. 3:51.
  2. Ruler of Colhuacan. 11:48 (huetzi), 12:15,17, 12:18 (huetzi).
  3. Ruler of Nonoalco. 81:50.
  4. See HUETL.

HUEXOCALCO or CUAUHTLA-HUEXOCALCO, pc.n., site of the ruler's palace in Cuauhtitlan town. 32:22, 41:34, 42:21, 44:14, 48:16 (huexocaltitlan = next to Huexocalco), 59:54 (coupled with TLAXOXIUHCO); quauhtla huexocalco, 48:53, 49:2 (cf. FC 11:176:13: quauhtla texcalco = in the wilds).

HUEXOLOTLAN, pc.n. 68:2, 121:20 (Huexollotlan), 122:4 (Huexollotlan).

HUEXOTLA, pc.n. 25:52, 33:16, 35:17, 45:37, 46:41, 57:10,34, 60:7,51, 64:3,33.

HUEXOTZINCATL, pl. HUEXOTZINCA, g.n. 13:11, 18:2,7,43, 24:8,21, 26:46, 27:7, 42:37, 43:37, 44:33,48, 45:10,13,22,29,42, 51:2, 57:15, 45, 58:39, 59:14, 61:46, 63:26; mohuexotzincachichiuhtinenca, 42:27, 42; mohuexotzincanotzaya, 42:38.

HUEXOTZINCO, pc.n. 3:40,44, 13:18, 24:9, 28:1, 34:15, 43:18–49
   passim, 44:21, 45:2, 46:17,33, 51:3, 52:35, 53:21, 57:19, 58:49,
   59:10,16,24, 60:42,52, 61:35, 63:57.
HUICTLOLINQUI, p.n. 76:21,55.
HUILACAPICHTEPEC, pc.n. 19:33.
HUILOC, pc.n. 65:17.
HUILOTEPEC, pc.n. 121:30 (Huillotepec).
HUIPILLAN, pc.n. 67:39, 121:21.
HUITZCO, name of a mountain. 4:38, 9:8 (huitzcoc = on Huitzco).
HUITZILATZIN, p.n. 63:52.
HUITZILIHUITL or HUITZILIHUITZIN, p.n.
   1. Leader of the Mexica prior to the founding of Mexico. 13:43,44,45, 17:7,
      83:41, 84:5.
   2. Second king of Tenochtitlan. 29:52, 30:21,25, 32:7, 65:56, 66:3, 84:21,
      25,26,38.
   3. One who cuckolded Nezahualpilli. 59:18.
HUITZILOPOCHCO, pc.n. 10:50, 15:36, 16:18, 63:52. See also 50:30
   (translation only).
HUITZILOPOCHTLI, p.n., god of the Mexica. 33:45, 57:42, 58:35, 61:58,
   78:13.
HUITZILPOPOCA, p.n. 81:49.
HUITZILTEPEC, pc.n. 18:32.
HUITZILTEUHCATZIN, p.n. 52:11.
HUITZITZILAPAN, pc.n. 66:40, 84:35.
HUITZNAHUA, g.n. (Aubin per SIM). 12:6 (huitznahua chichimeca), 29:10
   (xaltocameca ca huitznahua = Xaltocameca who are Huitznahua), 80:40,41
   (Huitznahua women).
HUITZNAHUAC, pc.n.
   1. 14:9 (tequixquinahuac huitznahuac viztopan).
   2. 80:29,44,49.
HUITZOCUITLAPILLAN, pc.n. 21:20 (huitzocuitlapilla).
HUITZTLAN, pc.n. 67:39,49, 121:23,31.
HUIXACHCUAUHYO- (incomplete owing to copyist's error?), pc.n. 21:21.
HUIXACHTLAN, pc.n. 60:6.
HUIXTOMPAN, pc.n. 12:33 (tepetlapan yn tequixquinahuac viztonpan), 14:9
   (tequixquinahuac huitznahuac viztopan), 17:45 (tequixquinahuac vixtōpa).
"HUIZTONPAN," see HUIXTOMPAN.

ICHCAPETLACOTLA, pc.n. 65:10.
ICHCATLAN, pc.n. 65:44.
ICHPOCHCO, pc.n. 19:35.
ICHPOCHTETITLAN, pc.n. 21:26.

ICNOTLACATL, p.n. 10:17,20; cf. 10:24,27 (play on the name Icnotlacatl, "poor man").

ICPATEPEC, pc.n. 61:22, 67:48, 121:32.

IHUIMECATL, p.n., one of the sorcerers who put Quetzalcoatl to flight. 5: 26,52,53, 6:10,37,47.

IHUITIMAL, p.n. 3:55.

IHUITL, p.n. (?).
 1. Name of one of the three hearthstones. 1:7, 3:27.
 2. See IHUITZIN.

IHUITLTEMOCTZIN, p.n. 14:52,53, 15:2,12.

IHUITZIN, p.n., one of the Tlahuaca founders. 13:5. Cf. IHUITL.

ILANCUEITL, female p.n. 24:23, 26:40, 26:44 (ellancueytl), 27:31 (idem), 27:39 (elancueytl), 27:51 (illancueyitl), 30:28 (yllancueytl).

ILHUICAMINA or ILHUICAMINATZIN, p.n.
 1. Epithet of MOTEUCZOMATZIN 1, q.v.
 2. Epithet of MOTEUCZOMATZIN 2 (FC 6:71:7: jlvicamjna).

ILTITLAN, pc.n. 13:51, 20:4.

IMEXAYAC, p.n. (?). 64:6 (should be y mexayac?, cf. MEXAYACATL).

IQUEHUAC (3:32) or IQUEHUACATZIN, p.n.
 1. An early Chichimec. 3:32.
 2. A prince of Cuauhtitlan. 28:10,10.
 3. Son of MOTEUCZOMATZIN 1. 50:24 (iquehuacatzin), 50:39.

ITZCAHUA or ITZCAHUATZIN, p.n. 58:5,10,16,19, 58:28 (ytzcohuatzin), 58:32, 63:47.

ITZCALPAN, pc.n. 62:25.

ITZCOATL (34:22) or ITZCOATZIN
 1. Fourth ruler of Tenochtitlan. 26:18, 30:25,26, 34:18,22,27, 36:2–29 passim, 37:1,39, 38:3, 40:2,10, 43:15, 45:25, 46:32, 47:37, 48:10, 28,33, 49:4,35,37,43, 62:50, 66:28,29,41, 84:31,32, 84:49, 121:7,14.
 2. Ruler of Cuauhnahuac. 59:45, 61:31.

ITZCUINCUITLAPILCO, pc.n. 67:4, 84:46.

ITZCUINTEPEC, pc.n. 68:8, 122:4.

ITZCUINTZIN, p.n. 29:20.

ITZMATLA, pc.n. 65:6,9.

ITZOCAN, pc.n., = ITZYOCAN (?). 82:10.

ITZPAPALOTL, female p.n., goddess of the Chichimecs. 1:9,12,15, 3:17, 4:21, 25:48, 50:36, 80:8, 80:19 (refers to fetish).

ITZTAPALAPAN, pc.n. 50:11,18, 61:4, 63:51.

ITZTAPALAPANECATL, g.n. 50:30.

ITZTAPALLOCAN, pc.n. 64:37.

ITZTEPEC, pc.n. 84:36.

ITZTLACOLIUHQUI, p.n. 3:31.

ITZTOLPANXOCHI or ITZTOLPANXOCHITL, female p.n. 22:5, 23:4.
ITZTOLTZIN, p.n. 60:13.
ITZYOCAN, pc.n., = ITZOCAN (?). 63:45, 67:2. Cf. ITZYOYOCAN.
ITZYOYOCAN, pc.n. 68:3. Cf. ITZYOCAN.
IXAHUATZIN, p.n. 19:12.
IXAPAZTLI TEUCTLI, p.n. 31:49.
IXAYOC, pc.n. 19:31, 29:12.
IXAYOCTONCA, g.n. 29:11.
IXAYOCTONCO, pc.n. 19:31, 29:14.
IXCOZAUHQUI, p.n. 63:44.
IXCUINAN, pl. IXCUINANME

1. A name for Tlazolteotl, the goddess of filth (FFCC bk. 1, ch. 12: Ixcuina), so
   called because there were four Tlazolteotls (FFCC: explanation not given;
   GKC, p. 77, derives ixcuinan from Huaxtec Maya, with the meaning "female
   kapok").
2. Pl., refers to a certain class of female supernaturals (i.e., the Tlazolteotls),
   said to "descend to the earth" (HG bk. 1, ch. 12, parag. 18: Ixcuiname).
3. Pl., female devils who came from Cuextlan. 9:30, 9:39 (ixcuiname), 9:40.

IXICAYAN, pc.n. 65:5.
IXTEHUEYO, p.n. 61:47, 63:27,31.
IXTLILCUECHAHUAC, pc.n. 64:15.
IXTLILTZIN, p.n., see MATEO IXTLILTZIN.
IXTLILXOCHITL or IXTLILXOCHITZIN, p.n.

1. The elder. 18:47, 23:49, 27:9, 32:31, 32:34 (ilxochitzin), 32:37,44,
   34:13, 35:23,29,34, 36:11, 38:21, 43:1, 46:30.
2. The younger.

IXTOMI (Fuzzy Face), p.n. 37:47.
IXTOTOMAHUATZIN, p.n. 57:30, 59:49, 60:2, 61:23,37,40,45, 63:50.
IYACTECUIZOTLAN, pc.n. 65:11.
IYAUHPOTONQUI, or YAUHQUEMEPOTONQUI, p.n. 61:47 (yyauhpo-
   lonqui), 63:27 (yauhquemepotonqui).
IYAUHTEPEC, pc.n. 84:42.
IYAUHTEPECA, g.n., pl. 28:26.
IYEHUACAN, pc.n. 19:47.
IZHUATLAN, pc.n. 67:38, 121:22.
IZQUITLAN, pc.n.

1. 9:15 (izquitlan atla).
2. = 1 (?). 19:12.

IZQUIXOCHITEPEC, pc.n. 61:22, 67:48.
IZTACALCO, pc.n. 15:53.
IZTACCHALCHIUHTLICUE, p.n., 78:32.
IZTACCOAC, pc.n. 19:46.

IZTACCOATL, p.n. (?). 63:17.

IZTAC MIXCOATL (White Mixcoatl), see MIXCOATL.

IZTAC TEUCTLI, p.n. 13:26.

IZTACTLALOCAN, pc.n. Iztactlallocan, 61:39,40, 67:35, 121:23,32.

IZTACTOTOTL or IZTACTOTOTZIN (22:25), p.n. 22:8,19,25,34,37,40,43, 48,51, 23:13, 26:5,7, 27:15,18,19.

IZTACXILOTZIN, female p.n. 9:14,19.

IZTATLAN, pc.n. 121:22.

IZTAUHYATLI, p.n. 64:15 (yztauhyatly yxtlilcuechahuac . . . , *should be* yztauhyatl y yxtlil. . . . ? Cf. IMEXAYAC).

IZTITLAN, pc.n. 60:40, 68:8, 122:4.

JUAN, abbrev. JU° (see NED: paha). See immediately below; see also SAN JUAN.

JUAN MATLALIHUITZIN, p.n., ruler of Apazco (= MATLALIHUITZIN 1?). 64:12 (Don ju° matlallihuitzi).

JUAN TLACOCHCALCATL, p.n. 63:56 (don Ju° tlacochcalcatl).

JUAN XALTEMOCTZIN, p.n. 15:40 (don Ju° Xaltemoctzin).

JUAN YOLLOCAMACHALTZIN, p.n. 19:10 (don ju° yollocamachaltzin).

JUDIOSME, g.n., pl., Span., judios, i.e., Jews. 59:3. See also marginal gloss at 51:12.

LUIS DE LA VEGA, p.n. 15:34 (don luis de la vega), 15:35 (don luis).

LUIS DE MANUEL MALOMITL, p.n. 16:19 (don luis de manuel mallomitl), 16:23,27 (Don luis de manuel).

MACUEXHUACAN (màcuexhuacan per 2:13), pc.n. 1:41 (macuexhuacan huehuetocan), 2:13, 2:52, 21:22, 56:5.

MACUEXTLAN, pc.n. 64:46.

MACUEXTZIN, p.n. 60:24.

MACUILOCOTLAN, pc.n. 60:27 (macuillocotlan).

MACUILOCTLAN, pc.n. 61:39.

MACUILTZINCO, pc.n. 61:6.

MACUILXOCHITL or MACUILXOCHITZIN, p.n.
   1. See PEDRO MACUILXOCHITL.
   2. A prince of Atlixco. 60:44,45.

MALIHUITZIN, p.n. 57:4,7 (mallihuitzin). Syn. MAXIHUITZIN.

MALINALCO, pc.n. 11:45.

MALINALLOCAN, pc.n. 19:35.

MALINALTEPEC, pc.n. 68:5, 121:34.

MALINTZIN, female p.n. 62:42.

"MALLOMITL," see LUIS DE MANUEL MALOMITL.

MALOMITL, see LUIS DE MANUEL MALOMITL.

MALPANTZIN TEUCTLI, p.n. 62:48.

MAMALHUAZYOCAN, pc.n. 66:53.

MAMALITZIN, p.n. 64:2 (mamallitzin).

MAMATZIN TEUCTLI, p.n.
1. Ruler of Cuitlahuac Tizic. 22:14, 24:6.
2. Ruler of the Tlahuacan Chalca in Xicco. 26:50.

MANUEL, see LUIS DE MANUEL MALOMITL.

MAPACH (Raccoon, see FC 11:9), p.n. 62:35.

MAPACHTEPEC, pc.n. 121:24.

MAQUIZPANTZIN, p.n. 63:3,6.

MAQUIZTECA, g.n., pl. 62:26.

MAQUIZTLI, p.n. 62:27.

MARIA, p.n.
1. Doña Maria of Huitzilopochco. 15:36, 16:17,24.
2. Doña Maria of Xochimilco. 61:17.

MARQUES or MARQUES DEL VALLE, i.e., Hernando Cortés (NED: malques). 15:44, 21:43 (marques del balle), 122:6.

MATEO IXTLILTZIN, p.n. Don mateo ixtliltzin, 57:32, 59:50.

MATLACCOATZIN, p.n. 8:24,31.

MATLACXOCHITL or MATLACXOCHITZIN, p.n. 5:23, 8:4,11.

MATLALIHUITZIN, p.n.
1. Ruler of Apazco (?, = JUAN MATLALIHUITZIN?). 64:5 (matlillihui-tzin—presumed copyist's error).
2. See HERNANDO MATLALIHUITZIN.

MATLATLAN, pc.n. 67:15, 121:2.

MATLATZINCATL, pl. MATLATZINCA, g.n. 57:11, 84:3.

MATLATZINCO, pc.n. 14:42, 52:1, 55:8,11, 57:26, 63:55, 67:23, 84:51, 121:10.

MAXALIUHYAN, see TEPETLMAXALIUHYAN.

MAXIHUITZIN, p.n. 57:3. Syn. MALIHUITZIN.

MAXTLA or MAXTLATON (6:14, etc.) or MAXTLATZIN (34:48), p.n.
1. A Toltec of Topiltzin's time. 6:14,17, 10:29.
2. A Chichimec captain. 18:52.
3. A Chichimec of Xallan. 26:33 (maxtlaton).
4. Tepaneca ruler, son of TEZOZOMOCTLI 1. 33:23–41 passim, 34:10,11, 48, 40:5,49, 42:24,47, 43:7,9,29,39, 44:13,31,36, 46:22, 66:8,16,17.
5. One who cuckolded Nezahualpilli. 59:18.
6. An official from Cuauhtitlan. 60:13,25, 60:28 (translation only).

MAYEHUATZIN, p.n. 59:34, 63:49.

MAZAAPAN, pc.n. 65:6.

MAZACIHUATL, see GABRIEL DE TAPIA MAZACIHUATL.

MAZACOYOTZIN, p.n. 63:55.

MAZAHUACAN, pc.n. 35:4, 84:2, 121:10.

MAZAMICAN, pc.n. 21:23.

MAZATEPEC, pc.n.
1. Where early Chichimecs "decorated themselves." 1:21.
2. Town controlled by Tetzcoco. 64:20.
3. Town conquered by Tizocicatzin (= 2?). 67:24.

MAZATLAN, pc.n. 11:2, 65:11, 67:39, 121:24.

MAZATZIN, p.n.
1. Chichimec ruler at Chapoltepec (= 2, below?). 12:43,45,47,49.
2. Ruler of Colhuacan. 12:57, 13:3.

MAZATZINTAMALCO, pc.n. 59:30.

MAZATZONCO, pc.n. 81:41.

MECELLOTL or MECELLOTZIN, p.n.
1. An early ruler of Cuauhtitlan. 8:25,34 (Mecellotzin).
2. A Chichimec captain. 18:52 (Mecellotl), 22:23 (idem).

MECITIN, g.n., pl., variant name for the MEXICA (see FC 10:189:6–10). 79:1. Syn. MEXITIN.

MECITLI, p.n. 78:40,40.

METEPEC, pc.n. 67:12, 84:53.

METZTITLAN, pc.n. 20:47, 21:6, 28:48,52, 49:25.

METZTITLANCALQUE, g.n., pl. 60:10.

MEXAYACATL, p.n. 61:36. Cf. IMEXAYAC.

MEXICATL, pl. MEXICA.
1. G.n. 12:14 (migrating Mexica reach Tollan), 12:23 (reach Ecatepec), 16:48 (at Chapoltepec), 16:51, 17:6 (timexica), 17:15,26,38, 18:26, 21:14 (mexica òtli = the Mexica road), 27:55 (war against the Chalca begins), 30:29, 33:51, 42:43, 43:22, 45:17, 47:25 (mexicatl), 49:7 (mexicatl), 49:13,40, 50:28,48,52,54, 51:10, 60:33,37,54, 65:4, 66:9,12,20, 66:50 (mexicatl), 79:1,1, 82:52, 83:9,10,17,29,45,49, 84:6,7,12,13; mexicatlalli, 26:32,34,36, 49:29; mexicatlatocayotl, 26:44, 27:52; Mexica tenochca, 42:25, cf. 48:30 (mexicatl tenochcatl), 34:8,24, 66:6,33; Mexica tlatilolca, 44:23. See also MEXITIN.
2. P.n. (?) or title (?). 24:47.

MEXICATZINCA, g.n., pl. 24:35, 50:29.

MEXICATZINCO, p.n. 33:19, 50:34, 61:4, 63:51.

MEXICAYOTL, Mexica people or Mexica nation. 51:53, 60:36.

MEXICO, pc.n. 26:21,24,30, 27:39,41,42,51, 28:28, 31:31, 37:17, 38:2, 41:43, 47:40, 49:8, 52:6,14,16,18, 57:18,22,22, 58:11,27, 59:30, 60:34, 61:55, 63:24,26,29, 64:48, 68:24; 122:8; tenochtitlan mexico, 53:26, 63:39, 65:21; mexico tenochtitlan, 22:15, 51:42, 56:44, 61:47.

MEXITIN, g.n., pl., variant name for the MEXICA (FC 10:189:6–10). 11:24, 27, 11:33 (mexiti), 11:34–43 passim, 12:3–52 passim, 13:23–48 passim,

14:28,48, 16:33,34,41,42, 17:3–43 passim, 18:23,28, 19:19, 20:43, 22:16, 24:3,19, 25:6, 27:26,29,54, 28:7,50, 29:5,8,42, 32:1, 47:28, 47:29 (mexiti), 82:50, 83:6,39. Syn. MECITIN.

MIACATLAN (TORQ bk. 13, ch. 5: vn Pueblo llamado Miacatlan, de la juris-diccion de Quauhnahuac, Cabeça de Marquesado), pc.n. 64:20 (miyacatla).

MIAHUAAPAN, pc.n. 65:14 (miyahuaapan).

MIAHUATAMALTZIN, see MIAHUATONALTZIN.

MIAHUATL (i.e., miyahuatl), female p.n. 3:33.

MIAHUATONALTZIN, (erroneous?) var. MIAHUATAMALTZIN (17:50), p.n. 13:21 (Miahuatonaltzin teuctli), 17:50.

MICCAAPAN, pc.n. 21:20.

MICCACALCATL, p.n. 13:11,19.

MICCACALCO, pc.n. 8:15 (tepotzotlan miccacalco).

MICHHUACAN, pc.n. 3:39.

MICQUETLAN, pc.n. 65:13, 67:17,24, 68:2, 121:4 (Miquetlan), 121:12 (Miquetlan).

MICTECA, g.n. Dead land people, denizens of the underworld. 76:34.

MICTLAN (the dead land), pc.n. 76:23.

MICTLANCIHUATL (the dead land lady), female p.n., a spirit or deity. 76:23.

MICTLANCUAUHTLA, pc.n. 58:3,41 (mictlanquauhtla tlaca).

MICTLANTEUCTLI (the dead land lord), p.n., a spirit or deity. 76:23–42 passim.

MIHUAQUE, g.n., one of five groups that settled Tlalmanalco (CHIM 165, ZCHIM 1:40). 13:15, 58:9,12,22,26. See also CHALCA MIHUAQUE.

MIMICH or MIMICHTZIN (27:43, 79:43), p.n.

1. Member of the legendary MIXCOA, companion to XIUHNEL. 79:36–54 passim, 80:9.

2. One of the early Cuauhtitlan Chichimecs (= 1, above?). 3:30.

3. A Colhua noble. 27:43.

MIMIXCOA, see MIXCOA.

MIQUETLAN, see MICQUETLAN.

MIQUIZTLAN, pc.n. 122:4.

MIXCOA, see MIXCOATL.

MIXCOAC, pc.n. 66:38, 84:34.

MIXCOAMAZATZIN, p.n. 1:55, 3:51.

MIXCOATEPETL or MIXCOATEPEC (50:49), pc.n.

1. A shrine in Colhuacan (FC 2:214:16).

2. A shrine in Tenochtitlan (cf. FC 2:172: mjxcoateupan). 50:49.

3. The Mixcoatl shrine of legend. 81:9.

MIXCOATL, pl. MIXCOA or MIMIXCOA

1. G.n., pl., a legendary band of Chichimecs (in the sense of CHICHIME-CATL 2). 1:10,11,13, 1:17 (mixcoã), 78:30 (mixcoâ), 78:32,35, 79:2, 14,36, 81:4.

2. P.n., sing., one of the Mixcoa, a legendary hero. 1:13 (yztac mixcoatl = White Mixcoatl), 1:14 (Mixcoatl the younger), 1:16, 78:24,36, 79:18,24, 80:16–44 passim.

3. Sing., name given to one of the three hearthstones in early Chichimec times. 1:7.

4. P.n., sing., Mixcoatl or Diablo Mixcoatl (the devil Mixcoatl) (who led the early Cuauhtitlan Chichimecs) (= 2, above?). 3:1, 25:47 (impersonated by ritualists), 26:4,5 (temple of in Cuauhtitlan), 27:18,24,48 (idem), 44:42 (god of the Cuauhtitlancalque), 56:25 (impersonated by warriors).

5. P.n., sing., one of the early Cuauhtitlan Chichimecs (= 2, above?). 3:30.

6. = 4, but as worshipped in Cuitlahuac. 50:34 (mixcoatl diablo), 50:42, 44,52 (refers to the idol or statue), 62:15–16 (also called White Mixcoatl or Mixcoatl the younger), 62:33, 66:37 (mixcohuatl diablo), 63:10, 63:10–11 (also called White Mixcoatl or Mixcoatl the younger). See also CAMAXTLE MIXCOATL, TETZAUH.

7. Sing., pyramid of Mixcoatl in Cuitlahuac Tizic, or the sanctuary at the top of this pyramid. 50:35 (tlecotihuetz yn icpac mixcoatl = he rushed to the top of the Mixcoatl), 50:40 (otlatlac yn mixcoatl yn xocoyotl = Mixcoatl the younger was burned), 59:46 (ynteocal mixcoatl = their temple, Mixcoatl).

8. Sing., idol of the early Chalca (ZCHIM 1:51 and CHIM 146). 12:8.

9. Sing., idol of the Huexotzinca (see note to the translation at 44:49). 57:20. See also CAMAXTLE.

MIXTECA, g.n., pl. 26:52, 66:49.

MIXTLAN, pc.n. 26:53, 67:17, 121:3.

MIYACATLA, see MIACATLAN.

MIYAHUATL, see MIAHUATL.

MIZQUIC, pc.n. 59:28, 63:17,48, 65:51, 66:37, 84:17,19,36.

MIZQUITLAN, pc.n. 67:40, 121:25.

MIZTLIIMA, p.n.

1. Brother of IXTOTOMAHUATZIN killed in Huexotzinco. 61:36.

2. Emigrant from Huexotzinco. 61:47, 63:27.

MIZTONTLAN, pc.n. 65:15.

MOCELTZIN, female p.n. 15:37.

MOLANCO, see MOLLANCO.

MOLLANCO (cf. FC 2:194: Molonco; FC 8:2: Mollonco; García Granados *Diccionario* 1:44: Mollanco; ibid., 3:229: Molango), pc.n.

1. Town that paid tribute to Tetzcoco. 64:41 (called Tecpan Mollanco? See note to the translation).

2. Town that performed labor for Mexico (= 1?). 65:19, 67:31 (conquered by Ahuitzotzin), 121:16 (Molanco, conquered by Ahuitzotzin).

MOMOZTITLAN, pc.n. 15:47.

MONAMIQUIYAN, see TEPETLIMONAMIQUIYAN.

MOQUIHUIXTLI or MOQUIHUIX, p.n. 55:18,21,23, 55:25 (moquihuix), 55:27,32,39,48, 67:10.

MOTEIZCOCOPIPINA, p.n. 28:27.

MOTEUCZOMA (51:43, etc.) or MOTEUCZOMATZIN, p.n. Syn. ILHUICAMINA.

    1. The elder Moteuczomatzin, ruler of Tenochtitlan. 15:4,9,11, 50:23, 51:43, 22:24,29,39,40,44, 54:3,41, 63:2, 67:6; huehue motecçumatzin, 36:24; huehue moteucçomatzin, 28:2, 30:27, 34:20, 51:34,47, 52:7,16, 53:29, 46, 54:43,46, 63:1, 84:41,49; moteucçomatzin huehue, 50:14; huehue moteucçomatzin ylhuicaminatzin, 49:44; huehue moteucçomatzin . . . ilhuicamina, 66:42; (ilhuicaminatzin huehue moteucçomatzin), 84:39; huehue Moteuczomatzin, 121:7,14.

    2. The younger Moteuczomatzin, ruler of Tenochtitlan. 15:21,37,39,40, 59:38, 60:35,56, 61:26,29,38,52,55,56, 62:9, 63:28, 65:42, 67:43 (ynic ome moteucçomatzin = Moteuczomatzin the second), 68:9,14,24,26,33, 121:28,29.

    3. Ruler of Tenayocan. 63:54.

MOTOZAHUICAN, pc.n. 26:38 (motoçahuica).

MOYOTEPEC, pc.n. 63:20.

MOYOTLAN, pc.n. 65:13.

MOZAUHQUI, p.n. 53:41.

NACAZHUEYOCAN, pc.n. 21:25.

NAHUACAN, p.n. 3:32.

NAHUALLIIAPAN, pc.n. 63:16 (nahualliyapan). Cf. CM fol. 33, line 10: nahualapan.

*NAHUALTEUCTLI, pl. NAHUALTEUCTIN or NAHUALTETEUCTIN. Pl., magician lords (another name for the Tzompanteuctin, see TZOMPANTEUCTLI), 62:12,45, 63:4.

NAHUIACATL, p.n. 63:46.

NAHUICALLOCAN, pc.n. 60:26.

NAHUITECPATL (4 Flint), a name for the moon. 77:38,46.

NANAHUATL or NANAHUATZIN, p.n.

    1. Spirit who split open Food Mountain, 77:19,23 (nanahuatl); who became the sun. 77:31,36,40,42,45,47 (nanahuatl).

    2. A noble of Cuauhtitlan. 15:15 (nanahuatzin).

NANTZINTLAN, pc.n. 121:22 (Nautzintlan).

NAPPATEUCTLI, p.n., a spirit or deity, 77:40.

"NATA," see TATA.

NAUHECATL TONATIUH (4-Wind Sun), p.n., a spirit or deity. 68:21.

NAUHTLAN, pc.n. 63:56.

NAUHYOTZIN, p.n.

1. Ruler of Tollan. 8:12,23.
2. Early ruler of the Colhuaque. 11:5,16,17,18,49.
3. Later ruler of Colhuacan. 27:42,44, 31:45, 42:49.

NECOC, epithet of TEZCATLIPOCA (see NED, cf. FC 3:12:19: necoc iaotl, FC 6:11:3:idem). 17:22. Cf. GLOS: necoc. See also GLOS: diablo.

NECUAMETL, p.n.
1. A Toltec of Huemac's time. 81:48.
2. One of the early Cuauhtitlan Chichimecs. 3:31.
3. A Chalca emissary. 52:18,38,40, 53:5.
4. See DIEGO NECUAMETZIN.

NECUAMETZIN, p.n., see DIEGO NECUAMETZIN.

NECUAMEXOCHITZIN, p.n. 8:14,22.

NECUAMEYOCAN, pc.n. 3:14,19.

NENE, female p.n., a mythical character. 75:46.

NEPANTLA, pc.n., one of the four quarters of Cuauhtitlan town. 29:35, 43:46, 46:47, 55:10. Cf. GLOS: nepantla.

NEPOPOHUALCO, pc.n. 10:44, 21:15,28, 52:30.

NEXPAN, pc.n. 67:35.

NEXTLALPAN, pc.n. 9:46, 20:4.

NEZAHUALCOYOTL or NEZAHUALCOYOTZIN, p.n. 29:49, 34:13,15, 35:30,42, 36:22,32,42, 37:2–49 passim, 38:2–44 passim, 39:16,16,39, 44,49,52, 43:10, 44:30,33, 45:4,8,11,28,30,33,42, 46:28,33, 47:33,37, 39, 48:32, 51:21,26, 52:20,24,33,41, 53:1,7,30,33,44, 54:10, 55:12, 64:17,32 (netzahualcoyotzin).

NEZAHUALPILLI or NEZAHUALPILTZINTLI, p.n. 53:8,22, 55:13, 58: 49, 59:18, 61:42, 64:18,32, 65:28,42.

NEZAHUALTEMOCATZIN, p.n. 13:47.

NOCHEZTLAN, pc.n. 67:47, 121:30.

NOCHPALLIICUE, female p.n., a deity. 78:14.

NOCHTONCO, pc.n. 21:23.

NONOALCA, g.n., pl. 14:27.

NONOALCATEPETL (Mount Nonoalco), pc.n. 4:39 (nonohualcatepec), 5:44, 6:41 (nonohualcatepec).

NONOALCATZIN, p.n. 12:16,27.

NONOALCO, pc.n. 10:52, 81:50.

NOPALLAN, pc.n. 68:2, 121:33.

NOPALTEPEC, pc.n. 21:23.

OCELOTEPEC, pc.n. 65:15.

OCELOTLAPAN, p.n. 31:27.

OCELOTLIXTACAN, pc.n. 21:18.

OCELOTZIN, p.n. 64:7.

OCOPETLAPAN, pc.n. 64:21.

OCOYACAC, pc.n. 67:14, 84:53.

OCOZACAYOCAN, pc.n. 19:30.

OCOYO, pc.n. (?). 63:14.

OCUILLAN, pc.n. 11:45, 57:12, 67:12, 121:2.

OCUILTECATL, g.n. 84:3.

OLINTEPEC, pc.n. 64:21.

OLLAN, pc.n. 65:9, 67:49.

OMACATLAN, pc.n. 65:17.

OMEACAC, pc.n. 62:24.

OMETLAN, pc.n. 65:6.

OMEYOCAN (Place of Duality), pc.n., otherwordly abode of supernaturals. 4:46 (ommeyocan).

OTLATITLAN, pc.n. 65:45.

OTLAYO, pc.n. 19:33 (òtlayo).

OTLAZPAN, pc.n. 12:51, 21:11,44 (òtlazpan), 29:18,22,38, 40:34, 46:49 (òtlazpan), 47:14 (idem), 64:9 (one of Cuauhtitlan's Four Lords).

OTLAZPANECA, g.n., pl. 40:44.

OTOMITL, pl. OTOMI (18:10), g.n. 9:53, 18:29,31 (refers to the Cuahuaque Otomi?), 49:21, 56:5,45,49 (refers to Tollan, Apazco, Xilotepec, Chiapan, and Cuahuacan). See also CUAHUAQUE OTOMI, TLAOTONXINTLI.

OTOMPAN, pc.n. 32:36, 32:38 (otompan tlaca), 32:42, 36:12, 54:33, 64:2, 33, 66:2, 84:22.

OTONQUILPAN, pc.n. 35:44.

OTONTEPEC, pc.n. 21:15.

OXITLAN, pc.n. 65:44, 121:31.

OXOMOCO, p.n., a mythical character. 1:27,27, 77:16,18,19.

OZOMATEPEC, pc.n. 21:24.

OZOMATEUCTLI, p.n.
1. 10:18.
2. 26:53.

OZTOMAN, pc.n. 67:13, 121:1.

OZTOTEMPAN, pc.n. 10:33.

OZTOTICPAC, pc.n. 29:45, 51:1, 52:31, 64:38, 67:15, 121:3.

OZTOTL (IXT 1:293), pc.n. 64:40 (or Oztotl Tlatlauhyan? See note to the translation).

OZTOTLAQUETZALLOCAN, pc.n. 21:26.

PABLO TLILLOTLINAHUAL, p.n. 15:32.

PABLO YAOTLAMIN, p.n. 64:14.

PACHYOCAN, pc.n. 21:22.

PALZOQUITLAN, pc.n. 64:44 (palçoquitla).

PANCO, pc.n. 68:4.

PANITZIN, p.n., ruler of Ecatepec. 63:55. Cf. PANTLI.

PANTEPEC, pc.n. 122:1.

PANTICTZIN TEUCTLI, p.n. 29:3.

PANTITLAN (Banner Place), pc.n.

    1. A whirlpool in the Lake of Mexico (TEZ chap. 80, p. 563; FC 2:42:9; FC 2:84:15). 12:39, 82:53, 83:11.

    2. = 1 (?). 63:13.

PANTLAN, pc.n. 64:36.

PANTLI, p.n., ruler of Xilotzinco. 29:24 (in 1395), 54:10 (in 1467). Cf. PANITZIN.

PANTZONTLAN, pc.n. 65:8.

PAPAHUACAN, pc.n. 19:35, 21:19, 54:34.

PAPALOTLAN (TORQ, IXT), pc.n. 64:37 (papallotla tetzcoco).

PAPATLAN, pc.n. 65:18.

PAPAZTAC, p.n. 78:18.

PATOLTETITLAN, pc.n. 65:15.

PEDRO DE SAN AUGUSTIN, p.n. 16:30 (Don Pedro de san augustin).

PEDRO MACUILXOCHITL or PEDRO MACUILXOCHITZIN, p.n. Don Pedro macuilxochitl, 61:18; Don Pedro macuilxochitzin, 15:37, 16:12,14,15; macuilxochitzin, 16:19.

PEDRO TLACAHUEPANTZIN, p.n. 64:15 (Don pedro tlacahuepantzin).

PEDRO TLACATEUCTZIN, p.n. 31:38 (don pedro tlacateuctzin).

PETLACALLI TEUCTLI, p.n. 26:49.

PETLAUHTOCATZIN, p.n. 15:16.

PIAZTLAN, see PIYAZTLAN.

PICHACATZIN TEUCTLI, vars. PICHATZIN, PICHATZIN TEUCTLI, p.n. 24:6, 28:36,38, 43:2.

PILLI TEUCTLI (Prince Lord), p.n. 62:41.

PINOTL, p.n. 68:16,30.

PIPILO, p.n. 26:29.

PIPIOLTEPEC, pc.n. 121:33.

PITZALLOTL, p.n. 19:39, 26:27.

PIYAZTLAN, pc.n. 67:49, 121:31 (Piaztlan).

POCHTECA, g.n., pl. 32:29.

POCHTLAN, pc.n. 80:27.

POCTEPECA, g.n. 57:14.

POCTLAN, pc.n. 65:44.

POHUAZANCO, pc.n. 65:18.

POLLOTLAN, pc.n. 65:16.

POLOC (Driblet), name of the person created by Mixcoatl from his own blood (cf. MOL: polocatl = leavings). 62:34.

POPOTLAN, pc.n. 12:39 (popotlan acolnahuac).
POXCAUHTLAN, pc.n. 121:4.
POYAUHTECATL, name of a mountain. 36:35.

QUECEHUACATZIN, p.n. 15:30.
QUECEHUATL, p.n. 63:57.
QUECHOLLAN, pc.n. 65:44.
QUEHUATL, p.n. 18:4.
QUETZALAYATZIN, p.n. 33:20,29,34, 34:47, 66:15.
QUETZALCOATL,
    1. P.n., deity. Creator of humans, 2:22; steals bones to make new race of humans, 76:22,22,26,36,41,43,48,54, 77:1; discovers maize in the mountain, 77:6,9,11,15.
    2. = 1? 68:21 (identified with NAUHECATL TONATIUH).
    3. P.n., refers to TOPILTZIN. 3:54–8:3 (life of), 4:1 (topiltzin tlamacazqui ce acatl quetzalcohuatl), 4:32 (quetzalcoatl topiltzin), 4:34 (yn topiltzin yn ce acatl quetzalcoatl), 9:57, 77:30.
    4. Title first held by Topiltzin, then by Huemac, who yielded it to Cuauhtli. 8:48,49, 8:50, 8:55 (quetzalcoatia = he becomes the Quetzalcoatl), 9:57.
QUETZALCOATONCO, pc.n. 65:17.
QUETZALCUIXIN, p.n. 33:19, 34:46.
QUETZALMAQUIZTLI, p.n. 33:15, 45:36.
QUETZALMAZATL or QUETZALMAZATZIN, p.n.
    1. A son of TEZOZOMOCTLI 1. 34:43.
    2. A chief lord (or skull rack lord) of the Cuitlahuaca. 62:49,50 (fought Itzcoatzin).
    3. A chief lord (or skull rack lord) of the Cuitlahuaca. 63:3,5,7 (executed by Moteuczomatzin the younger; see 61:52).
QUETZALMICHIN TEUCTLI, p.n. 21:51, 22:11.
QUETZALPETLATL, female p.n., sister of Topiltzin Quetzalcoatl. 6:40,42,49. See also GLOS: quetzalpetlatl.
QUETZALQUEN, female p.n. 10:30.
QUETZALTEPEC, pc.n.
    1. Way station of the migrating Cuauhtitlan Chichimecs. 1:39.
    2. = 1, above? 68:6 (conquered by Ahuitzotzin); 122:2 (Quezaltepec, conquered by the younger Moteuczomatzin).
QUETZAL TEUCTLI, p.n. 62:43,44,47.
QUETZALTOTOTL, p.n. 53:40.
QUETZALTZIN (?), see CUETZALTZIN.
QUETZALXILOTL, female p.n. 10:30.
QUETZALXOTZIN, female p.n. 83:6.
QUEZALTEPEC, see QUETZALTEPEC.

QUIAUHTEOPAN, pc.n. 67:3 (quiyauhteopan), 84:44 (quiyauhteopan).

QUIAUHTEPEC, pc.n. 67:2,48 (quiyauhtepec).

QUIAUHTZIN, p.n. 28:27 (quiyauhtzin).

QUILACHTLI, see QUILAZTLI.

QUILAZTLI, var. QUILACHTLI (76:52), female p.n., a spirit or deity. 4:9 (quillaztli), 76:52, 81:1 (quillaztli).

QUIMICHTEPEC, pc.n. 68:5, 121:34.

QUIMICHTLAN, pc.n. 61:28.

QUINAMETIN, pl., a race of giants that inhabited the earth in early times (DHIST ch. 2, parag. 14: quiname, IXT: quinametin), haunted the earth in later times (FC 5, ch. 11: qujnameti). 2:31.

QUINATZIN, p.n.
  1. Ruler of Cuauhtitlan. 12:32 (huehue quinatzin = the elder Quinatzin), 15:6 (idem).
  2. Ruler of Cuauhtitlan (= 1, above?). 13:27,38,41,49,54, 14:8,12,19,30,38, 46,50, 15:6 (?, see 1, above), 17:31, 17:46 (huehue quinatzin), 19:23.
  3. Grandson of 2, above. 14:43,51.
  4. Grandson of 3, founded Tepotzotlan dynasty. 15:1,13,13,16,23, 16:3,5, 9,10, 52:6, 59:41, 64:5.
  5. See DIEGO QUINATZIN.

SAN AUGUSTIN, p.n., see PEDRO DE SAN AUGUSTIN.

SAN JUAN, pc.n., a Chalca community (one of the boroughs of Tlalmanalco?). 58:7 (san ju°).

SANTO DOMINGO, pc.n. 59:3.

TAMAOC (cf. Codex Mendoza fol. 10: tamuoc, a town conquered by Axayacatl), pc.n. 64:45, 121:5 (Tamooc).

TAMAPACHCO, pc.n. 67:24, 121:11.

TAMAZOLAC, pc.n. 10:41, 11:1 (tamaçollac), 19:46 (idem), 51:39 (toltitlan tamaçolac).

TAMAZOLLAC, see TAMAZOLAC.

TAMAZOLLAN, pc.n. 64:42 (tamacollan for tamaçollan?).

TAMOANCHAN, pc.n. 76:51, 77:12,32.

TAMOOC, see TAMAOC.

TAMOMOX, pc.n. 67:18.

TAMPATEL, pc.n. 67:18 (tapatel), 121:5.

TANCHOL, pc.n. 64:41.

TAPATEL, see TAMPATEL.

TAPIA, see GABRIEL DE TAPIA MAZACIHUATL.

TATA, p.n., a mythical character. 75:45 (misspelled "nata?"), 76:6 (tataye = O Tata!).

TATAPACO, pc.n. 21:23.

TECALCO, pc.n. 53:41, 67:15, 121:1.

TECALLAPOHUATZIN, p.n. 36:24.

TECAMACHALCO, pc.n. 63:44.

TECAMAN, see TECANMAN.

TECANMAN, pc.n. Tecaman, 19:35, 20:46, 29:9; tecanmā, 28:48; tecamman, 49:27; tecanma, 80:21.

TECANMECATL, p.n. 52:4.

TECATLAN, pc.n. 64:44.

TECATLATOATZIN, p.n. 45:3.

TECAXIC, pc.n. 21:27, 67:22.

TECCIZAPAN, pc.n. 64:43.

TECHCUAUHTITLAN, pc.n. 63:20.

TECHICHCO, pc.n.
1. Where some Cuauhtitlan rulers had their residence. 9:21, 11:30, 12:32, 13:48, 18:41,50.
2. A Chalca outpost in Colhuacan. 24:13, 24:15 (techichco tlaca), 24:18 (techichco colhuacan), 27:28 (idem), 27:54.
3. = 2, above (?). 63:12,22.

TECHIMALCO, pc.n. 63:15.

TECHOTLALATZIN, p.n.
1. A Tetzcoco noble. 34:50.
2. Lord of Itztapalapan (TORQ bk. 2, ch. 62, p. 185; IXT 2:146). 61:3.

TECOAC, pc.n. 21:27 (controlled by Cuauhtitlan), 62:21 (visited by Mixcoatl).

TECOACTONCO, pc.n. 19:1,6.

TECOATL, p.n. 19:3.

TECOCOATZIN, p.n. Tecocohuatzin, 42:20, 43:14,40, 44:6, 45:44, 46:2,15, 32, 47:2,37,51, 48:24,45,52; tecoçohuatzin, 48:39.

TECOLLIQUENQUI, p.n. 4:45.

TECOLOTLAN, pc.n. 65:6.

TECOLOTZIN, p.n. 35:13,14, 37:34, 39:33.

TECOL TEUCTLI, p.n. 10:19.

TECOMA, p.n. 62:26.

TECOMAAPAN, pc.n. 65:14.

TECOZAUHTLAN, pc.n. 121:33.

TECPAN
1. Palace (MOL). See GLOS: tecpan.
2. Pc.n. 28:41, 33:2, 62:46, 63:50. See also CUITLAHUAC TECPAN.
3. Pc.n. 64:41 (paid tribute to Tetzcoco, should be Tecpan Mollanco? See note to the translation).
4. Pc.n. (= 3?). 66:40, 84:35.

TECPANCUAUHTLA, pc.n. 4:30.

TECPANECA, g.n., pl., see TECPANECATL 2.

TECPANECATL

1. An official title (see NED). 21:8 (huehue xaltemoctzin tecpanecatl). Cf. ATECPANECATL.

2. Pl., g.n. 28:43 (tecpaneca cuitlahuaca).

TECPANTEPEC, pc.n. 67:35 (conquered by Ahuitzotzin). Cf. TECPATEPEC.

TECPATLAN, pc.n. 122:1.

TECPATEPEC, pc.n. 84:43, 121:20 (conquered by Ahuitzotzin). Cf. TECPANTEPEC.

TECPAYOCAN, pc.n. 12:34 (chiquiuhtepetlapan tecpayocan).

TECUANI (Man-eater), p.n. 37:48.

TECUANTEPEC, pc.n. 59:13, 67:39, 121:21.

TEHUEHUELTZIN, p.n. 59:44.

TEHUEPANCO, pc.n. 19:34, 21:16.

TEHUILACATZIN, p.n. 41:29,42,46,48 (tehuillacatzin).

TEHUILOYOCAN, pc.n.

1. 11:29 (çimapan tehuiloyocan).

2. = 1 (?). 19:41, 40:30, 47:15, 60:55, 61:2, 61:8 (tehuilocan).

TEHUITZIN, p.n. 15:26, 59:7.

TEIZTLACOATZIN, p.n. 11:37, 12:30.

TELITL, p.n. 40:10, 46:20 (tellitl).

TELOLOIYACAC, pc.n. 19:47.

TELPOCH, p.n. 19:4.

TELPOCHTLI, epithet of the god TEZCATLIPOCA (HG bk. 2, ch. 24, parag. 1). 5:33. Cf. GLOS: telpochtli.

TEMACPALCO, pc.n. 10:44, 19:32, 46:20.

TEMAMATLAC, pc.n. 21:22.

TEMATLAHUACALCO, pc.n. 11:41.

TEMETZACOCUITZIN, p.n. 27:24,47.

TEMETZIN, p.n. 63:57.

TEMILCO, pc.n.

1. Body of water in CITLALTEPEC (FC 2:11,74).

2. Way station of the migrating Cuauhtitlan Chichimecs (?, probably should be XIMILCO; see note to the translation at 2:57).

3. Place in the city of Cuauhtitlan (?). 48:16 (see note to the translation).

TEMIZTZIN, p.n. 34:32, 51:7. Syn. CALTZIN TEUCTLI.

TENAMAZTZIN, p.n. 50:39.

TENAMITLIYACAC, pc.n. 10:45.

TENANCA, see CHALCA TENANCA.

TENANCO, pc.n. (in Chalco, see CHALCA TENANCA). 63:46.

TENANITLAN, see TONANITLAN.

TENANTZINCO, pc.n. 67:12, 84:52.

TENAYO, g.n. 84:1.

TENAYOCAN, pc.n. 15:9, 40:10, 46:20, 46:39 (a Tepaneca town), 63:54, 84:12,14.

TENEXCALCO, pc.n. 21:21.

TENEXOTLI, pc.n. (?, name of a particular road?), Lime Road (from MOL: tenextli = cal). 19:45 (tenexòtli), 49:37 (tenexotlica = along the Lime Road).

TENEXTICPAC, pc.n. 67:18, 121:4.

TENNECUILCO, pc.n. 63:21.

TENOCELOTL or TENOCELOTZIN, p.n. 27:8, 43:24,42, 44:22, 46:11,17, 33, 51:3.

TENOCHCATL, pl. TENOCHCA, g.n. 26:42, 30:22, 33:44,49,50, 47:13, 48:13 (tenochcatl), 49:20,30, 55:16, 56:2,3 (tenochcatl), 56:20, 62:49, 66:19; yn mexica yn tenochca, 34:8,24, 66:6,33; Mexica tenochca, 42:25; mexicatl tenochcatl, 48:30.

TENOCHTITLAN, pc.n. 15:21,45, 26:19,40,42, 27:12, 28:2, 29:42, 30:20, 21, 32:7,9,25, 33:3,6,30,42,46, 34:17,19, 37:6,21, 40:9, 43:6,15, 47: 26, 48:11,27,32,34, 49:5,43,44, 50:38,49, 53:28,28,33, 54:1,7, 55:22, 55:24 (= ruler?), 55:42, 56:11,14, 57:16,37,42,53, 58:35,45, 59:22,37, 60:22,54,56, 61:29, 65:42, 84:9; Mexico tenochtitlan, 22:15, 51:42, 56:44, 61:46; tenochtitlan Mexico, 53:26, 63:39, 65:21.

TENOPALTITLAN, pc.n. 20:3 (tenòpaltitlan).

TENTLIL, p.n. 68:31.

TEOATZINCO, pc.n. 122:1.

TEOCALHUIYACAN, pc.n. 66:36, 84:34.

TEOCHIAPAN (Codex Mendoza fol. 15), pc.n. 68:4 (teochiyappa), 122:1.

TEOCHIAUHTZINCO, pc.n. 68:4 (teochiyauhtzinco).

TEOCOMPAN (Place of the Pot Cactus), pc.n. 10:13.

TEOCUAUHTLA, pc.n. 64:42.

TEOCUITLATLAN, pc.n. 67:35, 121:20.

TEOHCATL, see TEUHCATL.

TEOHUA, p.n. 64:1.

TEOHUACAN, pc.n. 10:52, 26:52 (teohuacan tlaca).

TEONOCHTLAN, pc.n. 64:42.

TEOPAN

  1. Temple (MOL). See GLOS: teopan.

  2. Pc.n. (?) 28:24 (cimapā teopā).

  3. See QUIAUHTEOPAN.

TEOPANCALCA, see CUITLAHUACATL.

TEOPANCALCAN, pc.n. 55:4, 57:30, 59:50, 61:37, 62:46, 63:50. See also CUITLAHUAC TEOPANCALCAN.

TEOPANZOLCO, pc.n. 20:4.

TEOPIAZCO, pc.n. 37:11.

TEOPOCHTLAN, pc.n. 67:36.

TEOTENANCO, pc.n. 67:12, 84:53.

TEOTEXCALLI, spirit oven (mythical place where the sun was formed; FC 7: 4:25). 77:29 (teotexcalco), 77:34.

TEOTIHUACAN, pc.n. 64:2,34, 77:29, 78:15.

TEOTITLAN, pc.n. 65:9.

TEOTLAHUICA (Spirit Guide, see NED: tlahuīca), p.n. 62:36.

TEOTLILLAN, pc.n. 10:52 (teotlilan).

TEOZATZIN, p.n. 14:48.

TEOZTOC, pc.n. 63:21.

TEPANAHUILLOYAN, pc.n. 19:48, 20:3.

TEPANECATL, pl. TEPANECA, g.n. 16:39,41,52, 17:48, 21:37 (tepaneca-yaoyotl), 22:31,35,42, 24:18 (tepanecatl), 27:1,55, 28:7,38,43, 30:33,43, 46,47, 31:3 (tepanecayaoyotl), 31:18 (tepaneca yn toltitlancalque), 31:23, 32:32, 33:31,43, 34:36,37,40, 35:24,27, 39:36,42, 40:4,12, 40:40 (tepanecayaoyotl), 40:47 (moçentepanecaytohua), 41:6,10,33, 42:10,40 (tepanecatl), 42:45, 43:17, 43:19 (tepanecatl), 44:20,25,38,43,47, 45:7, 14,24,27,49, 46:35,36,39 (list of Tepaneca towns), 47:22, 47:24 (tepane-catl), 47:26,36, 48:2 (cuahuaque tepaneca), 48:22 (yn tepaneca yn tolti-tlancalque), 48:36, 60:33, 66:18.

TEPANECAYOTL, Tepanec nation. 31:20.

TEPANOHUAYAN, pc.n., synonym for Tepanecapan, i.e., the region of the Te-paneca (see NED: tepanēcapan, see also CHIM 93 and 238). 30:35, 32:1, 40:6, 41:17, 47:29, 63:40 (tlacopan tepanohuayan).

TEPANONOC, p.n. 30:51, 31:1.

TEPANQUIZQUI, p.n.
  1. Name of a deity. 76:21,55.
  2. Son of Tezozomoctli of Azcapotzalco. 33:24, 34:43, 46:25.

TEPECHPAN, pc.n. 64:34.

TEPECOMECATL, p.n. 55:10.

TEPECUACUILCO, pc.n. 66:39, 67:3, 84:37,45.

TEPEMAXALCO, pc.n. 19:32.

TEPEPOLCO, pc.n. 64:39 (tepepulco).

TEPETITLAN, pc.n. 21:27.

TEPETL, p.n. 60:46. Cf. GLOS: tepetl.

TEPETLAOZTOC, pc.n. 64:34.

TEPETLAPAN, pc.n. 12:33, 13:54, 15:27, 59:7, 65:7.

TEPETLAYACAC, pc.n. 10:40.

TEPETLIMONAMIQUIYAN (Where Mountains Come Together), pc.n. 11:33.

TEPETLMAXALCO, pc.n. 21:27.

TEPETLMAXALIUHYAN (Where Mountains Divide), pc.n. 11:34.

TEPETZINCO, pc.n. 59:29.

TEPEXIC, pc.n. 60:15, 64:4,9.

TEPEXITENCO, pc.n. 4:19.

TEPEYACAC, pc.n.
1. Town in Puebla region. 3:40, 12:26, 18:3,44, 51:5, 52:2 (tepeyacac tlaca), 52:3, 53:39,43, 63:44, 67:14, 121:1.
2. Place north of Mexico. 12:38, 22:22 (acahuacan tepeyacac), 22:28 (tepeayacac).
3. Place north of Mexico (= 2?). 49:31.

TEPEYACAHUAQUE, g.n., pl. 18:7, 51:4, 53:34,38.

TEPIXTLOCO, pc.n. 50:47.

TEPOLCO, pc.n. 21:54.

TEPOLITZMAITL, p.n. 28:45, 32:4.

TEPOLNEXCO, pc.n. 48:46.

TEPOLNEXTLI, p.n. 3:44.

TEPOLOMITZIN, p.n. 36:26.

TEPONAZCO, pc.n. 35:41.

TEPOTONILOYAN, pc.n. 62:23.

TEPOTZOTECA, g.n., pl. 40:43, 42:12.

TEPOTZOTLAN, pc.n. 8:15 (tepotzotlan miccacalco), 14:40, 15:1, 15:13 (tepotzontlan), 16:3–28 passim, 18:16,30, 21:44, 29:36, 46:48, 52:6,7, 59:40, 61:18, 64:4,10.

TEPOXACCO, pc.n. 29:33, 46:46, 47:14.

TEPOZTECA, g.n., pl. 40:42.

TEPOZTLAN, pc.n. 84:42.

TEPOZTLI or TEPOZ, p.n. Huehue tepoztli, 52:19, 53:5; huehue tepoz, 52:37,37.

TEQUIHUA, see GLOS.

TEQUIXQUIAC, pc.n. 13:34, 84:27.

TEQUIXQUINAHUAC, pc.n. 12:33 (tepetlapan yn tequixquinahuac vizton-pan), 14:9 (tequixquinahuac huitznahuac viztopan), 15:33 17:45 (tequix-quinahuac vixtōpa), 29:31 (one of the four quarters of Cuauhtitlan town), 43:44 (idem), 46:46 (idem), 55:9, 60:29.

TETEC TLAMACAZQUI, see TOTEC TLAMACAZQUI.

TETELPAN, pc.n. 28:26 (tetelpan tlaca).

TETELTITLAN, pc.n. 65:8.

TETLANMAN, pc.n. 15:50.

TETLIZTACAN (cf. IXT 1:384: Tetelyzlacan), pc.n. 64:40 (tetlyztacan).

TETLMOPACCAN, pc.n. 65:14.

TETLOLINCAN, pc.n. 10:45.

TETLPOZTECCAN, pc.n. 63:19 (tetlpotzteccā), 65:13.

TETZAPOTITLAN, pc.n. 121:3 (conquered by Axayacatl). Cf. TZAPOTITLAN.

TETZAUH (Terror), p.n., alternate name for the god MIXCOATL (in Cuitla-huaca legend). 62:32 (see note to the translation).

TETZCATLPOPOCA, see TEZCATLPOPOCA.

TETZCOCATL, pl. TETZCOCA, g.n. 12:53, 32:10,47, 46:41, 49:5,7,8,11, 54:11 (tetzcoca acolhuaque), 59:9. See also CHICHIMECATL 3.

TETZCOCO, pc.n. 1:37, 15:52, 18:47, 23:49, 26:40, 27:10, 29:49, 32:31, 44, 34:12,49, 35:7,11, 37:10, 38:7, 42:50, 43:9, 45:35, 46:33, 48:31, 35, 52:20, 53:1,7,23,30, 55:12,14, 59:19, 61:42,51, 62:22, 63:39 ·(tetzcoco acolhuacan), 64:17,19,32,48, 64:35 (teçoyocan tetzcoco), 64:35 (chiauhtla tetzcoco), 64:38 (papalotla tetzcoco), 65:28,42, 66:38, 84:23, 35; tetzcoco tlatolli = according to stories from Tetzcoco, 4:31, 8:38 gloss.

TETZCOCO ATENCO, pc.n. 59:29.

TETZCOTZIN, female p.n. 9:26.

TETZCOTZINCO, pc.n. 51:21.

TETZIHUACTLA, pc.n. 35:37.

TEUCTEPEC, pc.n. 60:40, 121:30.

TEUCTLACOZAUHQUI

1. Rattlesnake, see GLOS: teuctlacozauhqui.
2. P.n., ruler of Xaltocan. 29:4.
3. P.n., ruler of Cuauhtinchan. 29:41.

TEUCTLAHUACATZIN, p.n. 33:46.

TEUCTLAMACAZQUI, title of a high official (FC 12:119:6, FC 12:119:28), lit., lord priest. 43:44.

TEUCTLI, lord (title used with proper names or in combination with other titles). See APANTEUCTLI, ATECPANECATL TEUCTLI, ATZIN TEUCTLI, CALLI TEUCTLI, etc. See also GN sec. 3.4. Cf. GLOS: teuctli.

TEUCTONALLAN, pc.n. 65:19.

TEUCTZIN, p.n. 35:14, 37:34, 39:33.

TEUHCATL (?) or TEOHCATL (?), p.n. 50:46 (teuhcatl), 50:51 (teohcatl). Cf. HUITZILTEUHCATZIN.

TEUHTEPEC, pc.n. 67:46.

TEUHTLEHUACATZIN, p.n. 63:54.

TEXCALAPAN, pc.n. 9:52.

TEXCALYACAC, pc.n. 63:15.

TEXOCUAUHTLI TOTEC, p.n., a spirit or deity. 63:23.

TEXOPAN, pc.n. 68:3.

TEXOPECO, pc.n. 63:19.

TEXOTLAN, pc.n. 67:49, 121:32.

TEYAHUALCO, pc.n. (cf. TEYAYAHUALCO). 11:51.

TEYAHUALOATZIN, p.n. 54:9 (teyahuallohuatzin).

TEYAYAHUALCO, pc.n. (cf. TEYAHUALCO and see GN sec. 1.6: yaya *for* ya). 62:24.

TEYOLLOCOA, vars. TEYOLLOCOATZIN, TEYOLCOCOATZIN, p.n. 33: 17 (teyollocohua), 34:46 (teyollocohuatzin), 45:39 (teyolcocohuatzin).

TEYOLLOCOHUA, see TEYOLLOCOA.

TEZCACOAC, pc.n. 20:1,2, 64:13.

TEZCACOATL, name or title of HUEMAC. 83:30 (tezcacoatl huemac), 83:33 (tezcacoatl yehuatl in huemac).

TEZCATLIPOCA, p.n.
1. Deity. 14:31, 76:5,17. See also TEZCATL TEUCTLI, TITLACAHUAN, TITLAHUAN.
2. One of the sorcerers who put Quetzalcoatl to flight (evidently the deity in the role of a sorcerer). 5:26,29,31,39,51. See also TELPOCHTLI, NECOC.
3. Tezcatlipoca of Tzapotlan, one of the sorcerers who deceived Huemac (same as 1 and 2, above?). 8:53.

TEZCATLPOPOCA, p.n. 61:47 (tetzcatlpopoca), 63:27.

TEZCATL TEUCTLI, or TEZCATZIN TEUCTLI, p.n., child named in honor of the god Tezcatlipoca, became ruler of Cuauhtitlan. 14:31,34,37, 17:44, 46, 18:13, 18:29 (tezcatzin teuctli), 18:39, 19:23.

TEZIUHTECATITLAN, pc.n. 20:3.

TEZONCALTITLAN. pc.n., place within TLATILOLCO (?). 56:19 (teçòcaltitlan; *should be* teçōcaltitlan?), 61:7 (teçoncaltitlan).

*TEZONTLALTZIN, p.n. 61:35 (teçòtlaltzin; *should be* teçōtlaltzin?).

TEZONYOCAN, pc.n. 19:33, 21:16 (teçoyocan), 64:35 (teçoyocan tetzcoco).

TEZOYOCAN, see TEZONYOCAN.

TEZOZOMOC (41:5) or TEZOZOMOCTLI or TEZOZOMOCTZIN, p.n.
1. Ruler of Azcapotzalco. 18:38,48, 23:51, 24:5 (huehue tezozomoctli), 24:12,16, 28:36,44,46, 30:34,36,44, 31:5,9,13,17,46, 32:33,43,47, 33: 5,8,25, 34:34,41, 35:9,12, 36:13, 37:8–45 passim, 38:9,12,39,42,46, 48, 39:3–48 passim, 40:14,15, 42:46,50, 44:31,35, 45:32, 46:26,29, 66:14.
2. Ruler of Tlahuacan Chalca in Xicco. 26:50.
3. Ruler of Cuitlahuac Tizic. 30:30, 32:5, 49:9,54, 50:5,38,40,43, 57:47.
4. Ruler of Cuauhtitlan. 32:19, 40:8, 41:5,23,35,37,39,49, 42:2,14,17.
5. Ruler of Colhuacan. 57:41, 63:52.

TIACAPANTZIN, female p.n. 15:42.

TIANQUIZTENCO, pc.n.
1. See UAH sec. 89.
2. 4:19.

TIANQUIZZOLCO, pc.n. 8:26 (tianquizçolco quauhtlaapan), 18:34 (quauhtlaapan tianquizçolco), 30:1 (quauhapan tianquizçolco).

TICOC YAHUACATL, official title especially applicable to a judge or executioner (FC 8:55:18; FC 8:61–62; FC 8:74:23; FC 8:77:8; CF bk. 2, ch. 27, fols. 57v-58; Codex Mendoza fol. 65; TEZ ch. 29, p. 316: Ticoyahuacatl). 60:12, 60:24.

TICOCTZIN, p.n.
1. Father-in-law of AZTATZONTZIN. 15:30.
2. = TICOC YAHUACATL. 60:18.

-TILIHUICAN, see CHIUCNAUHTILIHUICAN.

TITLACAHUAN, p.n., alternate name for TEZCATLIPOCA. 76:5,22, 78:12. See also TITLAHUAN.

TITLAHUAN (error for TITLACAHUAN?), p.n. 75:45.

TIZAAPAN, vars. ATIZAPAN (17:39, 20:4), TIZACAPAN (17:20), pc.n.
1. 17:20 (tiçacapan), 17:39 (atiçapan), 83:42.
2. = 1 (?). 20:4 (atiçapan).

TIZAATZIN, see DIEGO TIZAATZIN.

TIZACAPAN, see TIZAAPAN.

TIZAPAN, pc.n. 65:9.

TIZAPAPALOTZIN, p.n. 63:47.

TIZAYOCAN, pc.n. 54:35,36, 64:39.

TIZIC, pc.n. 13:8, 50:43,46, 62:46, 63:50. See also CUITLAHUAC TIZIC.

TIZICATL, pl. TIZICA, g.n. 33:1 (cuitlahuaca tiçica), 49:54 (tiçica cuitla-huaca), 49:56, 50:2,3,8 (nitiçacatl), 50:17. See also CUITLAHUACATL.

TIZOC, see TIZOCICATZIN.

TIZOCICATZIN (given as Tizoc in IXT, TEZ, and TORQ), p.n. 57:37,43,52, 67:20,26, 121:9.

TLACAHUEPANTZIN, p.n.
1. Son of Axayacatzin, died fighting in Huexotzinco (MEX 135, AUB 49, NED). 59:10.
2. See PEDRO TLACAHUEPANTZIN.

TLACATECCATL, pl. TLATLACATECCA, an official title (for discussion see TLACOCHCALCATL). 15:26, 30:23 (motlacateccatlalli), 32:35, 34:26 (xinechtlacateccatlallican), 40:49 (tlatlacatecca), 50:24, 59:7, 60:24.

TLACATEOTL (40:8), or TLACATEOTZIN, p.n.
1. Ruler of Cuauhtitlan. 27:48, 28:20.
2. Ruler of Tlatilolco. 32:24, 34:6, 40:8, 43:3, 66:5,7, 66:32 (tlatateotzin).

TLACATEUCTLI, an official title (for discussion see TLACOCHTEUCTLI). 29:19. See also CUAUHCHICHITZIN TLACATEUCTZIN, TLACA-TEUCTZIN TZINCOPINTZIN.

TLACATEUCTZIN, see PEDRO TLACATEUCTZIN. See also TLACA-TEUCTLI.

TLACATEUCTZIN TZINCOPINTZIN, p.n. 59:55.

TLACATL, king, ruler. See GLOS.

TLACAYAOTZIN, p.n. 63:46 (tlàcayaotzin).

TLACHCO, pc.n. 26:38, 67:3, 84:45.

TLACHCUICALCO, pc.n. 49:32.

TLACHIHUALE, see GLOS.

TLACHQUIAHUITL TEUCTLI, p.n. 10:19.

TLACHQUIAUHCA, g.n., pl. 61:25.

TLACHQUIAUHCO, pc.n. 68:4 (tlachquiyauhco), 121:34.

TLACOAPAN, pc.n. 65:44.

TLACOC, pc.n. 21:16.

TLACOCHCALCA

1. See TLACOCHCALCATL.

2. Name applied to one or more Chalca groups (CHIM). 54:43. See also CHALCA TLACOCHCALCA.

TLACOCHCALCATL, pl. TLACOCHCALCA (41:1).

1. One of a pair of high commanders (the other is the TLACATECCATL), one of whom must be noble (pilli), the other a non-noble warrior (HG bk. 6, ch. 14, parag. 55; HG bk. 6, ch. 20, parag. 27; see also AC 15:24–27)—being two members of a group of four high officials (of which the other two are TLACATEUCTLI and TLACOCHTEUCTLI); in 15th-c. Matlatzinco the tlacateccatl and the tlacochcalcatl were, respectively, the 2d- and 3d-ranking officials after the tlatoani (Zorita, article 18). Note: For further discussion see Piho. 15:31, 33:46, 41:1, 43:47, 50:24.

2. P.n. See JUAN TLACOCHCALCATL.

3. See TLACOCHCALCA.

TLACOCHCALCO, pc.n.

1. Place controlled by Xaltocan. 19:34.

2. Place assoc. with CHALCO ATENCO (see CHIM 279). 49:40, 58:4 (chalco tlacochcalco), 66:10. See also CHALCO (re 63:47).

TLACOCHCUE, female p.n. 3:33.

TLACOCHTEUCTLI, one of a pair of high executives (the other is the TLA-CATEUCTLI), one of whom must be noble (pilli), the other a non-noble warrior (HG bk. 6, ch. 20, parag. 26)—being two members of a group of four high officials, of which the other two are TLACOCHCALCATL and TLACATECCATL (HG bk. 6, ch. 20, parag. 28). 61:8 (tehuilocan tlacochteuctli).

TLACOCHTZIN, p.n. 58:12.

TLACOCOUHCAN, pc.n., place within the city of Cuauhtitlan. 42:13.

TLACOPAN, pc.n. 16:39, 46:39, 63:39 (tlacopan tepanohuayan), 63:53, 64:49, 65:36,42, 66:36, 84:33.

TLACOPANTONCO XOLOTLIATLAUHYOC, pc.n. 18:15,30.

TLACOTEPEC, pc.n. 64:46, 67:11,41, 84:52, 121:25.

TLACOTZINTLI, p.n. (?, see note to the translation at 15:42). Cf. GLOS: tlacotzintli.

TLACOXOCHITLA, pc.n. 65:9.

TLACUATZIN, p.n. 18:53, 22:22,42.

TLAHUACA, g.n., apparently an alternate name for the CUITLAHUACA (see 13:4–8). 13:4, 32:27.

TLAHUACAN, pc.n., see CHALCA TLAHUACAN.

TLAHUAHUANQUI, p.n. 28:40.

TLAHUEXOLOTL, p.n. 34:17.

TLAHUITOL, p.n. 19:42.

TLAHUIZCALPANTEUCTLI, p.n., spirit or deity. 7:43 (translated: Lord of the Dawn), 78:7,9,11 (this Tlahuizcalpanteuctli is the frost).

TLAHUIZPOTONCATZIN, p.n. 13:45.

TLAILOTLACAN, pc.n.

    1. One of the original boroughs of TLALMANALCO (?, the "Tlayllotlaque" were one of five groups that settled Tlalmanalco, see CHIM 165, ZCHIM 1:40). 53:19, 58:7.

    2. A borough of AMAQUEMECAN (CHIM 184–282 passim).

TLAILOTLAQUE, g.n., pl., inhabitants of TLAILOTLACAN 1. 58:10,23,26.

TLALANAPAN, see TLALLANAPAN.

TLALCOCOMOCCO, pc.n. 18:23.

TLALCOZAUHTITLAN, pc.n. 67:3, 68:3, 84:44.

TLALCOZPAN, pc.n. 19:10,13,37, 26:27 (tlalcozpan hueytoctitlan).

TLALHUACPAN (the Dry Lands), pc.n., realm of the Tepaneca (NED). 23:51, 24:13.

TLALICHCATL, p.n., a spirit or deity. 4:45.

TLALLAMANAC, p.n., a spirit or deity (= TLALLAMANQUI?). 4:45, 77:1.

TLALLAMANQUI, p.n., a spirit or deity (= TLALLAMANAC?). 76:21.

TLALLANAPAN (cf. IXT 2:114: Tlalanapan), pc.n. 64:39.

TLALLI TEUCTLI, p.n.

    1. Ruler of Chalco. 12:20.

    2. = 1, above (?). 18:9.

TLALMANALCO, pc.n., Chalca capital (DHIST ch. 2, parag. 8). 59:42.

TLALOC, p.n.

    1. The rain god, the principal rain spirit (FFCC bk. 1, ch. 4), called "the master" (82:46). Syn.(?) TLALOCANTEUCTLI.

    2. One of the rain gods. 82:43.

    3. Pl., tlaloque, the rain gods. 77:21–23, 82:14,15,19,23,38, 83:9,13.

TLALOCAN, see IZTACTLALOCAN, TLALOCANTEUCTLI.

TLALOCANTEUCTLI, p.n., a spirit or deity. 77:39. Cf. TLALOC 1.

TLALOQUE, see TLALOC 3.

TLALTECAHUACAN, pc.n., one of the original boroughs of Tlalmanalco (?, the Tlaltecahuaque were one of five groups that settled Tlalmanalco, see CHIM 165, ZCHIM 1:40). 53:18, 58:13.

TLALTECAHUAQUE, g.n., pl., one of five groups that settled Tlalmanalco (CHIM 165, ZCHIM 1:40). = TLALTECAYOHUAQUE (?).

TLALTECATL, p.n. 64:1.

TLALTECATZIN, p.n. 81:48.

TLALTECAYOHUACAN, pc.n. Note: 58:5–13 implies that Tlaltecayohuacan = TLALTECAHUACAN. 16:1.

TLALTECAYOHUAQUE, g.n., pl., = TLALTECAHUAQUE (?, see also TLAL-TECAYOHUACAN). 13:15, 58:6 (tlaltecayohuaque chalca).

TLALTEPAN, pc.n. 19:44.

TLALTETELPAN, pc.n. 63:20.

TLALTEUCTLI, p.n., lit., earth lord. Note that Tlalteuctli is feminine (see 78:40 and 79:6). 38:5 (yn tonatiuh yn tlalteuctli), 76:19, 78:40 (identified with Mecitli), 79:6 (idem).

TLALTOCHTLI, p.n. 29:4.

TLALTOLCALTZIN, p.n., a prince of Colhuacan (should be TLATOLCAL-TZIN?). 27:44.

TLALTZIN TEUCTLI, p.n. 51:7, 53:12.

TLAMACAZCATEPEC, pc.n.
1. 6:24 (figurative usage?).
2. = 1, above (?). 19:45.

TLAMACAZCATZINCO, pc.n. 10:9.

TLAMACAZQUI, priest. 4:1, 5:33–43, 6:43. See TEUCTLAMACAZQUI, TOTEC TLAMACAZQUI. See also GLOS: tlamacazqui.

TLAMACAZTLAN, pc.n. 65:19.

TLAMAMATLATL, pc.n. 21:18.

TLANCUAXOXOUHQUI, p.n. 3:44.

TLANITZTLAN, pc.n., town conquered by Moteuczomatzin the younger (Carta de don Pablo Nazareo per García Granados *Diccionario* 1:565: Tlaniztlan). 67:47, 121:30 (Tlaniztlan).

TLANIZTLAN, see TLANITZTLAN.

TLANTZANATZTOC, see TLATZANATZTOC.

TLAOLLAN, pc.n. 67:16, 121:3.

TLAOTONXINTLI, one who is shorn or shaved as an Otomi (FC 12:88:2), a high-ranking warrior, possibly the same as a cuachic (shaven head; for details see NED: otomitl 2, cuāchic). 31:30.

TLAPACOYAN, pc.n. 64:47, 67:4, 84:46.

TLAPALICHCATLAN, pc.n. 64:46 (tlapalychcatla).

TLAPALLAN, pc.n. 29:11 (assoc. with TLILHUACAN), 78:29, 81:44. See also TLILLAN TLAPALLAN.

TLAPALLITLAN, pc.n. 65:5.

TLAPAN, pc.n. 121:11 (conquered by Tizocicatzin), 121:16 (conquered by Ahuitzotzin). Cf. TLAPPAN.

TLAPECHHUACAN, pc.n. 10:50 (tlapechhuacan quauhtenco), 11:19 (idem).

TLAPPAN, pc.n. 67:25,30 (conquered by Tizocicatzin and again by Ahuitzo-tzin). Cf. TLAPAN.

TLAPPANECA, g.n., pl. 58:2,38.

TLAQUILTENANCO, pc.n. 64:20.

TLATELOLCO (UAH passim but often written TLATILOLCO in Nahuatl documents), pc.n. See TLATILOLCO.

TLATILCO, pc.n. 19:5.

TLATILOLCA, g.n., pl. 44:21, 44:23 (Mexica tlatilolca), 45:1,23, 47:13, 49:30, 49:31 (tlatilolca atl), 50:29, 55:17, 55:50 (nitlatilolcatl), 56:30, 61:2 (tlatilolcatlalli), 67:8.

TLATILOLCO, pc.n. 29:43, 32:20,23, 33:1,6, 34:6, 40:8, 41:5, 43:3,8, 55:18,48, 56:45, 60:54, 61:1, 66:5,30, 67:9,10, 84:36,51.

TLATLACHPANALOYAN, pc.n. 21:20.

TLATLACUALOYAN, pc.n. 20:2.

TLATLATEPEC, pc.n. 121:33.

TLATLAUHQUITEPEC, pc.n. (GKC 306: einstmals bedeutender Ort im Gebirge nördlich von S. Juan de los Llanos). 64:47, 67:5, 84:46.

TLATLAUHQUITEPECA, g.n. 55:3.

TLATLAUHYAN, pc.n. 64:40 (*should be* Oztotl Tlatlauhyan? See note to the translation).

TLATLAYAN, pc.n., destination of Quetzalcoatl (FC 10:176:2: in tlapalla in tlatlaia). 7:32, 68:1. See also TLILLAN TLAPALLAN.

TLATOANI, king, ruler. See GLOS: tlatoani.

TLATOLCALTZIN, p.n.
1. A prince of Colhuacan (?, see TLALTOLCALTZIN). 27:44.
2. Ruler of Colhuacan. 57:9,40.
3. Ruler of Xochimilco. 63:49.

TLATOLOYAN, pc.n. 65:10. Cf. GLOS: tlatoloyan.

TLATZALLAN, pc.n. 21:22,32 (tlatzallan acatzintlan).

TLATZANATZTOC (He Rattles the Reeds, see 14:16, see GLOS: tlatzanatza), p.n. 14:15 tlaçanatztoc), 14:35 (idem), 14:38 (tlatzanatztoc), 14:41 (tlantzanatztoc), 14:51 (tlaçanaztoc), 17:47 (idem).

TLAXCALLAN, pc.n. 3:41, 20:48, 21:6, 28:48,52, 34:14, 45:6, 49:25, 63:56.

TLAXCALTECA, g.n., pl. 13:10, 18:3,7,44, 45:10,13,22,29,42.

TLAXIMALOYAN (NED), pc.n. 67:13 (tlaximalloyan), 121:2 (tlaximalloyan).

TLAXOXIUHCO, pc.n. 59:53 (coupled with HUEXOCALCO).

TLAZANATZTOC, see TLATZANATZTOC.

TLAZOHUALLAN, pc.n. 65:11.

TLAZOLTEOTL or TLAZOLTEOTZIN, p.n.
1. Ruler of Cuauhtinchan. 52:4.
2. Chief lord of the Cuitlahuaca. 62:51, 63:2.

TLAZOLYAOTZIN, p.n. 57:34 (tlahçolyaotzin).

TLECOYOTL, p.n. 34:16.

TLECUAUHTLA, pc.n. 65:45.

TLECUILQUE, g.n., pl. 32:28.

TLILCOATZIN, p.n.
1. Ruler of Tollan. 8:32,39.
2. One of the Tlahuaca founders. 13:5.

TLILHUACAN, pc.n.

1. 29:12 (assoc. with TLAPALLAN). Cf. TLILLAN TLAPALLAN.

2. Name of a Chalca community. 58:12.

TLILHUAQUE, g.n., pl.

1. Inhabitants of TLILHUACAN 1 (?). 32:28.

2. Inhabitants of TLILHUACAN 2. 58:22,26.

TLILHUATONICAC, pc.n. 19:31.

TLILIUHQUITEPEC, pc.n. 3:41, 34:14 (tliliuhquitepe), 45:6, 57:29.

TLILIUHQUITEPECA, g.n., pl. 45:10,12.

TLILIUHQUITEPETL, p.n. (?). 34:17.

TLILLAN TLAPALLAN, pc.n. 5:21, 7:24 (yn tlillan yn tlapallan yn tlatlayan).

TLILLOTLINAHUAL, p.n., see PABLO TLILLOTLINAHUAL.

TLILPOTONCATZIN, p.n., see ACHICATZIN TLILPOTONCATZIN.

TLILTEPEC, pc.n. 59:8, 68:2, 122:4.

TLILTZAPOAPAN, pc.n. 64:41.

TLOTEPE, var. TLOTEPETL, p.n. 78:37, 79:18,26.

TOCHIHUITZIN, p.n.

1. Son of ITZCOATL 1. 36:27.

2. Prince of Mexicatzinco. 61:5.

3. Ruler of Mexicatzinco (= 2, above?). 63:51.

TOCHMILCO, pc.n. 65:12.

TOCHPAN, pc.n. 65:12, 67:17, 121:5.

TOCHPANECAYOTL, pertaining to TOCHPAN (said of a certain kind of tilma) (CF bk. 9, cf. 2, fol. 5: vna carga de mantas de tochpanecaiotl). 64:50.

TOCHQUIHUA, see TOZQUIHUA.

TOCHTEPEC, pc.n. 65:45.

TOCHTZIN, p.n.

1. A child of Quinatzin and the Mexicatl woman. 14:49.

2. See TOCHTZIN TEUCTLI.

TOCHTZIN TEUCTLI, p.n., prince and governor of Chichimecacuicoyan. 18:12.

TOCI, female p.n., a supernatural (FFCC bk. 1, ch. 15). 24:44.

TOCUILTZIN, p.n. 15:17 (coupled with TOTEC YATETZIN).

TOLAPAN, pc.n. 65:16.

TOLLAN, pc.n. (lit., among the rushes, cf. GLOS: tolla). 3:52,56, 4:26, 4:32 (tollan colhuacan), 5:22, 6:20, 8:4,11,12,23,31,32,39,49, 9:29,35,40,45, 10:26, 12:13,54, 13:34, 21:33 (tollan tlaca), 40:45, 55:51, 63:36, 64:6 (xippacoyā tollan), 64:11,15, 66:1,39, 77:30, 78:28, 81:47, 82:29, 83:3; see also pictograph following 78:23 and note to the translation at 78:24. For g.n., see TOLTECATL 1.

TOLLANTZINCO, pc.n. 4:22, 15:46, 16:14, 59:55, 60:14, 64:35, 66:2, 84:23.

TOLLOCAN, pc.n. 67:11.

TOLNAHUACATZINTLI, p.n. 60:23.

TOLPETLAC, pc.n. 12:29.

TOLTECATEPEC, pc.n. (lit., Toltec mountain). 6:14,25 (figurative usage?), 10:29 (idem?).

TOLTECATL, pl. TOLTECA

1. G.n. (pertaining to Tollan). 2:14,54,55, 3:50, 4:25, 5:13, 9:4,47,48, 54, 10:5,15,23,39,44,47,49, 11:8,11,14, 12:41, 51:38,40 (of Tamazolac), 81:53, 82:27,32,40,44,51, 83:3,18,22,26,44; cf. tollan tlaca (21:33).

2. Craftsman, artisan (NED). 4:54.

3. P.n., one of the sorcerers who put Quetzalcoatl to flight (= 4, below?). 5:26, 6:12,47.

4. P.n., one of the 400 pulque gods (MAGL 203).

5. See TOLTECATZIN.

TOLTECATZACUALLI, pc.n. 21:17.

TOLTECATZIN, p.n., ruler of Chiauhtzinco. 57:16,18, 59:24.

TOLTEPEC, pc.n. 26:26, 49:30.

TOLTITLAN, pc.n., 21:45, 30:48,50,51, 31:4,6,16,20,24, 33:18, 40:7, 45: 40,46, 46:4,19,39, 48:20,42,44, 51:39 (toltitlan tamaçolac), 54:5,38, 64:4,9, 84:23.

TOLTITLANCALQUE, g.n., pl. 25:40, 27:1 (Tepaneca who are known as Tol-titlancalque), 30:41,46,49, 31:18 (tepaneca yn toltitlancalque), 31:22,25, 40:42, 41:33, 45:44, 46:1, 47:43,49,52, 48:23 (yn tepaneca yn toltitlan-calque), 48:45.

TONACACIHUATL, p.n. 4:44, 77:54.

TONACATEPETL (Food Mountain), pc.n. (in myth). 77:5,14,20.

TONACATEUCTLI, p.n. 4:44, 77:35,53.

TONALLAN, pc.n. 64:45.

TONALLIIMOQUETZAYAN, pc.n. 67:22, 121:9.

TONANITLAN or TONANIXILLAN or TENANITLAN, pc.n. 19:35 (tonan-ytlan), 21:17 (tenanytlan), 46:37 (tonanyxillan—where Tepaneca were ex-iled), 48:37 (tonanytlan—where Tepaneca were exiled).

TONANIXILLAN, see TONANITLAN.

TONATIUH, p.n., Sun (the deity). 38:4. See also GLOS: tonatiuh.

TOPAN, heaven, the hereafter (NED, cf. NED: tochān). Key word: our home. 62:5.

TOPILLAN, pc.n. 11:1.

TOPILTZIN, p.n. 3:57 (topiltzin tlamacazqui ce acatl quetzalcohuatl), 4:32,33, 77:30, 78:26, 81:50. See also CE ACATL, QUETZALCOATL 2.

TOQUIHUA TEUCTLI, see TOZQUIHUA.

TOTEC

1. The victim in a flaying ritual (FC 2:49:12). 9:55.

2. Name or title. See TEXOCUAUHTLI TOTEC, TOTEC IYAUHTEUH, TOTEC TLAMACAZQUI.

TOTEC IYAUHTEUH, var. TOTEC YATETZIN, p.n. 15:17 (totec yatetzin), 60:45 (totec yyauhteuh).

TOTEC TLAMACAZQUI

1. Name or title of a priest (in Tenochtitlan?) (FC 3:67, FC 6:54).

2. Name or title of a religious specialist in Colhuacan. 24:47 (tetec tlamacazqui).

TOTEC YATETZIN, see TOTEC IYAUHTEUH.

TOTEPEUH, p.n.

1. Father of Quetzalcoatl. 3:55.

2. Ruler of Cuitlahuac. 18:21 (totepeuh teuctli), 18:46.

TOTEPEUH TEUCTLI, see TOTEPEUH 2.

TOTOCALCO, see GLOS.

TOTOLAPAN, pc.n. 66:54, 84:43.

TOTOLAPANECA, g.n., pl. 58:50 (totollapaneca).

TOTOLLAN, pc.n.

1. 3:40.

2. = 1 (?), 29:11, 67:34.

TOTOLLOCAN, pc.n. 65:15.

TOTOMATLATZIN, p.n. 20:30, 24:50.

TOTOMIHUAQUE, g.n., pl. 18:3,7,44, 24:20, 26:46, 27:6.

TOTONACAHUIA:MO, to "Totonac" oneself, to come under the influence of the Totonaca (?, cf. CETOCHHUIA:MO), freely, to go to the Totonaque (?). 59:58.

TOTONACAPAN, pc.n. 59:59.

TOTONAQUE, g.n., pl. 54:29.

TOTOOMITL, p.n. 19:42 (totoòmitl).

TOTOQUIHUATZIN, p.n. 63:53, 65:36,42.

TOTOTEPEC, pc.n. 3:41, 67:31,47, 121:17.

TOTOTLAN, pc.n. 67:16.

TOXICO, pc.n. 67:23, 121:10.

TOZANTZIN, p.n. 30:4.

TOZCAUHTLAN, pc.n. 67:16.

TOZCUECUEX, p.n. 82:49, 83:13,14.

TOZPAN, name of one of the three hearthstones. 1:7, 3:27.

TOZPANTLAN, pc.n. 65:5.

TOZPOTONCO, pc.n. 65:18.

TOZQUEHUA TEUCTLI, see TOZQUIHUA.

TOZQUENITLAL, pc.n. 49:33.

TOZQUIHUA, vars. TOCHQUIHUA TEUCTLI, TOQUIHUA TEUCTLI, TOZQUEHUA TEUCTLI, etc., p.n.

1. An early ruler of Chalco. 11:31 (tozquehua teuctli), 12:1 (tozquivan).

2. A later ruler of Chalco. 18:9 (toquihua teuctli), 18:9 gloss (tochquihua teuctli), 24:10 (tozquihua).

TOZQUIHUAN, see TOZQUIHUA.

TOZTEPEC, pc.n. 68:1.

TZACATZIN, p.n. 36:26 (huehue tzacatzin).

TZACUALPAN, pc.n. 84:37.

TZAPOTECA, g.n., pl. 58:38.

TZAPOTITLAN, pc.n. 67:17 (conquered by Axayacatl). Cf. TETZAPOTITLAN.

TZAPOTLAN, pc.n. 8:53 (where the sorcerers Yaotl and Tezcatlipoca lived), 67:31 (conquered by Ahuitzotzin), 81:42 (place where Ce Acatl made conquests), 121:16 (conquered by Ahuitzotzin).

TZICTLA, pc.n. 26:29 (tzictlacopavic).

TZICUILTZIN, female p.n. 15:14,19.

TZIHUACPAPALOTZIN, p.n. 8:36, 9:12.

TZIHUACPOPOCATZIN, p.n. 61:1.

TZIHUACTLATONAC, p.n. 10:46.

TZINACANTEPEC, pc.n. 67:11, 84:52.

TZINACANTLAN, pc.n. 68:1 (tzinacatlan), 121:31 (Tzinacatlan).

TZINACAOZTOC, pc.n. 65:45.

TZINACATZLAN, see TZINACANTLAN.

TZINCOC, name of a mountain. 4:39.

TZINCOPINTZIN, p.n. 59:55 (tlacateuctzin tzincopintzin).

TZINTEMAZATL, p.n. 58:47.

TZIPALLE, p.n. 15:35.

TZIPPANTZIN, p.n. 12:45.

TZITZIMITL

1. Ogress (see Bierhorst, *Mythology of Mexico and Central America*, pp. 170–72). 80:4.

2. Creature comparable to a crocodile (AM 68: vel yuhquin tzitzimitl = [the crocodile] is like a tzitzimitl).

3. Pl., demons of the sky (HG bk. 6, ch. 8, parag. 17: demonios del aire; HG bk. 7, ch. 11, parag. 4: feísimas y terribles y que comerían a los hombres y mujeres; HMPP 234: fleshless females who will descend to eat people when the world ends; FC 7:38 and FC 8:2: they descend to eat people during a solar eclipse). Cf. TZITZIMITL/COLELETLI 1.

TZITZIMITL/COLELETLI

1. Any of the women who had died in childbirth and haunted the earth at night (FC 6:163:31). 78:19.

2. Xoxohuic tzitzimitl, yn xoxohuic colelectli = el verde espiritu, el verde genio (RUIZ 74) = verde espiritado y el verde demonio (Serna 321, Serna 322 adds: el verde colelectli que es algun idolillo embuelto en un emboltorio infernal).

TZITZINTEPEC, pc.n. 63:15.

TZIUHCOAC, pc.n. (CF bk. 8, ch. 1, fol. 2; NED). 58:46 (tzicoac), 64:46

(paid tribute to Tetzcoco), 67:30 (conquered by Ahuitzotzin), 121:16 (conquered by Ahuitzotzin).

TZIUHCOACA, g.n., pl. 58:2,40 (tziuhcohuaca).

TZIUHCOATL or TZIUHCOATZIN, p.n., a leader of NEPANTLA. 43:45 (in 1430), 55:10 (in 1471).

TZIUHMAZATL, p.n. 10:17.

TZIUHTECATZIN, p.n. 18:19,24,35.

TZOHUITZIN, see TZONHUITZIN.

TZOMPANCA, g.n., pl. 40:44, 53:47, 54:4,8,18,21.

TZOMPANCO, pc.n. 13:46, 19:36, 29:18, 54:30, 64:8 (one of Cuauhtitlan's Four Lords); coupled with CITLALTEPEC, 12:21, 13:35, 21:11,45, 29:18, 40:34, 47:9; coupled with TEPOXACCO, 29:33, 46:46.

TZOMPANTEUCTI, to be a skull rack lord. 62:42.

TZOMPANTEUCTLI, pl. TZOMPANTEUCTIN or TZOMPANTETEUCTIN. Lit., skull rack lord (from tzompantli = skull rack; see FC 2:166–75), i.e., a high official, or oracle, in Cuitlahuac (DHIST ch. 50, parag. 14: un gran señor que hubo en Cuitlahuac, que llamaron Tzompanteuctli, a quien los de Cuitlahuac honraron como a dios, porque les dijo las cosas por venir). Singular, 61:53,55, 62:2,9,11; pl., 62:12,13, 63:8. Syn. *NAHUAL-TEUCTLI.

TZOMPANTZIN, p.n. 36:25.

TZONCUAYE, p.n. 10:18.

TZONHUITZIN, p.n. 18:53 (tzohuitzin), 19:13.

TZONMOLCATL, p.n. 60:29.

TZONMOLCO, pc.n. 81:40.

TZONPANCO, see TZOMPANCO.

TZONTECOCHATZIN, p.n. 35:31,43, 36:30.

TZONTEMOC or TZONTEMOCTZIN, p.n.

    1. Spirit or deity. 77:1 (tzontemoc).

    2. Ruler of Huexotla. 60:50, 64:3.

TZOPALLOTZIN, p.n. 28:39.

VEGA, p.n., see LUIS DE LA VEGA.

XALAPAN, pc.n. 65:45, 68:7, 121:17 (Xallapan), 122:3 (Xallapan).

XALATLAUHCO, pc.n. 67:14 (xallatlauhco), 121:1 (xallatlauhco).

XALLAN, pc.n. 19:8,8 (xalla), 26:33 (xallā).

XALMIMILOLCO, pc.n. 59:29.

XALTEMOCTZIN, p.n.

    1. Son of TLATZANATZTOC. 14:42, 15:52 (?).

    2. A prince of Cuauhtitlan (= 3, below?). 28:10.

    3. Ruler of Cuauhtitlan. 17:47, 29:14,16,26; huehue xaltemoctzin, 17:47,

XICTLAN, pc.n. 63:18.

XIHUACAN, pc.n. 81:3, 121:17.

XIHUITLTEMOCTZIN, p.n. 18:36, 21:49.

XILOMANTZIN, p.n. 49:47 (xillomantzin), 51:11 (xomotzin), 57:2,5 (xillomantzin).

XILOTEPEC, pc.n. 40:46, 55:51, 64:6, 67:4, 84:45.

XILOTZINCA, g.n., pl. 53:47, 54:18,21.

XILOTZINCO, pc.n. 21:20,31, 29:23, 54:9.

XILOXOCHCATL, p.n. (?) or title (?). 24:46.

XIMILCO (?, paleography uncertain), pc.n. 2:57 (see note to the translation and cf. TEMILCO).

XIPEMETZTLI, p.n. 24:11, 27:11.

XIPPACOYAN, pc.n. 64:5 (xippacoyā tollan).

XIQUIPILCATL, g.n. 84:2.

XIQUIPILCO, pc.n. 57:27, 67:10, 84:52.

XIUHCAC, p.n. 26:25.

XIUHCACCO, pc.n. 26:26.

XIUHCOZCATL, var. XIUHCOZCATZIN, p.n.

1. A Toltec. 9:54 (xiuhcozcatl).
2. A friend of Yaotl (same as 1?). 10:18 (xiuhcozcatl).
3. One who was sent by Itzcoatzin. 40:1 (xiuhcozcatzin).

XIUHNEL, var. XIUHNELTZIN, p.n.

1. Member of the legendary Mixcoa, companion to Mimich. 79:36,38, 79:43 (xiuhneltzin), 79:46, 79:47 (xiuhneltzin).
2. Early ruler of Cuauhtitlan (identified with 1, above?). Xiuhneltzin, 2:56, 3:2,47.
3. One of the three hearthstones of the early Chichimecs. 3:27.
4. One of the early Cuauhtitlan Chichimecs (= 1 and/or 2, above?). 3:30.

XIUHTEPEC, pc.n. 66:38, 67:1, 84:36,44.

XIUHTEPECA, g.n., pl. 28:25.

XIUHTETEUCTIN, pl. of XIUHTEUCTLI. Key word: fire lords. 63:14, 80:8.

XIUHTEUCTLI, p.n., a deity, i.e., the fire god (FFCC bk. 1, ch. 13). 1:6, 3:27, 77:35. See also HUEHUE TEOTL. For pl. see XIUHTETEUCTIN.

XIUHTEUCZATLAN, pc.n. 121:20.

XIUHTLACUILOLXOCHITZIN, female p.n. 4:18,28.

XIUHTLAN, pc.n. 60:28, 67:34.

XIUHTLAPOCA, p.n. 28:40.

XIUHTLATONACTZIN, p.n. 28:27.

XIUHTOCHTLI, p.n. 3:44.

XIYATL, p.n. 19:13.

XOCHICALTITLAN, pc.n. 19:39.

XOCHICOZCATL

1. Female p.n. 30:2.
2. Male p.n. 52:4, 53:42.

XOCHIMILCA, g.n., pl. 11:50,51, 12:10,11, 13:24, 17:15,41, 46:40, 47:32, 58:48. See also XOCHMILCATL.

XOCHIMILCO (FC 11:147:4, FC 11:152:4, but often written xochmilco in Nahuatl documents), pc.n.
   1. Lakeside town 20 km. south of Mexico. 17:17,41, 33:24, 46:24,35, 59: 28, 61:17, 63:49, 65:51, 66:37, 84:16,18,36 (xochmilco). See XOCHMILCATL.
   2. "San Cristobal Xochimilco, im Distrikt Zacatlan des Staates Puebla, auf der linken Talseite des Rio Axaxal unterhalb von Zacatlan" (GKC 306). 64:43 (?).
   3. = 1, above (?). 65:16.

XOCHIOLOLTZIN, p.n.
   1. A Toltec elder. 10:47.
   2. Ruler of Cuitlahuac Tizic. 57:47.

XOCHIPAN, p.n. 18:52, 22:23.

XOCHIPAPALOTL, female p.n. 12:46.

XOCHIQUENTLAN, pc.n. 65:11.

XOCHIQUETZAL, female p.n., a spirit or deity. 9:7 (waters of), 24:45 (worshipped by Colhuaque). 78:13.

XOCHIQUILAZCO, pc.n. 11:27.

XOCHIQUILAZYO, pc.n. (?). 63:13.

XOCHITITLAN, pc.n. 65:19.

XOCHITLCOZAUHQUI, p.n. 47:45.

XOCHITONAL, p.n. 27:43.

XOCHITZETZELTZIN, p.n. 64:6.

XOCHIYACAN, pc.n. 67:12, 84:52.

XOCHIYETLAN, pc.n. 67:25, 121:12 (Xochiyetla).

XOCHMILCATL, g.n. 84:3. See also XOCHIMILCA.

XOCHMILCO, see XOCHIMILCO.

XOCHMITL, p.n. 22:32,35,43.

XOCHTLAN, pc.n. 59:11, 67:31, 121:19.

XOCOCAPAN, pc.n. 64:41.

XOCONOCHTZIN, p.n., see FRANCISCO CARLOS XOCONOCHTZIN.

XOCOTITLAN, pc.n. 64:7.

XOCUETZIN, p.n. 53:18.

XOLLAN, pc.n. 65:19 (but see note to the transcription).

XOLLOCHIUHCAN, pc.n. 121:18 (conquered by Ahuitzotzin). Cf. XOLLO-CHIYUHYAN.

XOLLOCHIYUHYAN (García Granados *Diccionario* 1:44 has xolochiuhyan), pc.n. 67:32 (conquered by Ahuitzotzin). Cf. XOLLOCHIUHCAN.

XOLOC, pc.n. Xolloc, 11:38, 18:33.

XOLOCHIUHYAN, see XOLLOCHIYUHYAN.
XOLOTLAN, pc.n. 67:39, 121:23 (Xollotlan).
XOLOTLIATLAUHYOC, see TLACOPANTONCO XOLOTLIATLAUHYOC.
XONACAPACOYAN, pc.n. 6:13, 40:29.
XONETZIN, p.n. 16:1.
XONTLAN (?), pc.n. See note to the transcription at 65:19.
XOPANTZIN, p.n. 30:51.
XOXOMALPAN, pc.n. 21:25.
XPIANOTIN (written xp̄ianotin or xp̄ianotin), abbrev. for Chri(s)tianotin, i.e.,
Christians. 68:17,19,23,25,32.

YACAPICHTLAN, pc.n. 67:5, 84:47.
YAHUACATL, see TICOC YAHUACATL.
YANCUITLAN, pc.n. 67:25, 68:1, 121:11.
YAOCIHUATL, female p.n. 3:33.
YAOCOTZITZITLI, p.n. 19:12.
YAOCUIXTLI, p.n.
    1. Warrior of Mexicatzinco. 50:35.
    2. Ruler of Cuauhnahuac. 61:33,43.
YAOMAHUITZIN, p.n. 63:48.
YAOPAN, p.n. 52:4.
YAOTL
    1. Enemy (MOL).
    2. P.n., one of the sorcerers who contributed to the downfall of Tollan. 8:52,
    9:46,49, 10:14,36.
    3. P.n., leader of the Chalca Tlacochcalca. 12:25.
YAOTLAMIN, see PABLO YAOTLAMIN.
YAPALLIICUE, female p.n., a spirit or deity. 78:14.
YATETZIN, see TOTEC IYAUHTEUH.
YAUHQUEMEPOTONQUI, see IYAUHPOTONQUI.
YECATEPEC, see ECATEPEC.
YECATL TEUCTLI, p.n., Chalco ruler. 27:12, 28:4 (yeccatl teuctli).
    Cf. ECATZIN.
YECCATL TEUCTLI, see YECATL TEUCTLI.
YEIITZCUINTLAN, pc.n. 65:5.
YOHUALLAN, pc.n. 66:39, 84:37.
YOHUALLATONAC, p.n. 18:5,18.
YOHUALPAINTZIN, p.n. 60:19.
YOHUALTEPEC, pc.n. 67:2, 84:44.
YOHUALTONATIUH, p.n. 31:32,33.
YOHUATZIN, female p.n. 63:1 (yohuātzin), 63:6.
YOLLOCAMACHALTZIN, see JUAN YOLLOCAMACHALTZIN.

YOLLOXONECUILCO, pc.n. 122:3 (conquered by the younger Moteuczomatzin). Cf. YOLLOXONECUILLAN.
YOLLOXONECUILLAN, pc.n. 68:7 (conquered by the younger Moteuczomatzin). Cf. YOLLOXONECUILCO.
YOPITZINCO, pc.n. 3:40.

ZACACALCO (Straw House Place), pc.n. 28:23.
ZACANCATLYAOTL, var. ZACANCATLYAOMITL, p.n. 35:9,11,17.
ZACANCO, pc.n. 81:40.
ZACATEPEC, pc.n.
  1. Way station of the wandering Mexica. 11:40.
  2. Town controlled by Tetzcoco (= 1, above?). 64:20.
  3. = 1, above? 68:6 (conquered by Ahuitzotzin); 122:2 (conquered by the
  younger Moteuczomatzin).
ZACATLAN, pc.n. 37:5.
ZACATLANTONCO, pc.n. 3:41.
ZACATLATILTITLAN, pc.n. 19:4.
ZACATZONTITLAN, pc.n. 62:21.
ZACUANTEPEC, pc.n. 121:33.
ZOLLAN, pc.n. 121:31.
ZOLTEPEC (Quail Hill), pc.n. 19:16,32, 21:27, 26:35, 67:47; cf. 19:16
(ynçoltepeuh = their quail hill).
ZOLTON, p.n. 81:11,33.
"ZONELTEUCTLI," p.n. (62:40: çonelteuctli). See *CONELTEUCTLI.
ZOYATEPEC, pc.n. 65:45.
ZOZOLLAN, pc.n. 59:60, 67:46, 121:30.
ZOZOTETLAN, pc.n. 64:43 (çocotetlan).

Subject Guide

References to the Codex are by side and line number. A lowercase 'n' immediately following a number means that the reference includes an accompanying footnote.

Adultery, 15:16, 35:5–26, 59:18

Agriculture, *see* Horticulture

Alcoholic beverages, *see* Drunkenness, Plant foods and crops

Animal foods: birds, 4:16; deer, 4:16; fish, 76:1; honey, 6:19; rabbits, 4:16; snakes, 4:16, 13:31; turkey tamale, 82:34; turkey eggs, 13:31

Animal products (*see also* Animal foods, Featherwork, Quetzal plumes): conch horn, 76:28; coyote skins, 65:25; feathers, 65:2; redshell, 4:35,51; skins, 65:32,39; whiteshell, 4:35,51

Animals (*see also* Animal foods, Animal products, Birds, Hunting, Sacrifice of animals): ant, 30:7, 77:4–10; bumblebees and honeybees, 76:31; coyotes, 51:32; deer, 37:37, 65:26,34,41, 79:35–41; dogs, 76:8,15; ducks, 65:25, 33; dragonfly nymphs, 2:25; eagle, 38:16; fish, 2:26, 75:39; gophers, 81:20; jaguars (*ocelotl*), 38:17, 75:7, 77:49, 79:8; monkeys, 2:40, 75:18; opossums, 10:33; rabbits, 37:37, 54:22, 65:26,34,41, 78:17; rattlesnake, 38:18; vultures, 51:32; wolf, 38:17, 77:52; worms, 76:30

Aqueduct, *see* Architecture and engineering

Architecture and engineering (*see also* Bridges, Buildings, City planning, Roads): construction of aqueduct, 53:24–36, 66:44; construction of pyramid or (pyramid) temple (*teocalli*), 5:2–4, 28:15–18, 29:26,27,38, 51:20–27, 53:44, 57:42–44, 59:41; enlarging of (pyramid) temple, 33:42–45, 59: 46; stream diversion, 25:37–43, 48:15–27,45–51, 49:14–19, 59:20–21n, 59:26–33

Banners and streamers, *see* Comet, Regalia of war, Ritual acts, Sacrifice of humans

Bathing, *see* Ritual acts

Beverages, *see* Plant foods and crops

Birds (*see also* Animal foods, Clothing and adornment, Featherwork, Quetzal plumes, Regalia of war, Sacrifice of animals): cotinga, 4:52, 6:6, 7:35, 79:5; cranes, 65:39; eagle, 77:49; egret, 79:4; falcon, 77:51, 78:2; heron, 4:53, 7:36; scarlet macaw, 7:36; green parrot, 7:36; white-fronted parrot, 7:36; quail, 13:31, 19:15–16, 76:45–47; *quechol*, 77:54; quetzal, 7:38; roseate spoonbill (*tlauhquechol*), 4:52, 6:6, 7:35, 79:5; *teoquechol*, 79:5;

trogon, 4:53; troupial, 4:52, 7:36, 79:4; turkeys, 13:31, 65:26,34,40, 75:27; king vulture, 81:7

Boats: canoes (*acalli*), 36:1,18, 56:31, 66:11; raft, 62:29

Bridges, 4:24, 39:8

Buildings and earthworks (*see also* Architecture and engineering, Bridges): altar of beaten earth, 14:6–9, 20:33, 24:43–25:1, 25:45; calpulli temple, 26:4, 57:21; council house (*tlatoloyan*), 43:25; house (*calli*), 19:10, 48:17–22; house of fasting, 4:23,33, 5:9; house of penance, 7:9; house of quetzal plumes, 4:35, 6:38; house of redshell, 4:35, 6:38; house of troupial, 6:38; house of turquoise beams, 4:23,34; house of whiteshell, 4:35; maguey house, 3:19; monastery (*monasterio*), 28:23; palace (*tecpan*), 41:34, 42:21, 44:15, 55:34; palace (*-tlatocachan*), 8:14,19,26,36; palace (*tlatocan*), 61:7; palace house or ruler's house (*tecpancalli*), 9:22, 12:32, 14:45, 16:13, 32:23; pavilion or straw hut (*xacalli*), 22:15, 33:39, 35:26; platform at base of pyramid, 56:26; rampart, 25:5; ruler's residence (*tlatocacalli*), 9:23, 18:42; straw-house (*zacacalli*), 4:19, 8:17, 9:15,22, 11:38, 26:3, 27:49, 28:23, 42:11; sweating room, 30:5; (pyramid) temple (*teocalli*), 13:18, 24:29, 25:29–30,44, 41:9, 47:10, 81:9,24; (pyramid) temple with serpent columns, 5:2; pyramid temple called "house of the devil" (*tlacatecolocalli*), 46:4,6, 59:42; (temple) mound, 4:9, 9:14; thorn house (*tzihuaccalli*), 3:19

Burial: in earth (sand), 81:5; in stone chest, 7:13–16; in pyramid temple, 81:9. For cremation, *see* Fire.

Calendar, *see* Months, Time counting and calendrical lore

Calpulli: temple of 26:4, 57:21; land held by, 26:17, 59:54

Cannibalism, 25:27; by deity or spirit power, 1:13, 79:49–7

Canoes, *see* Boats

Captives, *see* Sacrifice of humans, Slavery and servitude, Warfare, Women

Caves (*see also* Emergence from underworld), 35:28,36, 78:33, 79:33–34, 80:38; and Huemac, 10:9, 11:13

Ceramics: bowls, 26:10; sacred cup, 14:7; eating dishes, 4:55; drinking vessels, 4:55; burnished pot, 81:31; pots, 26:10; pottery or ceramic ware, 4:55, 26:10

Ceremonies (*see also* Ritual acts, Ritual games, Sacrifice of animals, Sacrifice of humans): arrow fast, 26:23; arrow shoot, 9:36–44, 48:4–5; new fire, 76:11–18; of three hearthstones, 1:1–10, 3:20–29; year-bundle feast (*toxiuh molpilia*), 11:25, 29:51, 51:27, 60:5 (with new fire); Xochilhuitl, 21:39, 49:34 (with dancing)

Chalk, *see* Ritual acts, Rocks and minerals

Chastity: daughters kept in cage, 10:31; pubic covering of jade, 51:45

Childbirth, *see* Ritual acts

5:31,45–50, 6:8, 14:31–33; oil, 55:37; pack baskets, 1:48; rabbit pot, 78:17; ropes, 77:15, 81:20, 82:5–13; "a kind of snake-arm," 28:32; brought by Spaniards, 68:32–39; stone chest, 7:13–16; stone of sacrifice, 44:49 ("eagle bowl"), 60:8 (round-stone), 82:37

Marriage, *see* Statecraft

Mask, *see* Regalia of gods

Mat of authority, 3:20, 5:8, 8:47. For matting, *see* Manufactures

Measurement, units of: cubit (*ceciyacatl*), 8:45; fathom (*matl*), 64:50, 65:22,29, 65:29; forearm (*cemolicpitl*), 41:21; *mecatl*, 38:32, 39:25; span (*cemiztitl*), 5:31

Minerals, *see* Rocks and minerals

Months (i.e., twenty-day feast periods): Izcalli, 9:40, 24:40, 47:41; list of, 24:38–41, 64:23–30; Quecholli, 24:39, 25:49, 64:29; Tecuilhuitl, 16:7, 56:28, 64:26, 82:29; Toxcatl, 25:24; Tozoztli, 75:48

Moon: origin of, 77:41–78:18

Morning star: called Lord of the Dawn (Tlahuizcalpantecutli), 7:43, 78:7–11 (identified with frost); influence of, 7:47–56; origin of, 7:37–47

Music (*see also* Dance, Songs): conch horn, 76:28–32

Mythology (*see also* Earth, Fire, Flood, Humans, Moon, Morning star, Nightfall, Sky, Sun): Hidden Corn myth, 77:3–26; origin of the skull rack lords, 62:11–47; Quetzalcoatl in the dead land, 76:22–54

Nagual, 76:36,49

Nightfall: origin of, 78:22

Omens and prognostications (*see also* Comet, Divination, Dreams, Earthquakes, Famine, Solar eclipse): connected with Venus, 7:47–56; evil omens in Tollan, 9:28,45, 81:51; military victory predicted, 36:33–40; nation's downfall predicted, 23:18–45, 55:31 (by woman's vulva), 62:2–9 (by skull rack lord), 82:51–83:3 (by gods); rulership predicted, 23:12–18; serpent deity as oracle, 20:15–28

Penance, *see* Ritual acts

Picture writing, 51:31, 65:47n, 78:24n

Plant foods and crops (*see also* Horticulture, Plant products, Plants): amaranth, 51:29, 77:25; fermented atole, 15:51; barrel cactus, 1:49; beans, 6:16, 77:25; beverage, 16:2; cacao, 4:53, 51:52, 65:46; chia, 77:25; chilis, 6:15, 65:2n, 65:25,33,40, 81:34 (hot pepper); corn, 4:14, 6:16, 50:20, 51:19, 59:59, 75:50, 77:5,12,24, 82:20, 82:40,48, 83:22–24; Food Mountain, 77:5–26; greens, 6:15, 6:27; maguey, 6:17; prickly pears, 1:48–49; pulque, 5:27, 6:19, 6:28–7:1, 79:10, 80:23; spine silk, 1:49;

Sky: as abode of gods, 4:43, 77:53–54; collapse of, 2:28, 75:39,48; as destination of Quetzalcoatl, 7:39; of nine layers, 4:46, 78:11(?); origin of, 2:18; re-establishment of, 76:10,14; smoking of, 76:4,8,15,17,19

Slavery and servitude (*see also* Communal labor, Tribute labor, Women): freed slaves, 15:32, 16:2; escape from, 44:5–12; pages (*tecpoyotl*), 5:7–7:23; king's personal servants, 41:28, 41:41; as refuge for defeated nation, 20:46–21:5; servant communities (*huicalli*), 26:32, 46:43–49; slave market, 40:23; slaves itemized in tribute list, 65:3,35,41; of war captives, 41:14, 44:7

Snow (*see also* Frost), 51:13, 59:15,17, 82:27

Solar eclipse, 23:31, 57:13,38, 58:53,55, 59:2, 59:47, 60:41

Songs, 6:38,49, 7:1,4,8, 17:5, 47:22; "sings and dances . . . like a woman," 77:46; of sorcerer, 9:51

Sorcerers (*tlatlacatecolo*): bring idolatry to Cuauhtitlan, 20:37; magician lords (*nahualteteuctin*) in Cuitlahuac, 62:12,45, 63:4; called "devils" (*diablome*), 3:1, 4:21, 9:42,46,49, 10:3,20,21,35, 17:22, 20:37, 56:46, 62:15; as females, 9:30–43; impersonate females, 8:50–55; Huitzilopochtli called "devil," 57:43; Itzpapalotl called "sorcerer," 25:48; in Mexico, 63:22–24; Mixcoatl called "devil," 26:4, 27:24, 28:15, 50:34, 62:15,37; Mixcoatl called "magician's staff" (*nahualcuauhtli*?) 12:8; Mixcoatl called "sorcerer," 56:27; aid Nezahualcoyotl, 36:33–40; Quetzalcoatl called "sorcerer," 68:20; require human sacrifice, 5:9–6:35 (in opposition to Quetzalcoatl), 9:6, 17:22; King Tezozomoctli addressed as a sorcerer, 37:31; god of Tizic called "devil," 50:46; in Tlalmanalco, 59:41; in Toltitlan, 46:4; and settlement of Xaltocan, 10:12–38

Spaniards, *see* Concordance: Caxtilteca, Españoles, Xpianotin

Stars (*see also* Comet, Morning star, Sun): appeared during solar eclipse, 58:53, 59:2,12

Statecraft (*see also* Executions and assassinations, Gifts of greeting, Gifts of obligation, Hospitality, Land, Legal system, Mat of authority, Tribute goods, Tribute labor, Warfare): ally cheated out of tribute, 50:22–31; ally consoled after defeat, 17:10–12; daughters given to allies as marriage partners, 25:11, 37:40, 61:26,30; privileged allies called "Four Lords," 50:29, 63:51, 64:8; edict of enmity, 14:18–22, 19:20; emissaries and ambassadors, 13:28–30, 41:34, 43:18–44:5, 44:12–19 (beaten on the rump), 44:20–45:9, 52:15–53:7, 55:39–42; high ruler grants dynasty, 14:53–15:13; high ruler selects or inaugurates lesser ruler, 15:20–24, 28:44–46, 52:5–10; enemy idol held captive, 50:37–51:1; nepotism, 31:10–15, 33:13–24,37, 40:15–18; ruler "comes out into the open," 48:27; seat of government rotated among three places, 43:27; woman establishes dynasty, 26:39–45, 27:38–45

Stewards, *see* Land, Plant foods and crops, Tribute goods

Stone carving (*see also* Manufactures), 7:13–16, 33:43

Suicide (*see also* Executions and assassinations): by hanging, 11:6–15; by poison, 33:49, 42:2

Sun (*see also* Solar eclipse): requires blood, 78:4–5, 79:2–28; coming of the first dawn, 2:50, 62:39; invoked as deity, 38:4; sun deity's head adorned with red border, 77:55; called "father," 79:15; myth of four previous suns, 2:5–10,20,24–41, 75:3–43; origin of fifth sun, 2:42–52; 77:27–23

Sweathouse or sweating room, *see* Buildings and earthworks

Textiles (*see also* Clothing and adornment): blankets (*cuachtli*), 60:17; precious cloth, 14:34; "streamers" of cloth, 41:21; twist-woven bands of fabric, 65:23,31

Time counting and calendrical lore (*see also* Ceremonies, Months): of Cuauhtitlan Chichimecs, 1:24,43; day signs, 2:5,23–51, 7:47–56, 29:49, 49:53, 50:11,13,31,32, 56:29, 59:21,47, 60:53, 61:23, 75:14,23,32,42; in Tetzcoco, 1:37; of Toltecs, 2:14; tutelaries of, 1:25–29; origin of the four year counters, 1:22

Tobacco, 83:15

Tools and utensils (*see also* Ceramics): jade bowl, 76:53; knives, 44:50; spindle, 28:33; weaver's reed, 28:31

Tribute goods: from coastlands, 51:37, 51:51–52 (list of); collectors or stewards of, 15:5, 30:4, 57:6; woman as collector of, 51:46–52:1; divided among triple-alliance members (with lists), 64:48–65:47; to honor Huitzilopochtli, 62:1; payment or deposit of, 37:48, 39:36, 53:17; schedule of payment, 41:17–22, 64:22–31 (with lists); roll of payees, 64:37–47; from steward lands, 59:54; warehouse, 18:17

Tribute labor (*see also* Communal labor, Slavery and servitude): apportioned, 32:45–33:7, 48:45; eighty days of, 41:15–17; granted, 53:20; performed, 47:26; requisitioned, 51:8–10; roll of payees, 65:4–19

Underworld (*see also* Emergence from underworld), 76:22–50; of nine layers, 78:11(?)

Venus, *see* Morning star

Warfare (*see also* Gifts of obligation, Regalia of war, Ritual acts, Slavery and servitude, Statecraft, Weapons and shields, Women): allies marked for identification, 45:15–21; chasing the enemy, 11:51, 12:11, 19:18, 20:7; children as warriors, 54:12; "crazed" warriors after battle, 56:40–43; declaration of war, 16:48–51, 17:26, 40:4, 48:10–12, 51:33, 66:11 (by breaking canoes); ears taken as trophies, 17:17–20; called "flood and blaze," 36:36, 38:23, cf. 54:18–25 (water and fire used as tactics); flower war, 27:28,55; informers held hostage, 47:49–48:1; to acquire land, 32:2 (eagle land),

34:28, 47:27–29 (eagle land), 54:34–39 (eagle land); mercenaries, 83:47; night battle, 50:10, 56:16; pillaging, 55:50–56:6, 56:39–40; prisoners taken or rescued, 13:37–54, 16:43, 17:7, 20:31, 22:36–23:8, 25:20, 30:11–12, 37:3–8 (taking of a "partial captive"), 60:41–47; surprise attack, 47:45–46, 49:50–50:6; sham battle to trick enemy, 16:45; squadrons of forty each, 56:12–14; surrounding the enemy, 13:22, 16:34, 18:6–8, 21:47, 56:2; treacherous abandonment of one's own leader, 32:12–17; ululating, 56:48; on water, 56:30–37

Weapons and shields (*see also* Regalia of war): arrows or darts, 7:49, 37:36, 38:34, 53:14, 56:18, 56:47, 78:10, 79:3,4,7,12, 80:31,39,45; bows, 56:18; dart thrower (*atlatl*), 80:31; harpoon staffs, 42:36; macana staffs, 42:36; shields, 17:5, 37:36, 41:2, 43:32, 44:28, 53:14, 54:16, 56:48, 60:17, 79:4,13, 80:31,45; sling, 44:44

Weather, *see* Frost, Lightning, Rain and drought, Snow, Wind

Weaving, *see* Clothing and adornment, Manufactures, Textiles, Tools and utensils

Wind, 53:9, 75:17,23

Women: abduction or rape of, 12:45–49, 16:37,46, 16:52–17:4, 40:33, 84:6; who were Chichimecs, 3:32; as concubines, 55:33–38, 63:28; as dangerous supernaturals, 9:28–43, 79:34–80:7; as establishers of dynasty, 26:39–45, 27:38–45, 30:28–29; of Huitznahua, 80:29–51; imitated or impersonated by males, 8:50, 77:46; as ladies in waiting, 9:16, 24:23; requisitioned by Cortés, 15:44; as ritualists, 14:2–7; as rulers, 4:17, 9:13, 27:17–23; as sacrificial victims, 13:51, 82:49–53; sister of Quetzalcoatl, 6:40–53; woman as skull rack lord, 62:42; in slavery, 15:32,41,50,51, 65:27,35,41; as sorcerers, 9:30; as spies, 45:47–46:5, 55:21–25; woman tribute collector, 51:46–52:1; valiant women (*mocihuaquetzqui*), 8:43; as war captives, 37:26, 45:44–46:19, 60:52; as warriors, 17:16, 54:12; accused of whoring, 27:22; work of, 57:25, 58:17

Writing, *see* Picture writing

Source Abbreviations

Sources cited in abbreviated form may be accompanied by a page number, as in CAR 500, indicating Carochi, *Arte de la lengua mexicana* (1892 ed.), p. 500. If the work in question has only one volume, a second number indicates the line. Thus CAR 500:23 shows that the citation is to be found at line 23. But HERN 1:205 means Hernández, *Historia natural de Nueva España*, vol. 1, p. 205; and FC 8:23:2 is Sahagún, *Florentine Codex* (Anderson and Dibble ed., 1st ed.), bk. 8, p. 23, line 2. Wholly numerical citations refer to the *Codex Chimalpopoca* itself; hence 32:21 is side 32, line 21 of the codex. For complete bibliographic data on all sources, see References.

AC	Annals of Cuauhtitlan (present edition)
AM	Kutscher, Brotherston, and Vollmer, eds., *Aesop in Mexico*
AND	Andrews, *Introduction to Classical Nahuatl*
AUB	Dibble, *Historia de la nación mexicana . . . Códice de 1576 (Códice Aubin)*
CAR	Carochi, *Arte de la lengua mexicana* (1892 ed.)
CAROC	Carochi, *Arte de la lengua mexicana* (1983 ed.)
CF	Sahagún, *Códice florentino* (1979 ed.)
CHIM	Chimalpain, *Relaciones* (Rendón ed.)
CM	Cantares mexicanos
DCAL	"El calendario antigua," in Durán, *Historia de las Indias*, vol. 1
DHIST	Durán, *Historia de las Indias*, vol. 2
FC	Sahagún, *Florentine Codex* (Anderson and Dibble ed.), 1st ed.
FFCC	Sahagún, *Florentine Codex* (Anderson and Dibble ed.), 2d ed.
GLOS	Glossary in Bierhorst, *Codex Chimalpopoca: The Text in Nahuatl with a Glossary and Grammatical Notes*
GKC	Lehmann, *Die Geschichte der Königreiche von Colhuacan und Mexico*
GN	Grammatical Notes in Bierhorst, *Codex Chimalpopoca: The Text in Nahuatl with a Glossary and Grammatical Notes*
GRAM	Grammatical Notes in Bierhorst, *A Nahuatl-English Dictionary*
HERN	Hernández, *Historia natural de Nueva España*
HG	Sahagún, *Historia general de las cosas de Nueva España* (Garibay ed.)
HMAI	*Handbook of Middle American Indians*
HMPP	"Historia de los mexicanos por sus pinturas"
HTCH	Kirchoff et al., *Historia Tolteca Chichimeca*

IXT   Alva Ixtlilxochitl, *Obras históricas* (O'Gorman ed.)

MAGL   Nuttall, *The Book of the Life of the Ancient Mexicans* [Codex Maglia-
           bechiano]

MEX   Tezozomoc, *Crónica mexicáyotl.*

MOL   The Nahuatl-Spanish section of Molina's *Vocabulario*

MOLS   The Spanish-Nahuatl section of Molina's *Vocabulario*

NED   Bierhorst, *A Nahuatl-English Dictionary.*

PAR   Paredes, *Compendio del Arte de la lengua mexicana del P. Horacio
           Carochi*

RITOS   "Libro de los ritos y ceremonias," in Durán, *Historia de las Indias*,
           vol. 1

RUIZ   Ruiz de Alarcón, "Tratado de las supersticiones" (Paso y Troncoso ed.
           of 1953)

RUIZA   Coe and Whitaker, *Aztec Sorcerers . . . : The Treatise on Superstitions by
           Hernando Ruiz de Alarcón*

RUIZAL Ruiz de Alarcón, *Treatise on the Heathen Superstitions* (Andrews and
           Hassig ed.)

SIM   Siméon, *Dictionnaire de la langue nahuatl ou mexicaine*

TEZ   Tezozomoc, *Crónica mexicana*

TORQ   Torquemada, *Monarquía indiana*

UAH   Mengin, "Unos annales históricos de la nación mexicana"

ZCHIM   Zimmermann, *Die Relationen Chimalpahin's*

References

Alva Ixtlilxochitl, Fernando de. *Obras históricas*, ed. Edmundo O'Gorman. 2 vols. Mexico: Universidad Nacional Autónoma de México, 1975–77.

Anales de Cuauhtitlan: Noticias históricas de México y sus contornos. Compiled by D. José Fernando Ramírez. Translations by Faustino Galicia Chimalpopoca, Gumesindo Mendoza, and Felipe Sánchez Solís. Publicación de los Anales del Museo Nacional. Mexico, 1885.

Andrews, J. Richard. *Introduction to Classical Nahuatl.* Austin: University of Texas Press, 1975.

Bierhorst, John. *Cantares Mexicanos: Songs of the Aztecs.* Stanford, Calif.: Stanford University Press, 1985.

———. *Codex Chimalpopoca: The Text in Nahuatl with a Glossary and Grammatical Notes.* Tucson: University of Arizona Press, 1992.

———. *Four Masterworks of American Indian Literature.* New York: Farrar, Straus & Giroux, 1974.

———. *The Mythology of Mexico and Central America.* New York: William Morrow, 1990.

———. *A Nahuatl-English Dictionary and Concordance to the Cantares Mexicanos, with an Analytic Transcription and Grammatical Notes.* Stanford, Calif.: Stanford University Press, 1985.

Boone, Elizabeth Hill. *The Codex Magliabechiano and the Lost Prototype of the Magliabechiano Group.* Berkeley and Los Angeles: University of California Press, 1983.

Boturini Benaduci, Lorenzo. *Idea de una nueva historia general de la América Septentrional.* Mexico: Porrúa, 1974.

Brundage, Burr Cartwright. *A Rain of Darts: The Mexica Aztecs.* Austin: University of Texas Press, 1972.

Burkhart, Louise M. "Aztecs in Limbo: The Harrowing of Hell in Nahua-Christian Literature." Paper presented at the 47th International Congress of Americanists, New Orleans, July 11, 1991.

———. *The Slippery Earth: Nahua-Christian Moral Dialogue in Sixteenth-Century Mexico.* Tucson: University of Arizona Press, 1989.

Cantares mexicanos. In MS 1628 bis, Biblioteca Nacional, Mexico, fols. 1–85.

Carochi, Horacio. *Arte de la lengua mexicana.* Mexico: Juan Ruyz, 1645 (original) ed.; Museo Nacional, 1892 ed.; Universidad Nacional Autónoma de México, 1983 ed. (facsimile of the original).

References

Chimalpain Cuauhtlehuanitzin, Francisco de San Antón Muñón. *Relaciones originales de Chalco Amaquemecan*, ed. S. Rendón. Mexico: Fondo de Cultura Económica, 1965.

Clavijero, Francisco Javier. *Historia antigua de México*, ed. Mariano Cuevas. 2d ed., rev. 4 vols. Mexico: Porrúa, 1958.

Codex Aubin. See Dibble, *Historia de la nación mexicana*.

Codex Mendoza: Aztec Manuscript, with commentaries by Kurt Ross. N.p.: Miller Graphics, 1978(?).

Códice Rámirez, *see* "Relación del origen de los indios que habitan esta Nueva España según sus historias."

"Códice Telleriano-Remensis." In Antonio Ortiz Mena, Agustín Yáñez, and José Corona Nuñez, eds., *Antigüedades de México (basadas en la recopilación de Lord Kingsborough)*, vol. 1. Mexico: Secretaría de Hacienda y Crédito Público, 1964.

"Códice Vaticanus 3738." In Antonio Ortiz Mena, Agustín Yáñez, and José Corona Nuñez, eds., *Antigüedades de México (basadas en la recopilación de Lord Kingsborough)*, vol. 3. Mexico: Secretaría de Hacienda y Crédito Público, 1964.

Coe, Michael D., and Gordon Whittaker. *Aztec Sorcerers in Seventeenth Century Mexico: The Treatise on Superstitions by Hernando Ruiz de Alarcón*. Albany: Institute for Mesoamerican Studies, State University of New York, 1982.

Cortés, Hernán. *Cartas de relación de la conquista de México*. Madrid: Espasa-Calpe, 1970.

Davies, Nigel. *The Toltecs Until the Fall of Tula*. Norman: University of Oklahoma Press, 1977.

de la Garza, Mercedes. "Análisis comparativo de la *Historia de los Mexicanos por sus Pinturas* y la *Leyenda de los Soles*," *Estudios de Cultura Náhuatl*, vol. 16 (1983), pp. 123–34.

Díaz del Castillo, Bernal. *Historia verdadera de la conquista de la Nueva España*. 11th ed. Mexico: Porrúa, 1976.

Dibble, Charles E. *Historia de la nación mexicana: Reproducción a todo color del Códice de 1576 (Códice Aubin)*. Madrid: José Porrúa Turanzas, 1963.

———. "Writing in Central Mexico." In *Handbook of Middle American Indians* (Robert Wauchope, general ed.), vol. 10 (1971), pp. 322–32.

Durán, Diego de. *Historia de las Indias de Nueva España e islas de la tierra firme*, ed. Angel M. Garibay K. Vol 1: *Libro de los ritos y ceremonias . . .* and *El calendario antiguo*. Vol. 2: *Historia*. Mexico: Porrúa, 1967.

García Granados, Rafael. *Diccionario biográfico de historia antigua de Méjico*. 3 vols. Mexico: Instituto de Historia, 1952–53.

García Icazbalceta, Joaquin. *Don fray Juan de Zumárraga*. 4 vols. Mexico: Porrúa, 1947.

Garibay K., Angel M. *Epica náhuatl*. 2d ed. Mexico: Universidad Nacional Autónoma de México, 1964.

———. *La literatura de los aztecas*. Mexico: Joaquín Mortiz, 1964.

————. *Teogonía e historia de los mexicanos: Tres opúsculos del siglo XVI*. Mexico: Porrúa, 1965; 2d printing 1979. Includes "Historia de los mexicanos por sus pinturas," Garibay's Spanish translation of "Histoyre du Mechique," and Pedro Ponce de León's "Breve relación de los dioses y ritos de la gentilidad."

————. *Veinte himnos sacros de los nahuas*. Mexico: Universidad Nacional Autónoma de México, 1958.

Gibson, Charles. *Tlaxcala in the Sixteenth Century*. Stanford, Calif.: Stanford University Press, 1967. Originally published in 1952.

Gillespie, Susan D. *The Aztec Kings: The Construction of Rulership in Mexica History*. Tucson: University of Arizona Press, 1989.

Gingerich, Willard. "Quetzalcoatl and the Agon of Time: A Literary Reading of the *Anales de Cuauhtitlan*," *New Scholar*, vol. 10 (1986), pp. 41–60.

————. "Three Nahuatl Hymns on the Mother Archetype: An Interpretive Commentary," *Mexican Studies/Estudios Mexicanos*, vol. 4 (1988), pp. 191–244.

Glass, John B. "A Survey of Native Middle American Pictorial Manuscripts." In *Handbook of Middle American Indians* (Robert Wauchope, general ed.), vol. 14 (1975), pp. 3–80.

Graulich, Michel. "Las peregrinaciones aztecas y el ciclo de Mixcóatl," *Estudios de Cultura Náhuatl*, vol. 11 (1974), pp. 311–54.

Handbook of Middle American Indians, Robert Wauchope, general ed. 16 vols. Austin: University of Texas Press, 1965–76.

Hernández, Francisco. *Historia natural de Nueva España*, tr. from the Latin by José Rojo Navarro. 2 vols. (Hernández, *Obras completas*, parts 2 and 3). Vol. 1: *Historia de las plantas*. Vol. 2: *Historia de las plantas* (cont.), *Historia de los animales*, and *Historia de los minerales*. Mexico: Universidad Nacional Autónoma de México, 1959.

"Historia de los mexicanos por sus pinturas." In Joaquín García Icazbalceta, ed., *Nueva Colección de documentos para la historia de México*, vol. 3, pp. 209–40. Mexico: Salvador Chavez Hayhoe, 1941. See also Garibay, *Teogonía e historia de los mexicanos*.

"Histoyre du Mechique: manuscrit français inédit du XVIᵉ siècle," ed. Edouard de Jonghe, *Journal de la Société des Américanistes de Paris*, n.s., vol. 2 (1905), pp. 1–41. See also Garibay, *Teogonía e historia de los mexicanos*.

Horcasitas, Fernando. "An Analysis of the Deluge Myth in Mesoamerica." In Alan Dundes, ed., *The Flood Myth*, pp. 183–219. Berkeley and Los Angeles: University of California Press, 1988.

Ixtlilxochitl, Fernando de Alva. *See* Alva Ixtlilxochitl.

Kirchhoff, Paul, Lina Odena Güemes, and Luis Reyes García, eds. *Historia Tolteca-Chichimeca*. Mexico: INAH, 1976.

Kutscher, Gerdt, Gordon Brotherston, and Günter Vollmer, eds. *Aesop in Mexico: Die Fabeln des Aesop in aztekischer Sprache / A 16th Century Aztec Version of Aesop's Fables*. Berlin: Gebr. Mann, 1987.

Launey, Michel. *Introduction à la langue et à la littérature aztèques.* 2 vols. Paris: L'Harmattan, 1979–80.

Lehmann, Walter. *Die Geschichte der Königreiche von Colhuacan und Mexico* [i.e., Codex Chimalpopoca]. Quellenwerke zur alten Geschichte Amerikas, vol. 1. Stuttgart: Kohlhammer, 1938; 2d ed. (with preface, errata list, and expanded index by Gerdt Kutscher), 1974.

León-Portilla, Miguel. *Quetzalcóatl.* Mexico: Fondo de Cultura Económica, 1968.

León y Gama, Antonio de. Copy of the Codex Chimalpopoca. FM 312. Département des Manuscrits, Bibliothèque Nationale, Paris.

López Avila, Carlos. *Tlacotenco: Tlahmachzaniltin ihuan tecuicame / Cuentos y canciones de mi pueblo.* Amerindia: Revue d'Ethnolinguistigue Amérindienne, numéro spécial 5. Paris, 1984.

Mendieta, Gerónimo de. *Historia eclesiástica indiana.* Mexico: Porrúa, 1971.

Mengin, Ernst. "Unos annales históricos de la nación mexicana: Die Manuscrits mexicains nr. 22 und 22 bis der Bibliothèque Nationale de Paris" [the "Anales de Tlatelolco"], *Baessler-Archiv,* vol. 22, nos. 2–3 (1939). Berlin.

Molina, Alonso de. *Vocabulario en lengua castellana y mexicana y mexicana y castellana.* Mexico: Porrúa, 1970. Facsimile of the 1880 ed.

Moreno de los Arcos, Roberto. "Los cinco soles cosmogónicos," *Estudios de Cultura Náhuatl,* vol. 7 (1967), pp. 183–210.

———. "La colección Boturini y las fuentes de la obra de Antonio León y Gama," *Estudios de Cultura Náhuatl,* vol. 9 (1971), pp. 253–70.

Motolinía [Fray Toribio de Benavente]. "Historia de los indios de la Nueva España." In *Colección de documentos para la historia de México,* ed. Joaquín García Icazbalceta, vol. 1, pp. 1–249. Mexico: Porrúa, 1971. Reprint of the 1858 ed.

———. *Memoriales o libro de las cosas de las Nueva España y de los naturales de ella,* ed. Edmundo O'Gorman. Mexico: Universidad Nacional Autónoma de México, 1971.

Muñoz Camargo, Diego. *Historia de Tlaxcala.* Mexico: Secretaría de Fomento, 1892.

Nuttall, Zelia. *The Book of the Life of the Ancient Mexicans* [i.e., the Codex Magliabechiano]. Berkeley and Los Angeles: University of California Press, 1983. Reprint of the 1903 ed.

Ojeda Díaz, María de los Angeles. *Documentos sobre Mesoamérica en el Archivo Histórico de la Biblioteca Nacional de Antropología e Historia.* Cuadernos de la Biblioteca, serie: Arch. Hist., no. 2. Mexico, 1979.

Paredes, Américo. *Folktales of Mexico.* Chicago: University of Chicago Press, 1970.

Paredes, Ignacio de. *Compendio del Arte de la lengua mexicana del P. Horacio Carochi.* Mexico: Imprenta de la Bibliotheca Mexicana, 1759.

Paso y Troncoso, Francisco del. "Leyenda de los soles, continuada con otras leyendas y noticias," *Biblioteca Nauatl,* vol. 5, no. 1 (1903), pp. 1–40. Florence,

Italy. Reprinted in Agustín Yáñez, *Mitos indígenas* (Universidad Nacional Autónoma de México, 1942, 3d ed. 1964), pp. 1–34.

Pérez de Ribas, Andrés. *Historia de los triunfos de nuestra santa fe entre gentes las más bárbaras* . . . 3 vols. Mexico: Editorial Layac, 1944. Originally published in 1645.

Piho, Virve. "Tlacatecutli, tlacochtecutli, tlacatéccatl y tlacochcálcatl," *Estudios de Cultura Náhuatl*, vol. 10 (1972), pp. 315–28.

Pomar, Juan Bautista. "Relación de Tezcoco." In *Nueva colección de documentos para la historia de México*, ed. Joaquín García Icazbalceta, vol. 3. pp. 1–64. Mexico: Salvador Chavez Hayhoe, 1941.

Ponce [de León], Pedro. "Breve relación de los dioses y ritos de la gentilidad" [ed. Francisco del Paso y Troncoso], *Anales del Museo Nacional de Mexico*, ep. 1, vol. 6 (1892), pp. 3–11.

———. "Breve relación de los dioses y ritos de la gentilidad." In *Tratado de las idolatrías, supersticiones* . . . , ed. Francisco del Paso y Troncoso, vol. 1, pp. 369–80. 2d ed. Mexico: Ediciones Fuente Cultural (Librería Navarro), 1953. See also Garibay, *Teogonía e historia de los mexicanos*.

"Relación del origen de los indios que habitan esta Nueva España según sus historias" [the Códice Rámirez]. In Hernando Alvarado Tezozomoc, *Crónica mexicana*, ed. Manuel Orozco y Berra. Mexico: Porrúa, 1975. Reprint of the 1878 ed.

Robertson, Donald. *Mexican Manuscript Painting of the Early Colonial Period: The Metropolitan Schools*. New Haven: Yale University Press, 1959.

Ruiz de Alarcón, Hernando. "Tratado de las supersticiones y costumbres gentílicas que oy viven entre los indios naturales desta Nueva España." In *Tratado de las idolatrías, supersticiones* . . . , ed. Francisco del Paso y Troncoso, vol. 2, pp. 17–180. 2d. ed. Mexico: Ediciones Fuente Cultural (Librería Navarro), 1953.

———. *Treatise on the Heathen Superstitions* . . . , tr. and ed. J. Richard Andrews and Ross Hassig. Norman: University of Oklahoma Press, 1984.

Sahagún, Bernardino de. *Códice florentino*. 3 vols. Mexico: Secretaría de Gobernación, 1979.

———. *Florentine Codex: General History of the Things of New Spain*, ed. Arthur J. O. Anderson and Charles E. Dibble. Parts 1–13 (introductory volume and books 1–12). 1st ed., 1950–82. Books 1–3 and 12, 2d. ed., rev., 1970–81. Santa Fe, N.M.: School of American Research and University of Utah Press.

———. *Historia general de las cosas de Nueva España*, ed. Angel M. Garibay K. 4 vols. 2d ed. Mexico: Porrúa, 1969.

Seler, Eduard. "Ueber die Worte Anauac und Nauatl." In his *Gesammelte Abhandlungen zur amerikanischen Sprach- und Alterthumskunde*, vol. 2, pp. 49–77. Berlin, 1904.

Serna, Jacinto de la. "Manual de ministros de indios." In *Tratado de las idolatrías, supersticiones* . . . , ed. Francisco del Paso y Troncoso, vol. 1, pp. 39–368. 2d ed. Mexico: Ediciones Fuente Cultural (Librería Navarro), 1953.

Siméon, Rémi. *Dictionnaire de la langue nahuatl ou mexicaine*. Graz, Austria: Akademische Druck- & Verlagsanstalt, 1963. Reprint of the 1885 ed.

Sullivan, Thelma. "Códice Chimalpopoca: Anales de Cuauhtitlan" [transcription and English translation of the first seven sides of the *Annals of Cuauhtitlan*]. Typescript. Dumbarton Oaks. Washington, D.C.

Taggart, James M. *Nahuat Myth and Social Structure*. Austin: University of Texas Press, 1983.

Tezozomoc, Fernando Alvarado. *Crónica mexicana*, ed. Manuel Orozco y Berra. Mexico: Porrúa, 1975. Reprint of the 1878 ed.

———. *Crónica mexicáyotl*, ed. Adrián León. Mexico: Universidad Nacional Autónoma de México, 1949.

Torquemada, Juan de. *Monarquía indiana*. 3 vols. Mexico: Porrúa, 1975. Facsimile of the 1723 ed. of Torquemada's *Monarchía indiana*.

Tschohl, Peter. "Das Ende der Leyenda de los Soles und die Ubermittlungsprobleme des Códice Chimalpopoca," *Baessler-Archiv*, n.s., vol. 37, no. 1, pp. 201–79. Berlin: Dietrich Reimer, 1989.

Velázquez, Primo Feliciano, ed. *Códice Chimalpopoca: Anales de Cuauhtitlan y Leyenda de los soles*. Mexico: Universidad Nacional Autónoma de México, 1945; 2d ed., 1975.

Yáñez, Agustín. *Mitos indígenas*. See Paso y Troncoso, "Leyenda de los soles."

Ziehm, Elsa, ed. *Nahua-Texte aus San Pedro Jícora in Durango*. 3 vols. Quellenwerke zur alten Geschichte Amerikas, vols. 9–11. Berlin: Gebr. Mann, 1968–76.

Zimmermann, Günter. *Die Relationen Chimalpahin's zur Geschichte México's*. 2 parts (Universität Hamburg, Abhandlungen aus dem Gebiet der Auslandskunde, vols. 68–69; series B, vols. 38–39). Part 1: *Die Zeit bis zur Conquista 1521*. Part 2: *Das Jahrhundert nach der Conquista (1522–1615)*. Hamburg: Cram, De Gruyter & Co., 1965.

Zorita, Alonso de. *Breve y sumaria relación de los señores de la Nueva España*. Mexico: Universidad Nacional Autónoma de México, 1963.